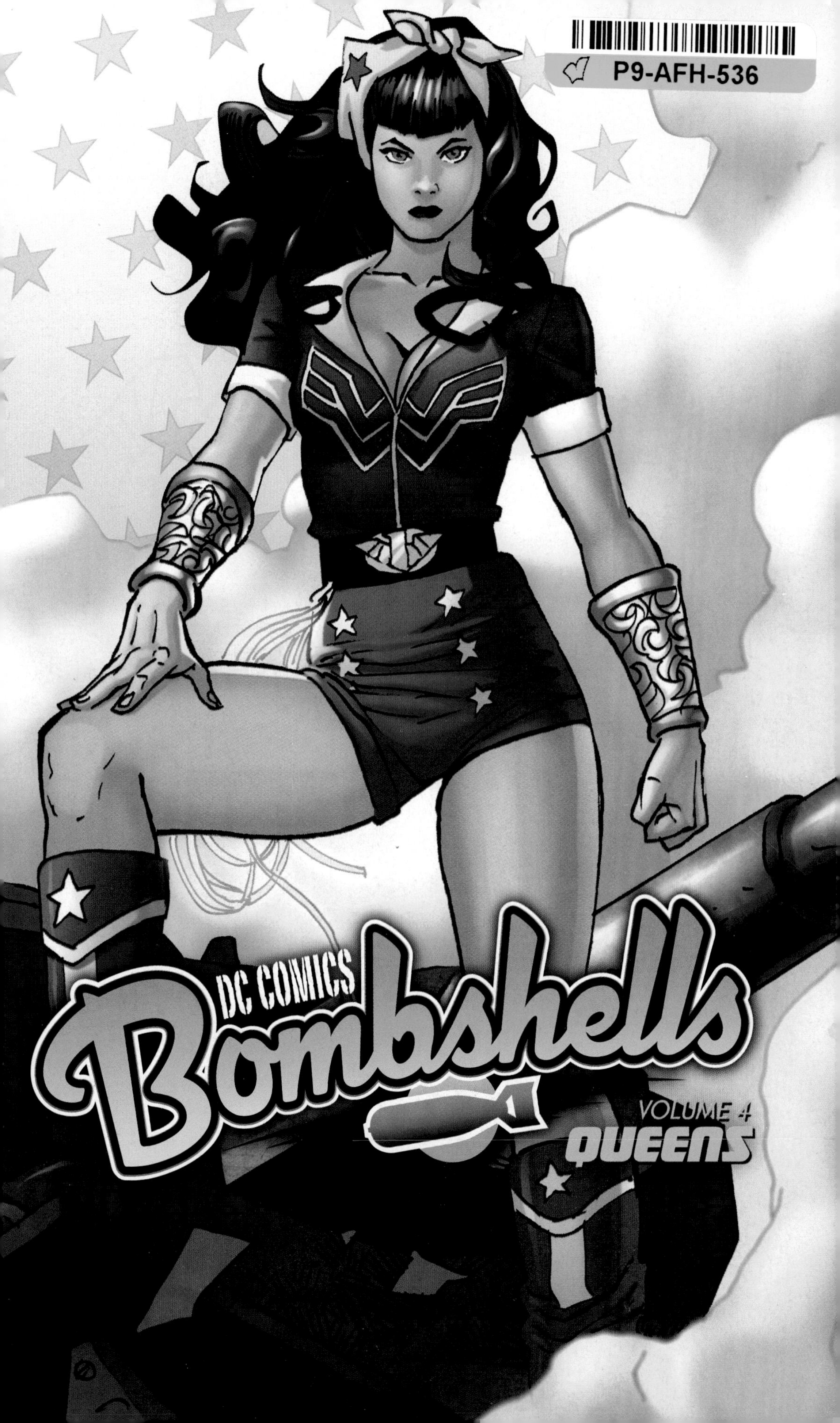
DC COMICS
Bombshells
VOLUME 4
QUEENS

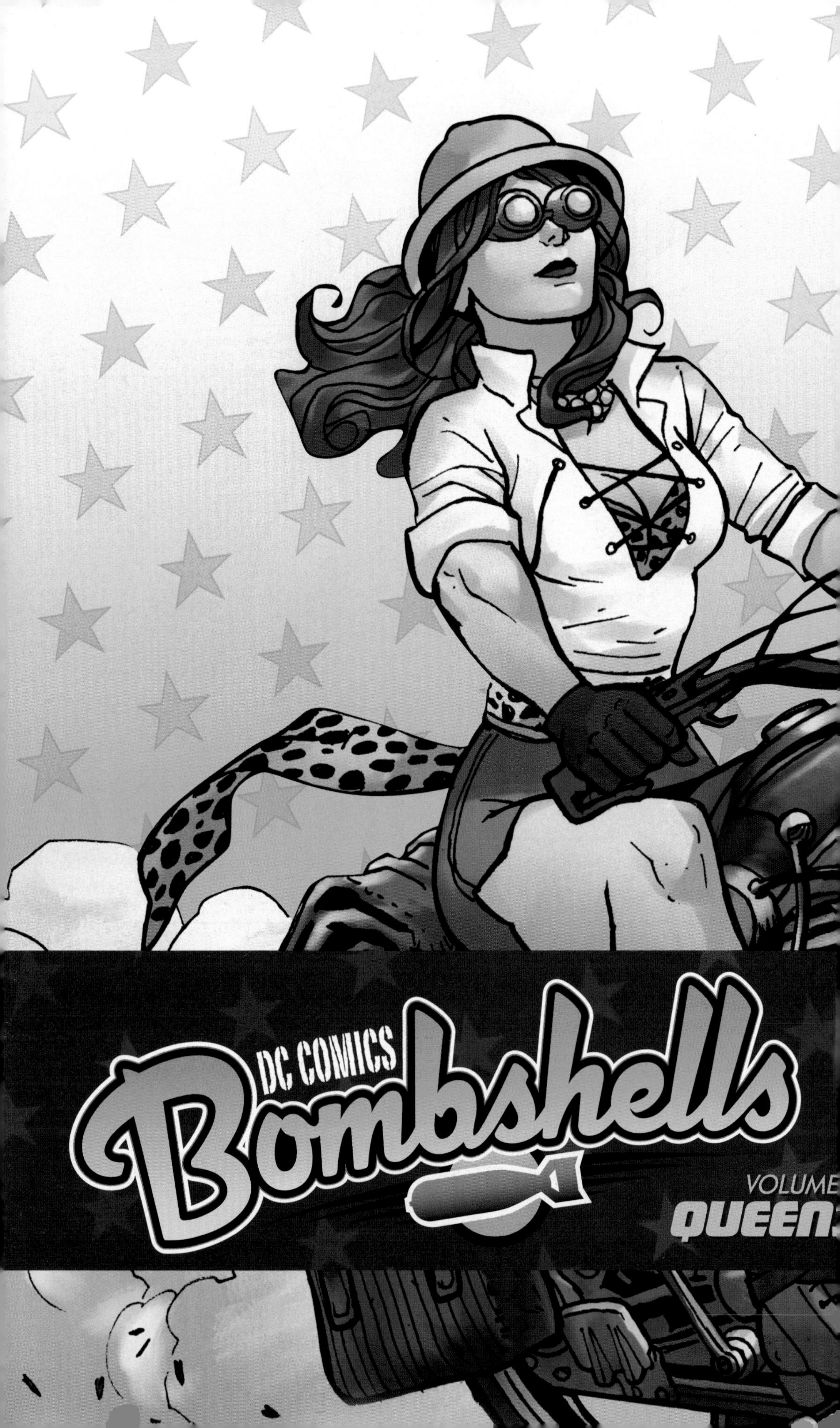
DC COMICS
Bombshells
VOLUME
QUEEN

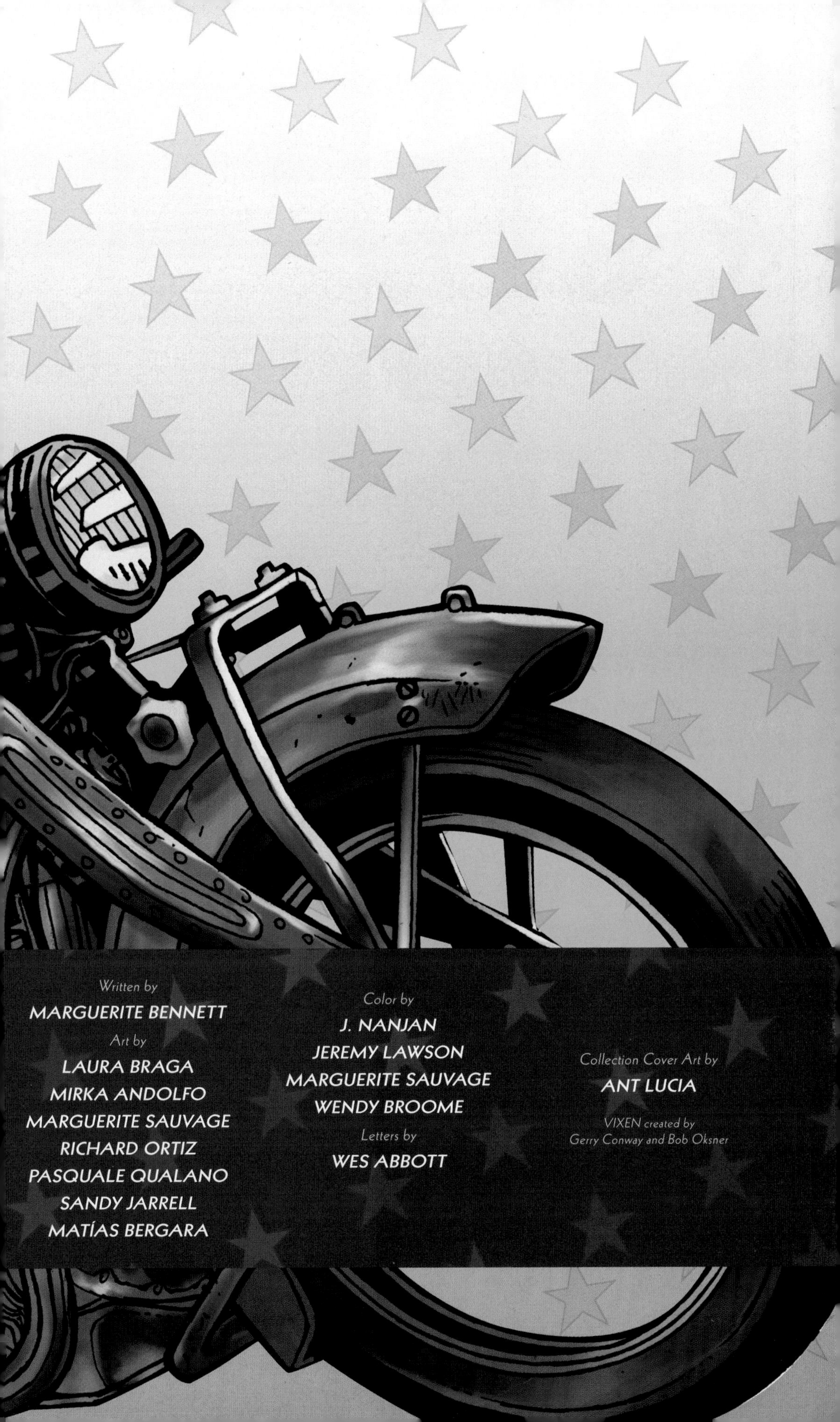

Written by
MARGUERITE BENNETT
Art by
LAURA BRAGA
MIRKA ANDOLFO
MARGUERITE SAUVAGE
RICHARD ORTIZ
PASQUALE QUALANO
SANDY JARRELL
MATÍAS BERGARA

Color by
J. NANJAN
JEREMY LAWSON
MARGUERITE SAUVAGE
WENDY BROOME
Letters by
WES ABBOTT

Collection Cover Art by
ANT LUCIA

VIXEN created by
Gerry Conway and Bob Oksner

JESSICA CHEN Editor – Original Series
JEB WOODARD Group Editor – Collected Editions
LIZ ERICKSON Editor – Collected Edition
STEVE COOK Design Director – Books
CURTIS KING JR. Publication Design

BOB HARRAS Senior VP – Editor-in-Chief, DC Comics

DIANE NELSON President
DAN DIDIO Publisher
JIM LEE Publisher
GEOFF JOHNS President & Chief Creative Officer
AMIT DESAI Executive VP – Business & Marketing Strategy,
Direct to Consumer & Global Franchise Management
SAM ADES Senior VP – Direct to Consumer
BOBBIE CHASE VP – Talent Development
MARK CHIARELLO Senior VP – Art, Design & Collected Editions
JOHN CUNNINGHAM Senior VP – Sales & Trade Marketing
ANNE DEPIES Senior VP – Business Strategy, Finance & Administrati
DON FALLETTI VP – Manufacturing Operations
LAWRENCE GANEM VP – Editorial Administration & Talent Relations
ALISON GILL Senior VP – Manufacturing & Operations
HANK KANALZ Senior VP – Editorial Strategy & Administration
JAY KOGAN VP – Legal Affairs
THOMAS LOFTUS VP – Business Affairs
JACK MAHAN VP – Business Affairs
NICK J. NAPOLITANO VP – Manufacturing Administration
EDDIE SCANNELL VP – Consumer Marketing
COURTNEY SIMMONS Senior VP – Publicity & Communications
JIM (SKI) SOKOLOWSKI VP – Comic Book Specialty Sales &
Trade Marketing
NANCY SPEARS VP – Mass, Book, Digital Sales & Trade Marketing

DC COMICS: BOMBSHELLS VOLUME 4: QUEENS

Published by DC Comics. Compilation and
all new material Copyright © 2017 DC Comics.
All Rights Reserved.

Originally published in single magazine form in DC COMICS: BOMBSHELLS 19-24
and online as DC COMICS: BOMBSHELLS Digital Chapters 55-72 Copyright © 2016
DC Comics. All Rights Reserved. All characters, their distinctive likenesses and
related elements featured in this publication are trademarks of DC Comics. The
stories, characters and incidents featured in this publication are entirely fictiona
DC Comics does not read or accept unsolicited ideas, stories or artwork.

DC Comics
2900 West Alameda Ave., Burbank, CA 91505
Printed by Vanguard Graphics, LLC, Ithaca, NY, USA. 5/19/17. First Printing.
ISBN: 978-1-4012-7407-8

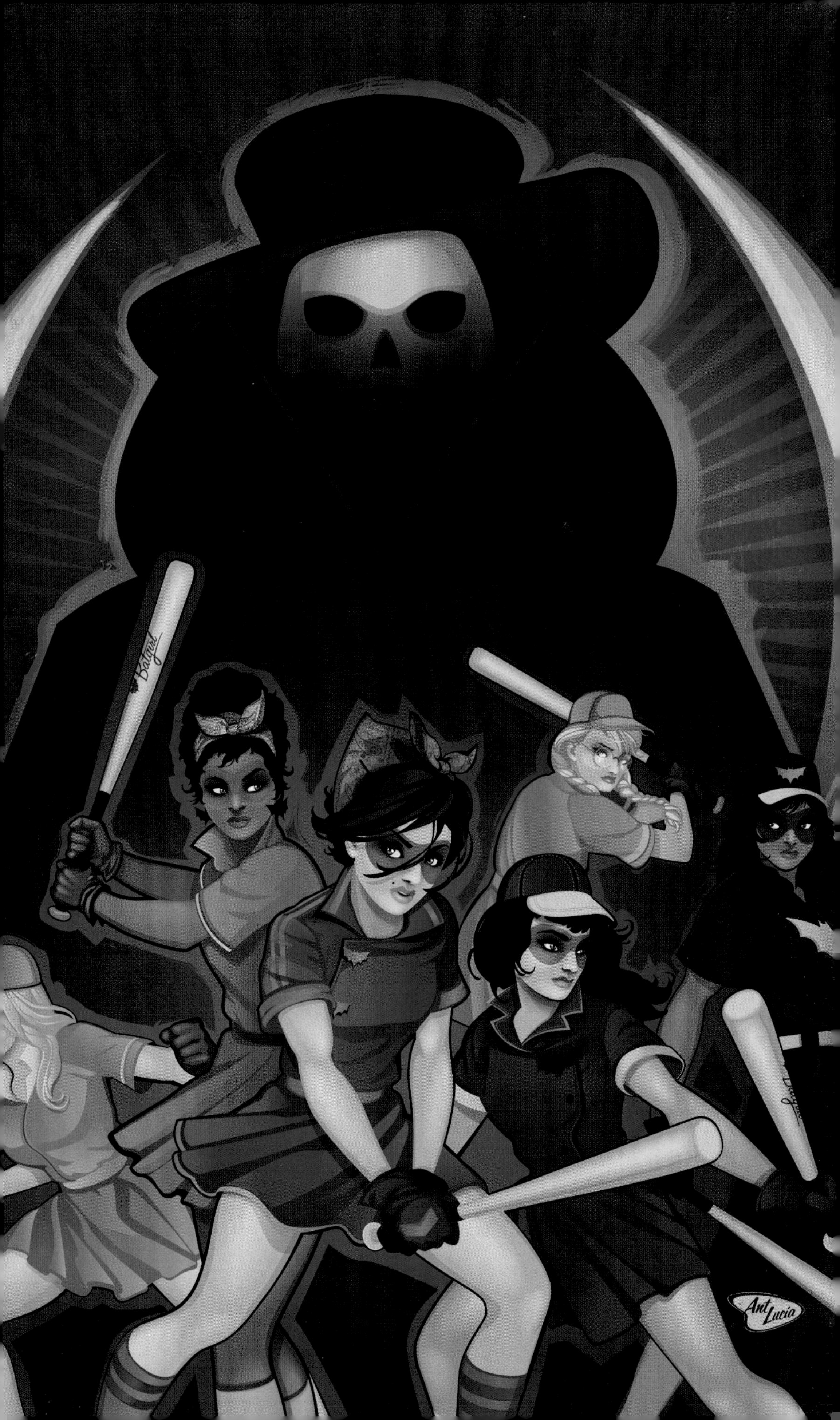
Batgirl
Ant Lucia

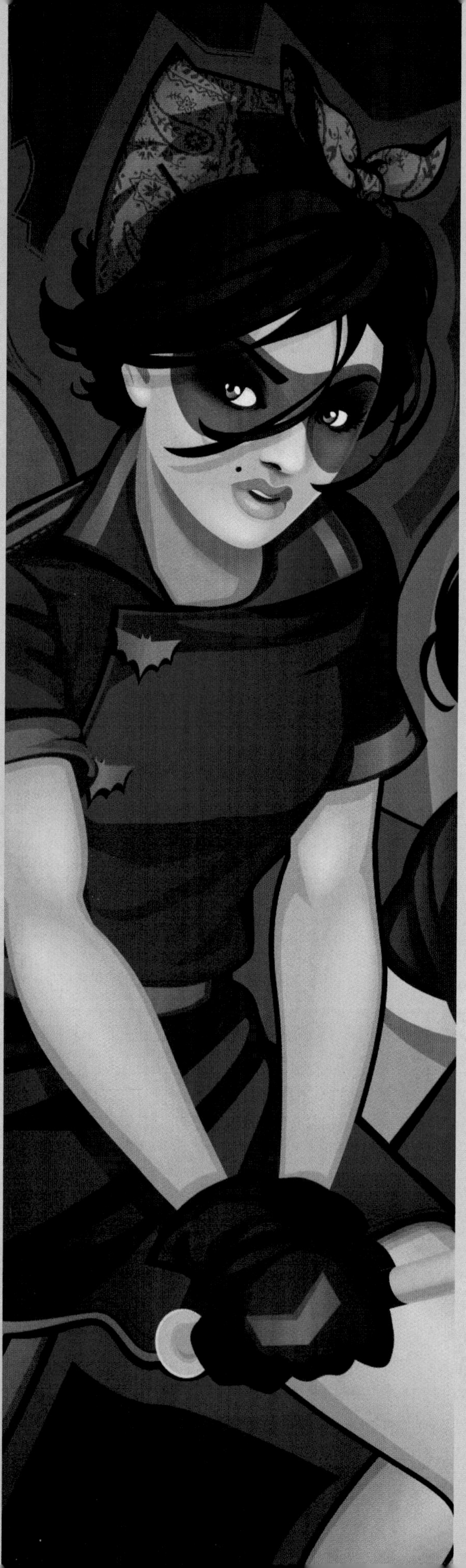

THE BATGIRLS FLY BY NIGHT

MARGUERITE BENNETT
Writer

MIRKA ANDOLFO
LAURA BRAGA
PASQUALE QUALANO
SANDY JARRELL
Artists

JEREMY LAWSON
Colorist

Cover by
ANT LUCIA

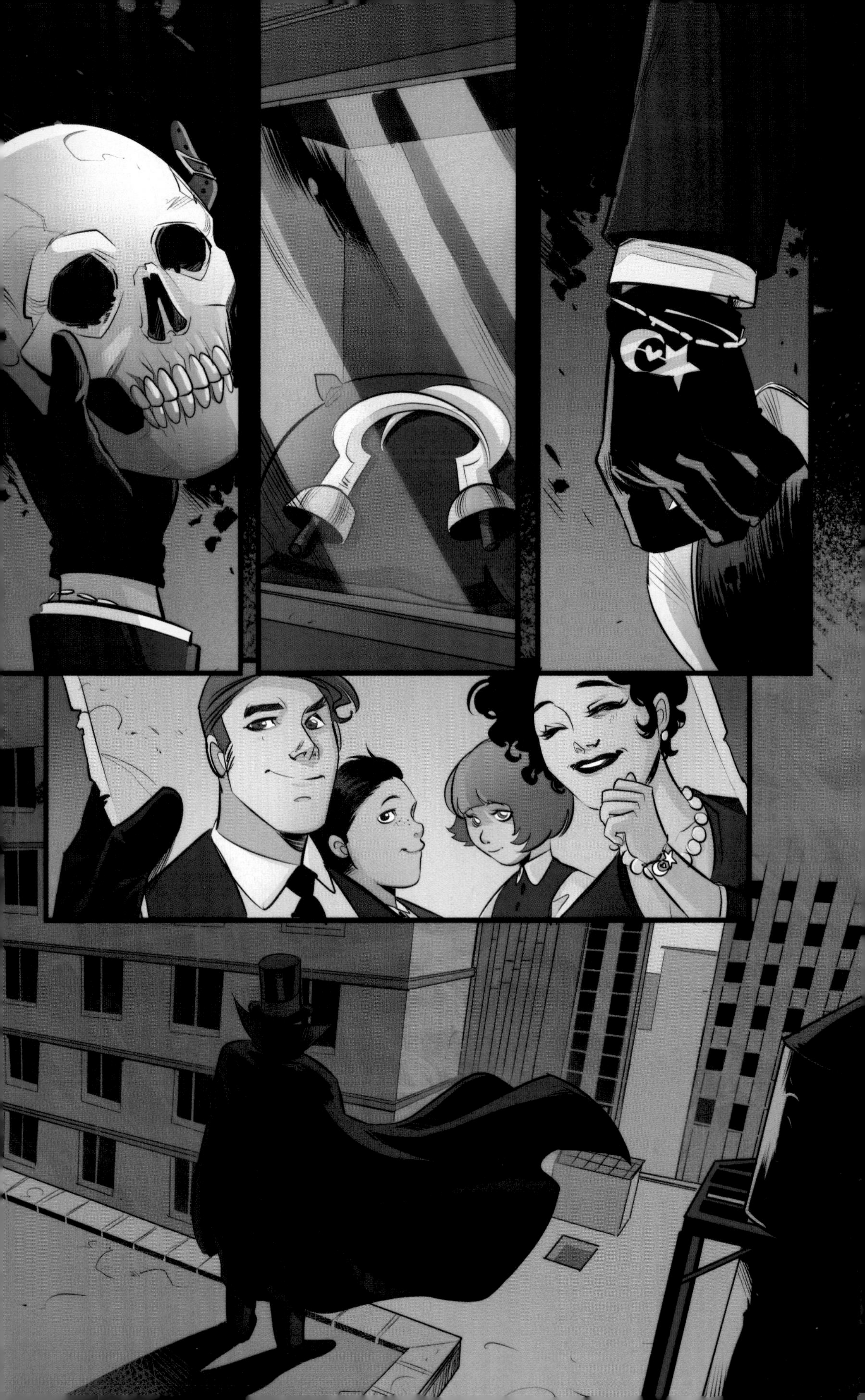

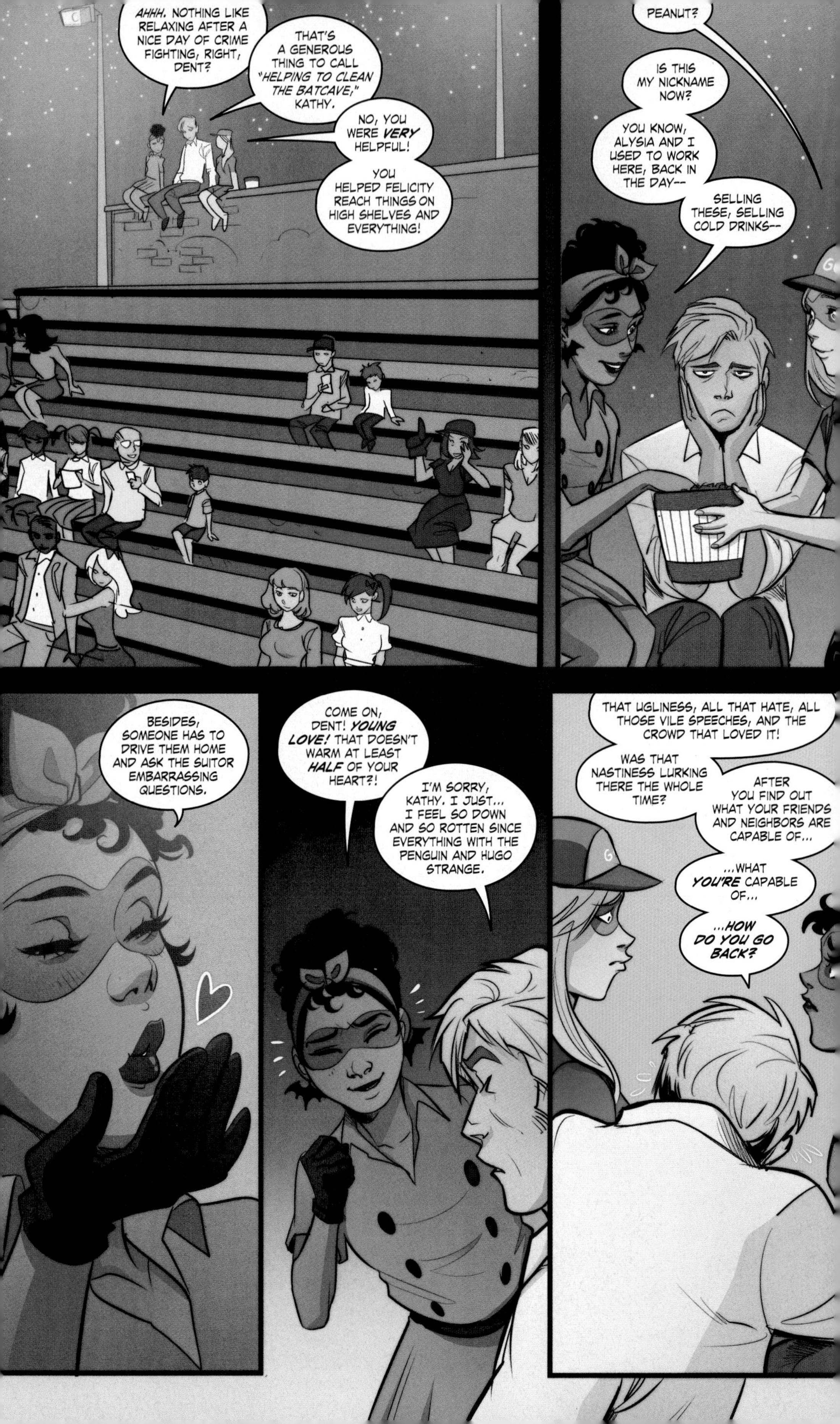
AHHH. NOTHING LIKE RELAXING AFTER A NICE DAY OF CRIME FIGHTING, RIGHT, DENT?
THAT'S A GENEROUS THING TO CALL "HELPING TO CLEAN THE BATCAVE," KATHY.
NO, YOU WERE VERY HELPFUL!
YOU HELPED FELICITY REACH THINGS ON HIGH SHELVES AND EVERYTHING!
PEANUT?
IS THIS MY NICKNAME NOW?
YOU KNOW, ALYSIA AND I USED TO WORK HERE, BACK IN THE DAY--
SELLING THESE, SELLING COLD DRINKS--
BESIDES, SOMEONE HAS TO DRIVE THEM HOME AND ASK THE SUITOR EMBARRASSING QUESTIONS.
COME ON, DENT! YOUNG LOVE! THAT DOESN'T WARM AT LEAST HALF OF YOUR HEART?!
I'M SORRY, KATHY. I JUST... I FEEL SO DOWN AND SO ROTTEN SINCE EVERYTHING WITH THE PENGUIN AND HUGO STRANGE.
THAT UGLINESS, ALL THAT HATE, ALL THOSE VILE SPEECHES, AND THE CROWD THAT LOVED IT!
WAS THAT NASTINESS LURKING THERE THE WHOLE TIME?
AFTER YOU FIND OUT WHAT YOUR FRIENDS AND NEIGHBORS ARE CAPABLE OF...
...WHAT YOU'RE CAPABLE OF...
...HOW DO YOU GO BACK?

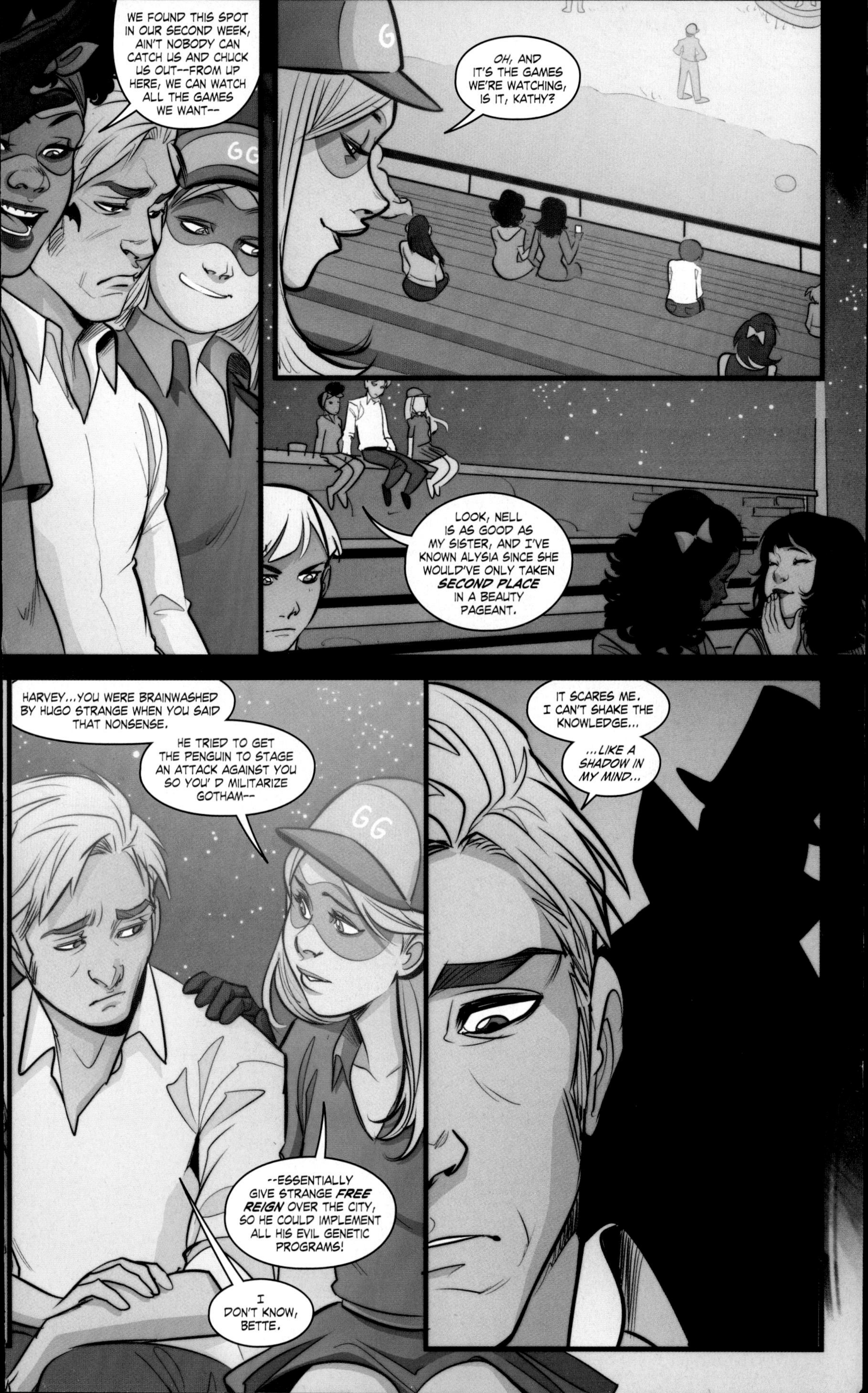
WE FOUND THIS SPOT IN OUR SECOND WEEK, AIN'T NOBODY CAN CATCH US AND CHUCK US OUT--FROM UP HERE, WE CAN WATCH ALL THE GAMES WE WANT--
OH, AND IT'S THE GAMES WE'RE WATCHING, IS IT, KATHY?
LOOK, NELL IS AS GOOD AS MY SISTER, AND I'VE KNOWN ALYSIA SINCE SHE WOULD'VE ONLY TAKEN SECOND PLACE IN A BEAUTY PAGEANT.
HARVEY...YOU WERE BRAINWASHED BY HUGO STRANGE WHEN YOU SAID THAT NONSENSE.
HE TRIED TO GET THE PENGUIN TO STAGE AN ATTACK AGAINST YOU SO YOU'D MILITARIZE GOTHAM--
--ESSENTIALLY GIVE STRANGE FREE REIGN OVER THE CITY, SO HE COULD IMPLEMENT ALL HIS EVIL GENETIC PROGRAMS!
I DON'T KNOW, BETTE.
IT SCARES ME. I CAN'T SHAKE THE KNOWLEDGE...
...LIKE A SHADOW IN MY MIND...

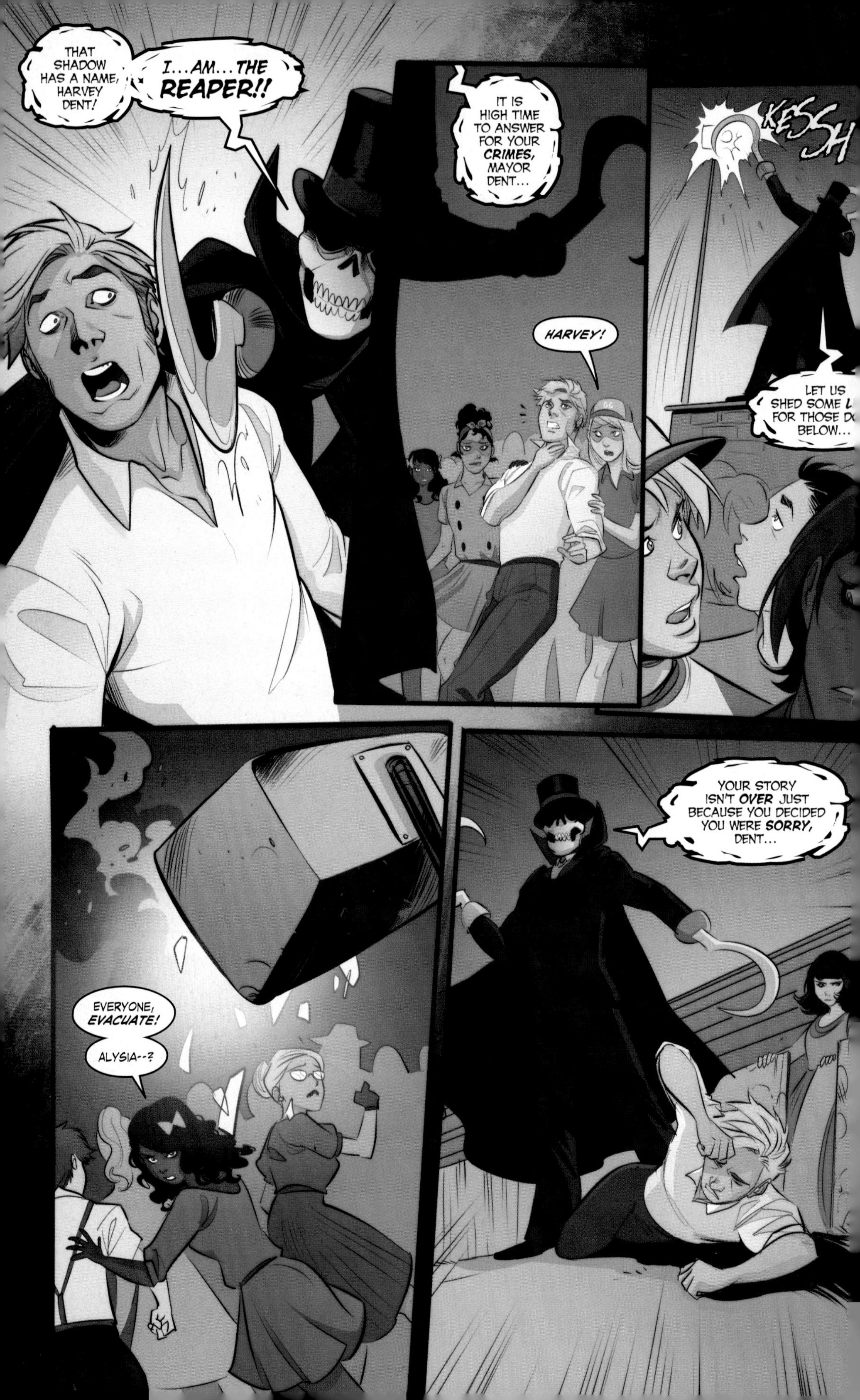

THAT SHADOW HAS A NAME, HARVEY DENT!
I...AM...THE REAPER!!
IT IS HIGH TIME TO ANSWER FOR YOUR CRIMES, MAYOR DENT...
HARVEY!
KESSSH
LET US SHED SOME L
FOR THOSE D
BELOW...
EVERYONE, EVACUATE!
ALYSIA--?
YOUR STORY ISN'T OVER JUST BECAUSE YOU DECIDED YOU WERE SORRY, DENT...

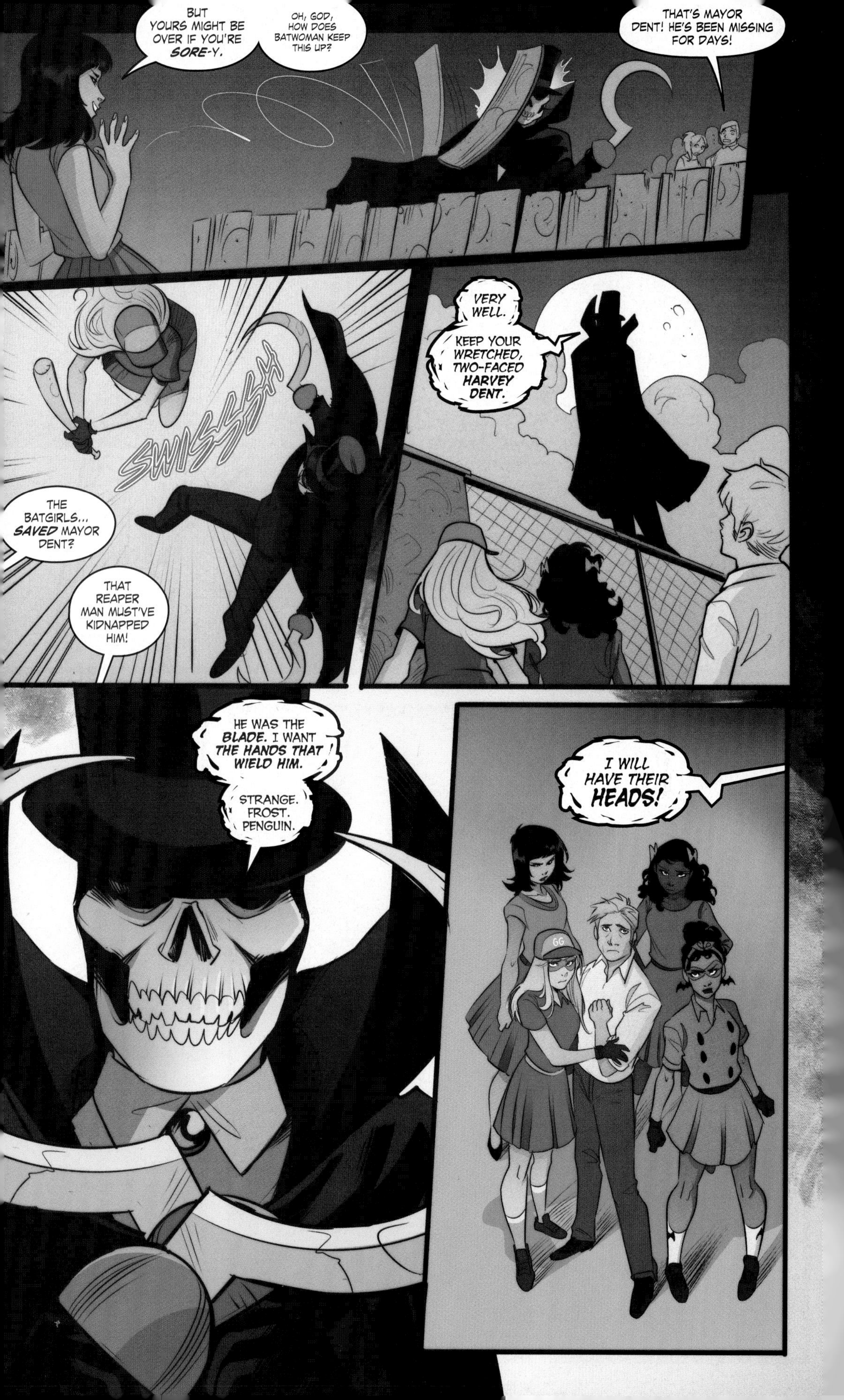
BUT YOURS MIGHT BE OVER IF YOU'RE SORE-Y.
OH, GOD, HOW DOES BATWOMAN KEEP THIS UP?
THAT'S MAYOR DENT! HE'S BEEN MISSING FOR DAYS!
SWISSSH
THE BATGIRLS... SAVED MAYOR DENT?
THAT REAPER MAN MUST'VE KIDNAPPED HIM!
VERY WELL.
KEEP YOUR WRETCHED, TWO-FACED HARVEY DENT.
HE WAS THE BLADE. I WANT THE HANDS THAT WIELD HIM.
STRANGE. FROST. PENGUIN.
I WILL HAVE THEIR HEADS!
GG

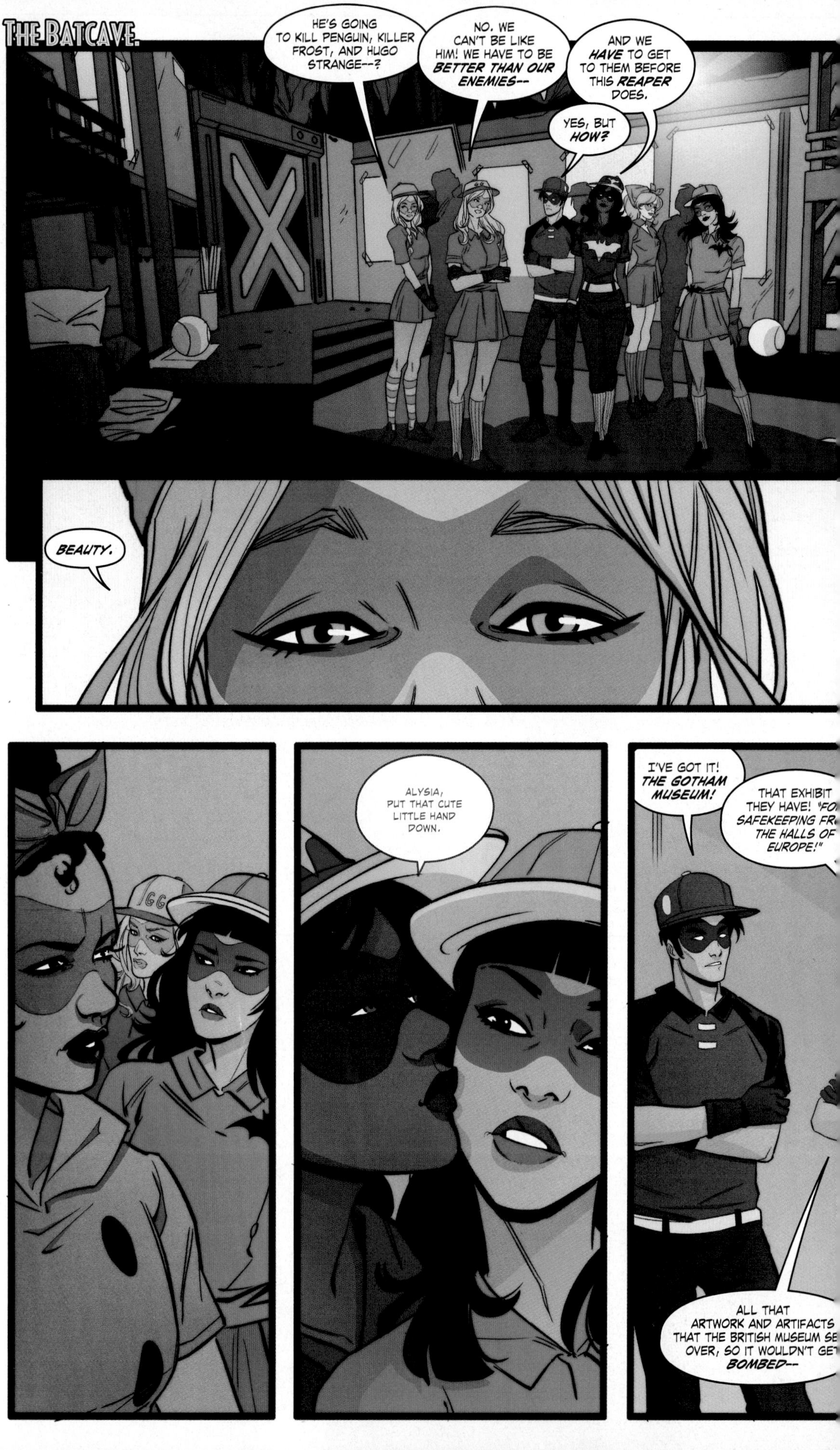
THE BATCAVE.
HE'S GOING TO KILL PENGUIN, KILLER FROST, AND HUGO STRANGE--?
NO. WE CAN'T BE LIKE HIM! WE HAVE TO BE BETTER THAN OUR ENEMIES--
AND WE HAVE TO GET TO THEM BEFORE THIS REAPER DOES.
YES, BUT HOW?
BEAUTY.
ALYSIA, PUT THAT CUTE LITTLE HAND DOWN.
I'VE GOT IT! THE GOTHAM MUSEUM!
THAT EXHIBIT THEY HAVE! "FO SAFEKEEPING FR THE HALLS OF EUROPE!"
ALL THAT ARTWORK AND ARTIFACTS THAT THE BRITISH MUSEUM SE OVER, SO IT WOULDN'T GET BOMBED--

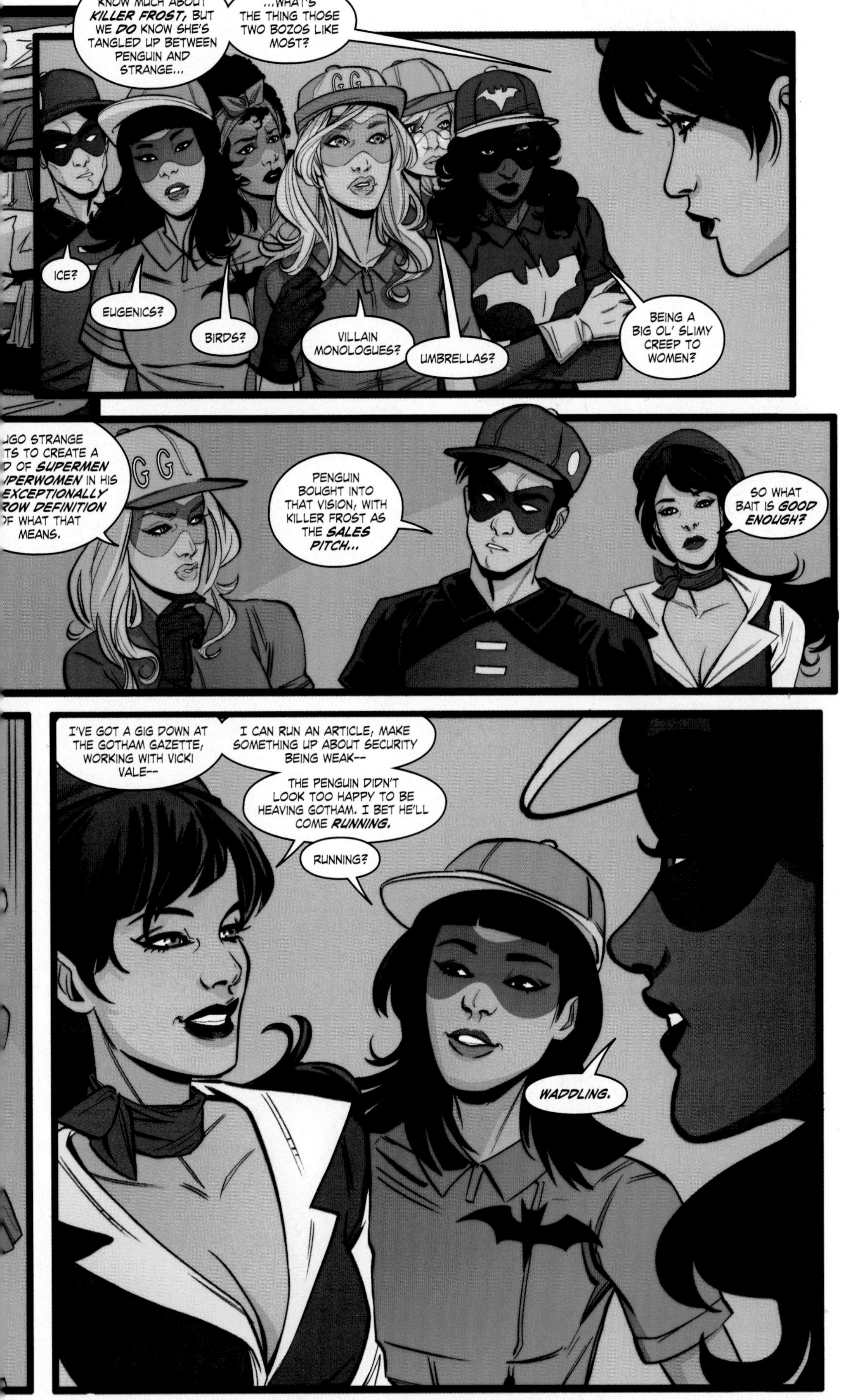
WE DON'T KNOW MUCH ABOUT ***KILLER FROST,*** BUT WE ***DO*** KNOW SHE'S TANGLED UP BETWEEN PENGUIN AND STRANGE...
...WHAT'S THE THING THOSE TWO BOZOS LIKE MOST?
ICE?
EUGENICS?
BIRDS?
VILLAIN MONOLOGUES?
UMBRELLAS?
BEING A BIG OL' SLIMY CREEP TO WOMEN?
UGO STRANGE TS TO CREATE A D OF ***SUPERMEN*** ***PERWOMEN*** IN HIS ***EXCEPTIONALLY*** ***ROW DEFINITION*** F WHAT THAT MEANS.
PENGUIN BOUGHT INTO THAT VISION, WITH KILLER FROST AS THE ***SALES PITCH...***
SO WHAT BAIT IS ***GOOD ENOUGH?***
I'VE GOT A GIG DOWN AT THE GOTHAM GAZETTE, WORKING WITH VICKI VALE--
I CAN RUN AN ARTICLE, MAKE SOMETHING UP ABOUT SECURITY BEING WEAK--
THE PENGUIN DIDN'T LOOK TOO HAPPY TO BE HEAVING GOTHAM. I BET HE'LL COME ***RUNNING.***
RUNNING?
WADDLING.

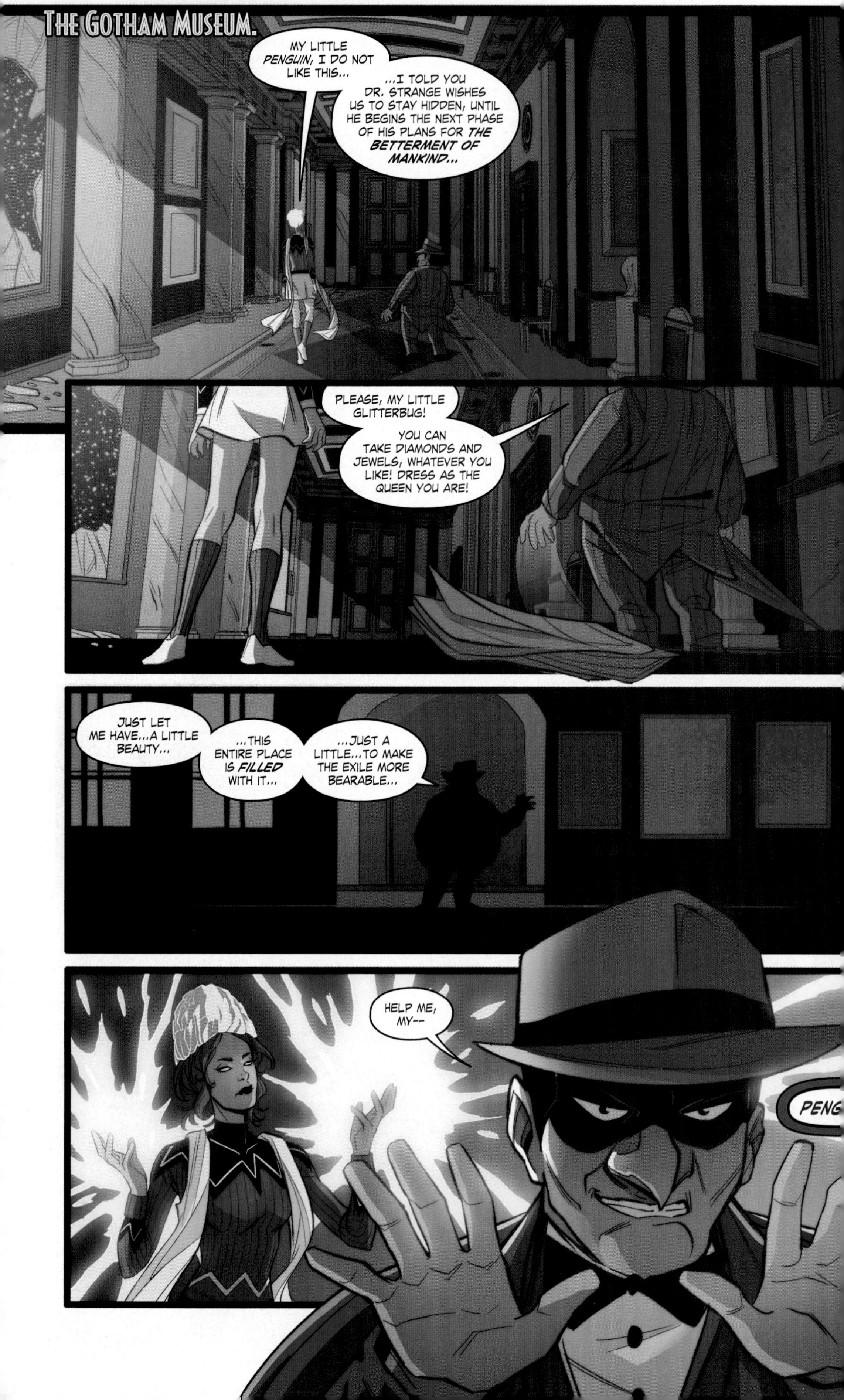
THE GOTHAM MUSEUM.
MY LITTLE PENGUIN, I DO NOT LIKE THIS...
...I TOLD YOU DR. STRANGE WISHES US TO STAY HIDDEN, UNTIL HE BEGINS THE NEXT PHASE OF HIS PLANS FOR THE BETTERMENT OF MANKIND...
PLEASE, MY LITTLE GLITTERBUG!
YOU CAN TAKE DIAMONDS AND JEWELS, WHATEVER YOU LIKE! DRESS AS THE QUEEN YOU ARE!
JUST LET ME HAVE...A LITTLE BEAUTY...
...THIS ENTIRE PLACE IS FILLED WITH IT...
...JUST A LITTLE...TO MAKE THE EXILE MORE BEARABLE...
HELP ME, MY--
PENG

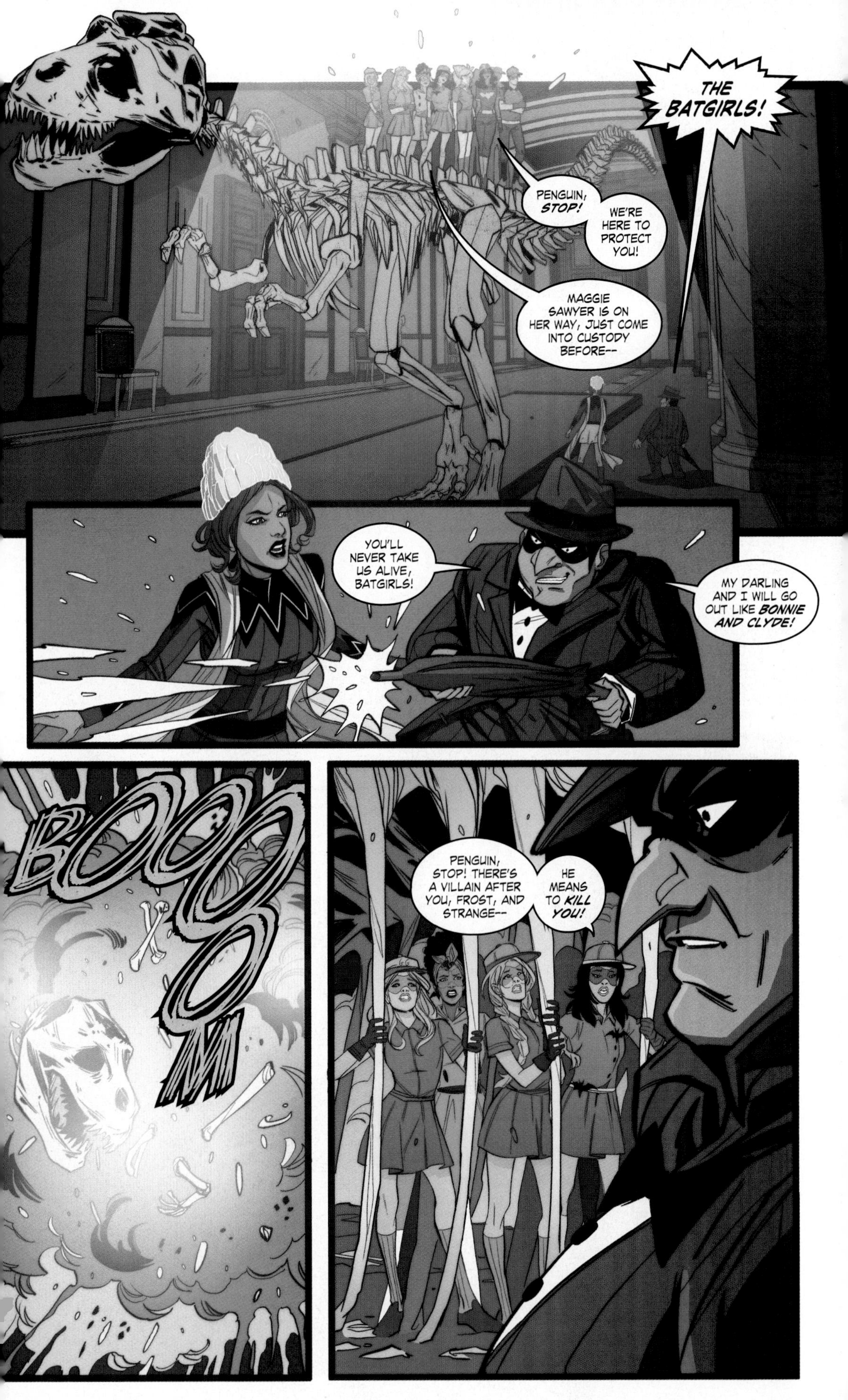
THE BATGIRLS!
PENGUIN, STOP!
WE'RE HERE TO PROTECT YOU!
MAGGIE SAWYER IS ON HER WAY, JUST COME INTO CUSTODY BEFORE--
YOU'LL NEVER TAKE US ALIVE, BATGIRLS!
MY DARLING AND I WILL GO OUT LIKE BONNIE AND CLYDE!
BOOOOM
PENGUIN, STOP! THERE'S A VILLAIN AFTER YOU, FROST, AND STRANGE--
HE MEANS TO KILL YOU!

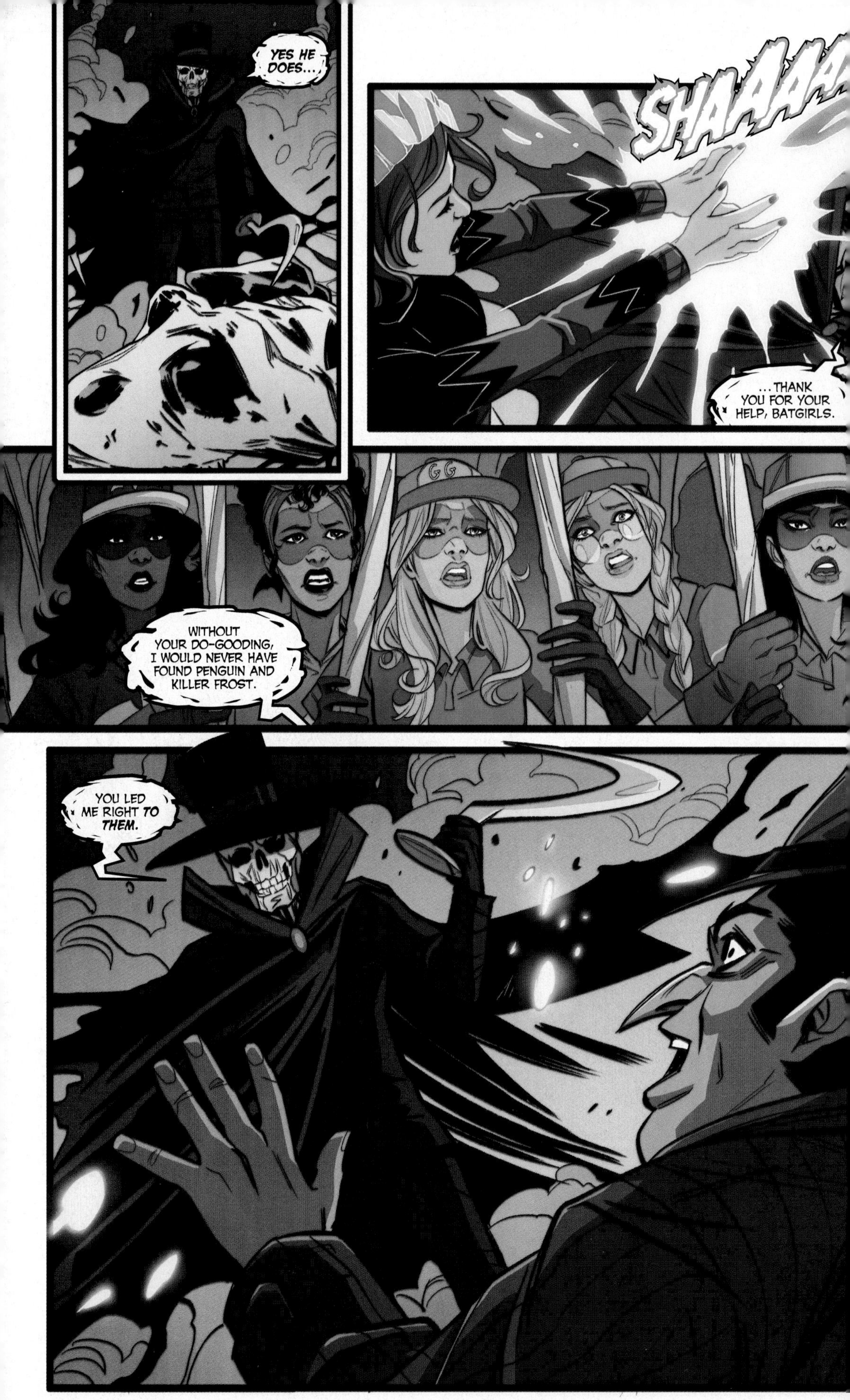
YES HE DOES...
SHAAAA
...THANK YOU FOR YOUR HELP, BATGIRLS.
WITHOUT YOUR DO-GOODING, I WOULD NEVER HAVE FOUND PENGUIN AND KILLER FROST.
YOU LED ME RIGHT TO THEM.

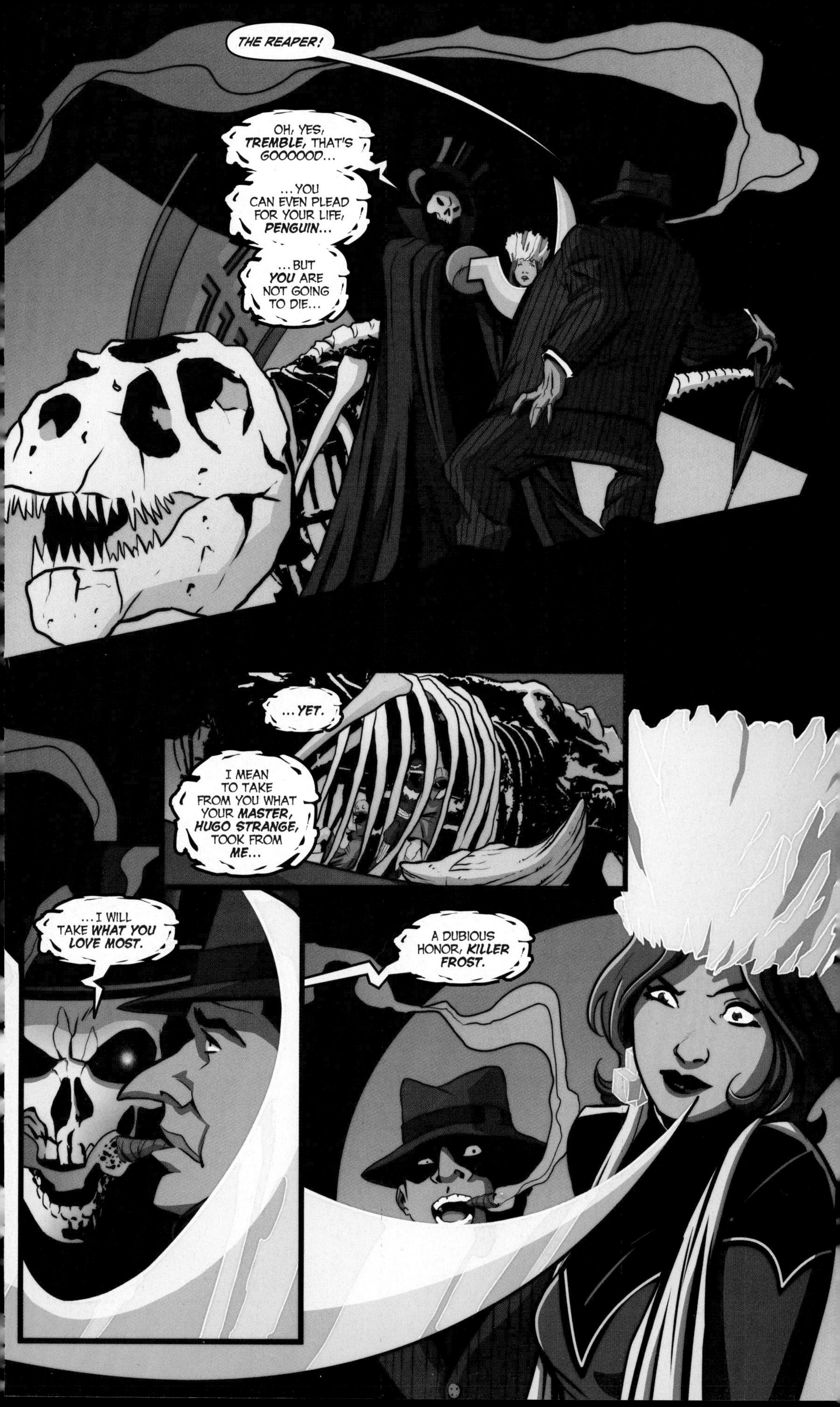
THE REAPER!
OH, YES, TREMBLE, THAT'S GOOOOOD...
...YOU CAN EVEN PLEAD FOR YOUR LIFE, PENGUIN...
...BUT YOU ARE NOT GOING TO DIE...
...YET.
I MEAN TO TAKE FROM YOU WHAT YOUR MASTER, HUGO STRANGE, TOOK FROM ME...
...I WILL TAKE WHAT YOU LOVE MOST.
A DUBIOUS HONOR, KILLER FROST.

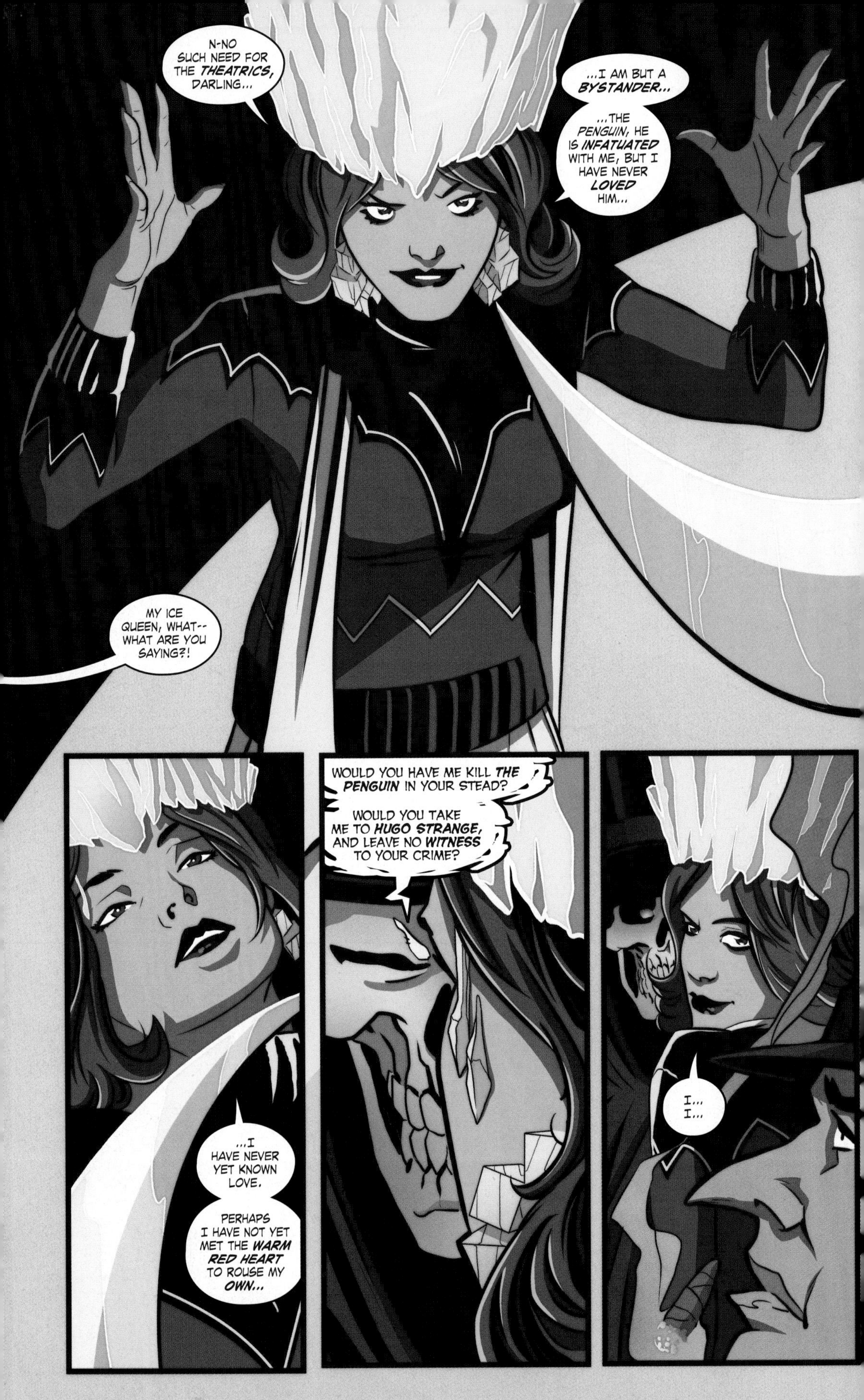
N-NO SUCH NEED FOR THE THEATRICS, DARLING...
...I AM BUT A BYSTANDER...
...THE PENGUIN, HE IS INFATUATED WITH ME, BUT I HAVE NEVER LOVED HIM...
MY ICE QUEEN, WHAT--WHAT ARE YOU SAYING?!
...I HAVE NEVER YET KNOWN LOVE.
PERHAPS I HAVE NOT YET MET THE WARM RED HEART TO ROUSE MY OWN...
WOULD YOU HAVE ME KILL THE PENGUIN IN YOUR STEAD?
WOULD YOU TAKE ME TO HUGO STRANGE, AND LEAVE NO WITNESS TO YOUR CRIME?
I... I...

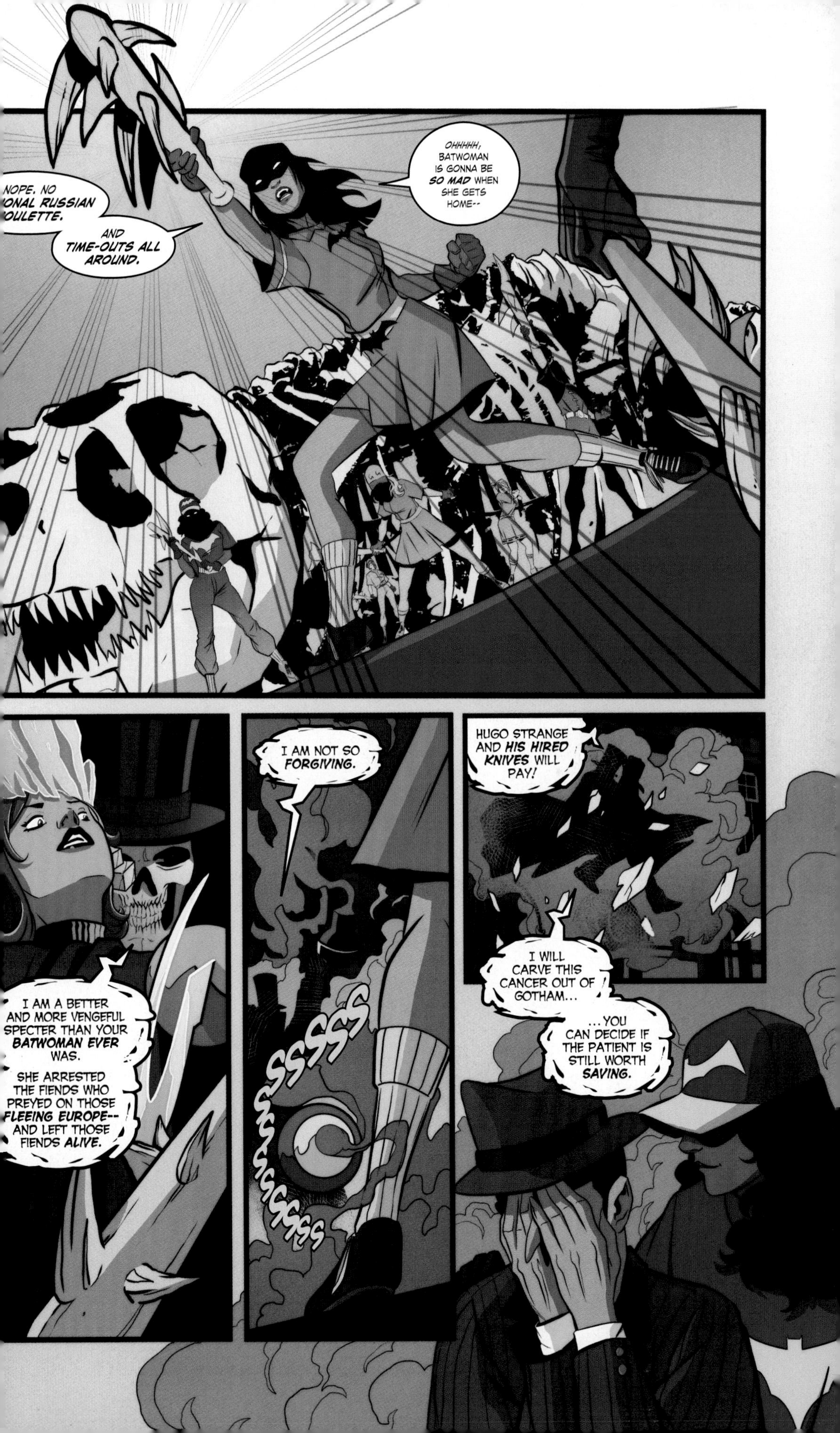
NOPE. NO
ONAL RUSSIAN
OULETTE.
AND TIME-OUTS ALL AROUND.
OHHHHH, BATWOMAN IS GONNA BE SO MAD WHEN SHE GETS HOME--
I AM A BETTER AND MORE VENGEFUL SPECTER THAN YOUR BATWOMAN EVER WAS.
SHE ARRESTED THE FIENDS WHO PREYED ON THOSE FLEEING EUROPE-- AND LEFT THOSE FIENDS ALIVE.
I AM NOT SO FORGIVING.
SSSSSS
SSSSSSSSSSS
HUGO STRANGE AND HIS HIRED KNIVES WILL PAY!
I WILL CARVE THIS CANCER OUT OF GOTHAM...
...YOU CAN DECIDE IF THE PATIENT IS STILL WORTH SAVING.

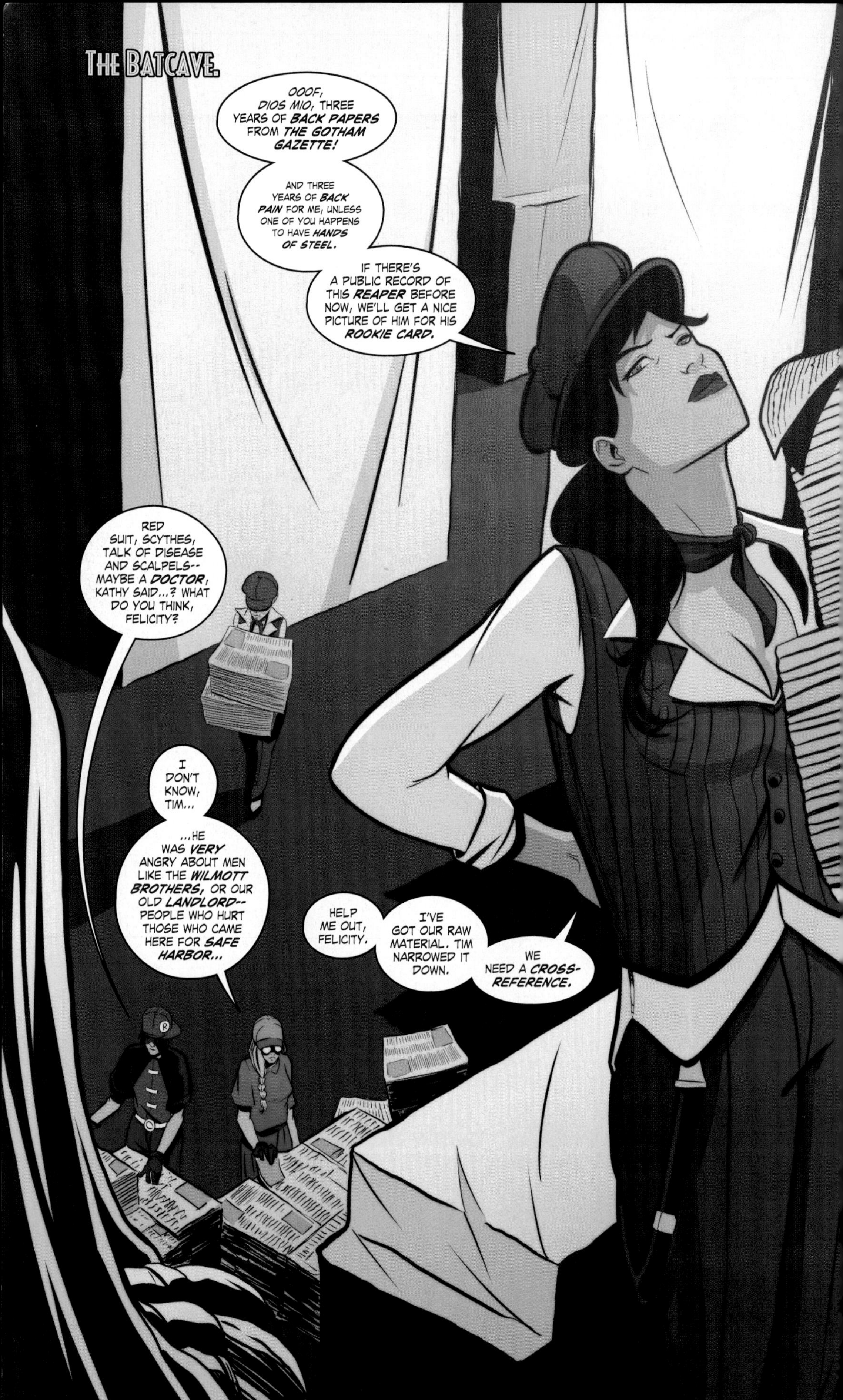
THE BATCAVE.
OOOF, DIOS MIO, THREE YEARS OF BACK PAPERS FROM THE GOTHAM GAZETTE!
AND THREE YEARS OF BACK PAIN FOR ME, UNLESS ONE OF YOU HAPPENS TO HAVE HANDS OF STEEL.
IF THERE'S A PUBLIC RECORD OF THIS REAPER BEFORE NOW, WE'LL GET A NICE PICTURE OF HIM FOR HIS ROOKIE CARD.
RED SUIT, SCYTHES, TALK OF DISEASE AND SCALPELS-- MAYBE A DOCTOR, KATHY SAID...? WHAT DO YOU THINK, FELICITY?
I DON'T KNOW, TIM...
...HE WAS VERY ANGRY ABOUT MEN LIKE THE WILMOTT BROTHERS, OR OUR OLD LANDLORD-- PEOPLE WHO HURT THOSE WHO CAME HERE FOR SAFE HARBOR...
HELP ME OUT, FELICITY.
I'VE GOT OUR RAW MATERIAL. TIM NARROWED IT DOWN.
WE NEED A CROSS-REFERENCE.

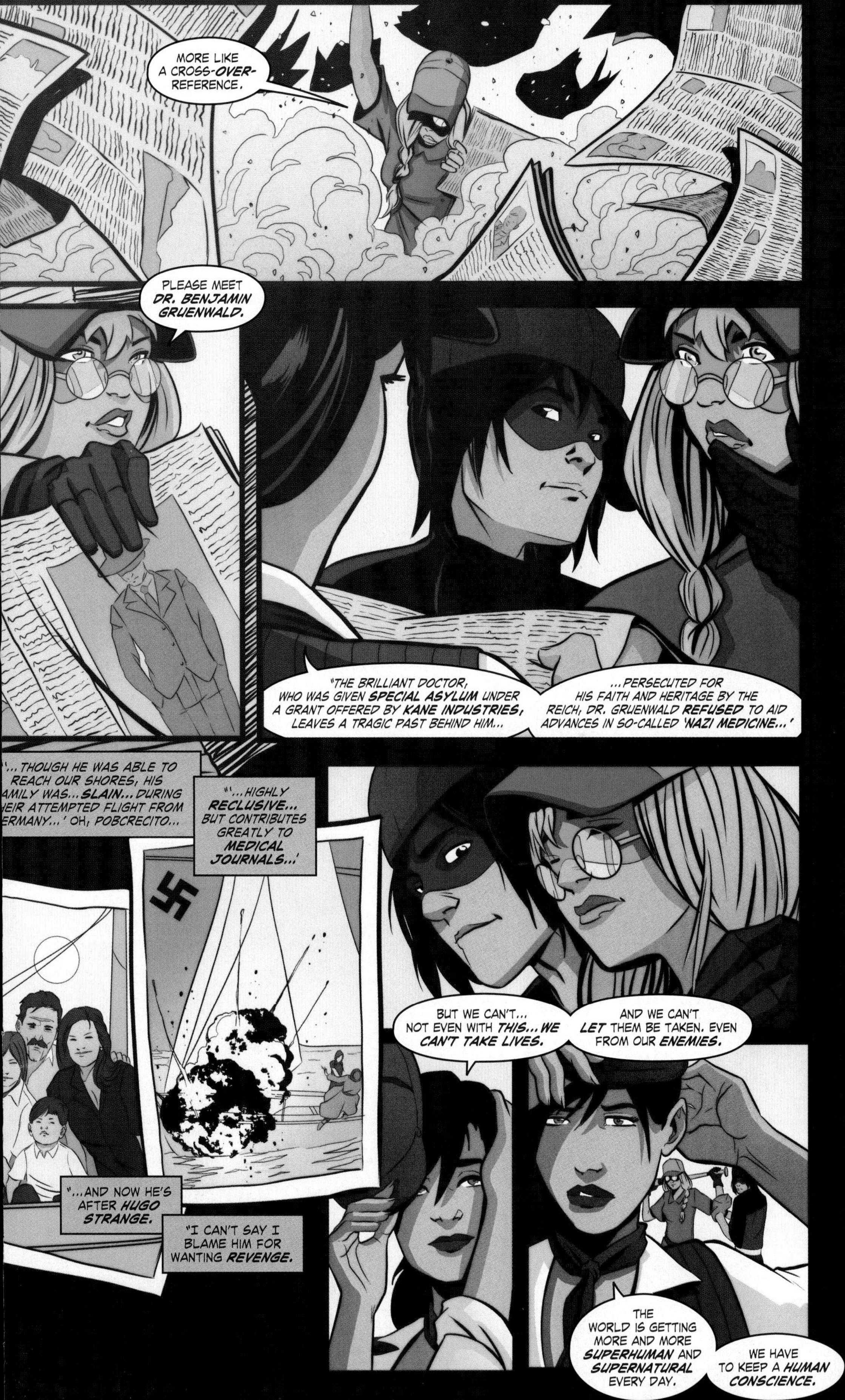
MORE LIKE A CROSS-OVER-REFERENCE.
PLEASE MEET DR. BENJAMIN GRUENWALD.
"THE BRILLIANT DOCTOR, WHO WAS GIVEN SPECIAL ASYLUM UNDER A GRANT OFFERED BY KANE INDUSTRIES, LEAVES A TRAGIC PAST BEHIND HIM...
...PERSECUTED FOR HIS FAITH AND HERITAGE BY THE REICH; DR. GRUENWALD REFUSED TO AID ADVANCES IN SO-CALLED 'NAZI MEDICINE...'
"...THOUGH HE WAS ABLE TO REACH OUR SHORES, HIS AMILY WAS...SLAIN...DURING HEIR ATTEMPTED FLIGHT FROM ERMANY...' OH, POBCRECITO...
"...HIGHLY RECLUSIVE... BUT CONTRIBUTES GREATLY TO MEDICAL JOURNALS...'
"...AND NOW HE'S AFTER HUGO STRANGE.
"I CAN'T SAY I BLAME HIM FOR WANTING REVENGE.
BUT WE CAN'T... NOT EVEN WITH THIS...WE CAN'T TAKE LIVES.
AND WE CAN'T LET THEM BE TAKEN. EVEN FROM OUR ENEMIES.
THE WORLD IS GETTING MORE AND MORE SUPERHUMAN AND SUPERNATURAL EVERY DAY.
WE HAVE TO KEEP A HUMAN CONSCIENCE.

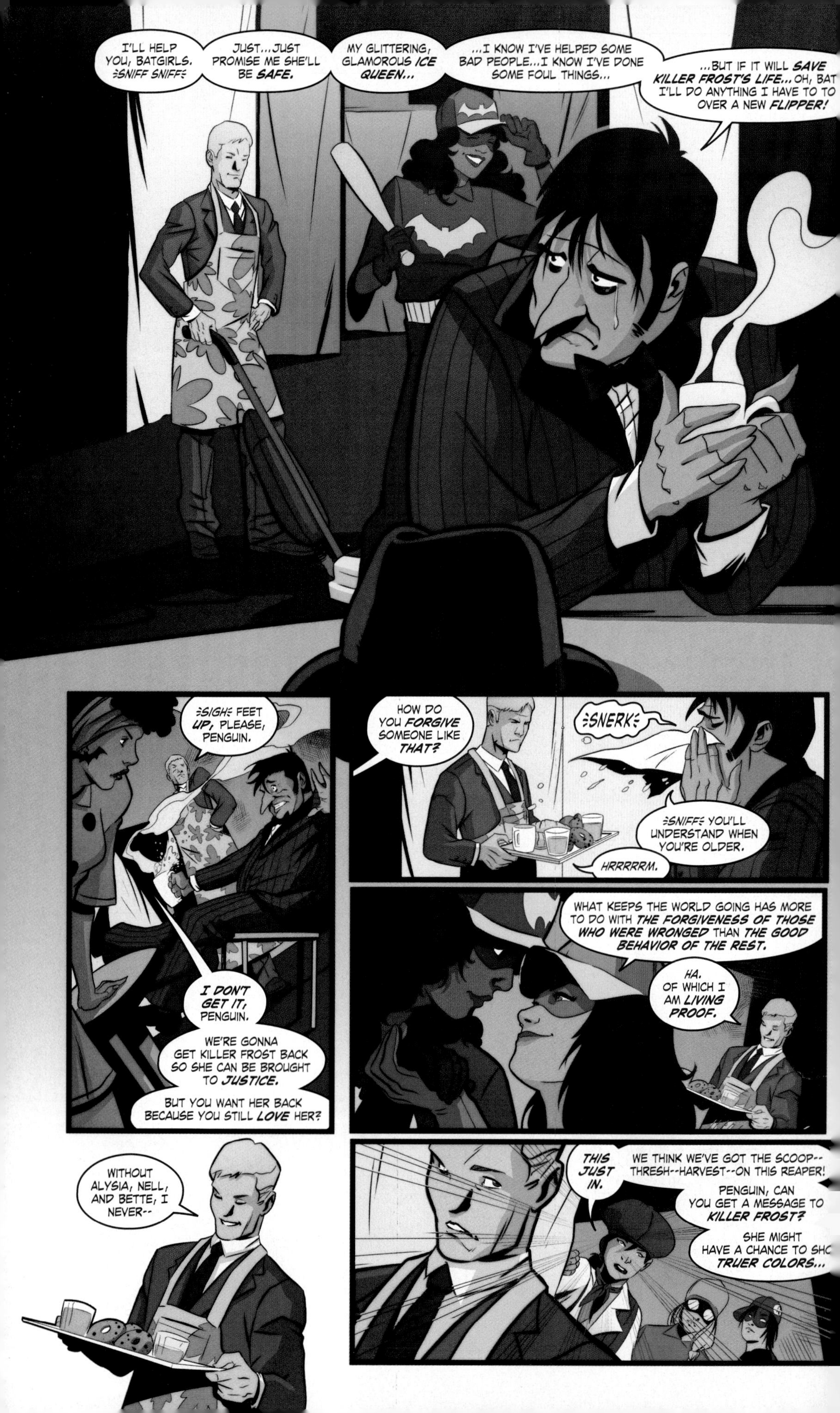
I'LL HELP YOU, BATGIRLS. ≈SNIFF SNIFF≈
JUST...JUST PROMISE ME SHE'LL BE SAFE.
MY GLITTERING, GLAMOROUS ICE QUEEN...
...I KNOW I'VE HELPED SOME BAD PEOPLE...I KNOW I'VE DONE SOME FOUL THINGS...
...BUT IF IT WILL SAVE KILLER FROST'S LIFE...OH, BAT I'LL DO ANYTHING I HAVE TO TO OVER A NEW FLIPPER!
≈SIGH≈ FEET UP, PLEASE, PENGUIN.
I DON'T GET IT, PENGUIN.
WE'RE GONNA GET KILLER FROST BACK SO SHE CAN BE BROUGHT TO JUSTICE.
BUT YOU WANT HER BACK BECAUSE YOU STILL LOVE HER?
HOW DO YOU FORGIVE SOMEONE LIKE THAT?
≈SNERK≈
≈SNIFF≈ YOU'LL UNDERSTAND WHEN YOU'RE OLDER.
HRRRRRM.
WHAT KEEPS THE WORLD GOING HAS MORE TO DO WITH THE FORGIVENESS OF THOSE WHO WERE WRONGED THAN THE GOOD BEHAVIOR OF THE REST.
HA. OF WHICH I AM LIVING PROOF.
WITHOUT ALYSIA, NELL, AND BETTE, I NEVER--
THIS JUST IN.
WE THINK WE'VE GOT THE SCOOP-- THRESH--HARVEST--ON THIS REAPER!
PENGUIN, CAN YOU GET A MESSAGE TO KILLER FROST?
SHE MIGHT HAVE A CHANCE TO SHO TRUER COLORS...

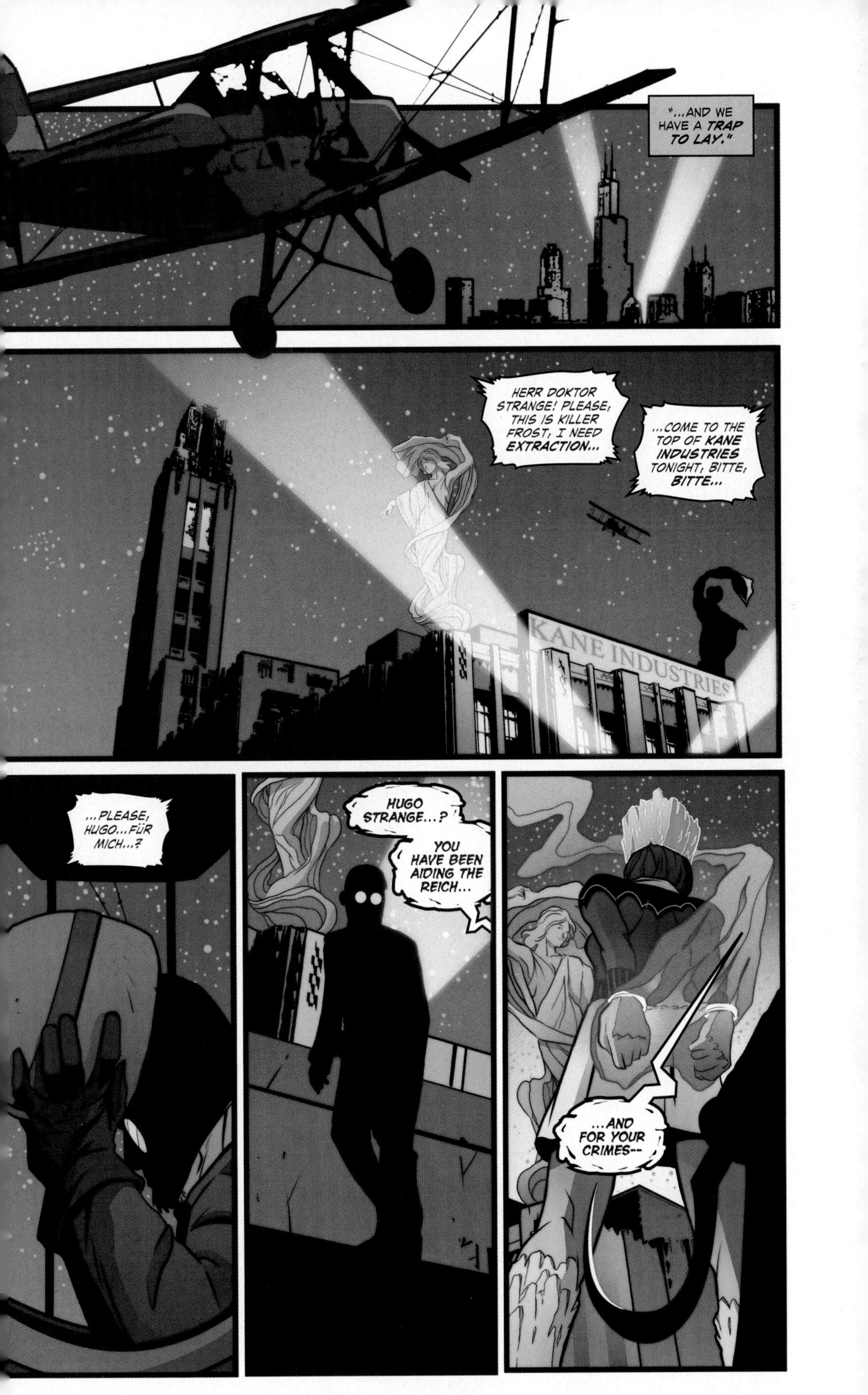
"...AND WE HAVE A TRAP TO LAY."
HERR DOKTOR STRANGE! PLEASE, THIS IS KILLER FROST, I NEED EXTRACTION...
...COME TO THE TOP OF KANE INDUSTRIES TONIGHT, BITTE, BITTE...
KANE INDUSTRIES
...PLEASE, HUGO...FÜR MICH...?
HUGO STRANGE...?
YOU HAVE BEEN AIDING THE REICH...
...AND FOR YOUR CRIMES--

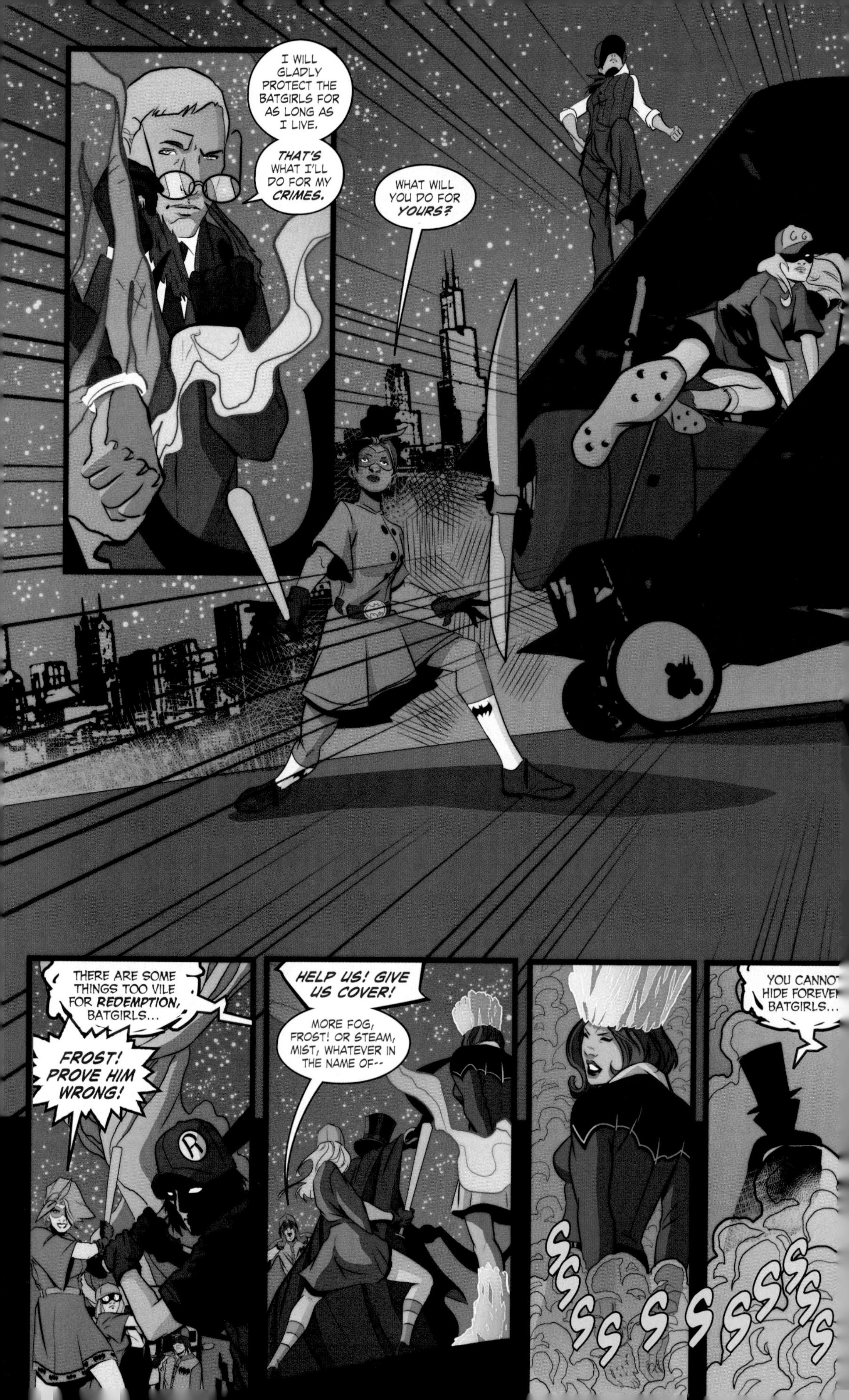
I WILL GLADLY PROTECT THE BATGIRLS FOR AS LONG AS I LIVE.
THAT'S WHAT I'LL DO FOR MY *CRIMES.*
WHAT WILL YOU DO FOR *YOURS?*
THERE ARE SOME THINGS TOO VILE FOR *REDEMPTION,* BATGIRLS...
FROST! PROVE HIM WRONG!
HELP US! GIVE US COVER!
MORE FOG, FROST! OR STEAM, MIST, WHATEVER IN THE NAME OF--
YOU CANNOT HIDE FOREVER BATGIRLS...
SSSSSSSSSSSSSSS

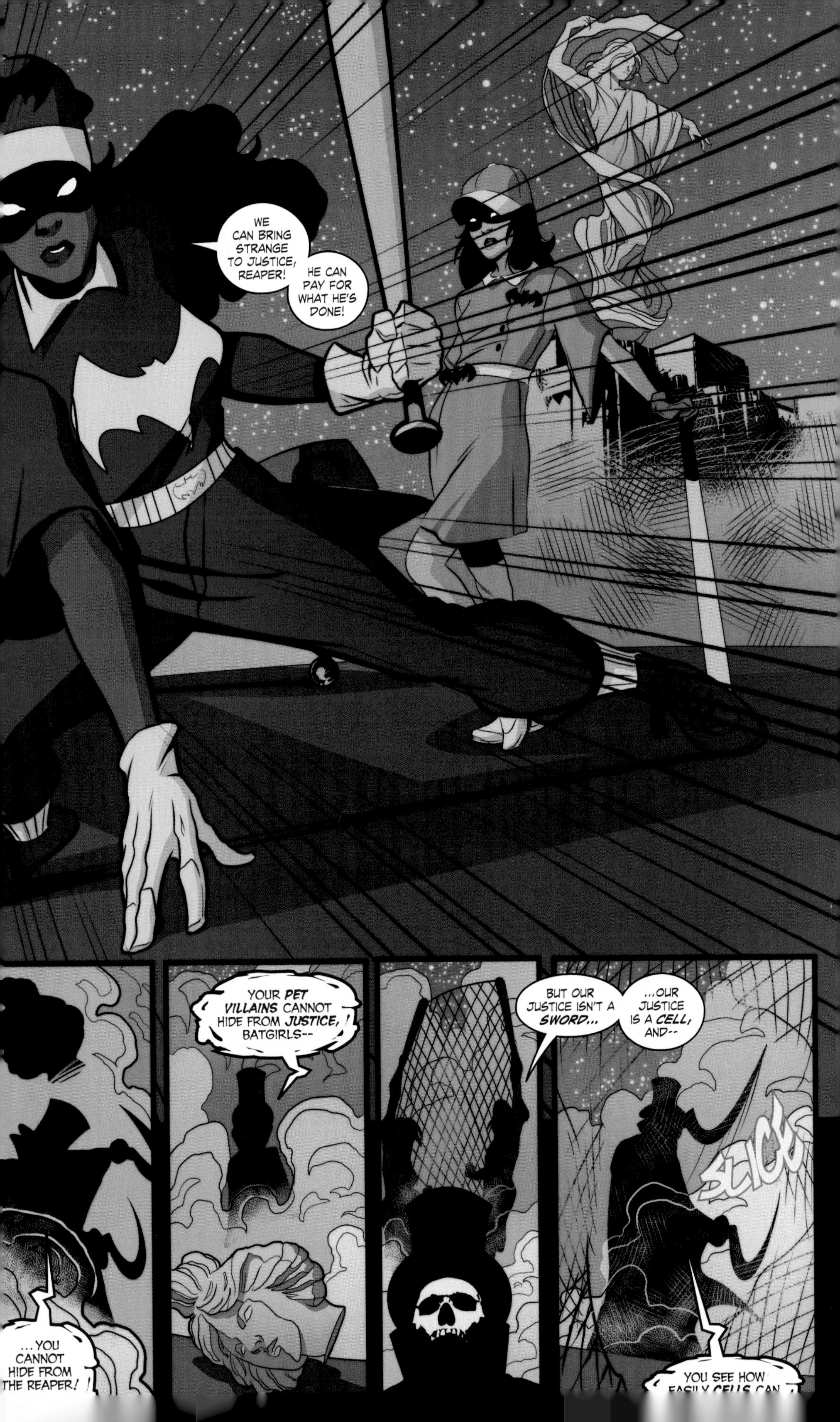
WE CAN BRING STRANGE TO JUSTICE, REAPER!
HE CAN PAY FOR WHAT HE'S DONE!
YOUR PET VILLAINS CANNOT HIDE FROM JUSTICE, BATGIRLS--
...YOU CANNOT HIDE FROM THE REAPER!
BUT OUR JUSTICE ISN'T A SWORD...
...OUR JUSTICE IS A CELL, AND--
SLICE
YOU SEE HOW EASILY CELLS CAN

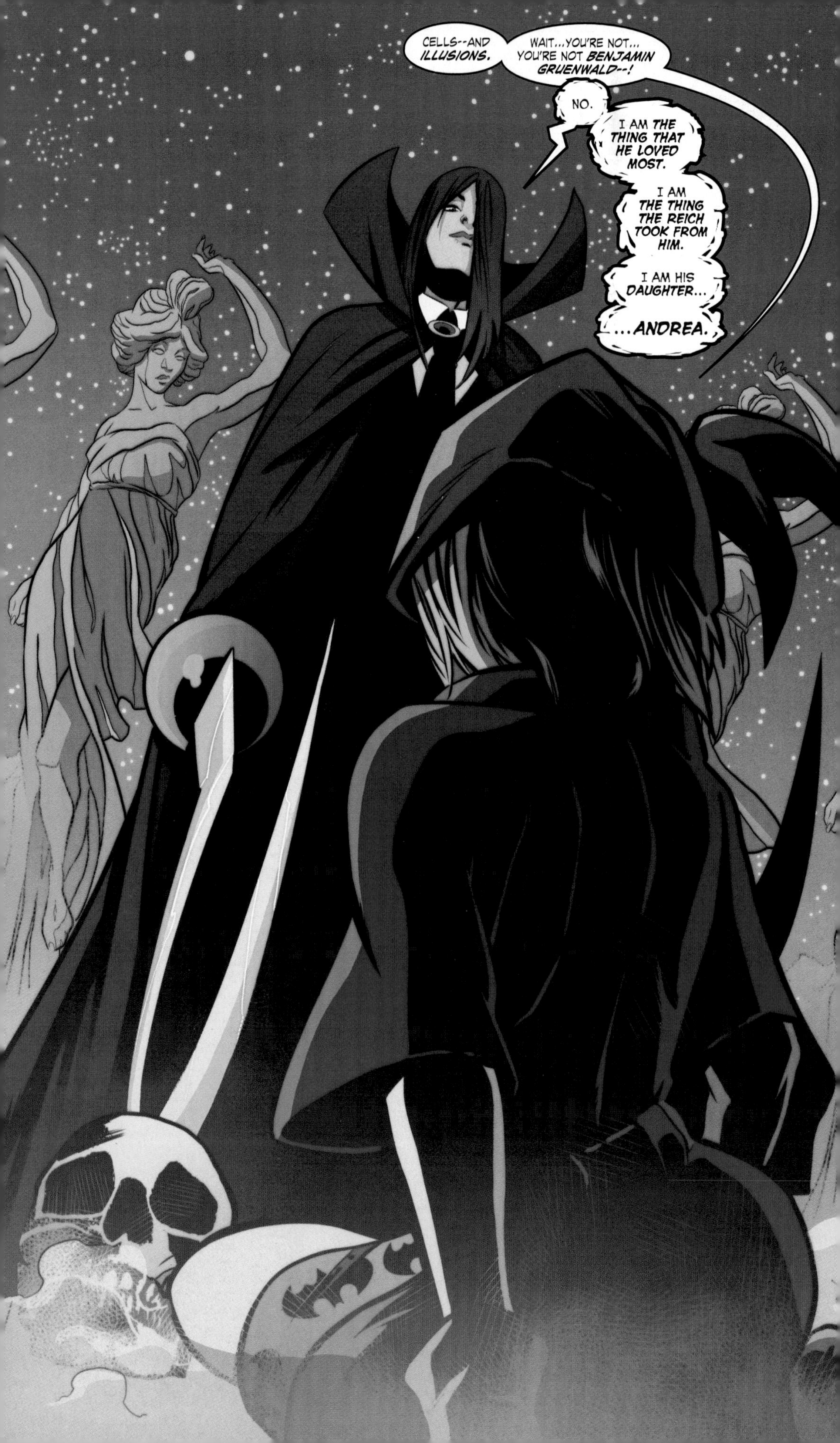
CELLS--AND *ILLUSIONS.*
WAIT...YOU'RE NOT... YOU'RE NOT *BENJAMIN GRUENWALD--!*
NO.
I AM *THE THING THAT HE LOVED MOST.*
I AM *THE THING THE REICH TOOK FROM HIM.*
I AM HIS *DAUGHTER...*
...ANDREA.

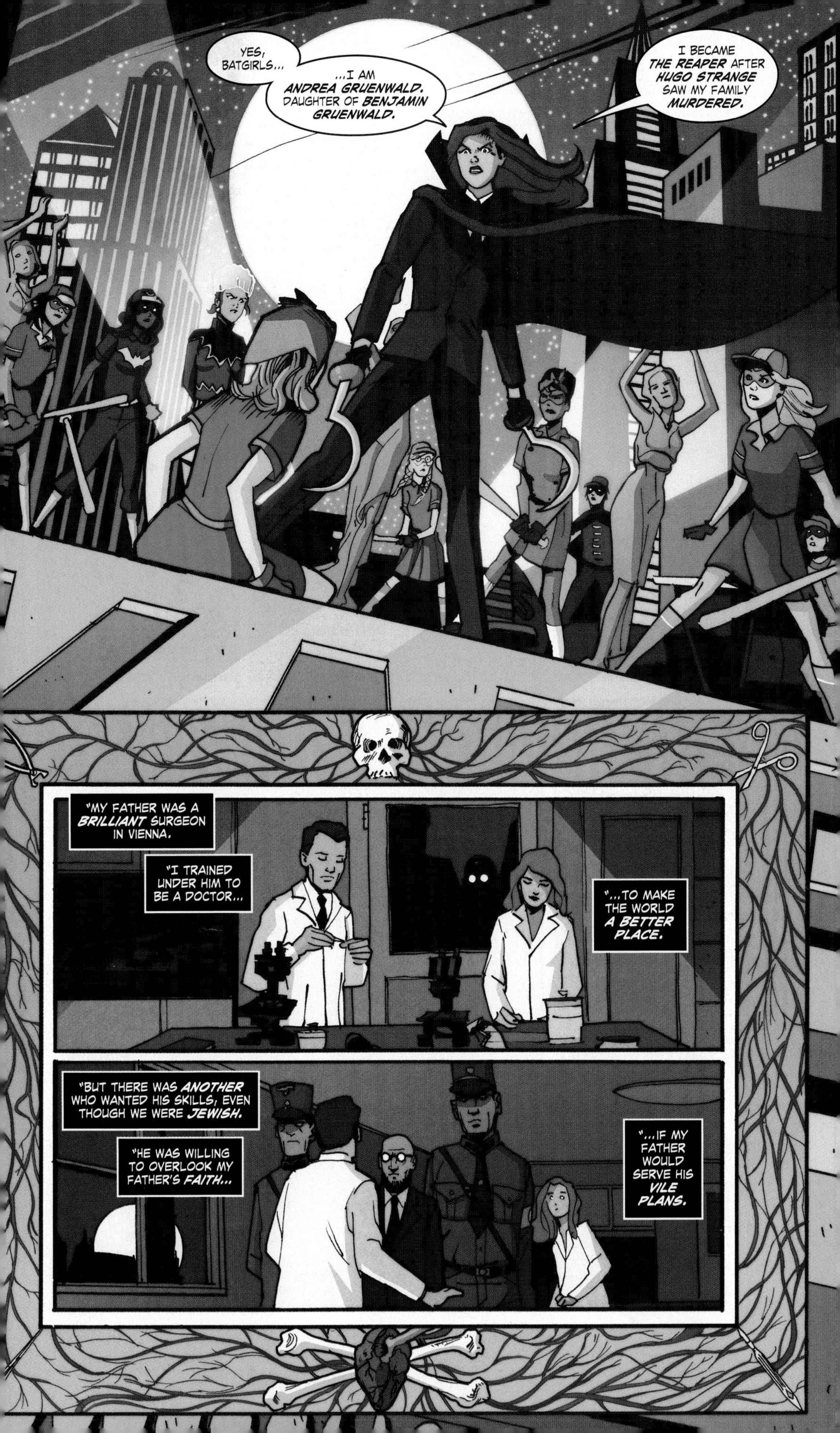
YES, BATGIRLS...
...I AM ANDREA GRUENWALD. DAUGHTER OF BENJAMIN GRUENWALD.
I BECAME THE REAPER AFTER HUGO STRANGE SAW MY FAMILY MURDERED.
"MY FATHER WAS A BRILLIANT SURGEON IN VIENNA.
"I TRAINED UNDER HIM TO BE A DOCTOR...
"...TO MAKE THE WORLD A BETTER PLACE.
"BUT THERE WAS ANOTHER WHO WANTED HIS SKILLS, EVEN THOUGH WE WERE JEWISH.
"HE WAS WILLING TO OVERLOOK MY FATHER'S FAITH...
"...IF MY FATHER WOULD SERVE HIS VILE PLANS.

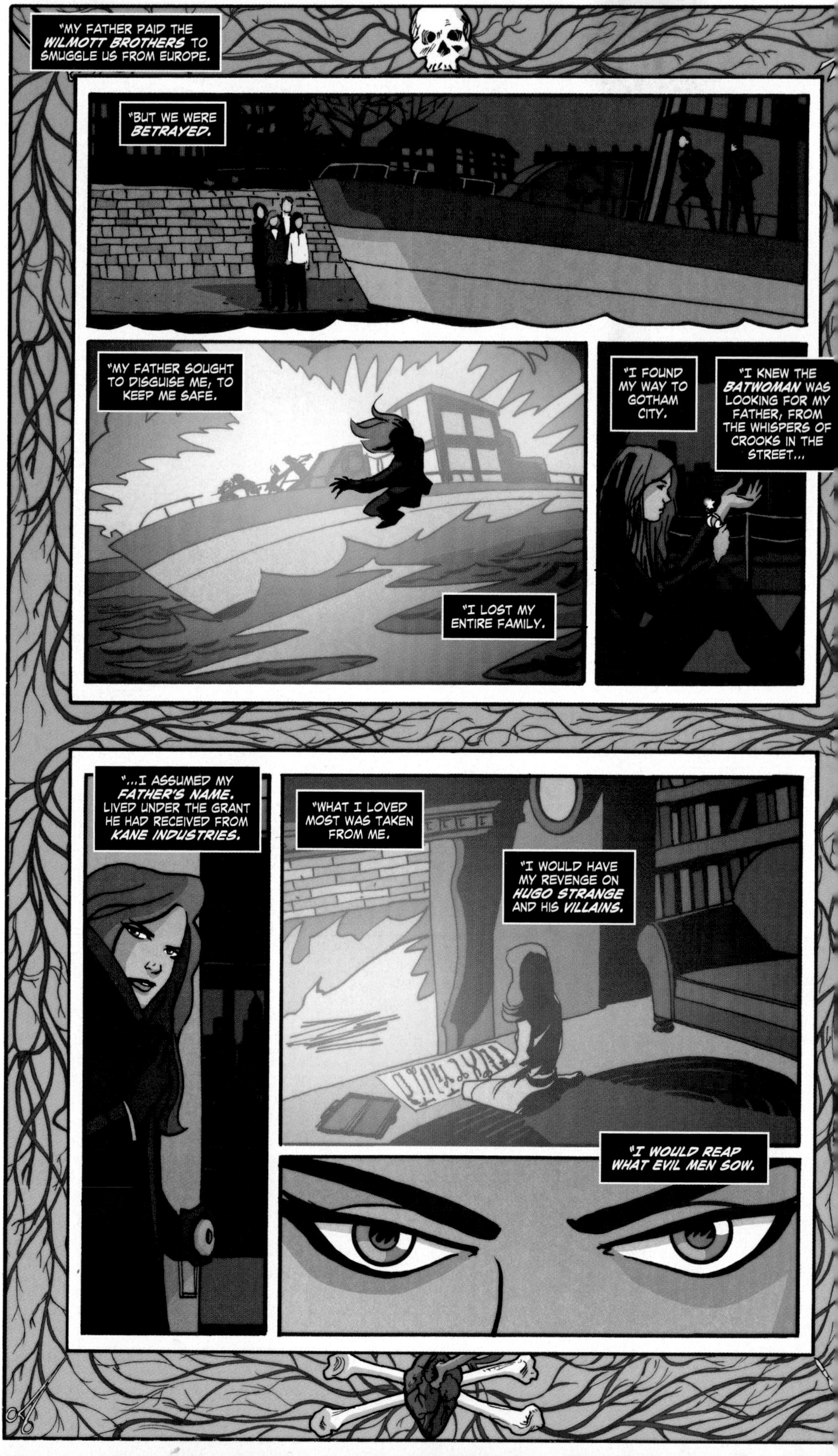
"MY FATHER PAID THE *WILMOTT BROTHERS* TO SMUGGLE US FROM EUROPE.
"BUT WE WERE *BETRAYED.*
"MY FATHER SOUGHT TO DISGUISE ME, TO KEEP ME SAFE.
"I LOST MY ENTIRE FAMILY.
"I FOUND MY WAY TO GOTHAM CITY.
"I KNEW THE *BATWOMAN* WAS LOOKING FOR MY FATHER, FROM THE WHISPERS OF CROOKS IN THE STREET...
"...I ASSUMED MY *FATHER'S NAME.* LIVED UNDER THE GRANT HE HAD RECEIVED FROM *KANE INDUSTRIES.*
"WHAT I LOVED MOST WAS TAKEN FROM ME.
"I WOULD HAVE MY REVENGE ON *HUGO STRANGE* AND HIS *VILLAINS.*
"I WOULD REAP WHAT EVIL MEN SOW.

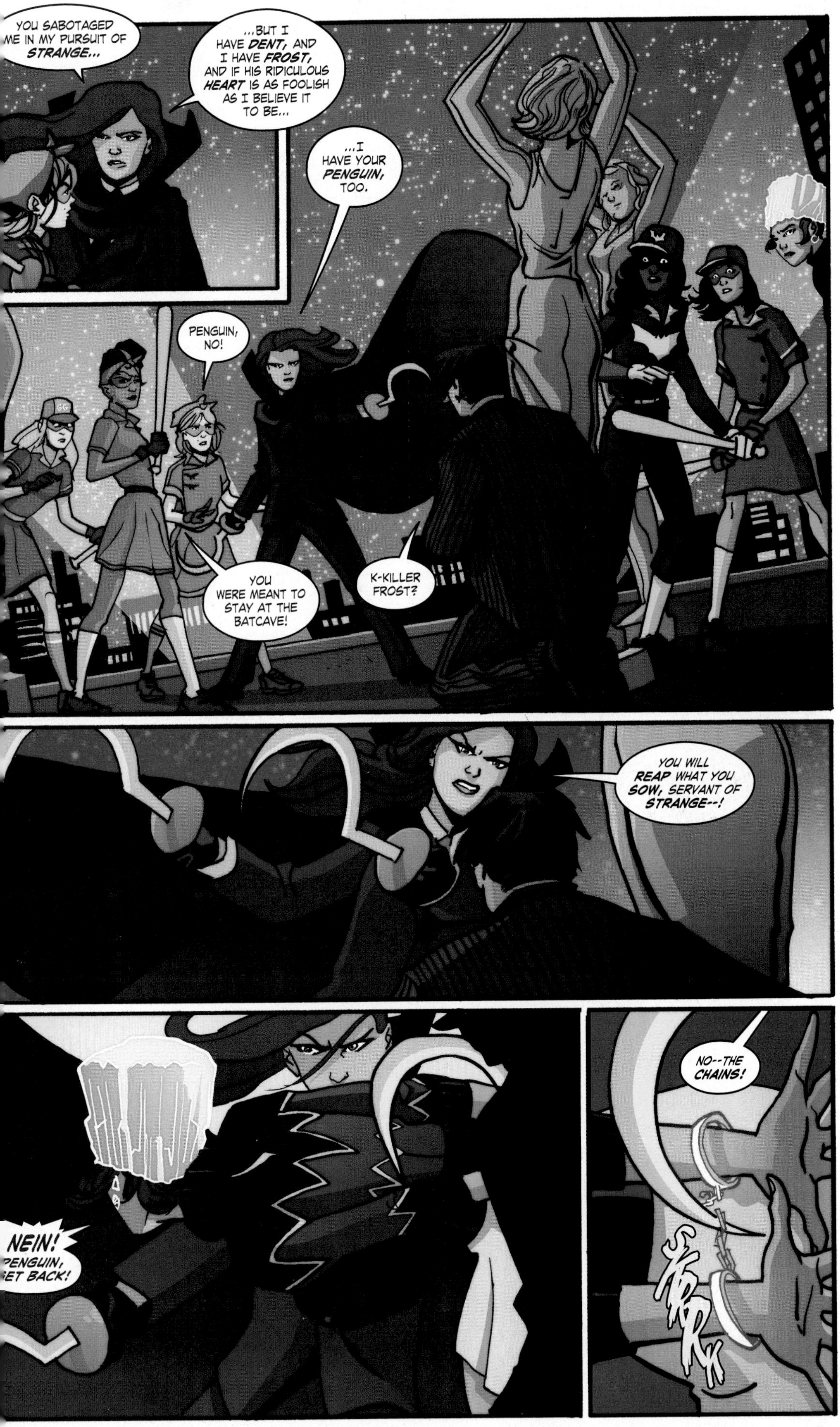
YOU SABOTAGED ME IN MY PURSUIT OF STRANGE...
...BUT I HAVE DENT, AND I HAVE FROST, AND IF HIS RIDICULOUS HEART IS AS FOOLISH AS I BELIEVE IT TO BE...
...I HAVE YOUR PENGUIN, TOO.
PENGUIN, NO!
YOU WERE MEANT TO STAY AT THE BATCAVE!
K-KILLER FROST?
YOU WILL REAP WHAT YOU SOW, SERVANT OF STRANGE--!
NEIN! PENGUIN, GET BACK!
NO--THE CHAINS!
SKRRKK

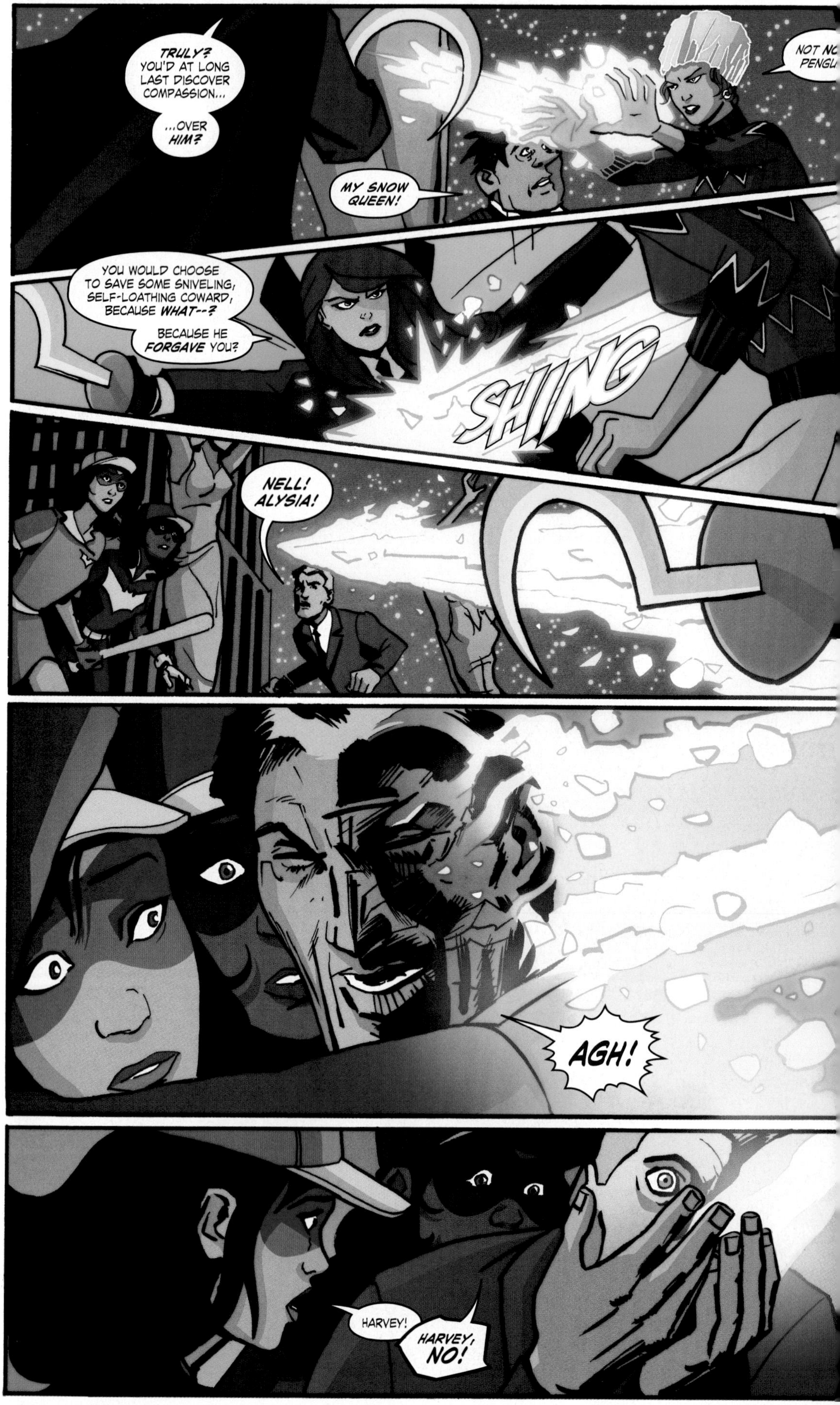
TRULY? YOU'D AT LONG LAST DISCOVER COMPASSION...
...OVER HIM?
MY SNOW QUEEN!
YOU WOULD CHOOSE TO SAVE SOME SNIVELING, SELF-LOATHING COWARD, BECAUSE WHAT--?
BECAUSE HE FORGAVE YOU?
SHING
NELL! ALYSIA!
AGH!
HARVEY!
HARVEY, NO!

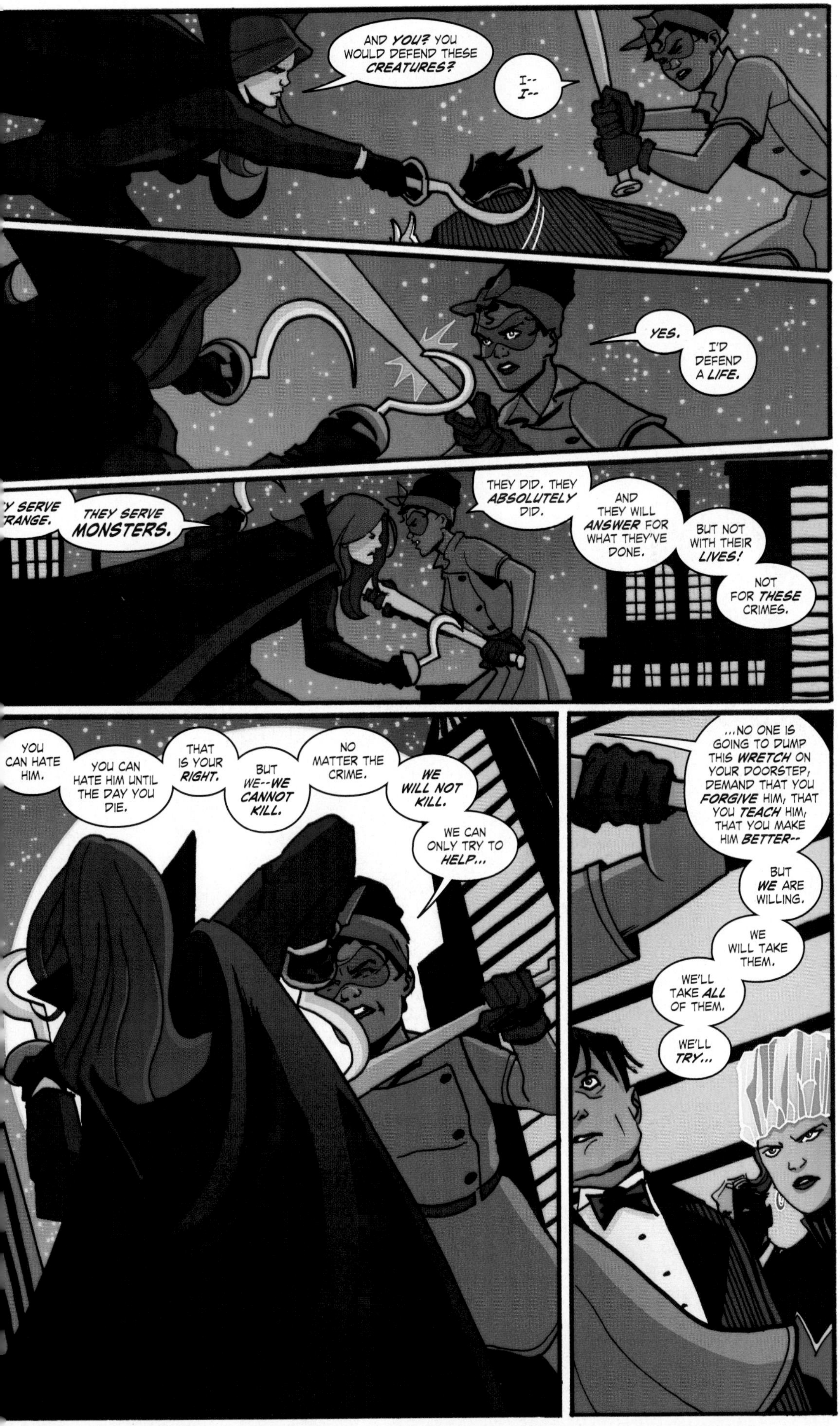
AND YOU? YOU WOULD DEFEND THESE CREATURES?
I-- I--
YES.
I'D DEFEND A LIFE.
Y SERVE RANGE.
THEY SERVE MONSTERS.
THEY DID. THEY ABSOLUTELY DID.
AND THEY WILL ANSWER FOR WHAT THEY'VE DONE.
BUT NOT WITH THEIR LIVES!
NOT FOR THESE CRIMES.
YOU CAN HATE HIM.
YOU CAN HATE HIM UNTIL THE DAY YOU DIE.
THAT IS YOUR RIGHT.
BUT WE--WE CANNOT KILL.
NO MATTER THE CRIME.
WE WILL NOT KILL.
WE CAN ONLY TRY TO HELP...
...NO ONE IS GOING TO DUMP THIS WRETCH ON YOUR DOORSTEP, DEMAND THAT YOU FORGIVE HIM, THAT YOU TEACH HIM, THAT YOU MAKE HIM BETTER--
BUT WE ARE WILLING.
WE WILL TAKE THEM.
WE'LL TAKE ALL OF THEM.
WE'LL TRY...

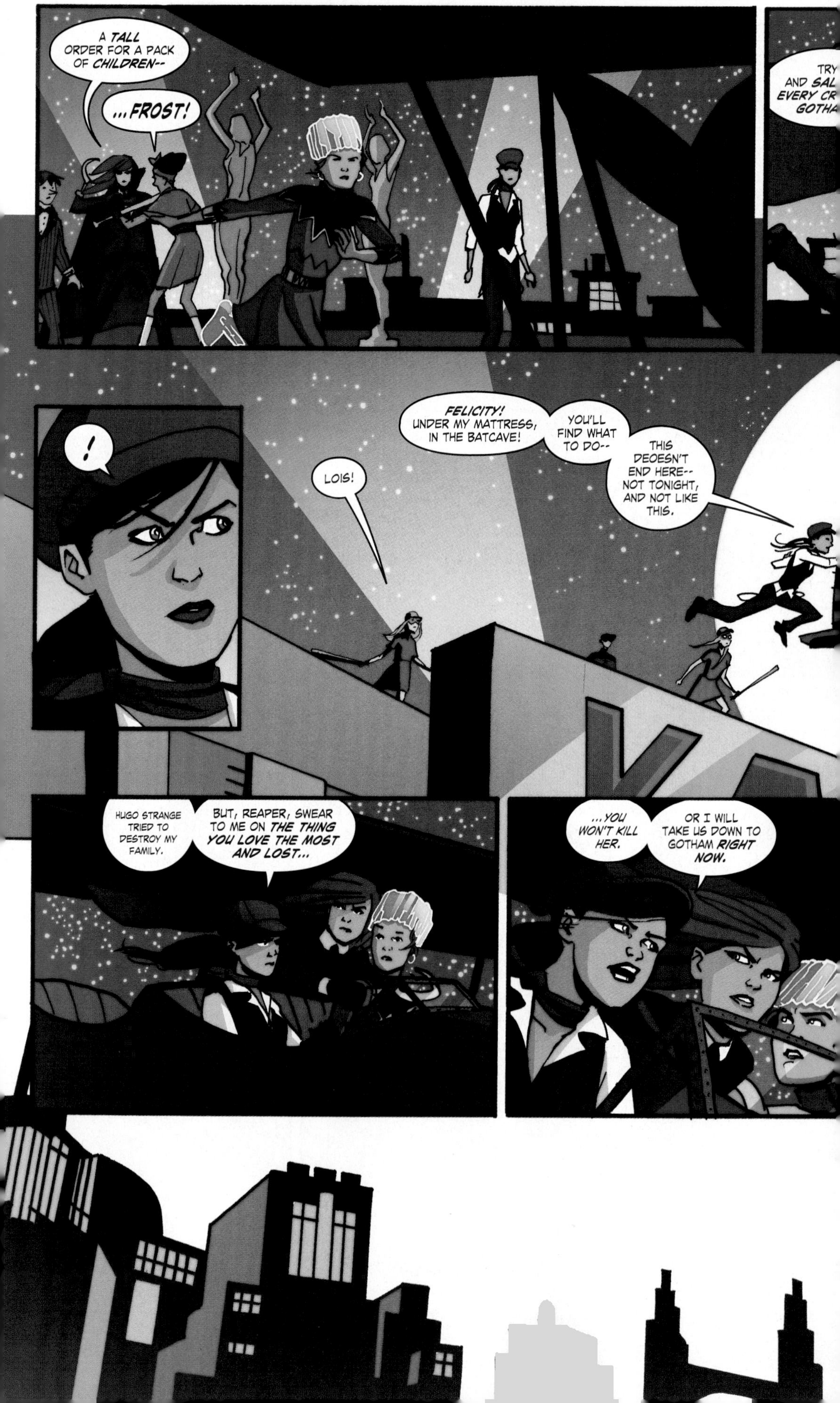
A TALL ORDER FOR A PACK OF CHILDREN--
...FROST!
!
LOIS!
FELICITY! UNDER MY MATTRESS, IN THE BATCAVE!
YOU'LL FIND WHAT TO DO--
THIS DEOESN'T END HERE-- NOT TONIGHT, AND NOT LIKE THIS.
HUGO STRANGE TRIED TO DESTROY MY FAMILY.
BUT, REAPER, SWEAR TO ME ON THE THING YOU LOVE THE MOST AND LOST...
...YOU WON'T KILL HER.
OR I WILL TAKE US DOWN TO GOTHAM RIGHT NOW.

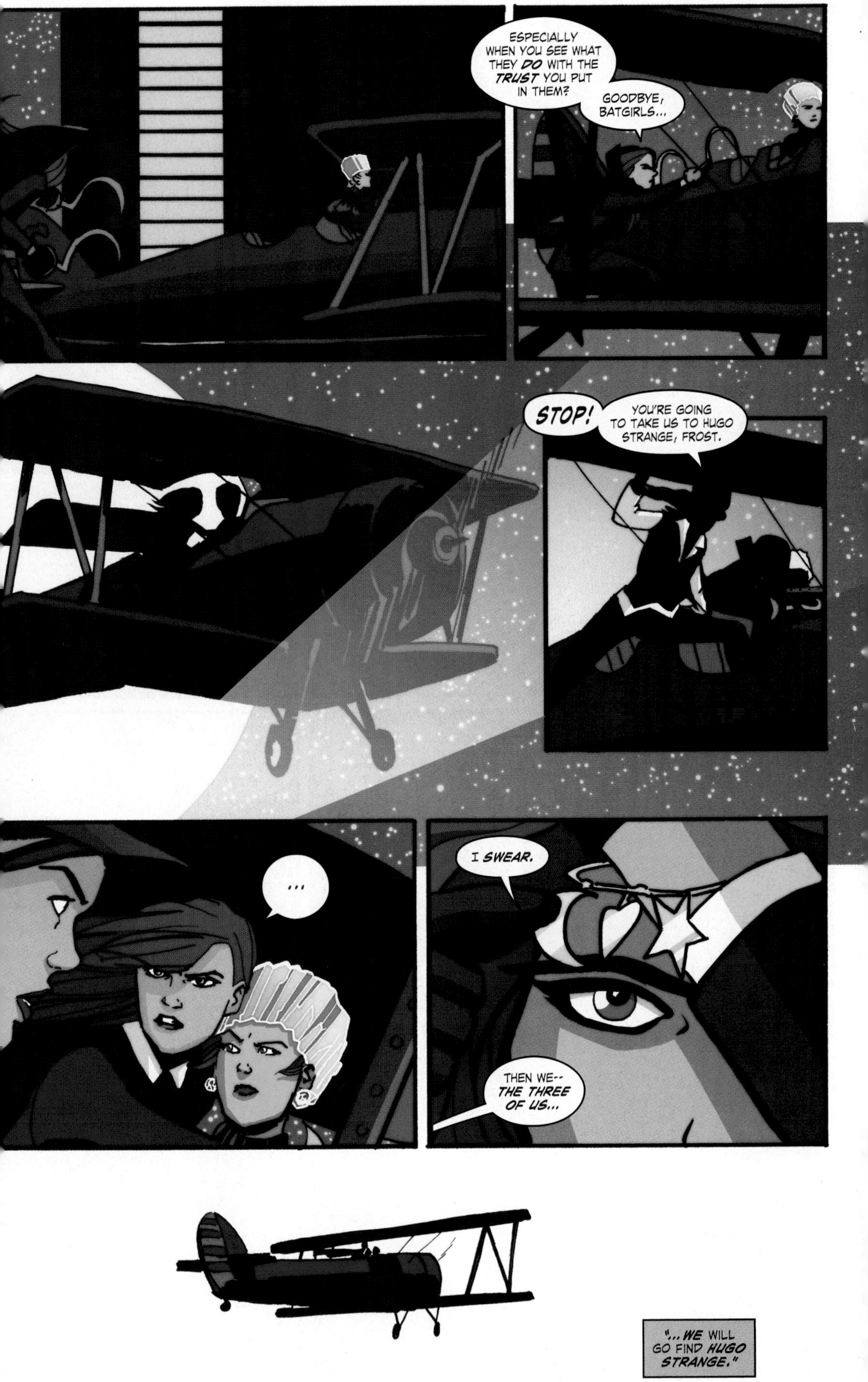
ESPECIALLY WHEN YOU SEE WHAT THEY *DO* WITH THE *TRUST* YOU PUT IN THEM?
GOODBYE, BATGIRLS...
STOP!
YOU'RE GOING TO TAKE US TO HUGO STRANGE, FROST.
...
I *SWEAR.*
THEN WE-- *THE THREE OF US...*
"...*WE* WILL GO FIND *HUGO STRANGE.*"

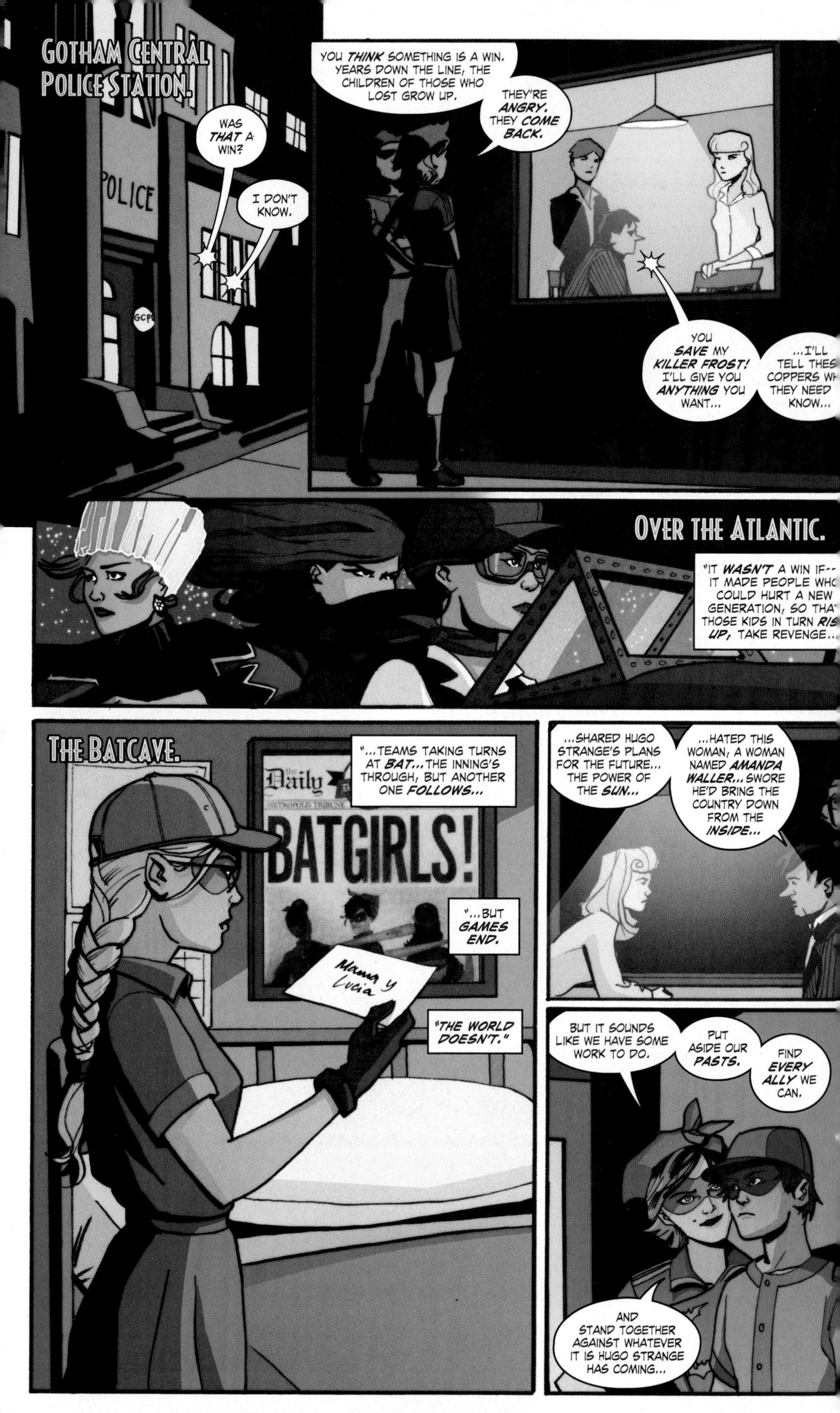
GOTHAM CENTRAL POLICE STATION.
WAS *THAT* A WIN?
I DON'T KNOW.
POLICE
GCPD
YOU *THINK* SOMETHING IS A WIN. YEARS DOWN THE LINE, THE CHILDREN OF THOSE WHO LOST GROW UP.
THEY'RE *ANGRY.* THEY *COME BACK.*
YOU *SAVE* MY *KILLER FROST!* I'LL GIVE YOU *ANYTHING* YOU WANT...
...I'LL TELL THES COPPERS WH THEY NEED KNOW...
OVER THE ATLANTIC.
"IT *WASN'T* A WIN IF-- IT MADE PEOPLE WHO COULD HURT A NEW GENERATION, SO THAT THOSE KIDS IN TURN *RIS UP,* TAKE REVENGE...
THE BATCAVE.
"...TEAMS TAKING TURNS AT *BAT...* THE INNING'S THROUGH, BUT ANOTHER ONE *FOLLOWS...*
the Daily
METROPOLIS TRIBUNE
BATGIRLS!
"...BUT *GAMES END.*
Mama y Lucia
"THE WORLD DOESN'T."
...SHARED HUGO STRANGE'S PLANS FOR THE FUTURE... THE POWER OF THE *SUN...*
...HATED THIS WOMAN, A WOMAN NAMED *AMANDA WALLER...* SWORE HE'D BRING THE COUNTRY DOWN FROM THE *INSIDE...*
BUT IT SOUNDS LIKE WE HAVE SOME WORK TO DO.
PUT ASIDE OUR *PASTS.*
FIND *EVERY ALLY* WE CAN.
AND STAND TOGETHER AGAINST WHATEVER IT IS HUGO STRANGE HAS COMING...

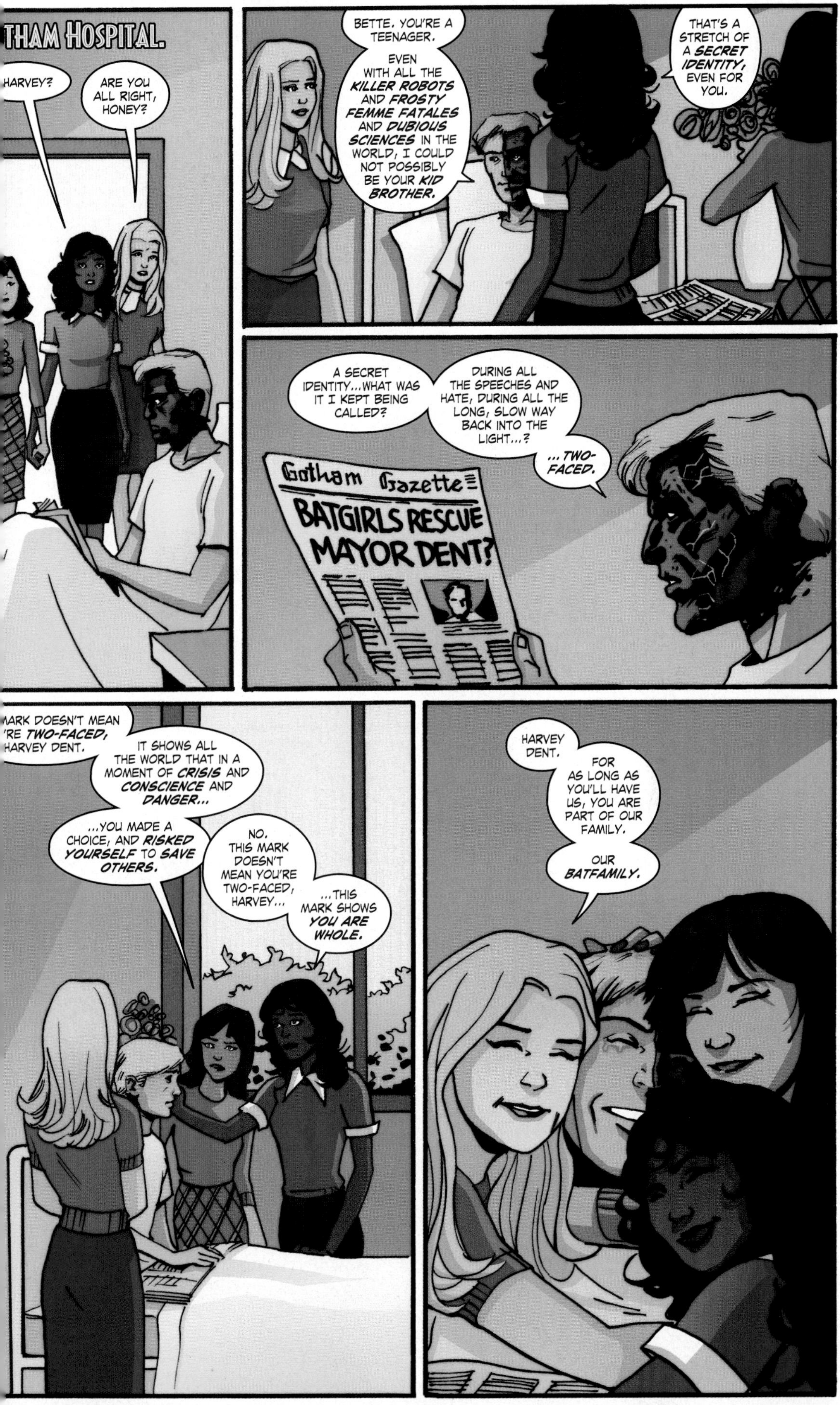

THAM HOSPITAL.
HARVEY?
ARE YOU ALL RIGHT, HONEY?
BETTE, YOU'RE A TEENAGER.
EVEN WITH ALL THE KILLER ROBOTS AND FROSTY FEMME FATALES AND DUBIOUS SCIENCES IN THE WORLD, I COULD NOT POSSIBLY BE YOUR KID BROTHER.
THAT'S A STRETCH OF A SECRET IDENTITY, EVEN FOR YOU.
A SECRET IDENTITY...WHAT WAS IT I KEPT BEING CALLED?
DURING ALL THE SPEECHES AND HATE, DURING ALL THE LONG, SLOW WAY BACK INTO THE LIGHT...?
...TWO-FACED.
Gotham Gazette
BATGIRLS RESCUE MAYOR DENT?
MARK DOESN'T MEAN 'RE TWO-FACED, HARVEY DENT.
IT SHOWS ALL THE WORLD THAT IN A MOMENT OF CRISIS AND CONSCIENCE AND DANGER...
...YOU MADE A CHOICE, AND RISKED YOURSELF TO SAVE OTHERS.
NO. THIS MARK DOESN'T MEAN YOU'RE TWO-FACED, HARVEY...
...THIS MARK SHOWS YOU ARE WHOLE.
HARVEY DENT.
FOR AS LONG AS YOU'LL HAVE US, YOU ARE PART OF OUR FAMILY.
OUR BATFAMILY.

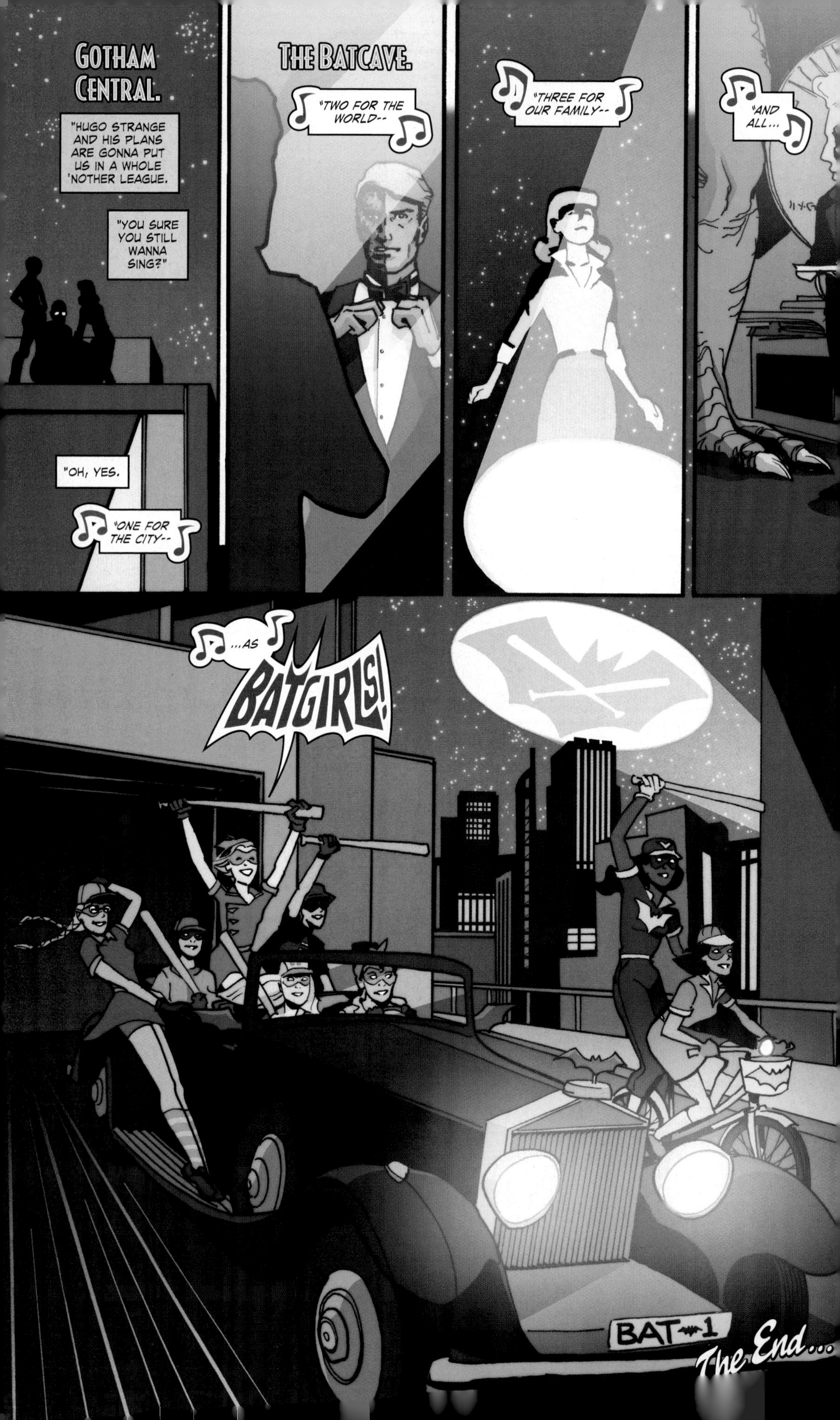
GOTHAM CENTRAL.
"HUGO STRANGE AND HIS PLANS ARE GONNA PUT US IN A WHOLE 'NOTHER LEAGUE.
"YOU SURE YOU STILL WANNA SING?"
"OH, YES.
"ONE FOR THE CITY--
THE BATCAVE.
"TWO FOR THE WORLD--
"THREE FOR OUR FAMILY--
"AND ALL...
...AS
BATGIRLS!
BAT-1
The End...

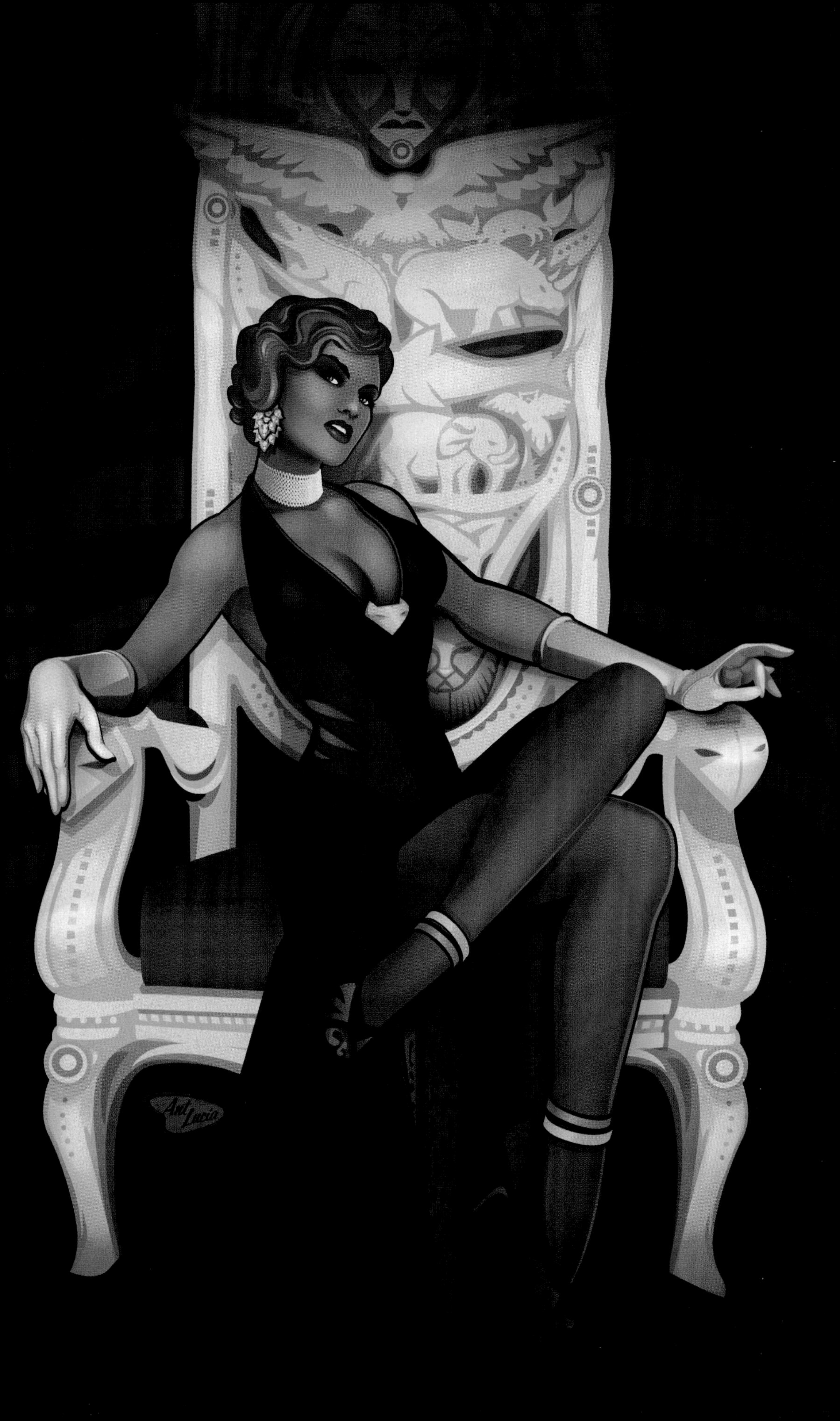
Ant Lucia

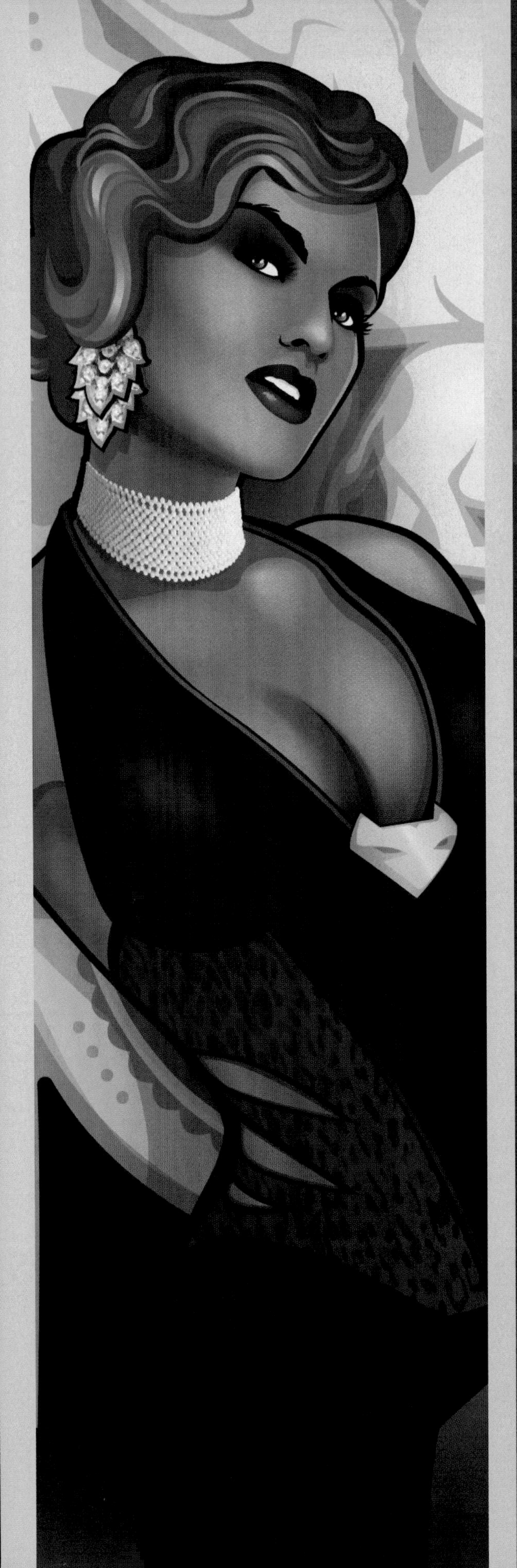

MEN WHO WOULD BE KINGS

MARGUERITE BENNETT

Writer

MARGUERITE SAUVAGE
MIRKA ANDOLFO
LAURA BRAGA

Artists

MARGUERITE SAUVAGE
WENDY BROOME
J. NANJAN

Colorists

Cover by
ANT LUCIA

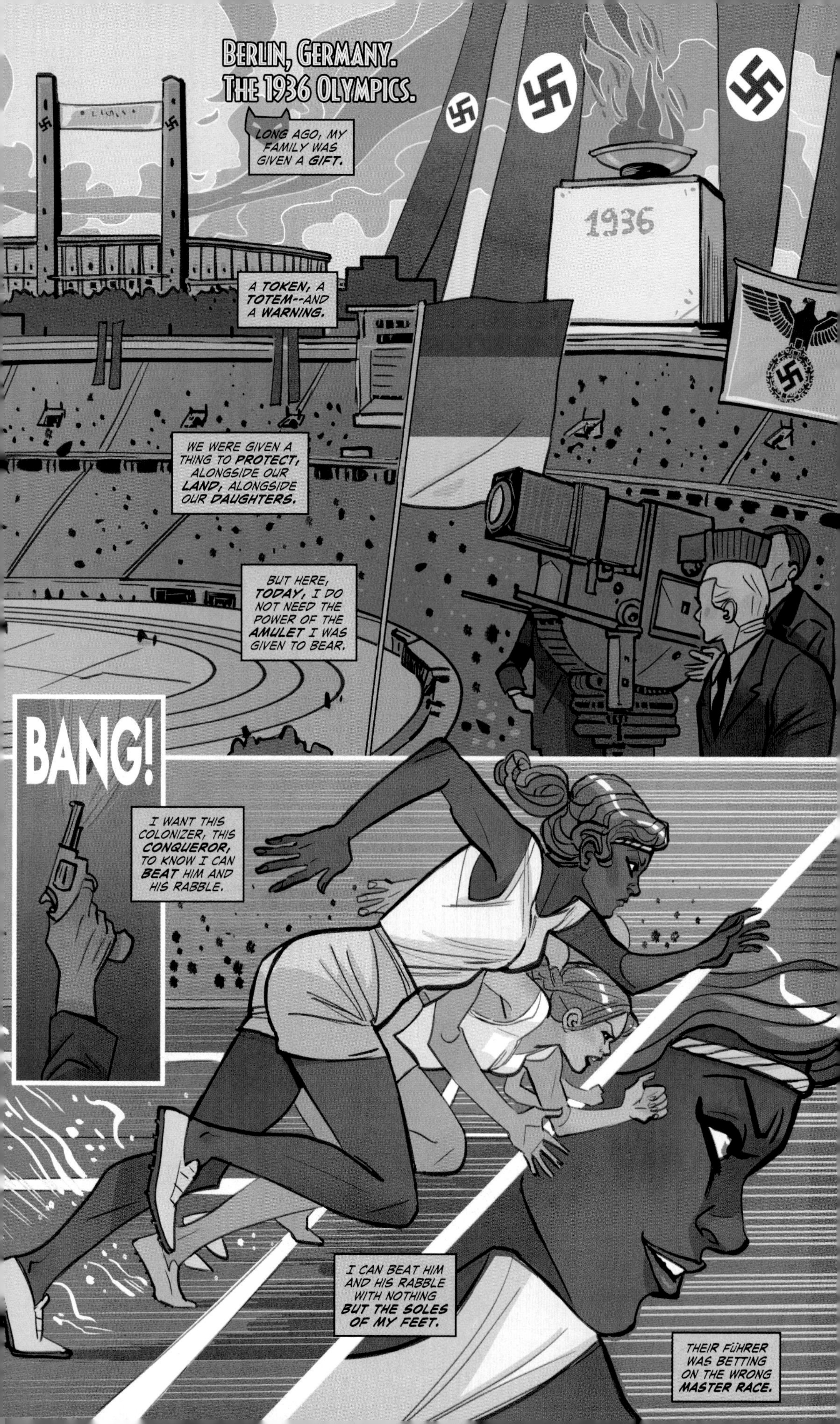
BERLIN, GERMANY.
THE 1936 OLYMPICS.
LONG AGO, MY FAMILY WAS GIVEN A GIFT.
1936
A TOKEN, A TOTEM--AND A WARNING.
WE WERE GIVEN A THING TO PROTECT, ALONGSIDE OUR LAND, ALONGSIDE OUR DAUGHTERS.
BUT HERE, TODAY, I DO NOT NEED THE POWER OF THE AMULET I WAS GIVEN TO BEAR.
BANG!
I WANT THIS COLONIZER, THIS CONQUEROR, TO KNOW I CAN BEAT HIM AND HIS RABBLE.
I CAN BEAT HIM AND HIS RABBLE WITH NOTHING BUT THE SOLES OF MY FEET.
THEIR FÜHRER WAS BETTING ON THE WRONG MASTER RACE.

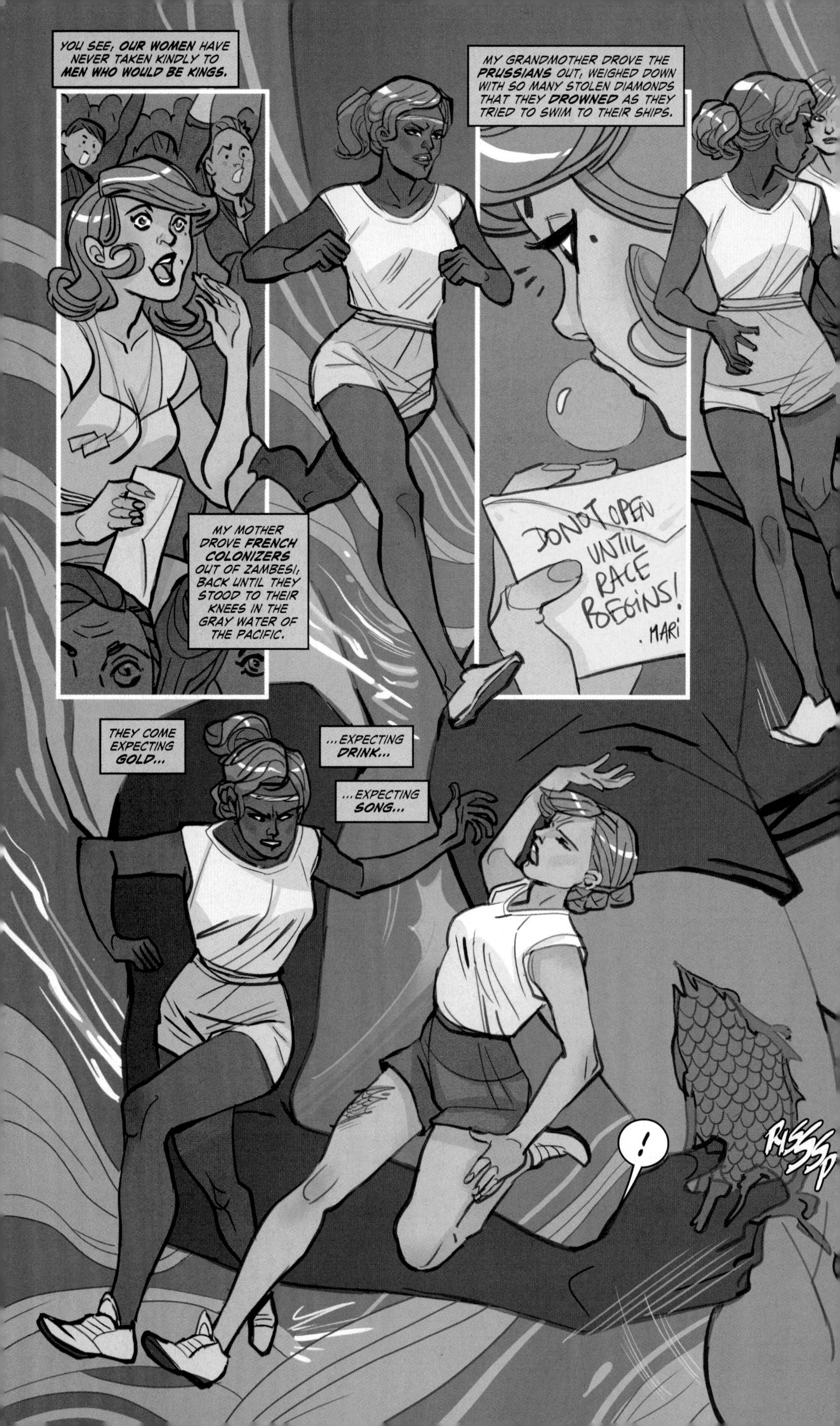

YOU SEE, OUR WOMEN HAVE NEVER TAKEN KINDLY TO MEN WHO WOULD BE KINGS.
MY MOTHER DROVE FRENCH COLONIZERS OUT OF ZAMBESI, BACK UNTIL THEY STOOD TO THEIR KNEES IN THE GRAY WATER OF THE PACIFIC.
MY GRANDMOTHER DROVE THE PRUSSIANS OUT, WEIGHED DOWN WITH SO MANY STOLEN DIAMONDS THAT THEY DROWNED AS THEY TRIED TO SWIM TO THEIR SHIPS.
DO NOT OPEN UNTIL RACE BEGINS! . MARI
THEY COME EXPECTING GOLD...
...EXPECTING DRINK...
...EXPECTING SONG...
!
RASSSP

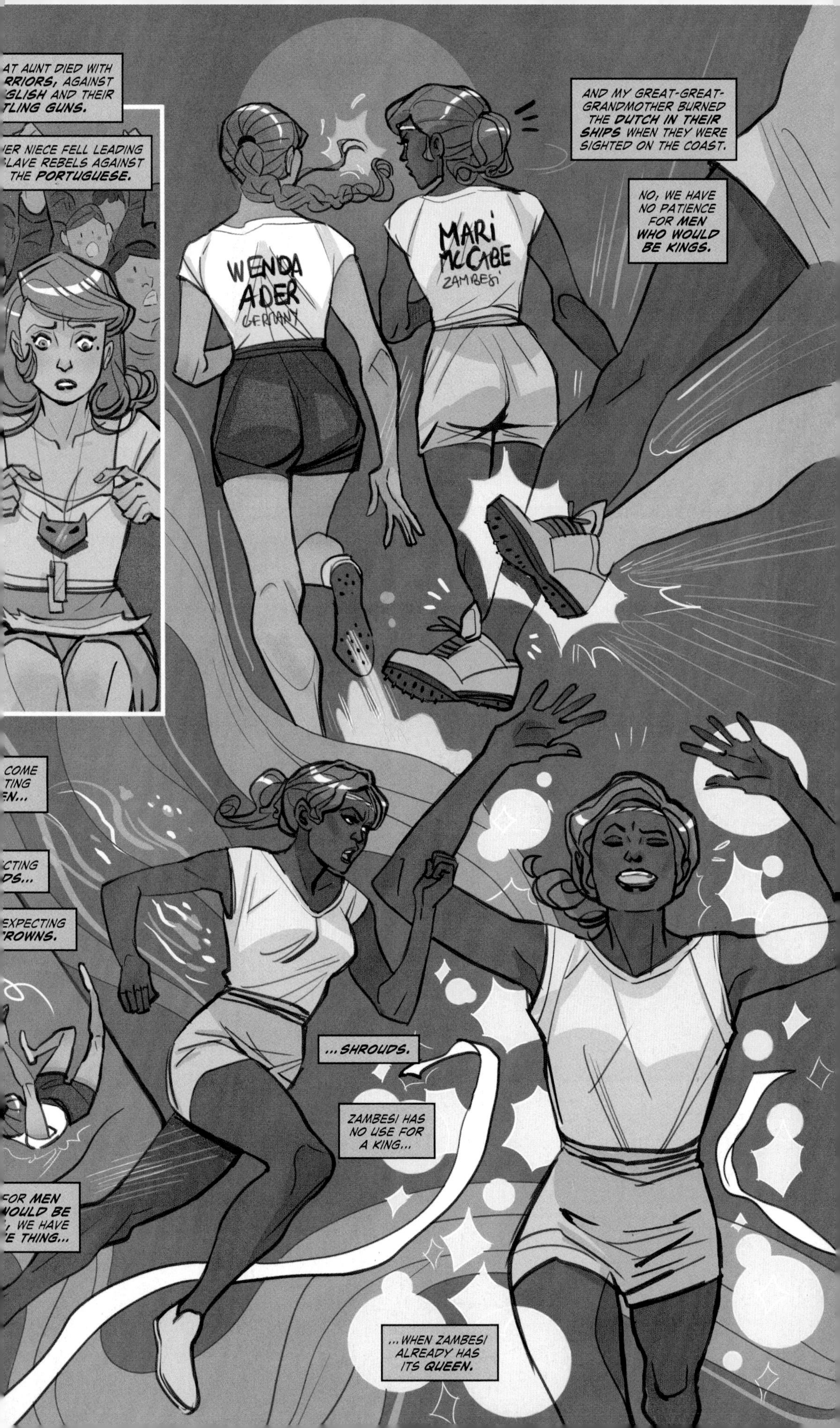

AT AUNT DIED WITH
RRIORS, AGAINST
IGLISH AND THEIR
TLING GUNS.
ER NIECE FELL LEADING
SLAVE REBELS AGAINST
THE PORTUGUESE.
AND MY GREAT-GREAT-GRANDMOTHER BURNED THE DUTCH IN THEIR SHIPS WHEN THEY WERE SIGHTED ON THE COAST.
NO, WE HAVE NO PATIENCE FOR MEN WHO WOULD BE KINGS.
WENDA ADER GERMANY
MARI McCABE ZAMBESI
COME
TING
EN...
CTING
DS...
EXPECTING
CROWNS.
FOR MEN
WOULD BE
, WE HAVE
E THING...
...SHROUDS.
ZAMBESI HAS NO USE FOR A KING...
...WHEN ZAMBESI ALREADY HAS ITS QUEEN.

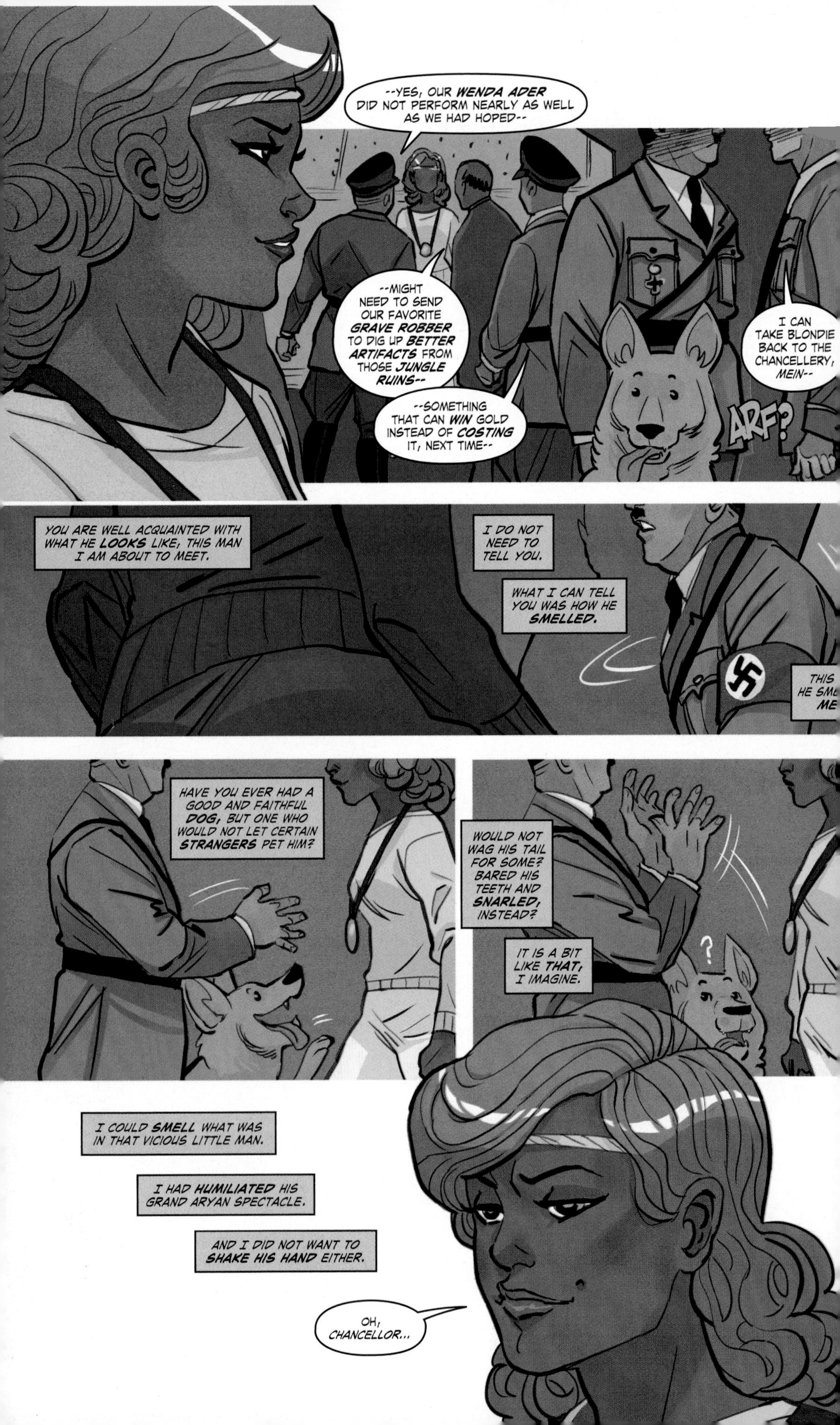

--YES, OUR WENDA ADER DID NOT PERFORM NEARLY AS WELL AS WE HAD HOPED--
--MIGHT NEED TO SEND OUR FAVORITE GRAVE ROBBER TO DIG UP BETTER ARTIFACTS FROM THOSE JUNGLE RUINS--
--SOMETHING THAT CAN WIN GOLD INSTEAD OF COSTING IT, NEXT TIME--
I CAN TAKE BLONDIE BACK TO THE CHANCELLERY, MEIN--
ARF?
YOU ARE WELL ACQUAINTED WITH WHAT HE LOOKS LIKE, THIS MAN I AM ABOUT TO MEET.
I DO NOT NEED TO TELL YOU.
WHAT I CAN TELL YOU WAS HOW HE SMELLED.
HAVE YOU EVER HAD A GOOD AND FAITHFUL DOG, BUT ONE WHO WOULD NOT LET CERTAIN STRANGERS PET HIM?
WOULD NOT WAG HIS TAIL FOR SOME? BARED HIS TEETH AND SNARLED, INSTEAD?
IT IS A BIT LIKE THAT, I IMAGINE.
?
I COULD SMELL WHAT WAS IN THAT VICIOUS LITTLE MAN.
I HAD HUMILIATED HIS GRAND ARYAN SPECTACLE.
AND I DID NOT WANT TO SHAKE HIS HAND EITHER.
OH, CHANCELLOR...

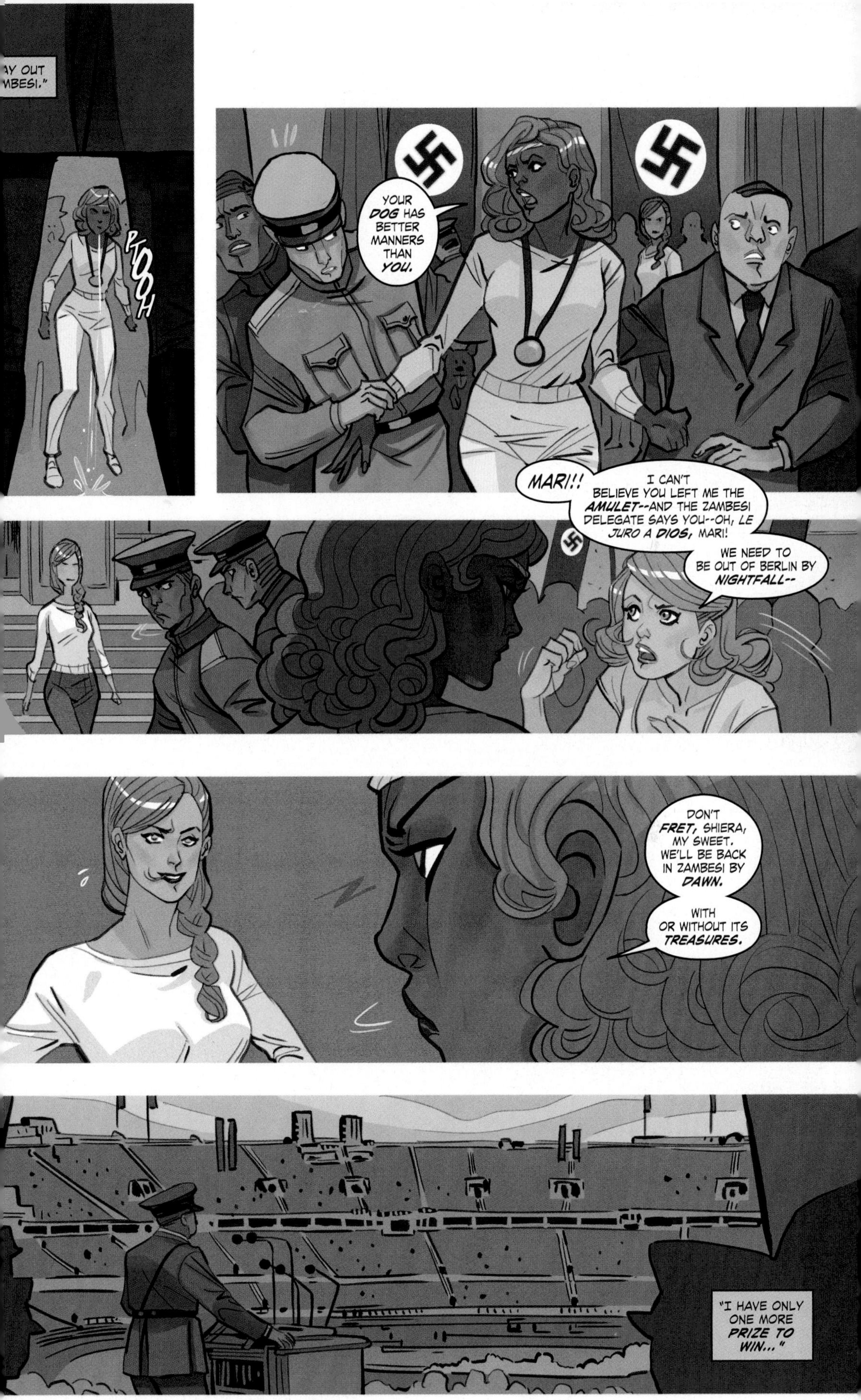

AY OUT
MBESI."
PTOOH
YOUR DOG HAS BETTER MANNERS THAN YOU.
MARI!!
I CAN'T BELIEVE YOU LEFT ME THE AMULET--AND THE ZAMBESI DELEGATE SAYS YOU--OH, LE JURO A DIOS, MARI!
WE NEED TO BE OUT OF BERLIN BY NIGHTFALL--
DON'T FRET, SHIERA, MY SWEET. WE'LL BE BACK IN ZAMBESI BY DAWN.
WITH OR WITHOUT ITS TREASURES.
"I HAVE ONLY ONE MORE PRIZE TO WIN..."

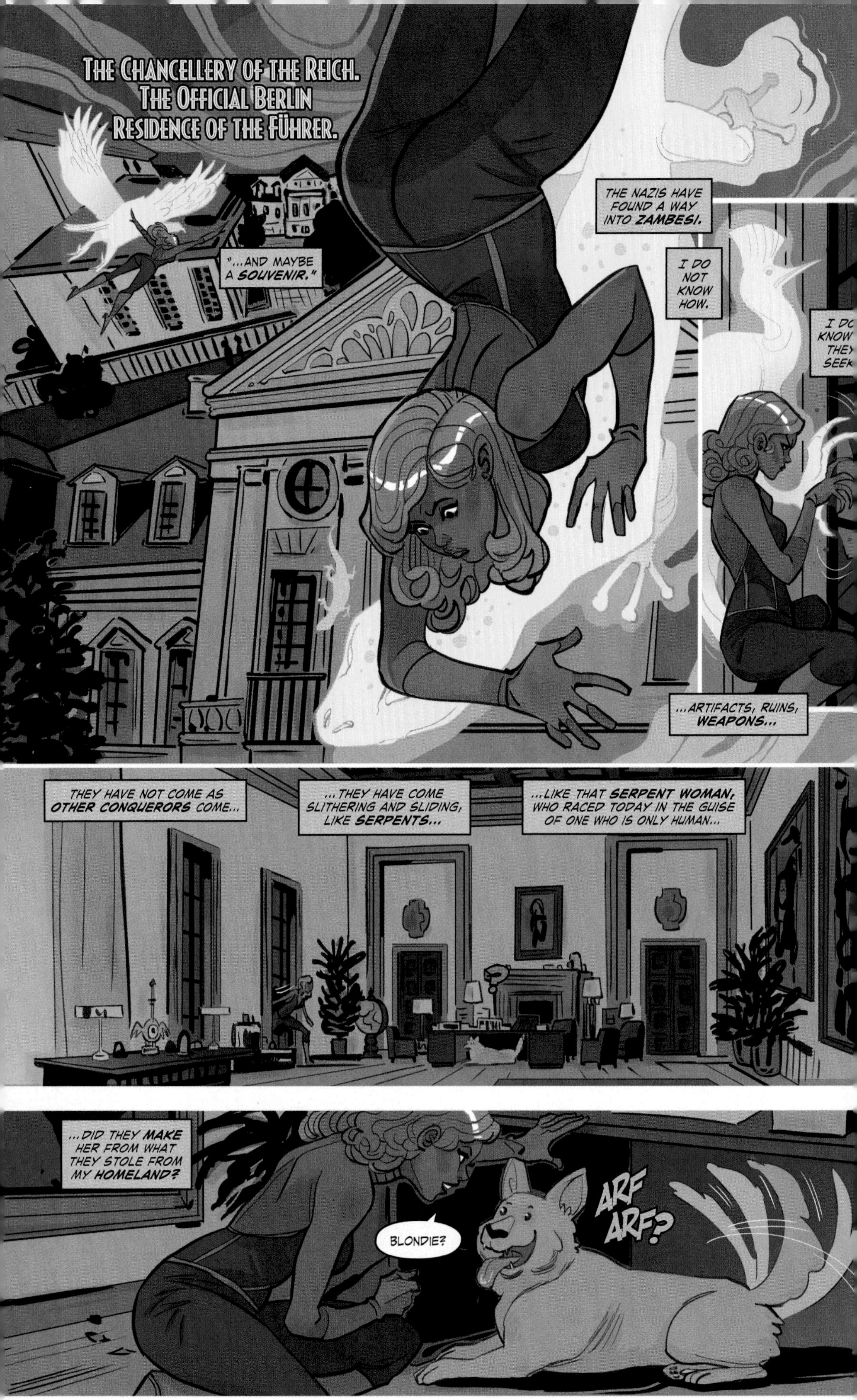

The Chancellery of the Reich. The Official Berlin Residence of the Führer.
"...AND MAYBE A SOUVENIR."
THE NAZIS HAVE FOUND A WAY INTO ZAMBESI.
I DO NOT KNOW HOW.
...ARTIFACTS, RUINS, WEAPONS...
THEY HAVE NOT COME AS OTHER CONQUERORS COME...
...THEY HAVE COME SLITHERING AND SLIDING, LIKE SERPENTS...
...LIKE THAT SERPENT WOMAN, WHO RACED TODAY IN THE GUISE OF ONE WHO IS ONLY HUMAN...
...DID THEY MAKE HER FROM WHAT THEY STOLE FROM MY HOMELAND?
BLONDIE?
ARF ARF?

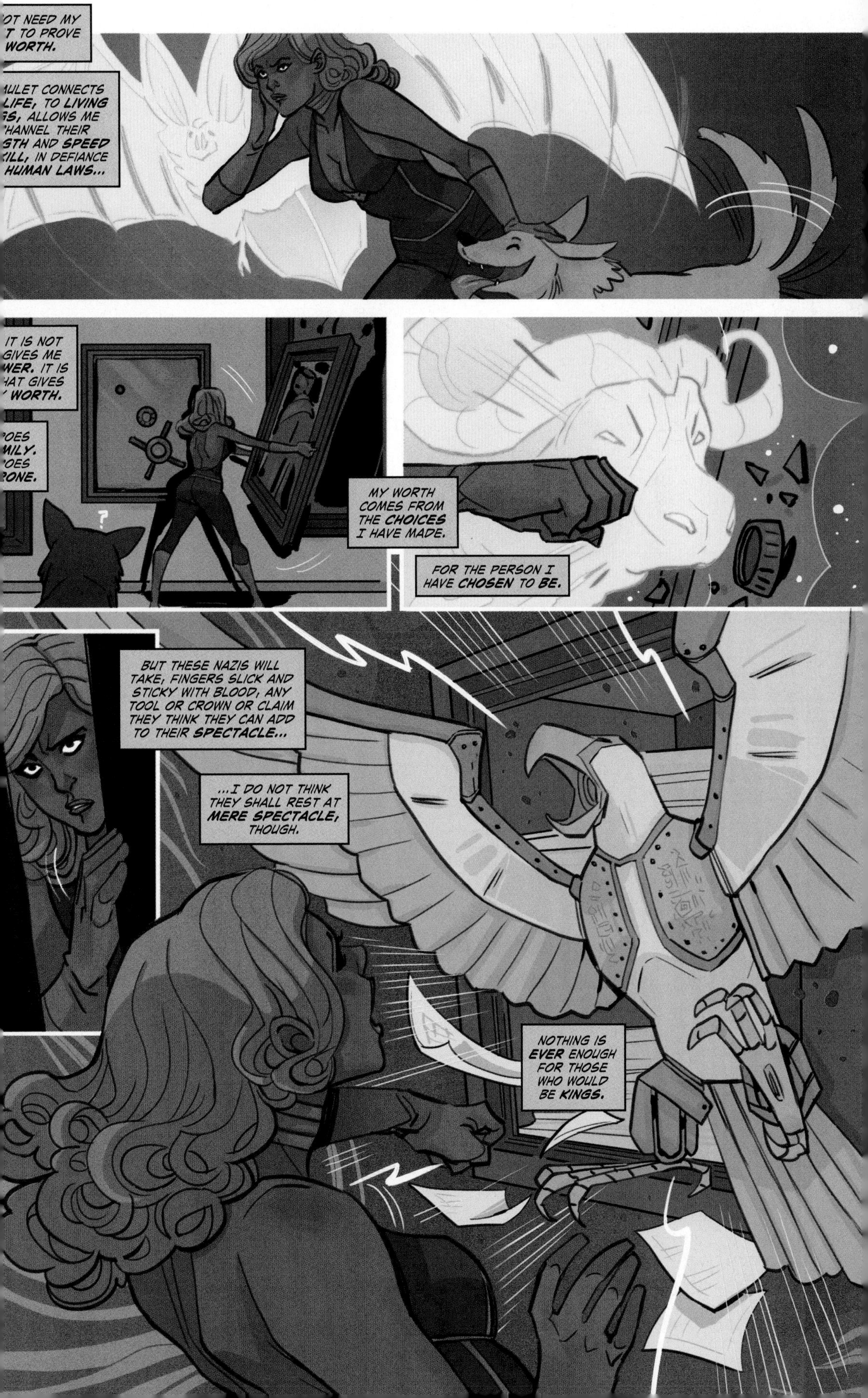
OT NEED MY
T TO PROVE
WORTH.
ULET CONNECTS
LIFE, TO LIVING
GS, ALLOWS ME
HANNEL THEIR
GTH AND SPEED
KILL, IN DEFIANCE
HUMAN LAWS...
IT IS NOT
GIVES ME
WER. IT IS
HAT GIVES
WORTH.
OES
MILY.
OES
ONE.
?
MY WORTH COMES FROM THE CHOICES I HAVE MADE.
FOR THE PERSON I HAVE CHOSEN TO BE.
BUT THESE NAZIS WILL TAKE, FINGERS SLICK AND STICKY WITH BLOOD, ANY TOOL OR CROWN OR CLAIM THEY THINK THEY CAN ADD TO THEIR SPECTACLE...
...I DO NOT THINK THEY SHALL REST AT MERE SPECTACLE, THOUGH.
NOTHING IS EVER ENOUGH FOR THOSE WHO WOULD BE KINGS.

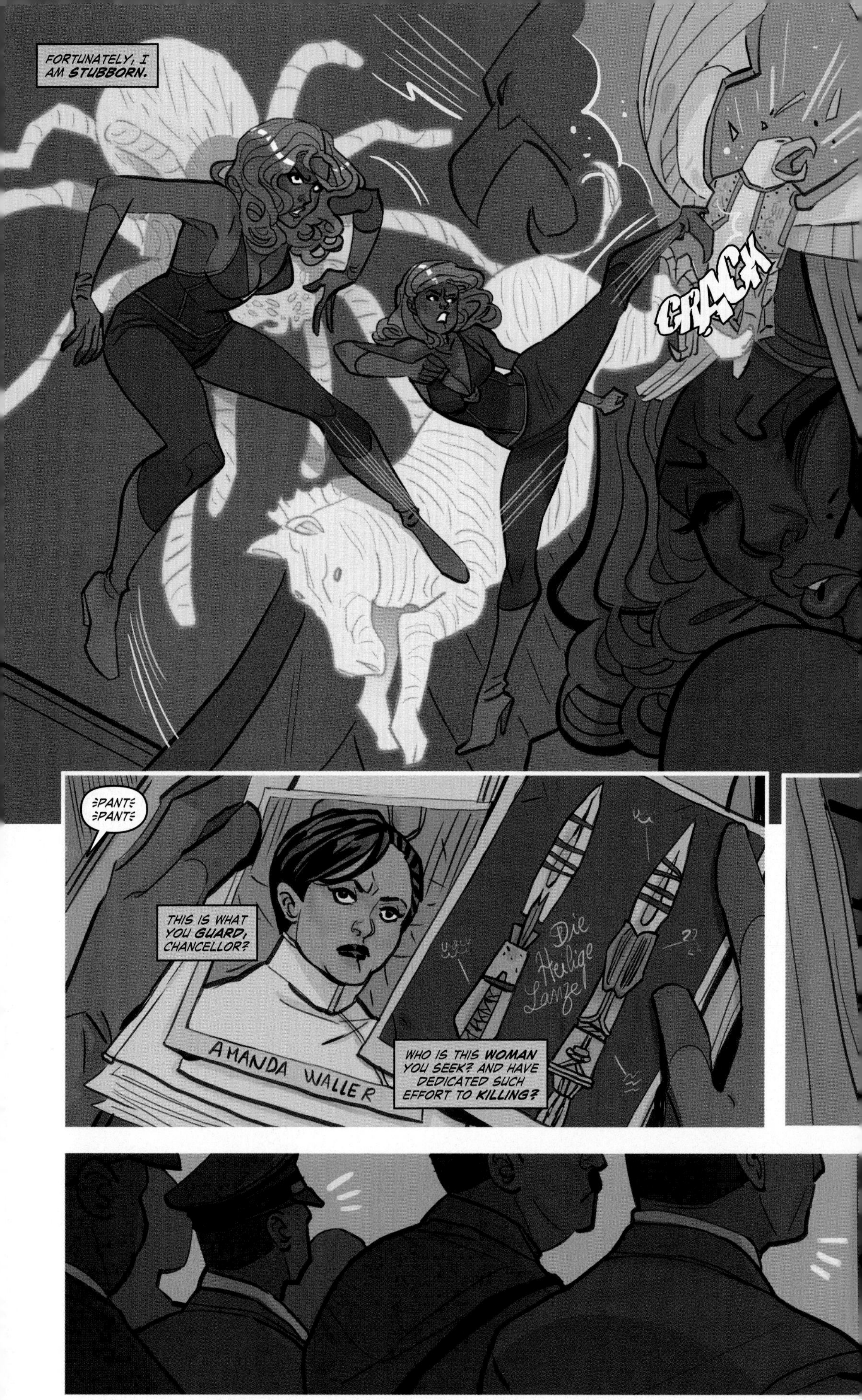

FORTUNATELY, I AM STUBBORN.
CRACK
≡PANT≡ ≡PANT≡
THIS IS WHAT YOU GUARD, CHANCELLOR?
AMANDA WALLER
Die Heilige Lanze
WHO IS THIS WOMAN YOU SEEK? AND HAVE DEDICATED SUCH EFFORT TO KILLING?

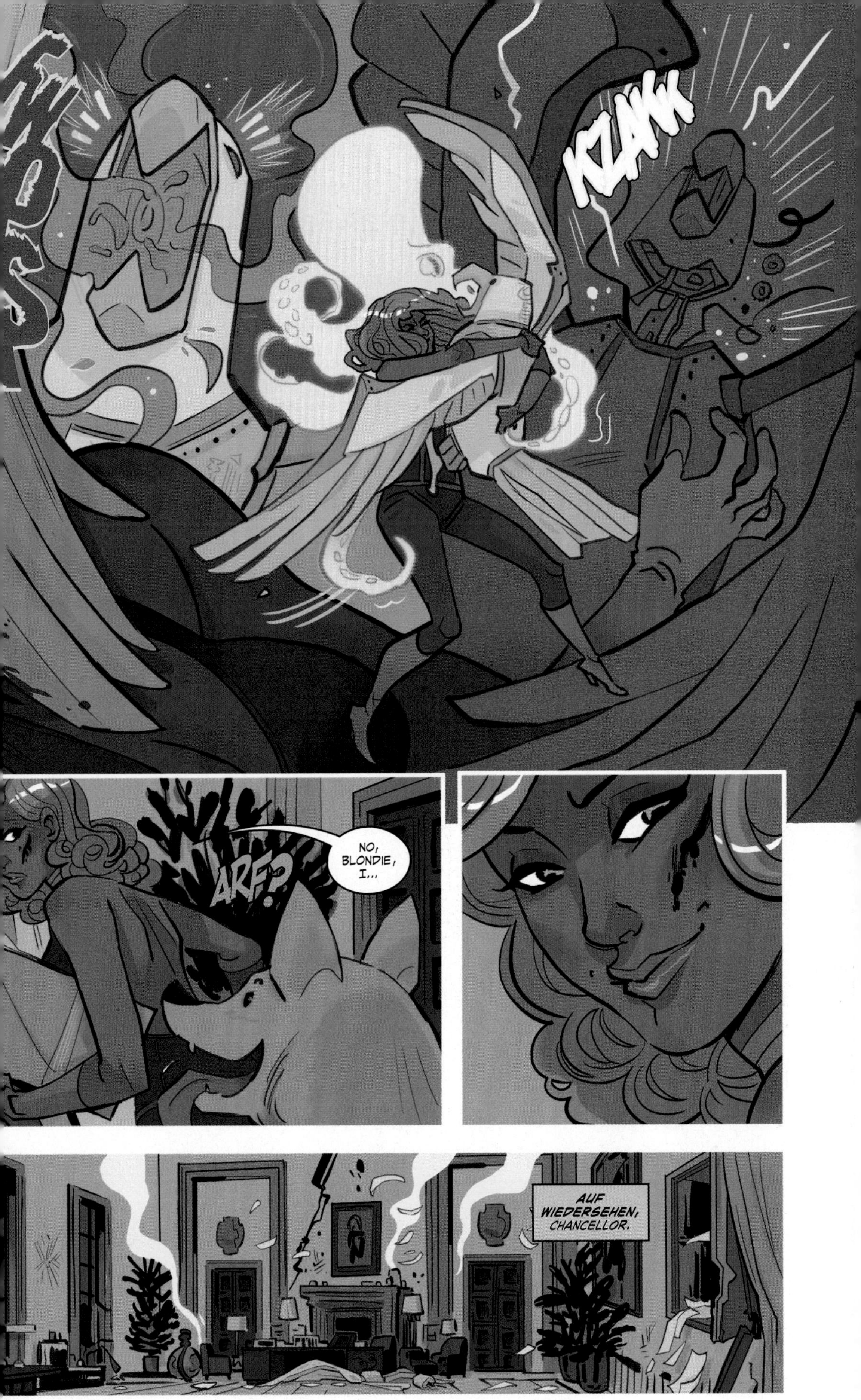
KZAKK
ARF?
NO, BLONDIE, I...
AUF WIEDERSEHEN, CHANCELLOR.

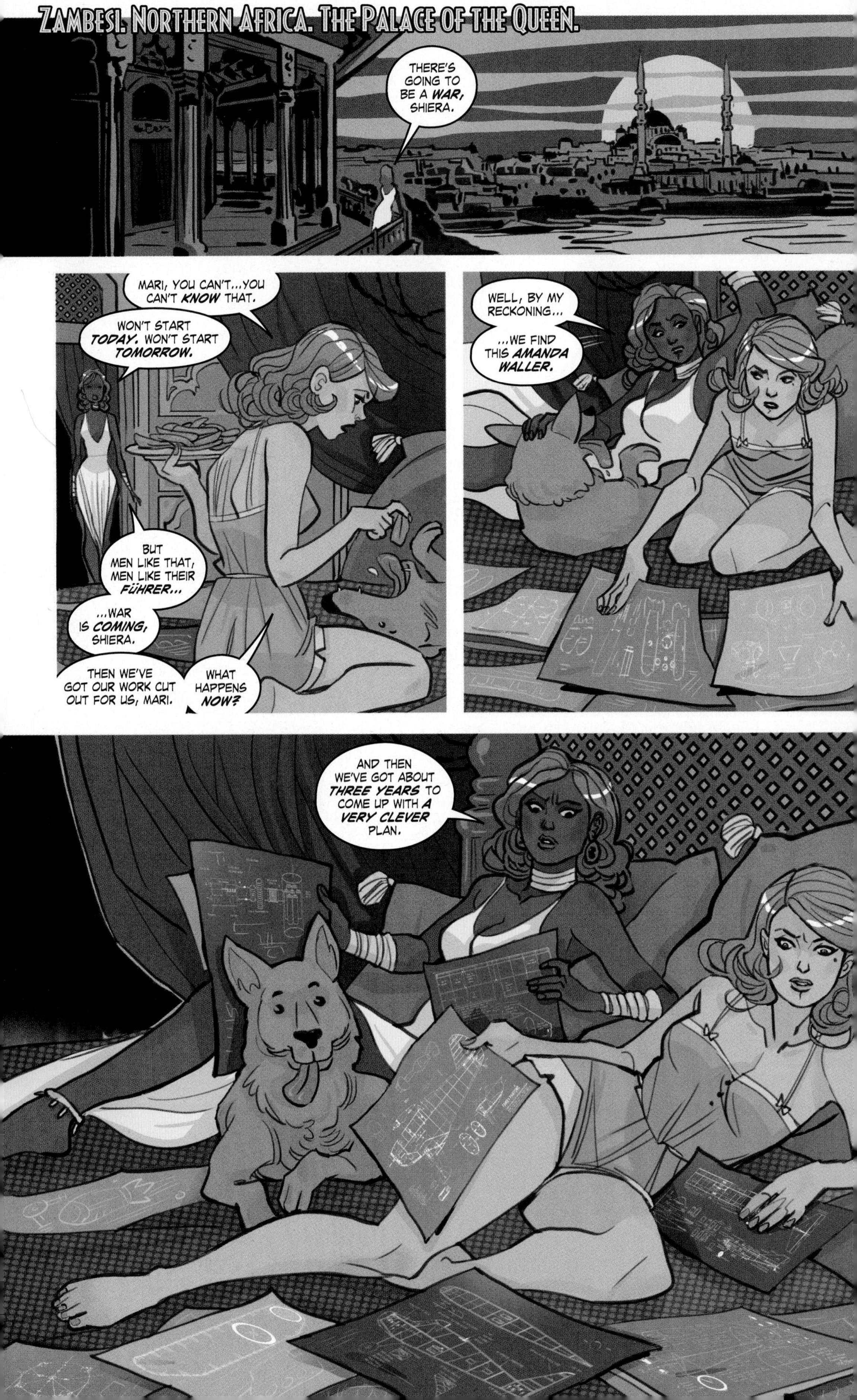
ZAMBESI. NORTHERN AFRICA. THE PALACE OF THE QUEEN.
THERE'S GOING TO BE A *WAR,* SHIERA.
MARI, YOU CAN'T...YOU CAN'T *KNOW* THAT.
WON'T START *TODAY.* WON'T START *TOMORROW.*
BUT MEN LIKE THAT, MEN LIKE THEIR *FÜHRER...*
...WAR IS *COMING,* SHIERA.
THEN WE'VE GOT OUR WORK CUT OUT FOR US, MARI.
WHAT HAPPENS *NOW?*
WELL, BY MY RECKONING...
...WE FIND THIS *AMANDA WALLER.*
AND THEN WE'VE GOT ABOUT *THREE YEARS* TO COME UP WITH *A VERY CLEVER* PLAN.

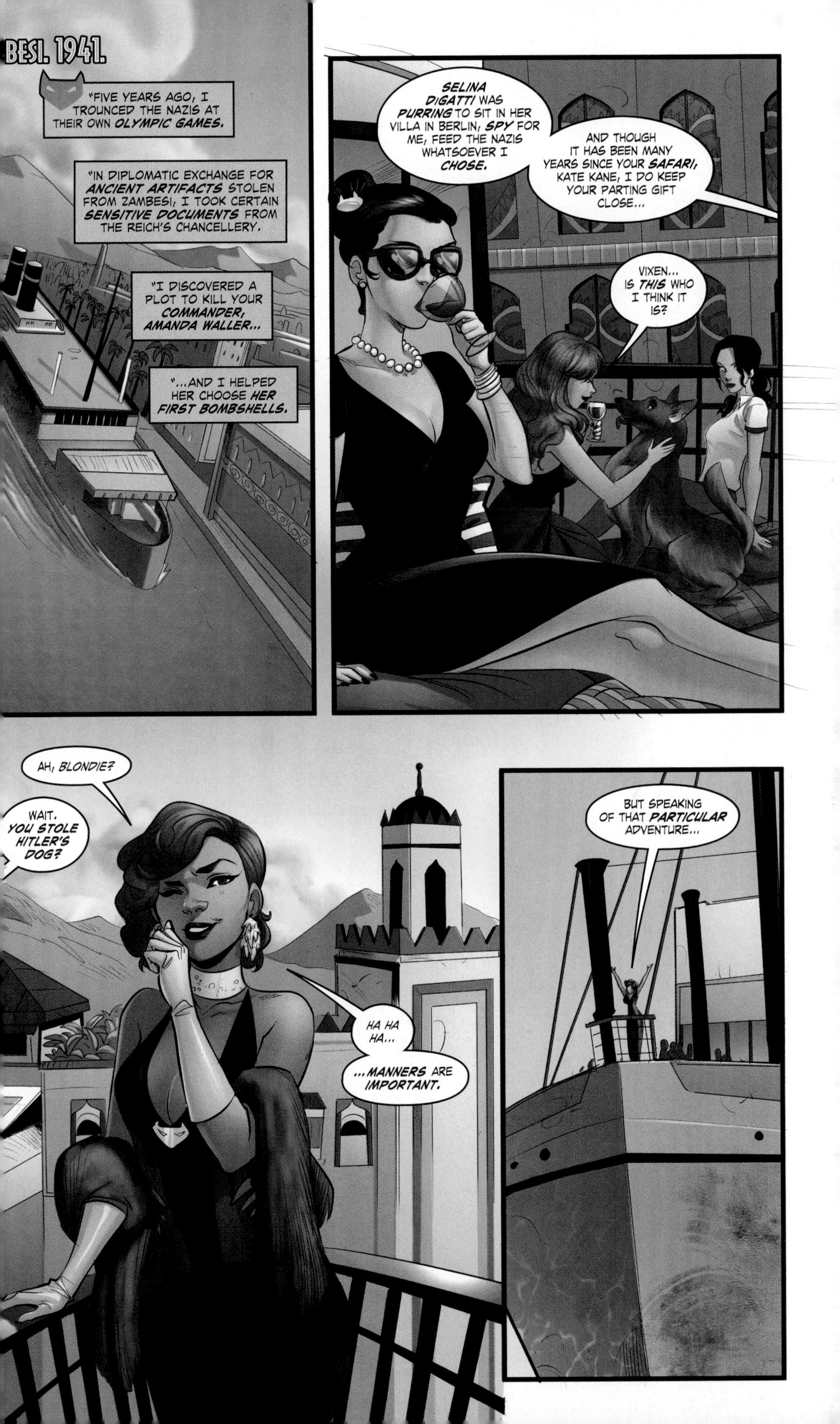
BESI. 1941.
"FIVE YEARS AGO, I TROUNCED THE NAZIS AT THEIR OWN OLYMPIC GAMES.
"IN DIPLOMATIC EXCHANGE FOR ANCIENT ARTIFACTS STOLEN FROM ZAMBESI, I TOOK CERTAIN SENSITIVE DOCUMENTS FROM THE REICH'S CHANCELLERY.
"I DISCOVERED A PLOT TO KILL YOUR COMMANDER, AMANDA WALLER...
"...AND I HELPED HER CHOOSE HER FIRST BOMBSHELLS.
SELINA DIGATTI WAS PURRING TO SIT IN HER VILLA IN BERLIN, SPY FOR ME, FEED THE NAZIS WHATSOEVER I CHOSE.
AND THOUGH IT HAS BEEN MANY YEARS SINCE YOUR SAFARI, KATE KANE, I DO KEEP YOUR PARTING GIFT CLOSE...
VIXEN... IS THIS WHO I THINK IT IS?
AH, BLONDIE?
WAIT. YOU STOLE HITLER'S DOG?
HA HA HA...
...MANNERS ARE IMPORTANT.
BUT SPEAKING OF THAT PARTICULAR ADVENTURE...

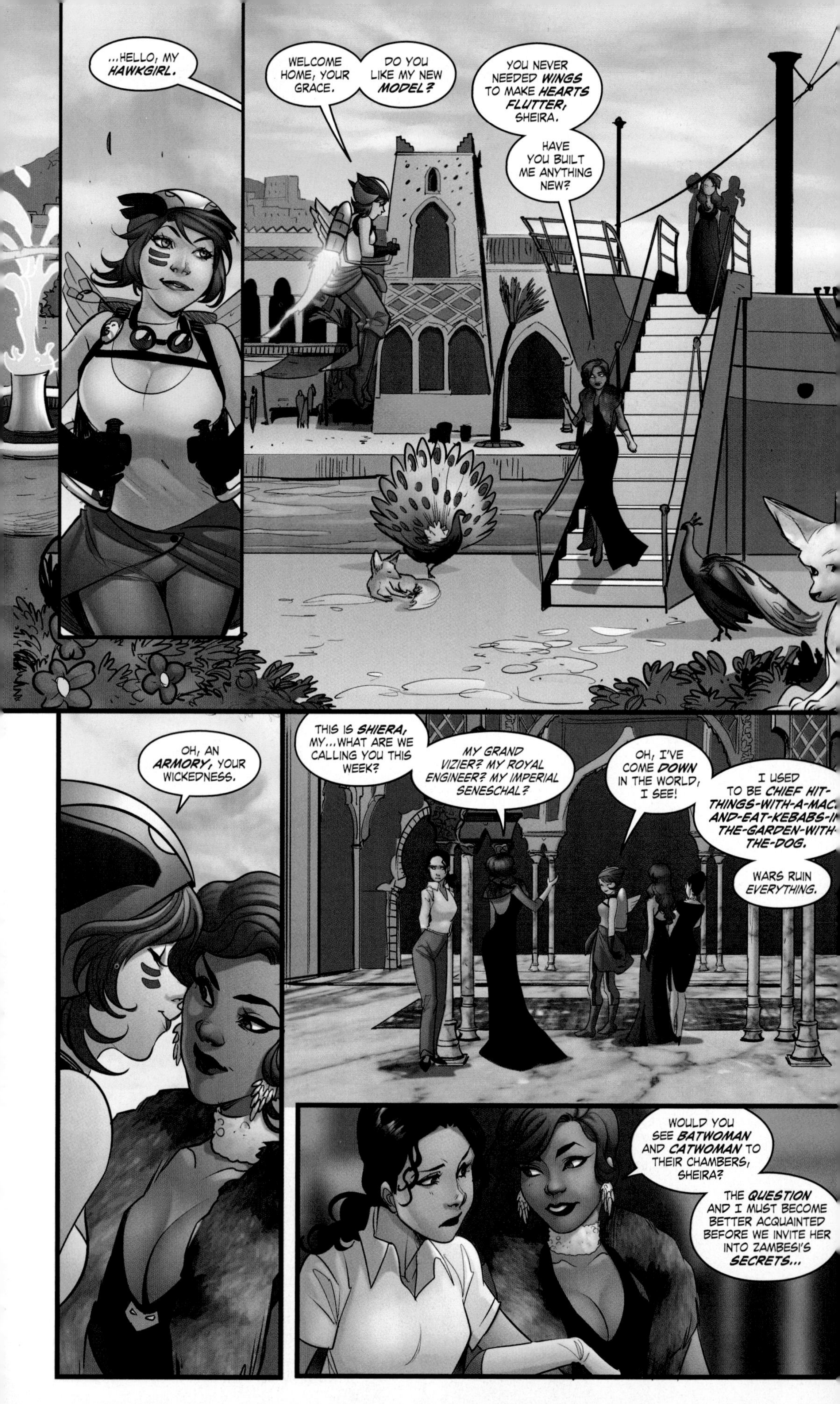
...HELLO, MY HAWKGIRL.
WELCOME HOME, YOUR GRACE.
DO YOU LIKE MY NEW MODEL?
YOU NEVER NEEDED WINGS TO MAKE HEARTS FLUTTER, SHEIRA.
HAVE YOU BUILT ME ANYTHING NEW?
OH, AN ARMORY, YOUR WICKEDNESS.
THIS IS SHIERA, MY...WHAT ARE WE CALLING YOU THIS WEEK?
MY GRAND VIZIER? MY ROYAL ENGINEER? MY IMPERIAL SENESCHAL?
OH, I'VE COME DOWN IN THE WORLD, I SEE!
I USED TO BE CHIEF HIT-THINGS-WITH-A-MAC AND-EAT-KEBABS-IN THE-GARDEN-WITH-THE-DOG.
WARS RUIN EVERYTHING.
WOULD YOU SEE BATWOMAN AND CATWOMAN TO THEIR CHAMBERS, SHEIRA?
THE QUESTION AND I MUST BECOME BETTER ACQUAINTED BEFORE WE INVITE HER INTO ZAMBESI'S SECRETS...

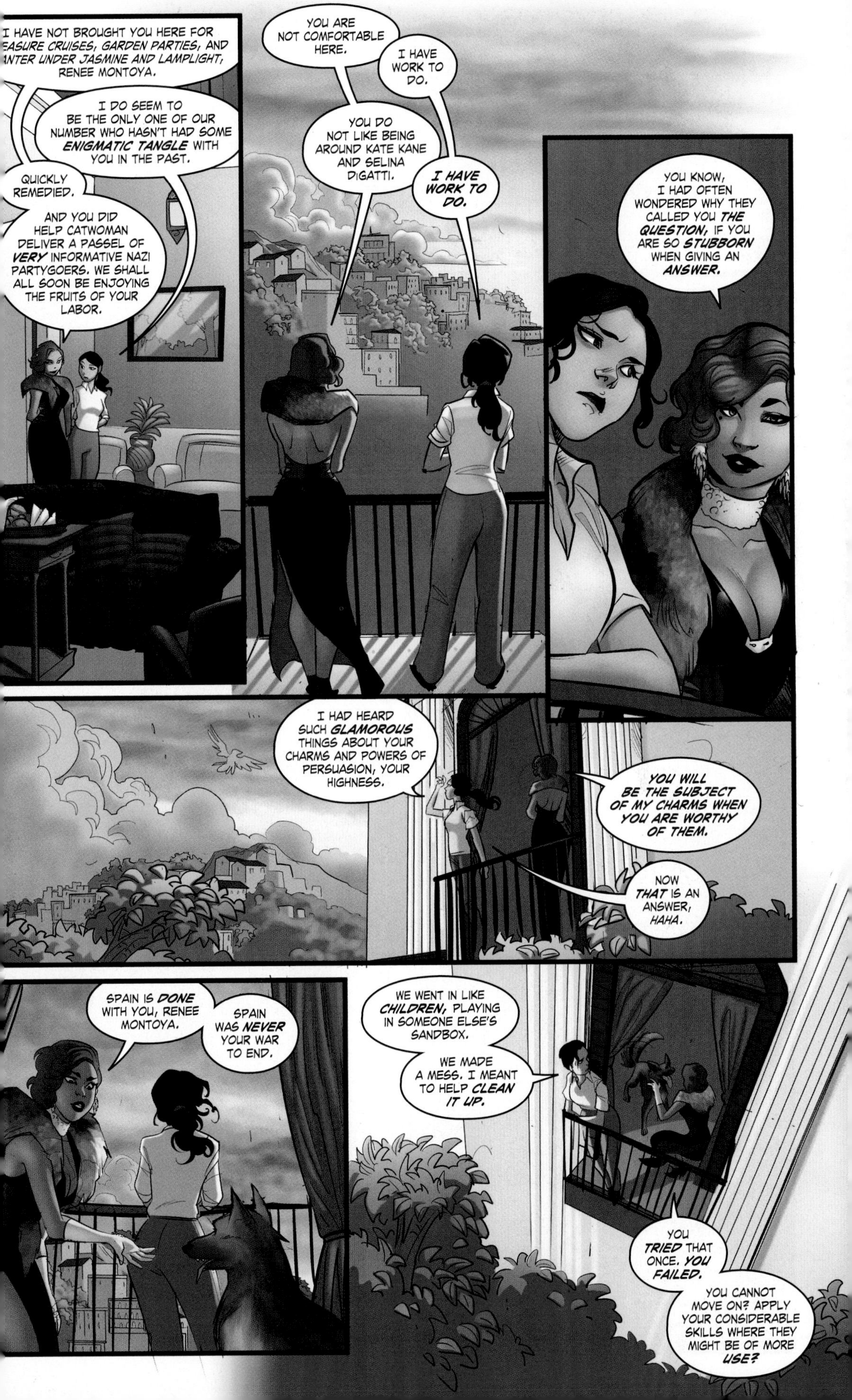
I HAVE NOT BROUGHT YOU HERE FOR
EASURE CRUISES, GARDEN PARTIES, AND
ANTER UNDER JASMINE AND LAMPLIGHT, RENEE MONTOYA.
I DO SEEM TO BE THE ONLY ONE OF OUR NUMBER WHO HASN'T HAD SOME ENIGMATIC TANGLE WITH YOU IN THE PAST.
QUICKLY REMEDIED.
AND YOU DID HELP CATWOMAN DELIVER A PASSEL OF VERY INFORMATIVE NAZI PARTYGOERS. WE SHALL ALL SOON BE ENJOYING THE FRUITS OF YOUR LABOR.
YOU ARE NOT COMFORTABLE HERE.
I HAVE WORK TO DO.
YOU DO NOT LIKE BEING AROUND KATE KANE AND SELINA DIGATTI.
I HAVE WORK TO DO.
YOU KNOW, I HAD OFTEN WONDERED WHY THEY CALLED YOU THE QUESTION, IF YOU ARE SO STUBBORN WHEN GIVING AN ANSWER.
I HAD HEARD SUCH GLAMOROUS THINGS ABOUT YOUR CHARMS AND POWERS OF PERSUASION, YOUR HIGHNESS.
YOU WILL BE THE SUBJECT OF MY CHARMS WHEN YOU ARE WORTHY OF THEM.
NOW THAT IS AN ANSWER, HAHA.
SPAIN IS DONE WITH YOU, RENEE MONTOYA.
SPAIN WAS NEVER YOUR WAR TO END.
WE WENT IN LIKE CHILDREN, PLAYING IN SOMEONE ELSE'S SANDBOX.
WE MADE A MESS. I MEANT TO HELP CLEAN IT UP.
YOU TRIED THAT ONCE. YOU FAILED.
YOU CANNOT MOVE ON? APPLY YOUR CONSIDERABLE SKILLS WHERE THEY MIGHT BE OF MORE USE?

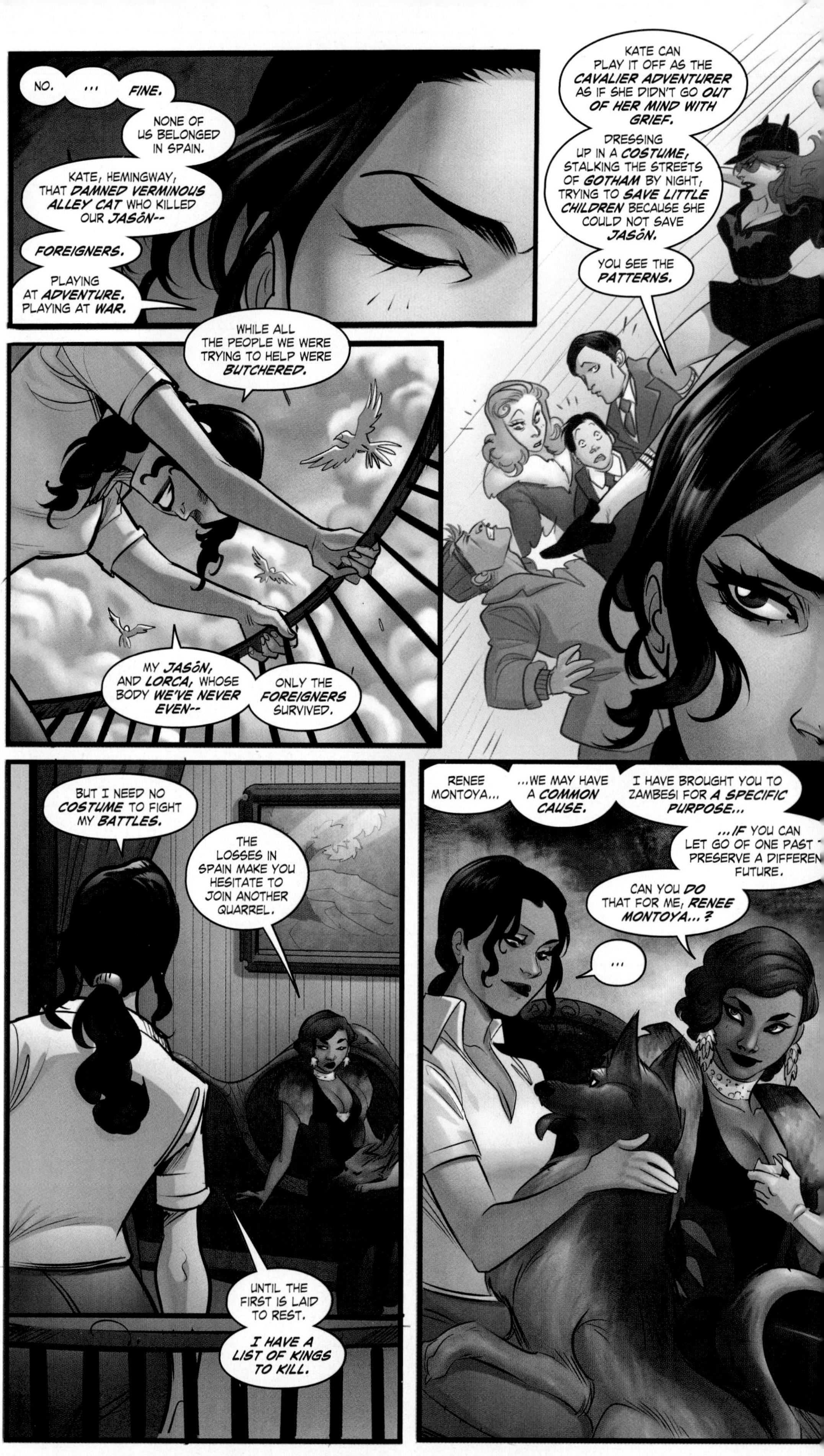
NO.
...
FINE.
NONE OF US BELONGED IN SPAIN.
KATE, HEMINGWAY, THAT DAMNED VERMINOUS ALLEY CAT WHO KILLED OUR JASÓN--
FOREIGNERS.
PLAYING AT ADVENTURE. PLAYING AT WAR.
KATE CAN PLAY IT OFF AS THE CAVALIER ADVENTURER AS IF SHE DIDN'T GO OUT OF HER MIND WITH GRIEF.
DRESSING UP IN A COSTUME, STALKING THE STREETS OF GOTHAM BY NIGHT, TRYING TO SAVE LITTLE CHILDREN BECAUSE SHE COULD NOT SAVE JASÓN.
YOU SEE THE PATTERNS.
WHILE ALL THE PEOPLE WE WERE TRYING TO HELP WERE BUTCHERED.
MY JASÓN, AND LORCA, WHOSE BODY WE'VE NEVER EVEN--
ONLY THE FOREIGNERS SURVIVED.
BUT I NEED NO COSTUME TO FIGHT MY BATTLES.
THE LOSSES IN SPAIN MAKE YOU HESITATE TO JOIN ANOTHER QUARREL.
UNTIL THE FIRST IS LAID TO REST.
I HAVE A LIST OF KINGS TO KILL.
RENEE MONTOYA...
...WE MAY HAVE A COMMON CAUSE.
I HAVE BROUGHT YOU TO ZAMBESI FOR A SPECIFIC PURPOSE...
...IF YOU CAN LET GO OF ONE PAST TO PRESERVE A DIFFEREN FUTURE.
CAN YOU DO THAT FOR ME, RENEE MONTOYA...?
...

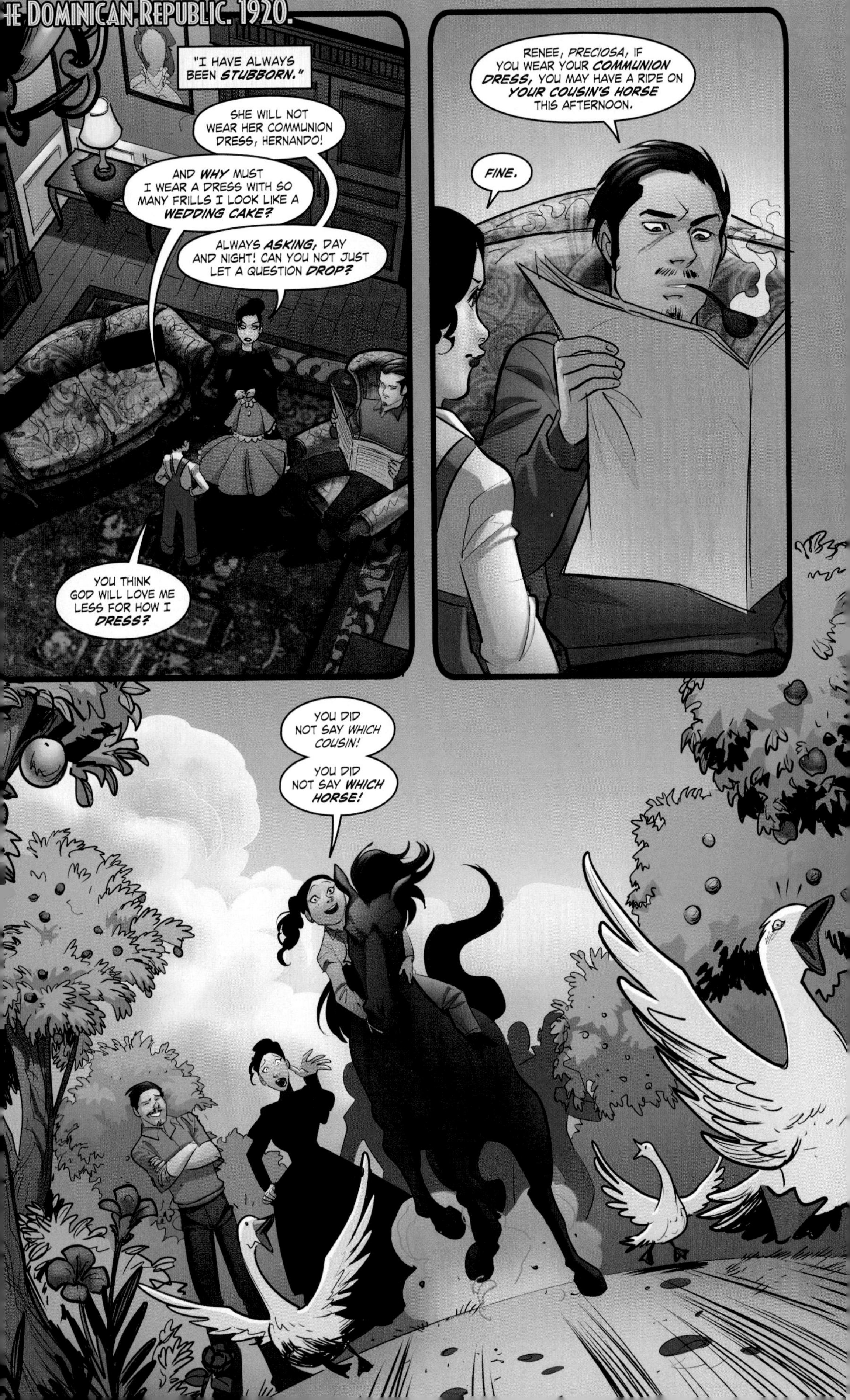
HE DOMINICAN REPUBLIC. 1920.
"I HAVE ALWAYS BEEN STUBBORN."
SHE WILL NOT WEAR HER COMMUNION DRESS, HERNANDO!
AND WHY MUST I WEAR A DRESS WITH SO MANY FRILLS I LOOK LIKE A WEDDING CAKE?
ALWAYS ASKING, DAY AND NIGHT! CAN YOU NOT JUST LET A QUESTION DROP?
YOU THINK GOD WILL LOVE ME LESS FOR HOW I DRESS?
RENEE, PRECIOSA, IF YOU WEAR YOUR COMMUNION DRESS, YOU MAY HAVE A RIDE ON YOUR COUSIN'S HORSE THIS AFTERNOON.
FINE.
YOU DID NOT SAY WHICH COUSIN!
YOU DID NOT SAY WHICH HORSE!

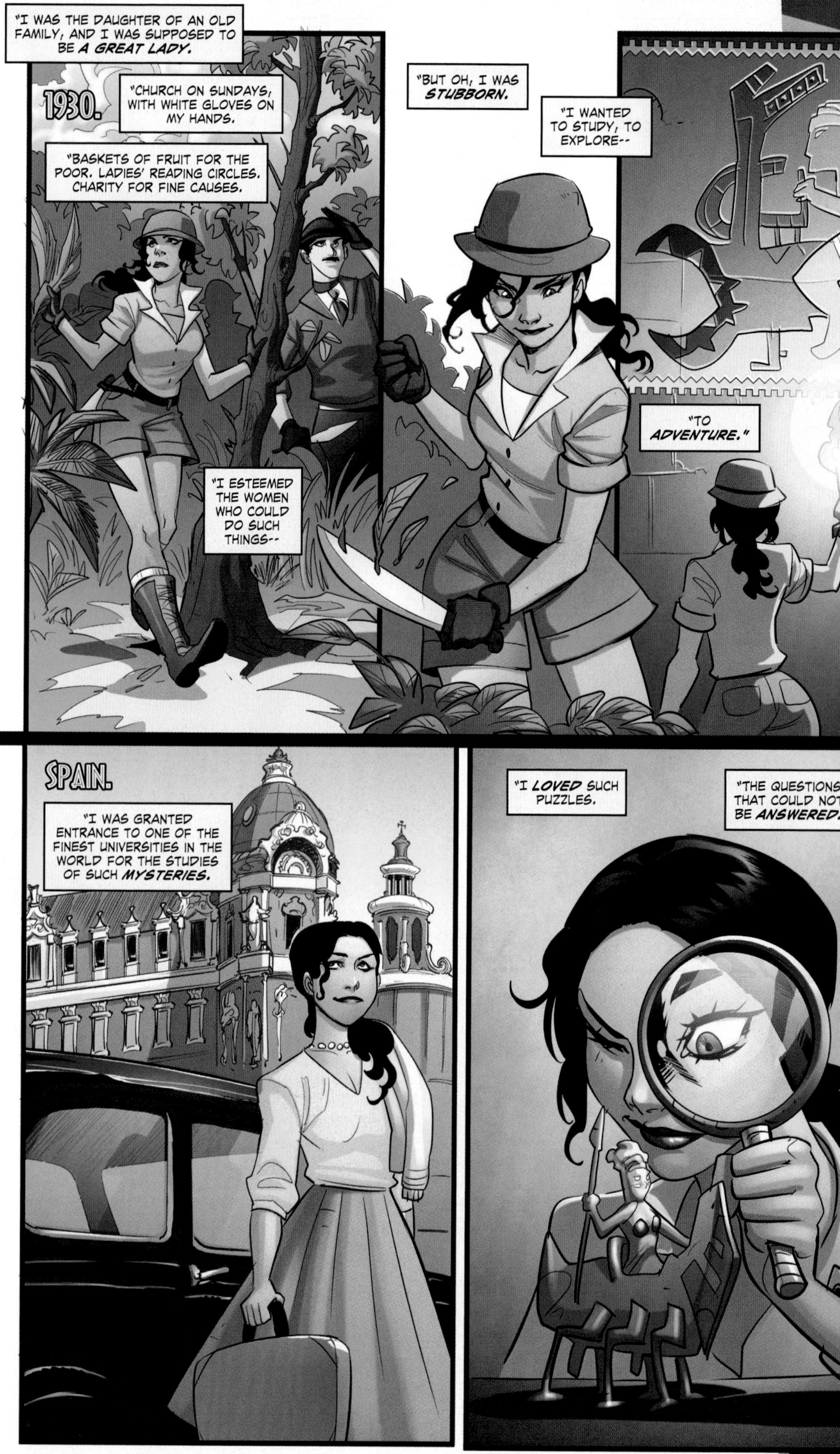

"I WAS THE DAUGHTER OF AN OLD FAMILY, AND I WAS SUPPOSED TO BE *A GREAT LADY.*
1930.
"CHURCH ON SUNDAYS, WITH WHITE GLOVES ON MY HANDS.
"BASKETS OF FRUIT FOR THE POOR. LADIES' READING CIRCLES. CHARITY FOR FINE CAUSES.
"I ESTEEMED THE WOMEN WHO COULD DO SUCH THINGS--
"BUT OH, I WAS *STUBBORN.*
"I WANTED TO STUDY, TO EXPLORE--
"TO *ADVENTURE.*"
SPAIN.
"I WAS GRANTED ENTRANCE TO ONE OF THE FINEST UNIVERSITIES IN THE WORLD FOR THE STUDIES OF SUCH *MYSTERIES.*
"I *LOVED* SUCH PUZZLES.
"THE QUESTIONS THAT COULD NOT BE *ANSWERED.*

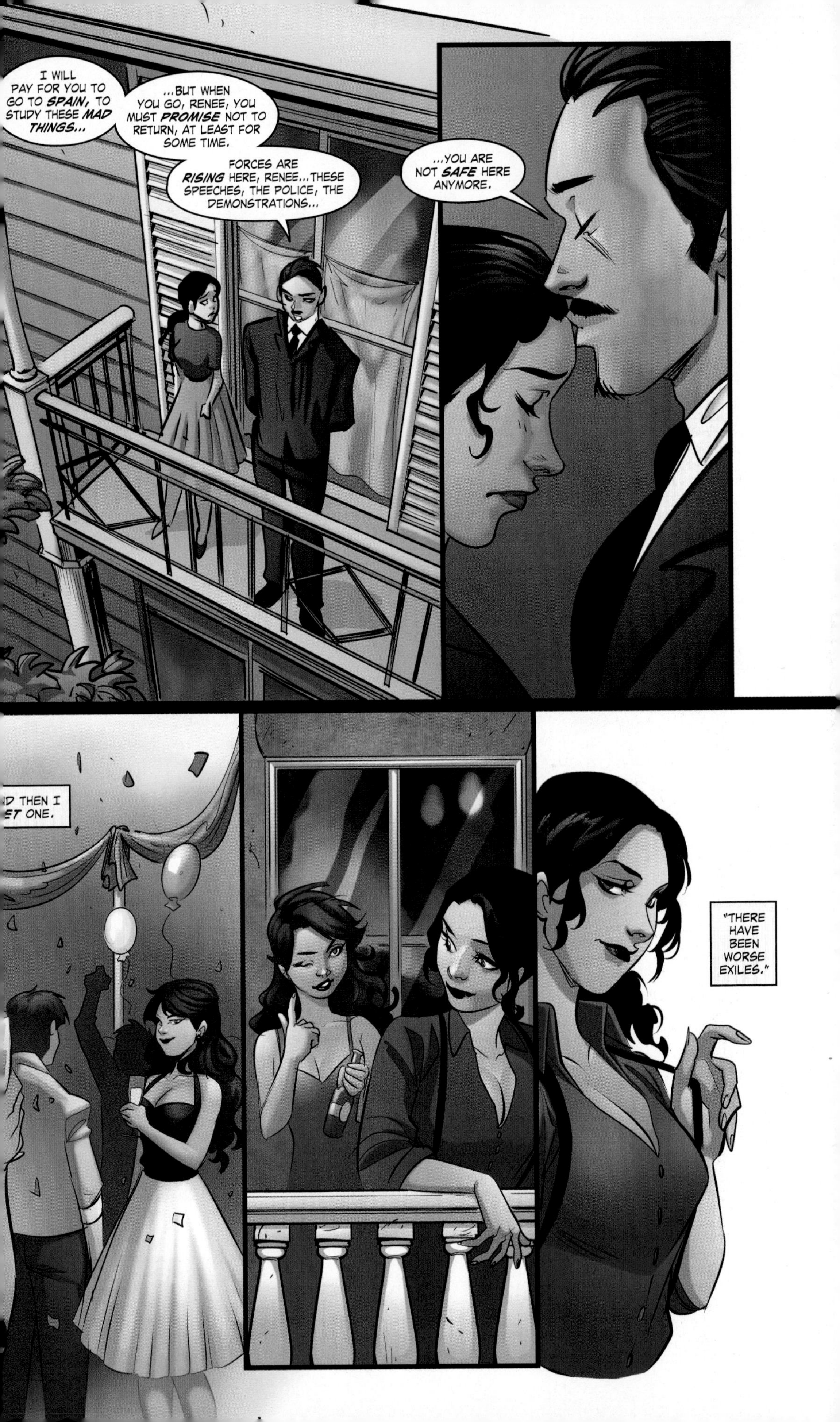
I WILL PAY FOR YOU TO GO TO SPAIN, TO STUDY THESE MAD THINGS...
...BUT WHEN YOU GO, RENEE, YOU MUST PROMISE NOT TO RETURN, AT LEAST FOR SOME TIME.
FORCES ARE RISING HERE, RENEE...THESE SPEECHES, THE POLICE, THE DEMONSTRATIONS...
...YOU ARE NOT SAFE HERE ANYMORE.
D THEN I
ET ONE.
"THERE HAVE BEEN WORSE EXILES."

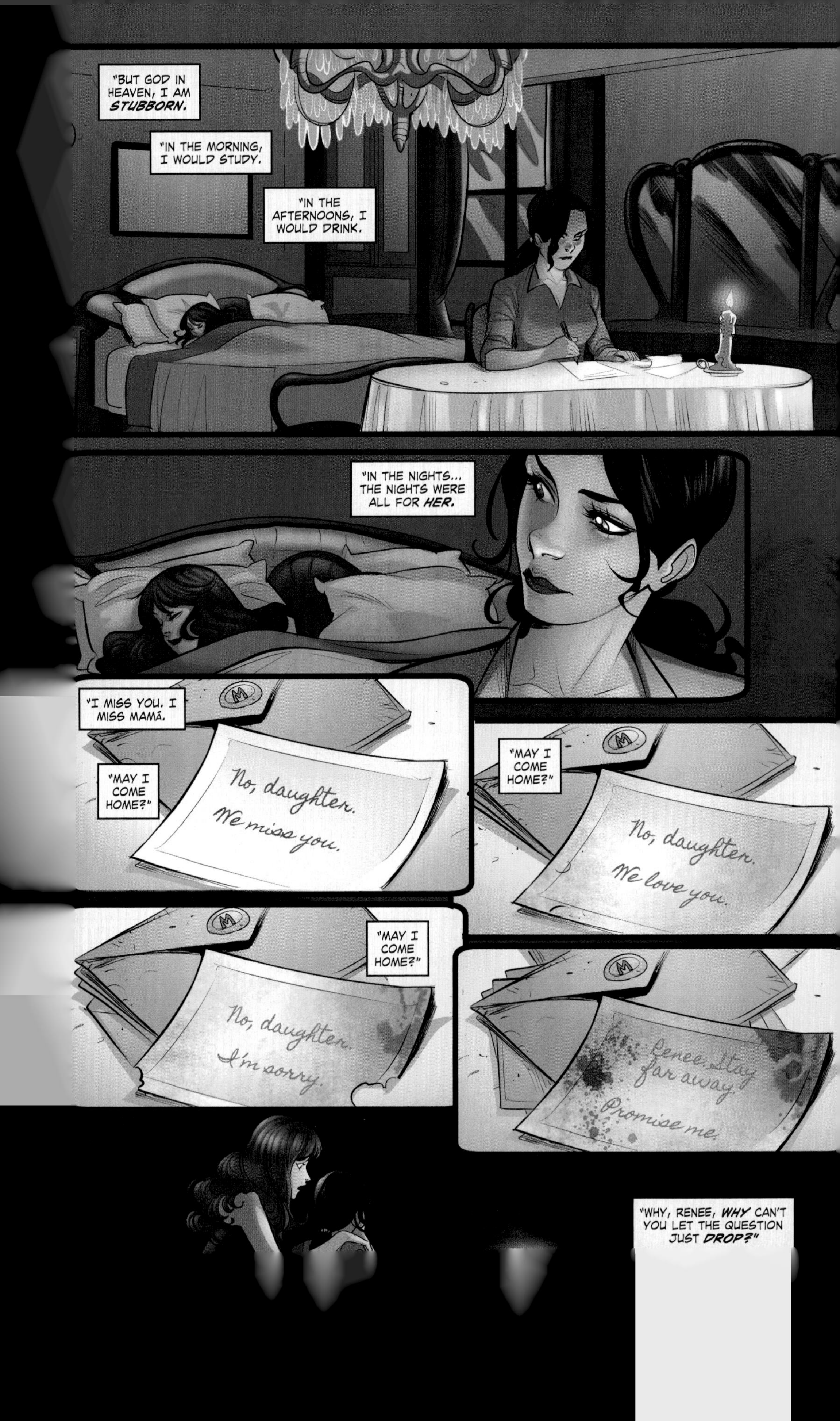
"BUT GOD IN HEAVEN, I AM STUBBORN.
"IN THE MORNING, I WOULD STUDY.
"IN THE AFTERNOONS, I WOULD DRINK.
"IN THE NIGHTS... THE NIGHTS WERE ALL FOR HER.
"I MISS YOU. I MISS MAMÁ.
"MAY I COME HOME?"
No, daughter. We miss you.
"MAY I COME HOME?"
No, daughter. We love you.
"MAY I COME HOME?"
No, daughter. I'm sorry.
Renee. Stay far away. Promise me.
"WHY, RENEE, WHY CAN'T YOU LET THE QUESTION JUST DROP?"

NE MILE
ROM SITE B.
A TYRANT TOOK MY HOMELAND.
A TYRANT TOOK SPAIN.
AND ANOTHER TYRANT IS TRYING TO TAKE THE REST OF THE FREE WORLD.
I DO NOT SEEK TO DENY YOU YOUR QUEST, RENEE MONTOYA.
BUT LET US FIND THE HEAD OF THIS SERPENT THAT POISONS THE WORLD.
LET US REMOVE IT FOR HIM.
WHY DO YOU EVEN WANT ME?
YOU HAPPENED TO EXPLORE SOME SITES THAT WERE DOCUMENTED BY ANOTHER YOUNG ADVENTURER.
A WEST POINT LIEUTENANT BY THE NAME OF FRANCINE CHARLES.
LT. CHARLES IS CURRENTLY ENGAGED... ELSEWHERE.
BUT SHE SPOKE OF PAPERS YOU HAD WRITTEN AT UNIVERSITY.
AND YOUR STRENGTH, YOUR LEADERSHIP, YOUR CLEVERNESS, AND, YES--YOUR STUBBORNNESS...
...MIGHT HELP US WITH WHAT WE HAVE FOUND HERE.

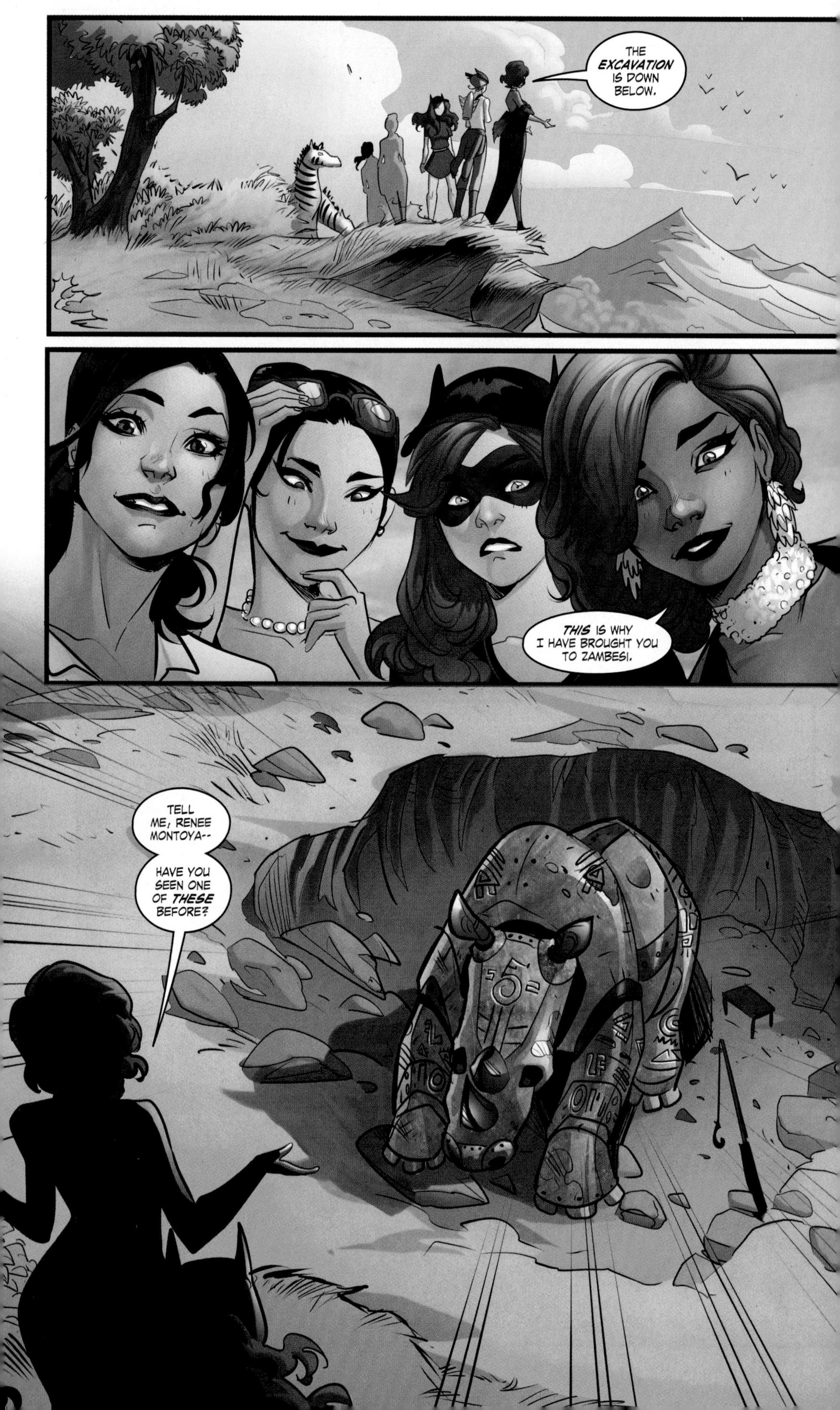
THE EXCAVATION IS DOWN BELOW.
THIS IS WHY I HAVE BROUGHT YOU TO ZAMBESI.
TELL ME, RENEE MONTOYA--
HAVE YOU SEEN ONE OF THESE BEFORE?

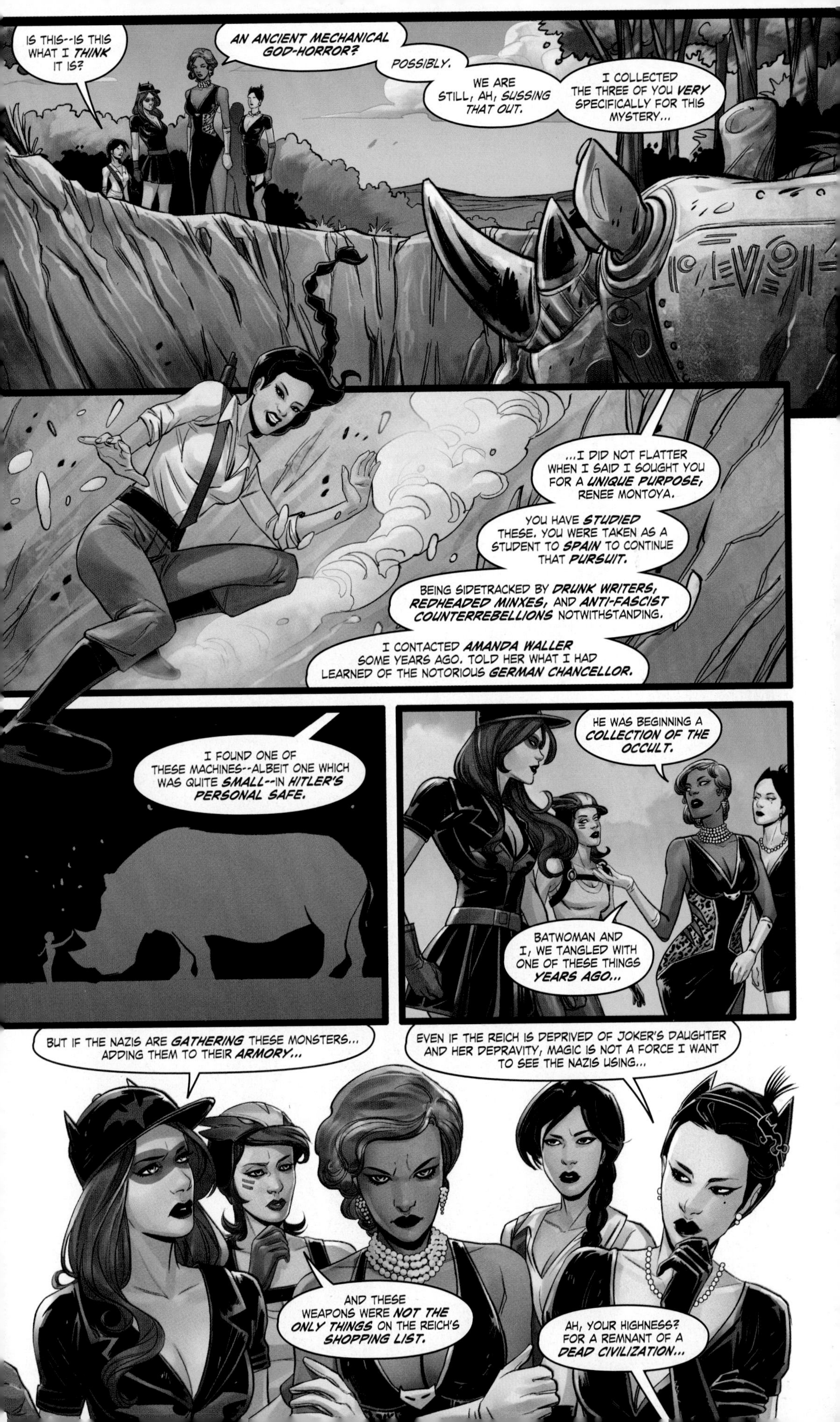
IS THIS--IS THIS WHAT I THINK IT IS?
AN ANCIENT MECHANICAL GOD-HORROR?
POSSIBLY.
WE ARE STILL, AH, SUSSING THAT OUT.
I COLLECTED THE THREE OF YOU VERY SPECIFICALLY FOR THIS MYSTERY...
...I DID NOT FLATTER WHEN I SAID I SOUGHT YOU FOR A UNIQUE PURPOSE, RENEE MONTOYA.
YOU HAVE STUDIED THESE. YOU WERE TAKEN AS A STUDENT TO SPAIN TO CONTINUE THAT PURSUIT.
BEING SIDETRACKED BY DRUNK WRITERS, REDHEADED MINXES, AND ANTI-FASCIST COUNTERREBELLIONS NOTWITHSTANDING.
I CONTACTED AMANDA WALLER SOME YEARS AGO. TOLD HER WHAT I HAD LEARNED OF THE NOTORIOUS GERMAN CHANCELLOR.
I FOUND ONE OF THESE MACHINES--ALBEIT ONE WHICH WAS QUITE SMALL--IN HITLER'S PERSONAL SAFE.
HE WAS BEGINNING A COLLECTION OF THE OCCULT.
BATWOMAN AND I, WE TANGLED WITH ONE OF THESE THINGS YEARS AGO...
BUT IF THE NAZIS ARE GATHERING THESE MONSTERS... ADDING THEM TO THEIR ARMORY...
EVEN IF THE REICH IS DEPRIVED OF JOKER'S DAUGHTER AND HER DEPRAVITY, MAGIC IS NOT A FORCE I WANT TO SEE THE NAZIS USING...
AND THESE WEAPONS WERE NOT THE ONLY THINGS ON THE REICH'S SHOPPING LIST.
AH, YOUR HIGHNESS? FOR A REMNANT OF A DEAD CIVILIZATION...

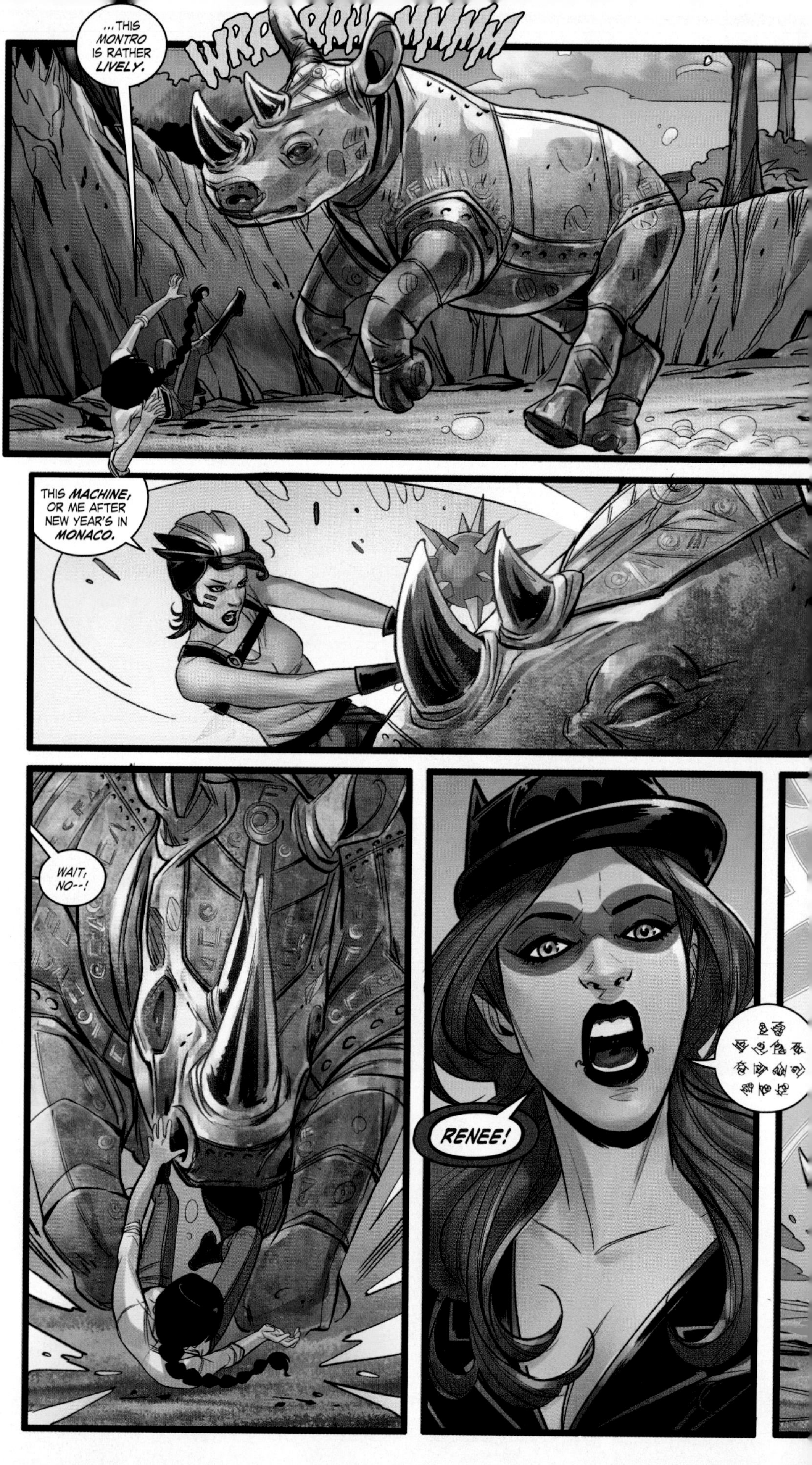
...THIS MONTRO IS RATHER LIVELY.
WRAAARRAAHHMMMM
THIS MACHINE, OR ME AFTER NEW YEAR'S IN MONACO.
WAIT, NO--!
RENEE!

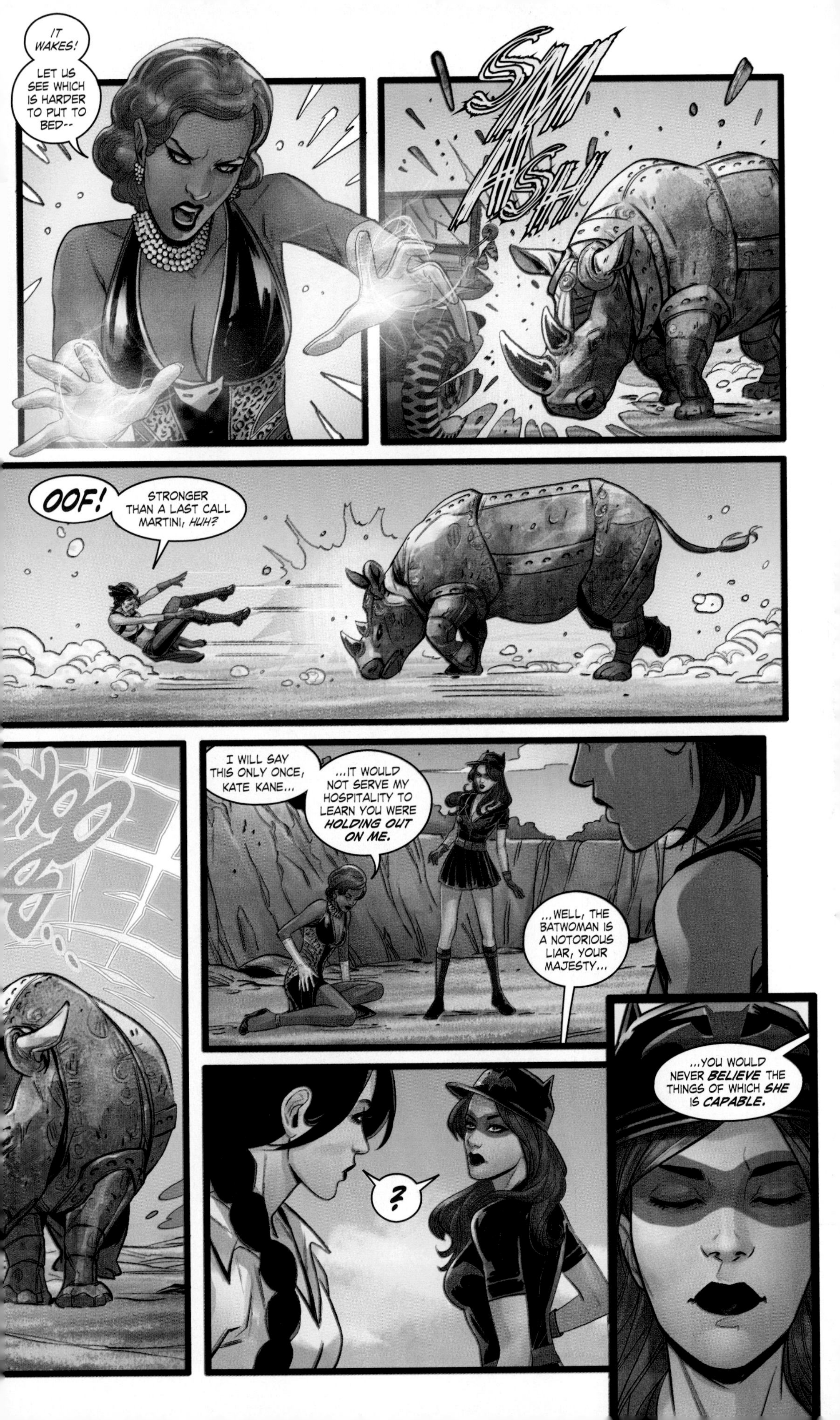
IT WAKES!
LET US SEE WHICH IS HARDER TO PUT TO BED--
SMASH
OOF!
STRONGER THAN A LAST CALL MARTINI, HUH?
I WILL SAY THIS ONLY ONCE, KATE KANE...
...IT WOULD NOT SERVE MY HOSPITALITY TO LEARN YOU WERE HOLDING OUT ON ME.
...WELL, THE BATWOMAN IS A NOTORIOUS LIAR, YOUR MAJESTY...
?
...YOU WOULD NEVER BELIEVE THE THINGS OF WHICH SHE IS CAPABLE.

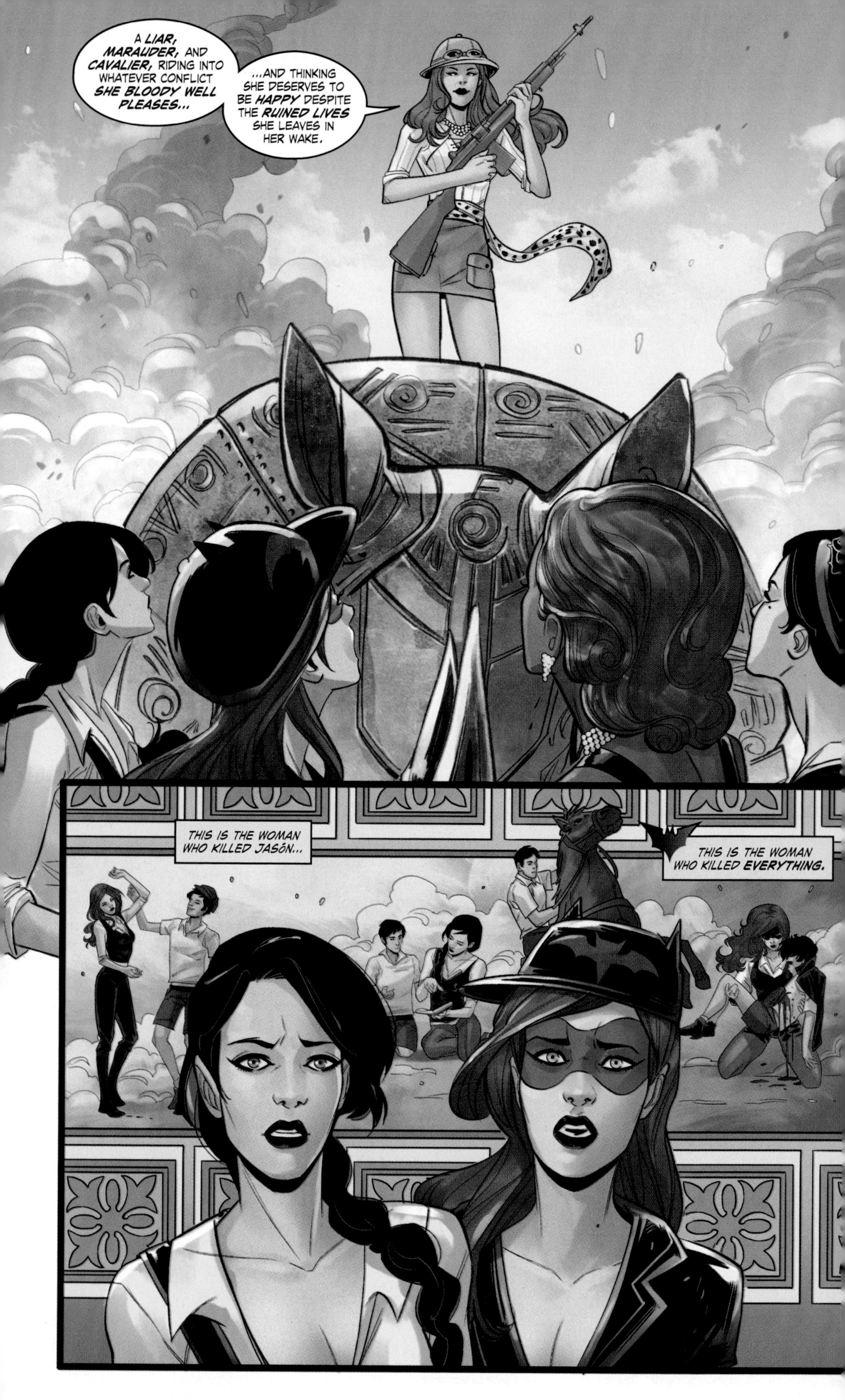

A LIAR, MARAUDER, AND CAVALIER, RIDING INTO WHATEVER CONFLICT SHE BLOODY WELL PLEASES...
...AND THINKING SHE DESERVES TO BE HAPPY DESPITE THE RUINED LIVES SHE LEAVES IN HER WAKE.
THIS IS THE WOMAN WHO KILLED JASÓN...
THIS IS THE WOMAN WHO KILLED EVERYTHING.

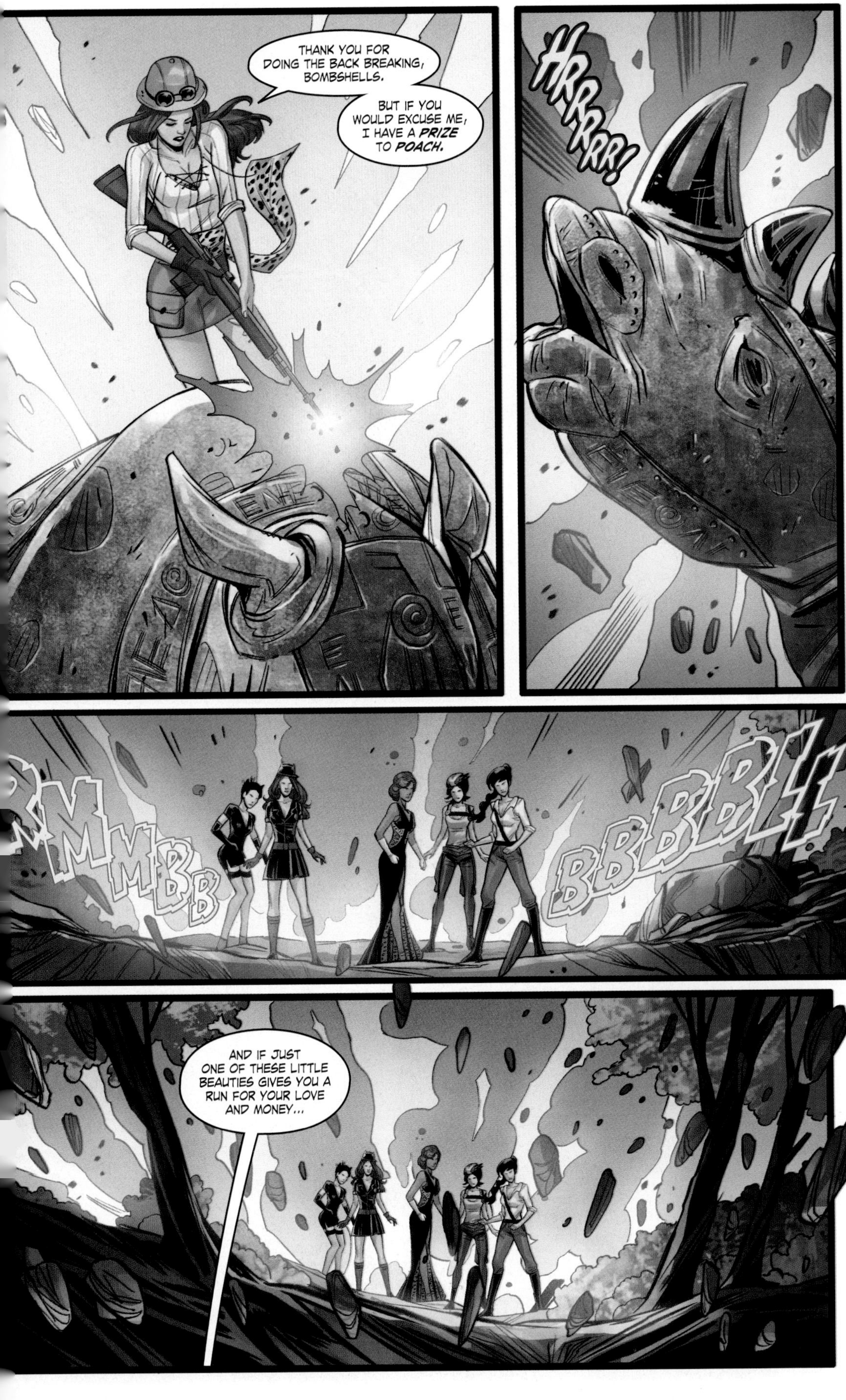
THANK YOU FOR DOING THE BACK BREAKING, BOMBSHELLS.
BUT IF YOU WOULD EXCUSE ME, I HAVE A *PRIZE* TO *POACH.*
HRRRRRR!
RMMBB
BBBBBL!
AND IF JUST ONE OF THESE LITTLE BEAUTIES GIVES YOU A RUN FOR YOUR LOVE AND MONEY...

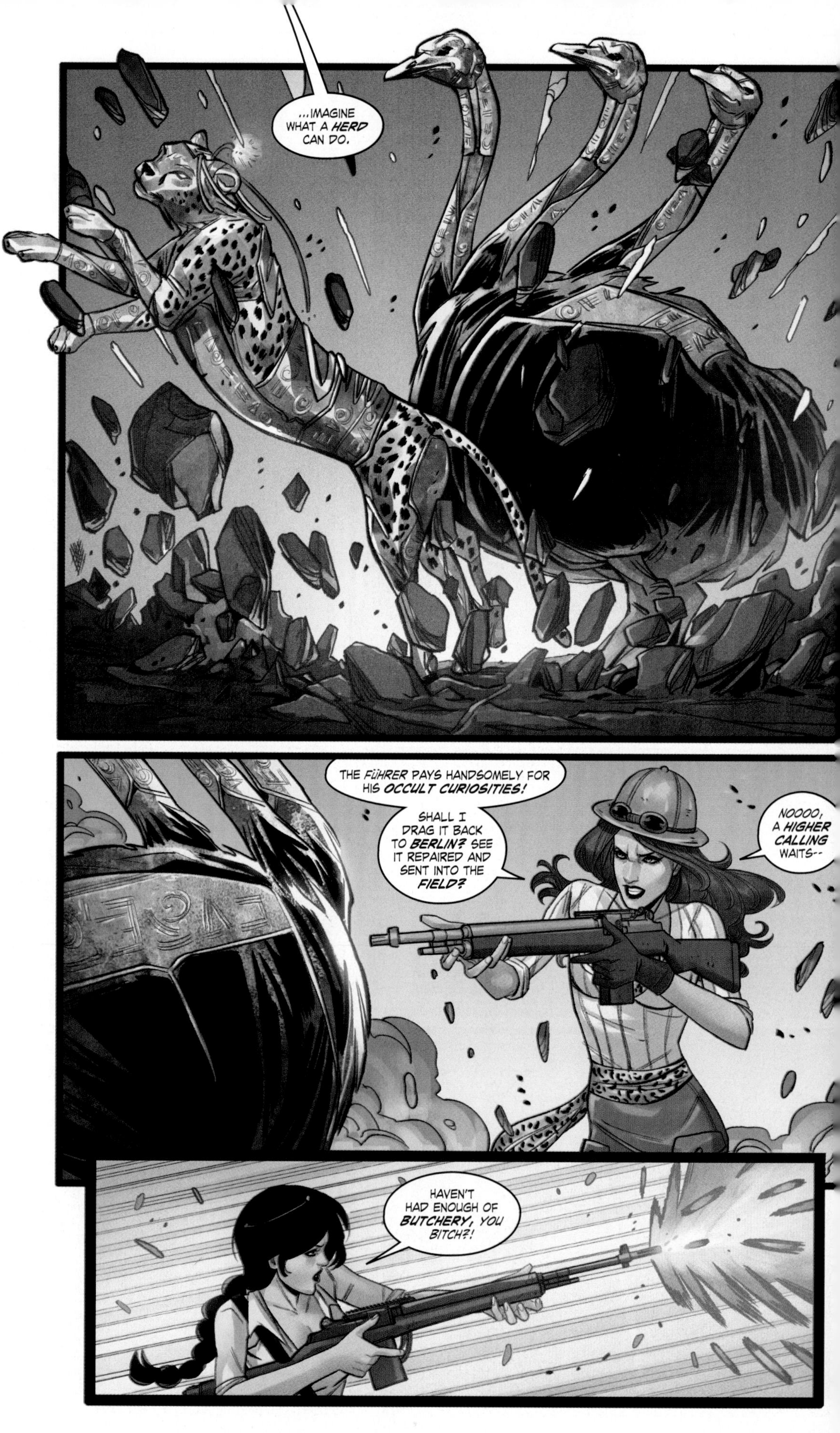
...IMAGINE WHAT A HERD CAN DO.
THE FÜHRER PAYS HANDSOMELY FOR HIS OCCULT CURIOSITIES!
SHALL I DRAG IT BACK TO BERLIN? SEE IT REPAIRED AND SENT INTO THE FIELD?
NOOOO, A HIGHER CALLING WAITS--
HAVEN'T HAD ENOUGH OF BUTCHERY, YOU BITCH?!

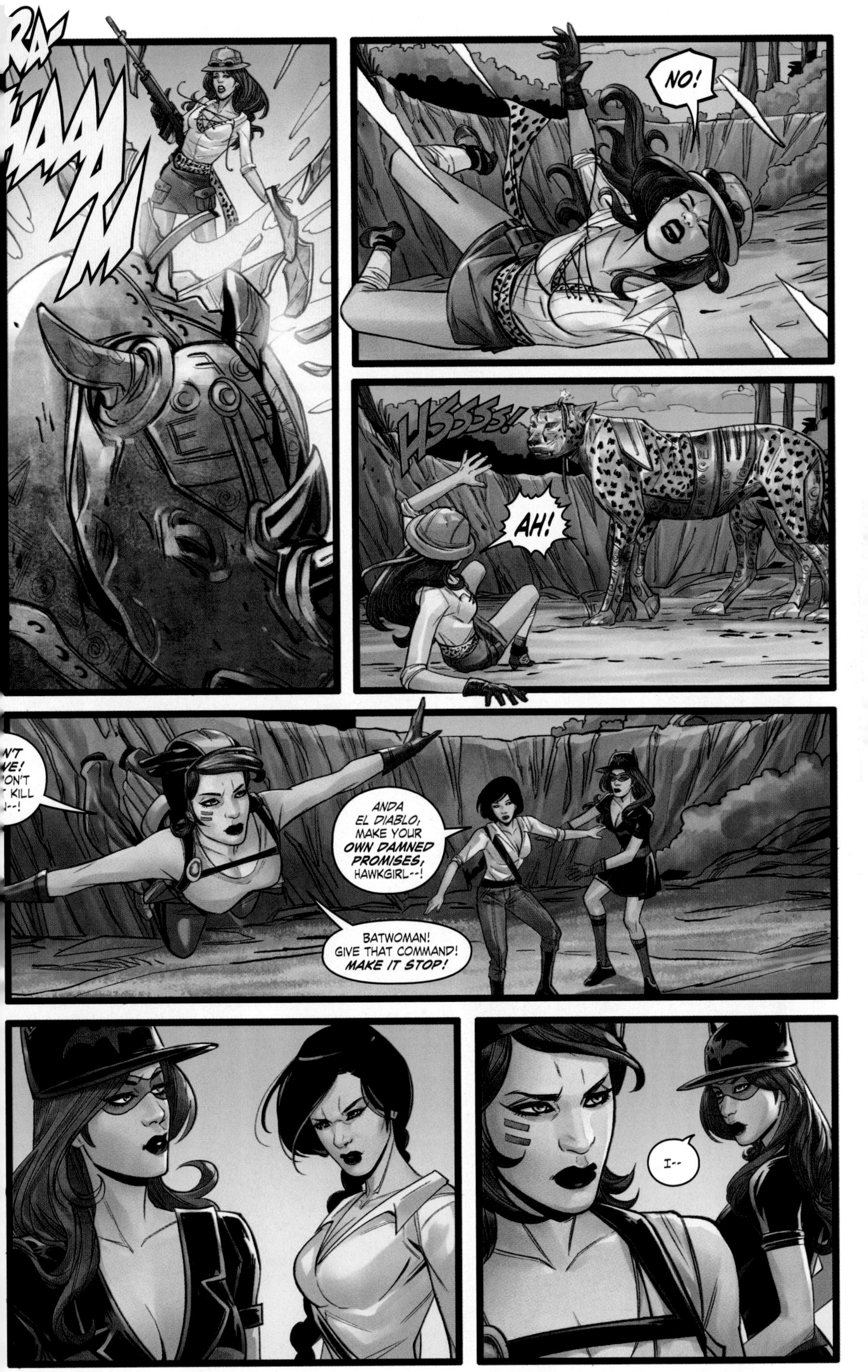
NO!
AH!
ANDA EL DIABLO, MAKE YOUR OWN DAMNED PROMISES, HAWKGIRL--!
BATWOMAN! GIVE THAT COMMAND! MAKE IT STOP!
I--

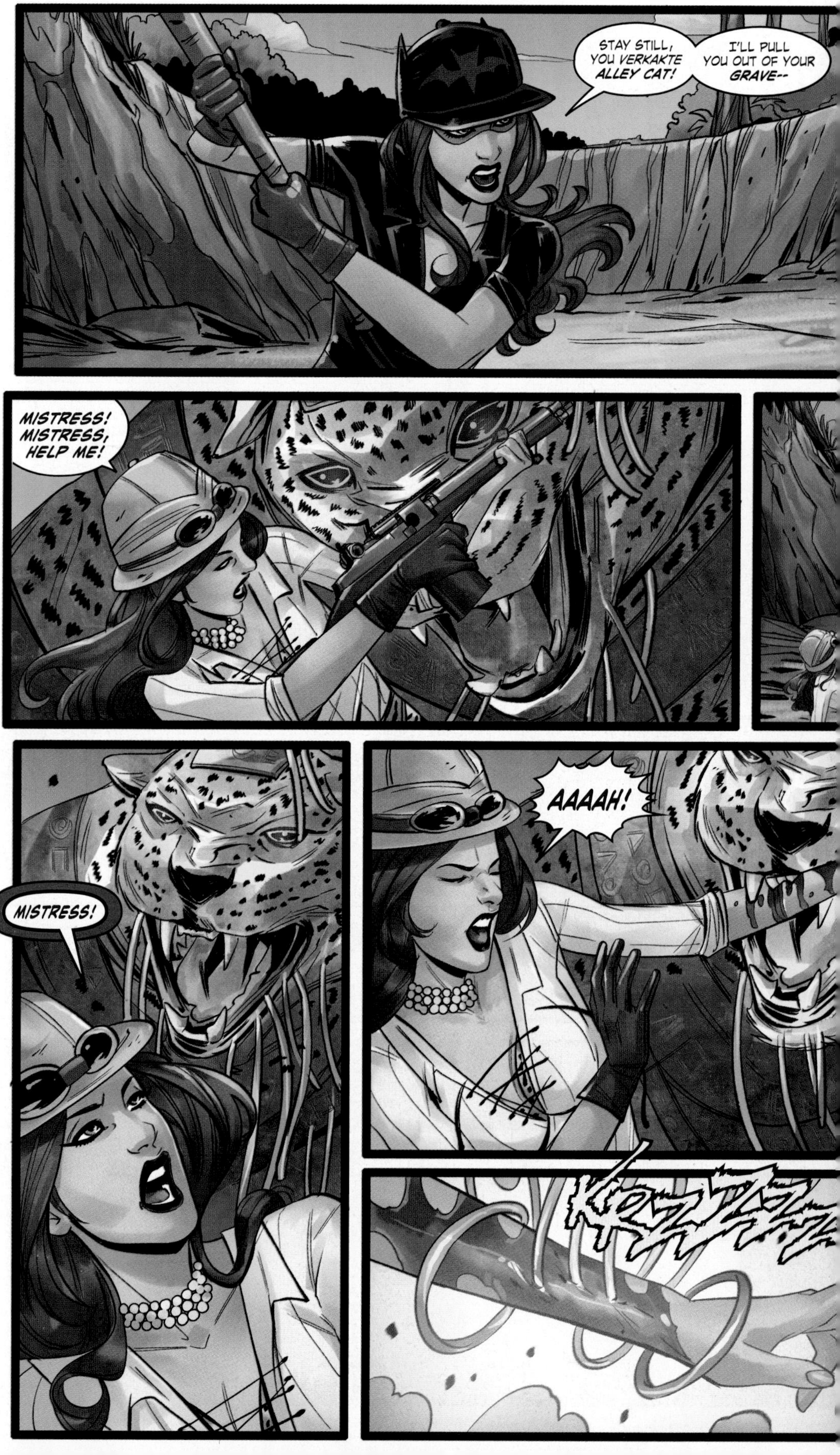
STAY STILL, YOU VERKAKTE ALLEY CAT!
I'LL PULL YOU OUT OF YOUR GRAVE--
MISTRESS! MISTRESS, HELP ME!
MISTRESS!
AAAAH!

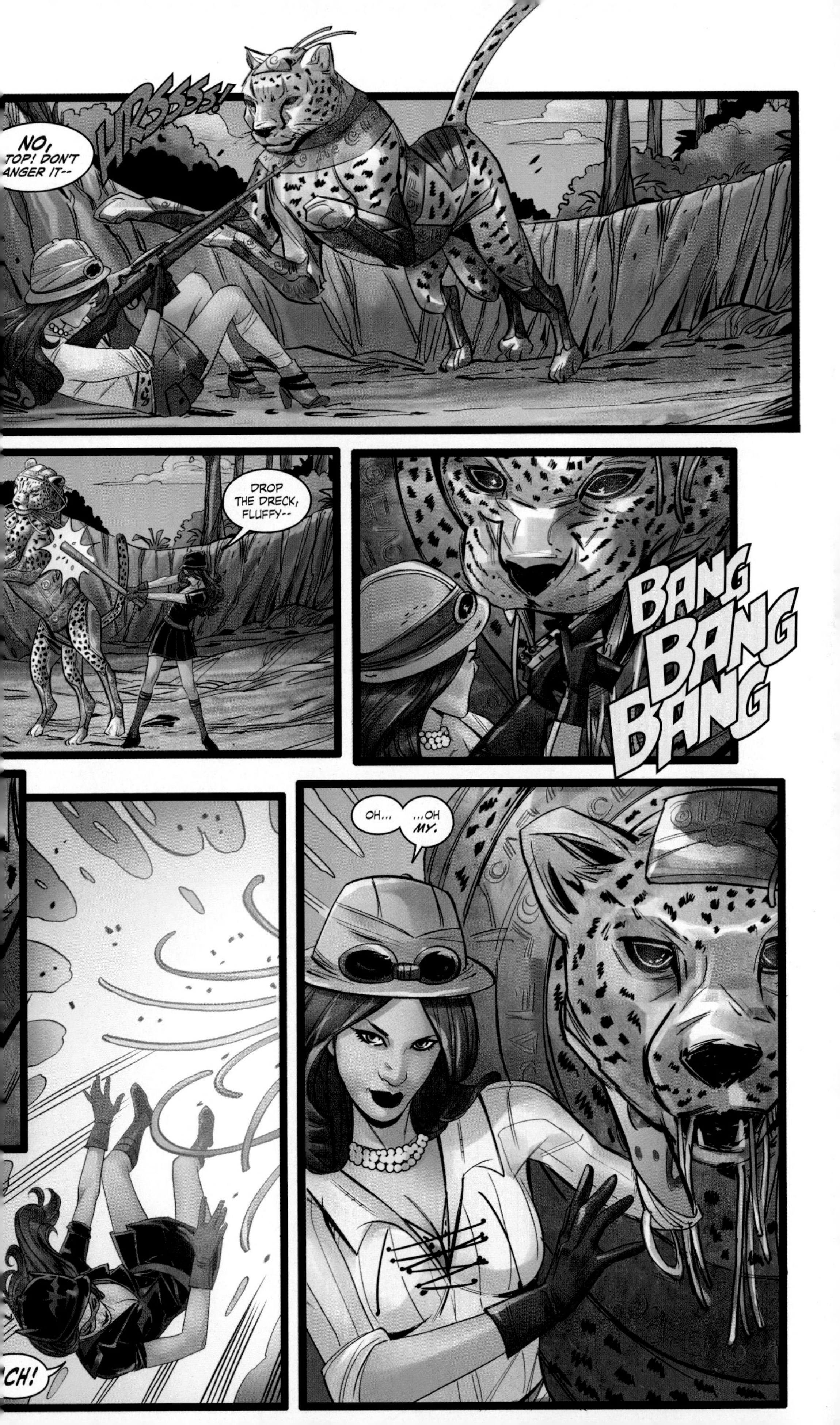

NO, TOP! DON'T ANGER IT--
URSSSS!
DROP THE DRECK, FLUFFY--
BANG BANG BANG
OH... ...OH MY.
CH!

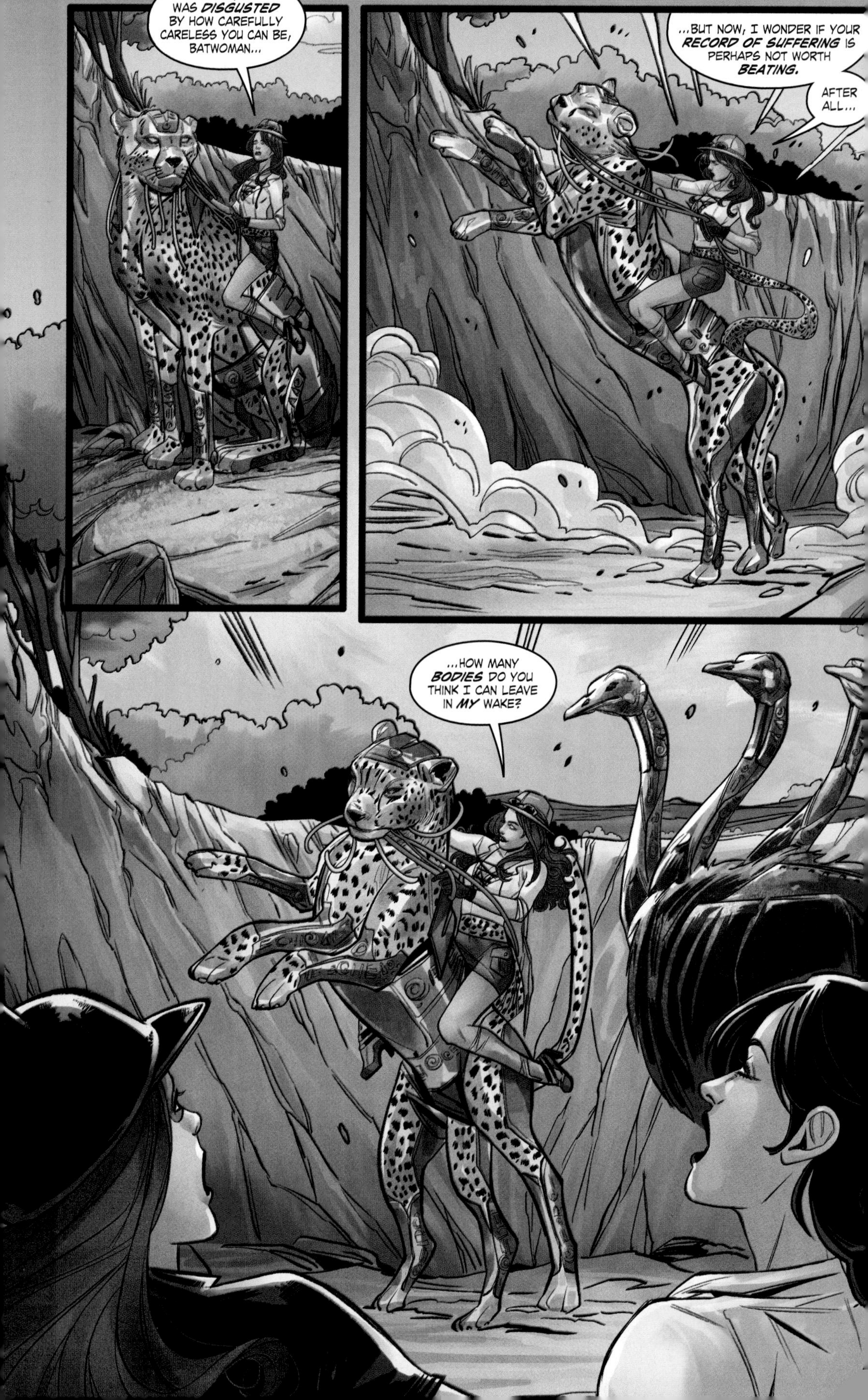
ONCE, I WAS DISGUSTED BY HOW CAREFULLY CARELESS YOU CAN BE, BATWOMAN...
...BUT NOW, I WONDER IF YOUR RECORD OF SUFFERING IS PERHAPS NOT WORTH BEATING.
AFTER ALL...
...HOW MANY BODIES DO YOU THINK I CAN LEAVE IN MY WAKE?

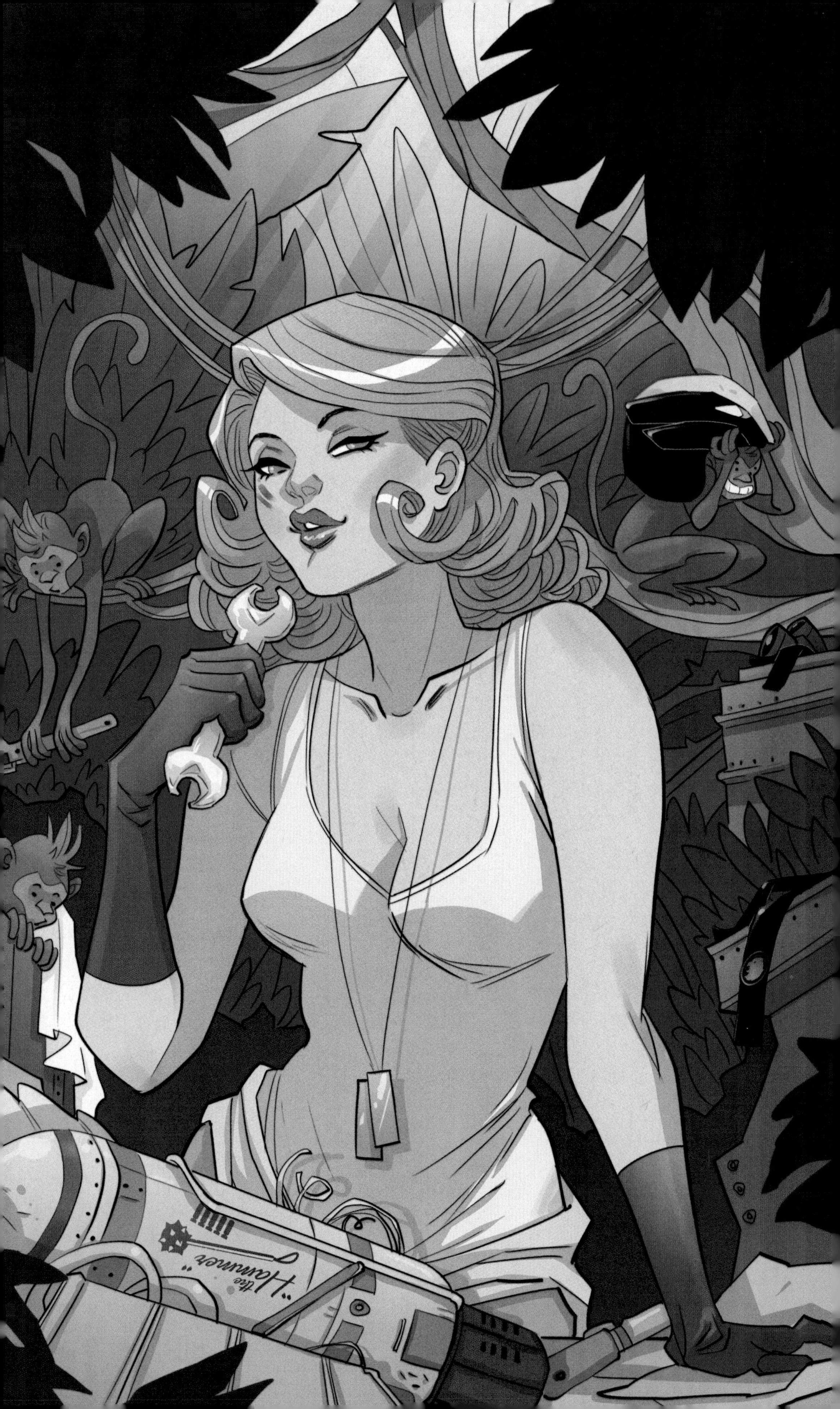
the Hammer

BIG CATS

MARGUERITE BENNETT
Writer

MIRKA ANDOLFO
RICHARD ORTIZ
LAURA BRAGA
Artists

J. NANJAN
Colorist

Cover by
MARGUERITE SAUVAGE

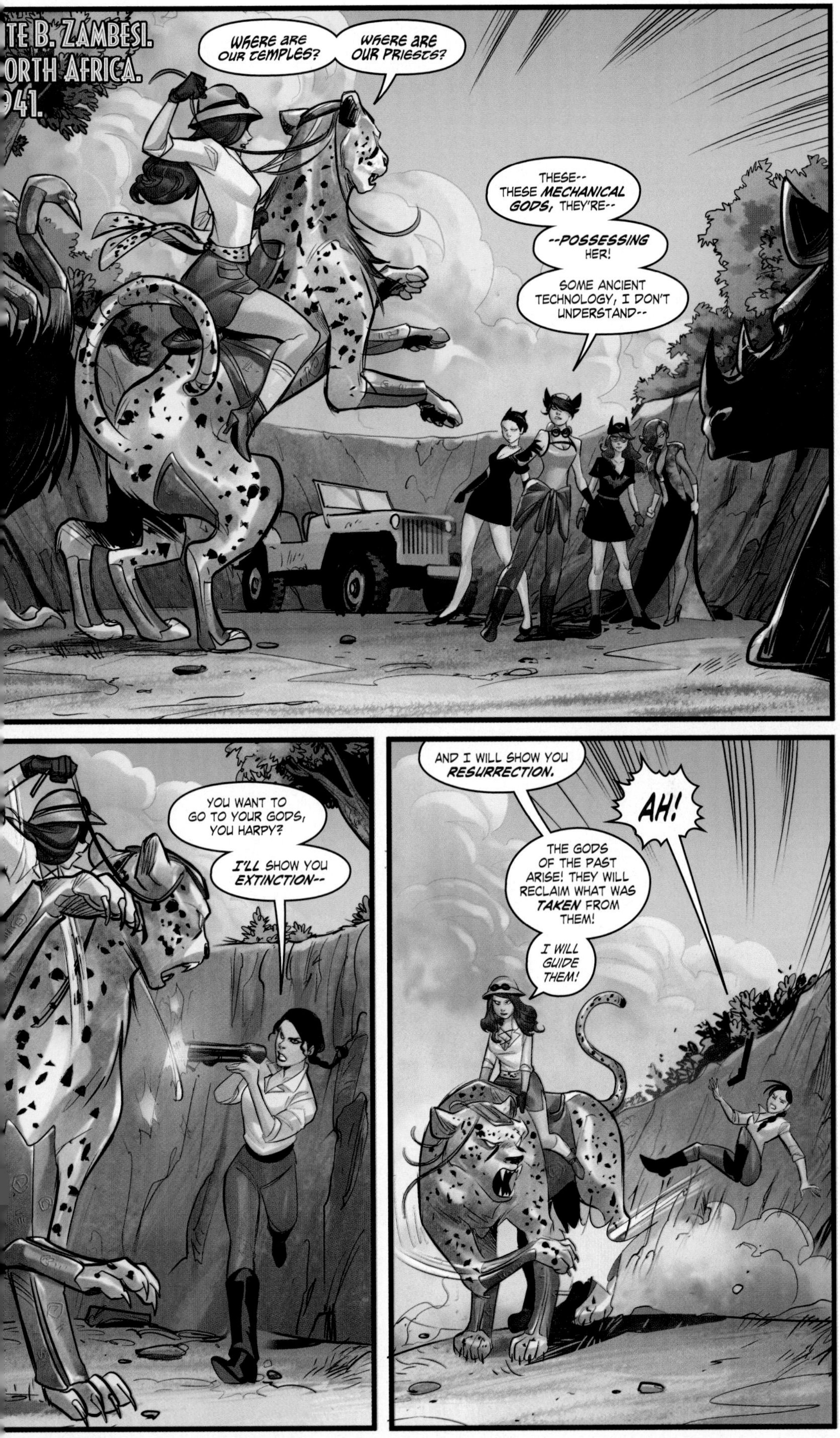
TE B. ZAMBESI.
ORTH AFRICA.
941.
WHERE ARE OUR TEMPLES?
WHERE ARE OUR PRIESTS?
THESE-- THESE MECHANICAL GODS, THEY'RE--
--POSSESSING HER!
SOME ANCIENT TECHNOLOGY, I DON'T UNDERSTAND--
YOU WANT TO GO TO YOUR GODS, YOU HARPY?
I'LL SHOW YOU EXTINCTION--
AND I WILL SHOW YOU RESURRECTION.
AH!
THE GODS OF THE PAST ARISE! THEY WILL RECLAIM WHAT WAS TAKEN FROM THEM!
I WILL GUIDE THEM!

HA! YOU BRING A WHIP TO FIGHT *GODS*?

"OOOH, LOOK AT ME, I'M A CRAZY CHEETAH LADY, I'M BETTER THAN A CAT-O'-NINE-TAILS--"

LISTEN, GLAMOURPUSS, YOU DON'T NEED THE OTHER EIGHT PIECES OF TAIL...

...ONCE YOU FIND THE *ONE* YOU'RE REALLY AFTER.

FWEEEM

CRSSSH

YOU WANT TO SEE A MONSTER?!

DON'T MISS YOUR SHOT, PUSSYCAT--

GRNGH

Y TRIE KILL D

SKREEE

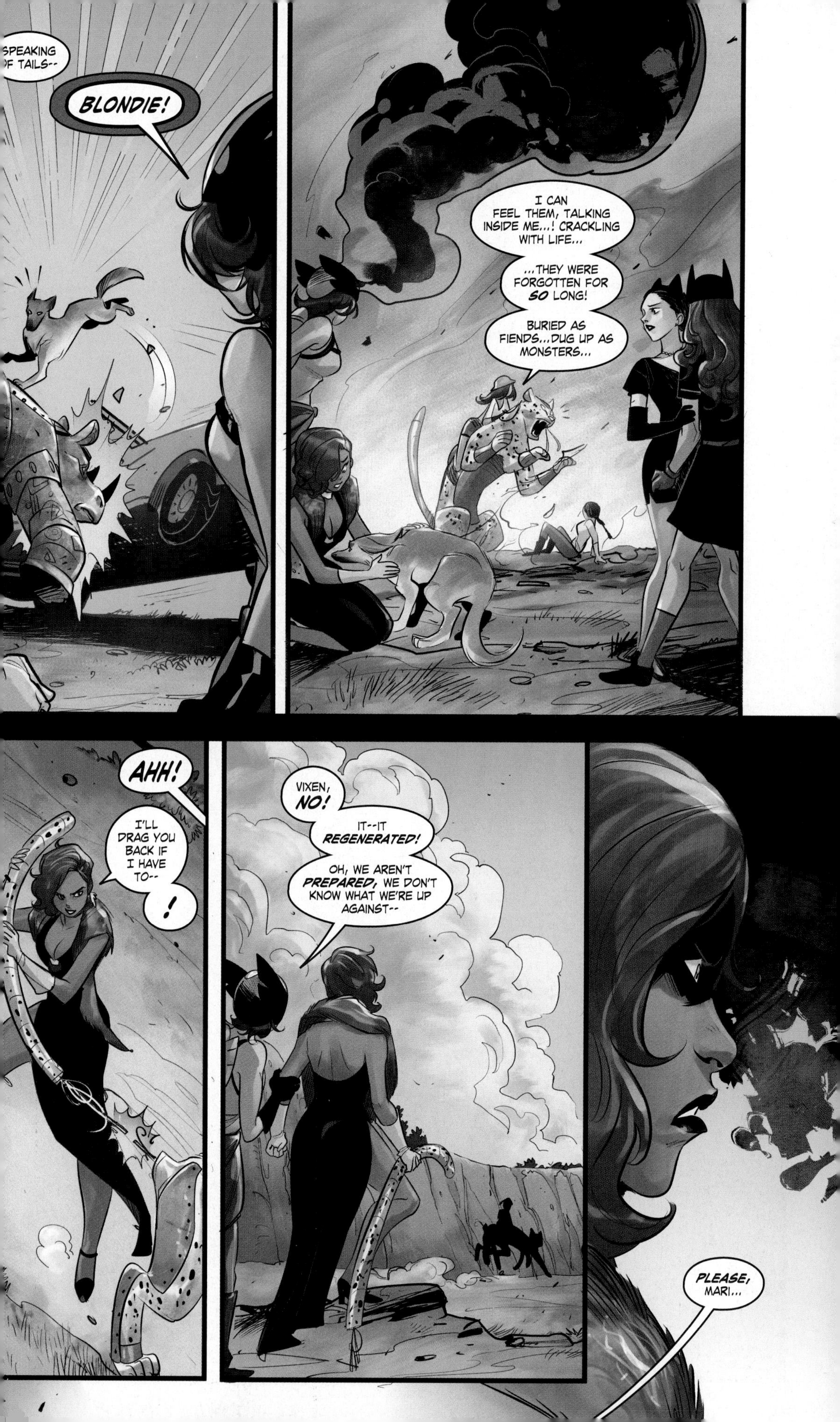
SPEAKING OF TAILS--
BLONDIE!
I CAN FEEL THEM, TALKING INSIDE ME...! CRACKLING WITH LIFE...
...THEY WERE FORGOTTEN FOR SO LONG!
BURIED AS FIENDS...DUG UP AS MONSTERS...
AHH!
I'LL DRAG YOU BACK IF I HAVE TO--
!
VIXEN, NO!
IT--IT REGENERATED!
OH, WE AREN'T PREPARED, WE DON'T KNOW WHAT WE'RE UP AGAINST--
PLEASE, MARI...

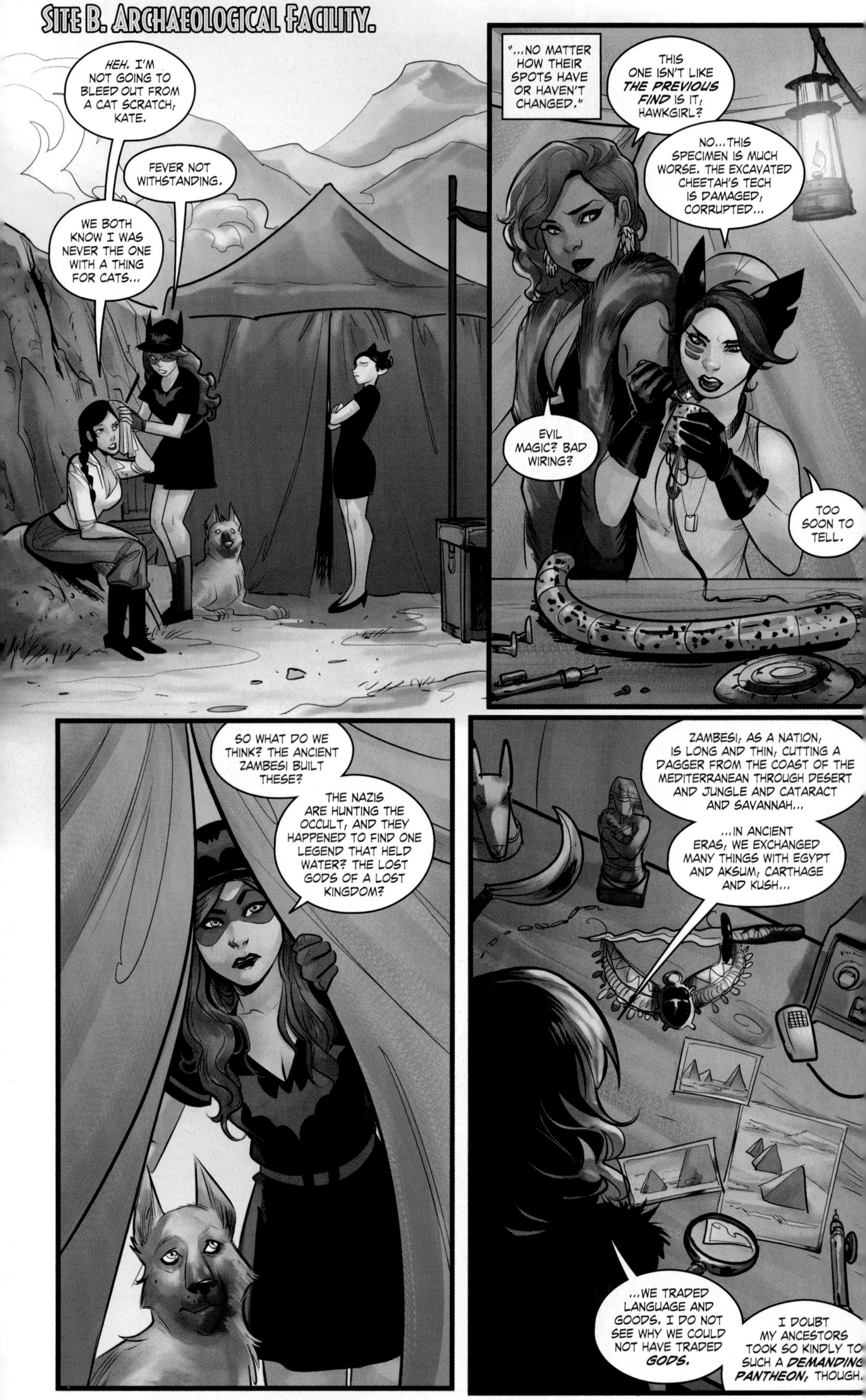
SITE B. ARCHAEOLOGICAL FACILITY.
HEH. I'M NOT GOING TO BLEED OUT FROM A CAT SCRATCH, KATE.
FEVER NOT WITHSTANDING.
WE BOTH KNOW I WAS NEVER THE ONE WITH A THING FOR CATS...
"...NO MATTER HOW THEIR SPOTS HAVE OR HAVEN'T CHANGED."
THIS ONE ISN'T LIKE THE PREVIOUS FIND IS IT, HAWKGIRL?
NO...THIS SPECIMEN IS MUCH WORSE. THE EXCAVATED CHEETAH'S TECH IS DAMAGED, CORRUPTED...
EVIL MAGIC? BAD WIRING?
TOO SOON TO TELL.
SO WHAT DO WE THINK? THE ANCIENT ZAMBESI BUILT THESE?
THE NAZIS ARE HUNTING THE OCCULT, AND THEY HAPPENED TO FIND ONE LEGEND THAT HELD WATER? THE LOST GODS OF A LOST KINGDOM?
ZAMBESI, AS A NATION, IS LONG AND THIN, CUTTING A DAGGER FROM THE COAST OF THE MEDITERRANEAN THROUGH DESERT AND JUNGLE AND CATARACT AND SAVANNAH...
...IN ANCIENT ERAS, WE EXCHANGED MANY THINGS WITH EGYPT AND AKSUM, CARTHAGE AND KUSH...
...WE TRADED LANGUAGE AND GOODS. I DO NOT SEE WHY WE COULD NOT HAVE TRADED GODS.
I DOUBT MY ANCESTORS TOOK SO KINDLY TO SUCH A DEMANDING PANTHEON, THOUGH.

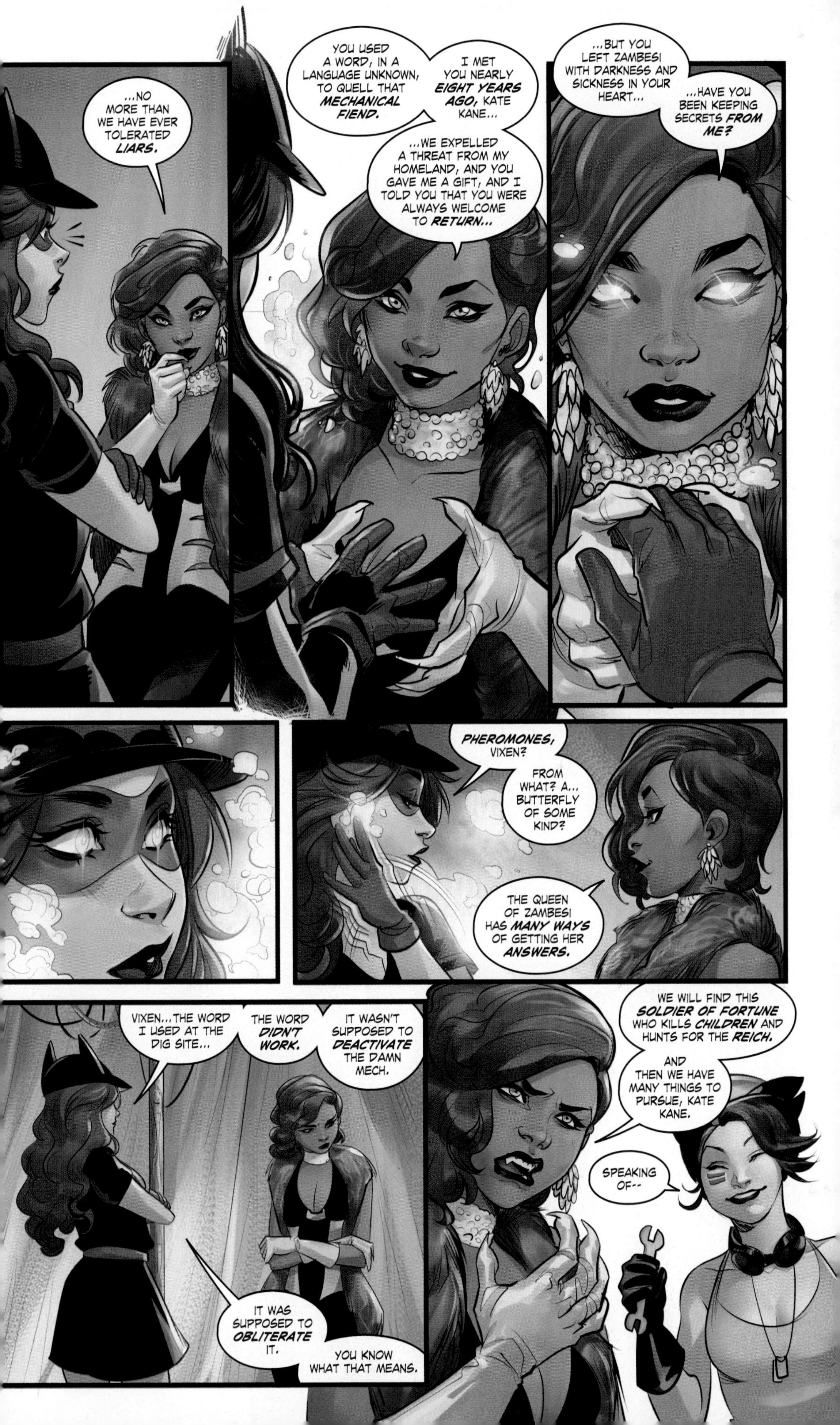
...NO MORE THAN WE HAVE EVER TOLERATED LIARS.
YOU USED A WORD, IN A LANGUAGE UNKNOWN, TO QUELL THAT MECHANICAL FIEND.
I MET YOU NEARLY EIGHT YEARS AGO, KATE KANE...
...WE EXPELLED A THREAT FROM MY HOMELAND, AND YOU GAVE ME A GIFT, AND I TOLD YOU THAT YOU WERE ALWAYS WELCOME TO RETURN...
...BUT YOU LEFT ZAMBESI WITH DARKNESS AND SICKNESS IN YOUR HEART...
...HAVE YOU BEEN KEEPING SECRETS FROM ME?
PHEROMONES, VIXEN?
FROM WHAT? A... BUTTERFLY OF SOME KIND?
THE QUEEN OF ZAMBESI HAS MANY WAYS OF GETTING HER ANSWERS.
VIXEN...THE WORD I USED AT THE DIG SITE...
THE WORD DIDN'T WORK.
IT WASN'T SUPPOSED TO DEACTIVATE THE DAMN MECH.
IT WAS SUPPOSED TO OBLITERATE IT.
YOU KNOW WHAT THAT MEANS.
WE WILL FIND THIS SOLDIER OF FORTUNE WHO KILLS CHILDREN AND HUNTS FOR THE REICH.
AND THEN WE HAVE MANY THINGS TO PURSUE, KATE KANE.
SPEAKING OF--

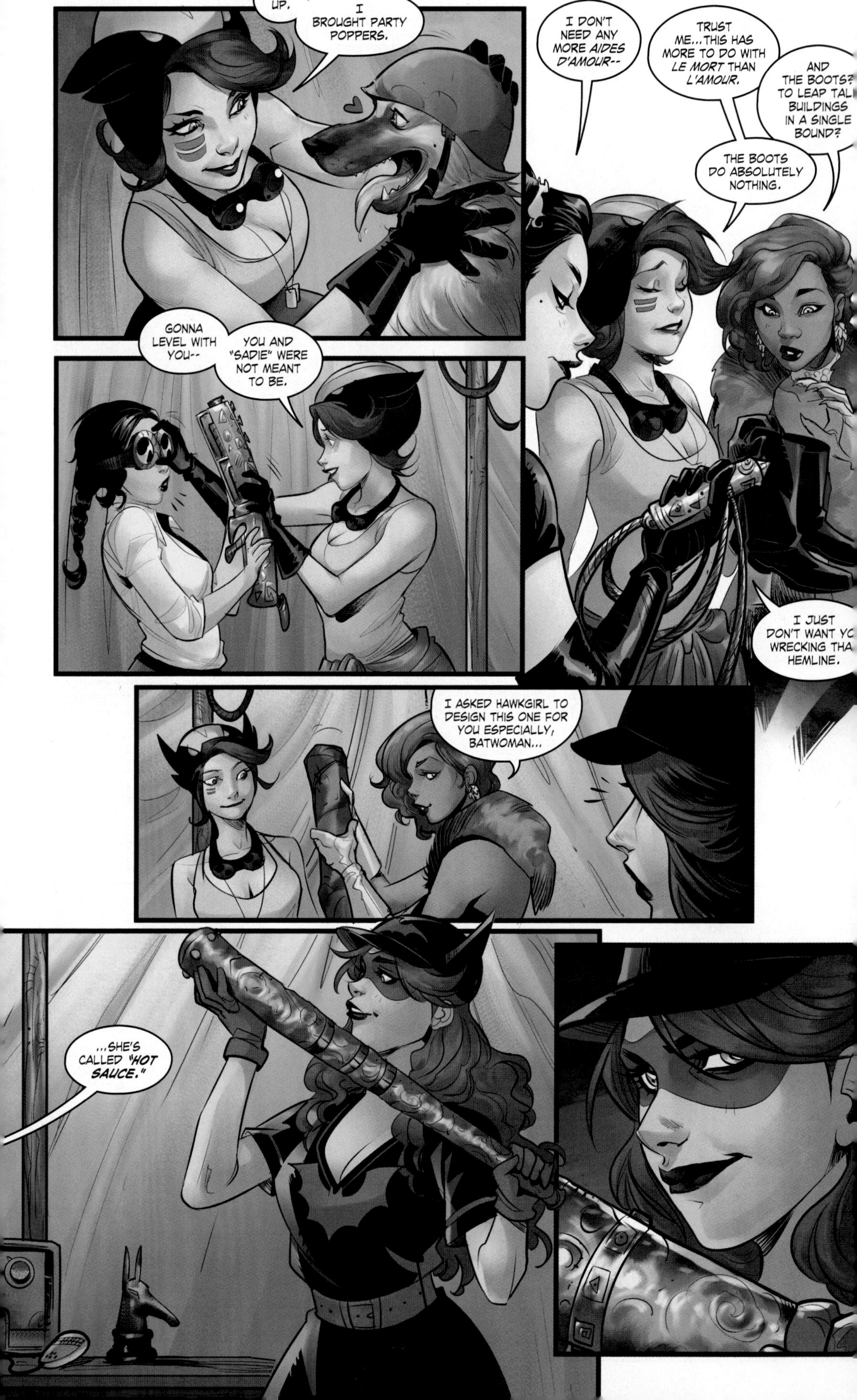
SUIT UP.
I BROUGHT PARTY POPPERS.
I DON'T NEED ANY MORE *AIDES D'AMOUR*--
TRUST ME...THIS HAS MORE TO DO WITH *LE MORT* THAN *L'AMOUR*.
AND THE BOOTS? TO LEAP TAL BUILDINGS IN A SINGLE BOUND?
THE BOOTS DO ABSOLUTELY NOTHING.
GONNA LEVEL WITH YOU--
YOU AND "SADIE" WERE NOT MEANT TO BE.
I JUST DON'T WANT YO WRECKING THA HEMLINE.
I ASKED HAWKGIRL TO DESIGN THIS ONE FOR YOU ESPECIALLY, BATWOMAN...
...SHE'S CALLED *"HOT SAUCE."*

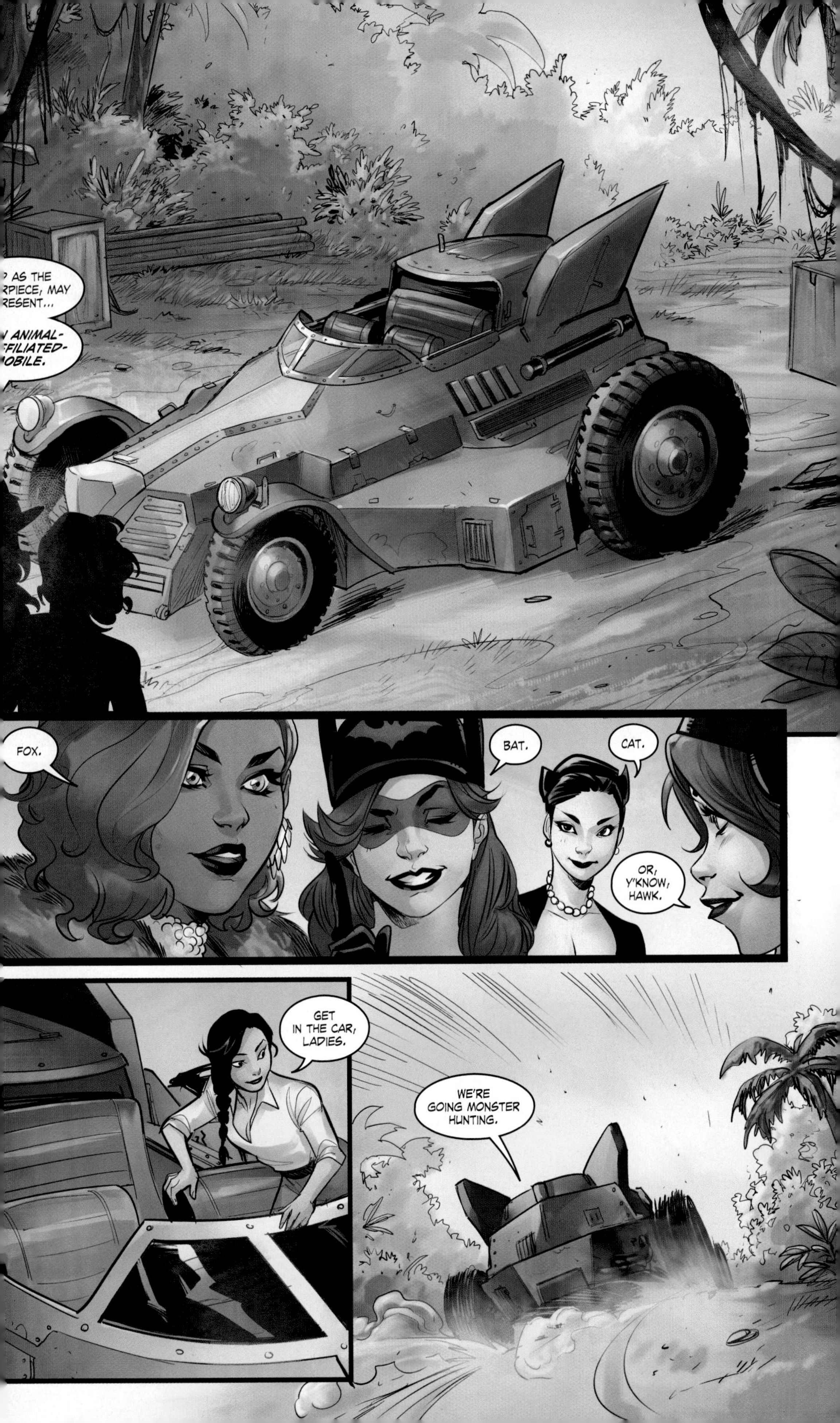

P AS THE RPIECE, MAY RESENT...
N ANIMAL- FFILIATED- OBILE.
FOX.
BAT.
CAT.
OR, Y'KNOW, HAWK.
GET IN THE CAR, LADIES.
WE'RE GOING MONSTER HUNTING.

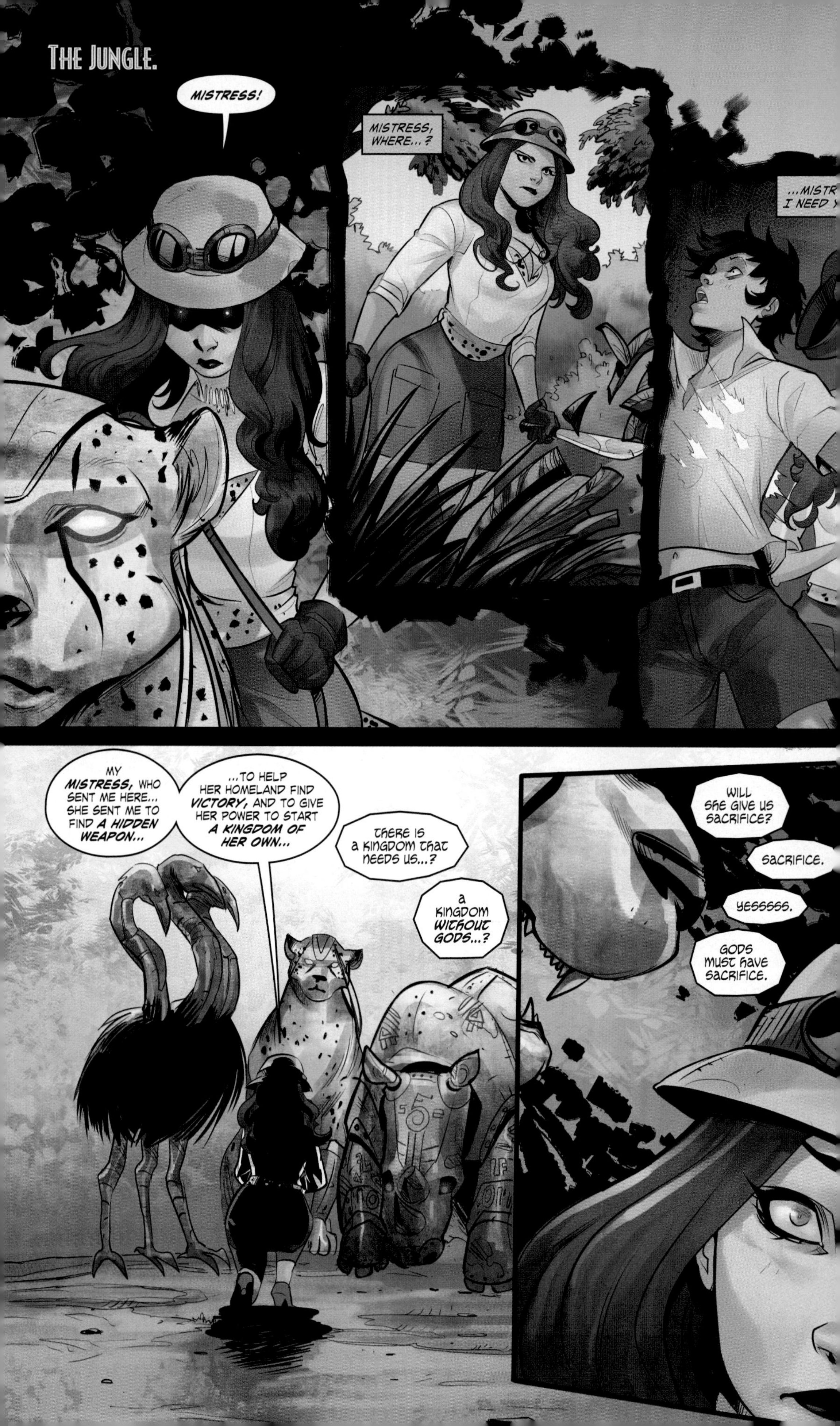
THE JUNGLE.
MISTRESS!
MISTRESS, WHERE...?
...MISTR I NEED Y
MY MISTRESS, WHO SENT ME HERE... SHE SENT ME TO FIND A HIDDEN WEAPON...
...TO HELP HER HOMELAND FIND VICTORY, AND TO GIVE HER POWER TO START A KINGDOM OF HER OWN...
THERE IS A KINGDOM THAT NEEDS US...?
A KINGDOM WITHOUT GODS...?
WILL SHE GIVE US SACRIFICE?
SACRIFICE.
YESSSSS.
GODS MUST HAVE SACRIFICE.

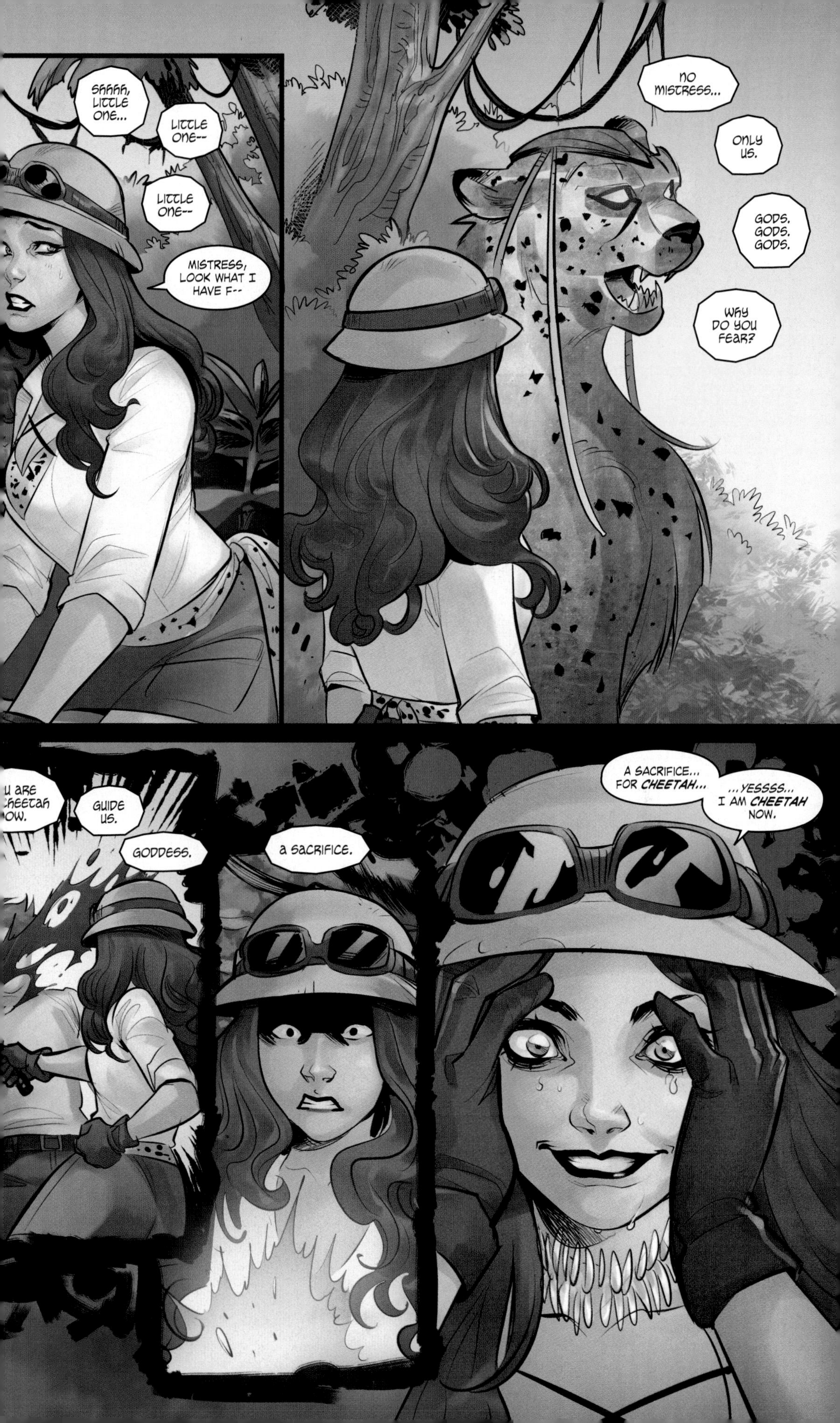
SHHHH, LITTLE ONE...
LITTLE ONE--
LITTLE ONE--
MISTRESS, LOOK WHAT I HAVE F--
NO MISTRESS...
ONLY US.
GODS. GODS. GODS.
WHY DO YOU FEAR?
u are cheetah ow.
GUIDE US.
GODDESS.
a SACRIFICE.
A SACRIFICE... FOR **CHEETAH**...
...YESSSS... I AM **CHEETAH** NOW.

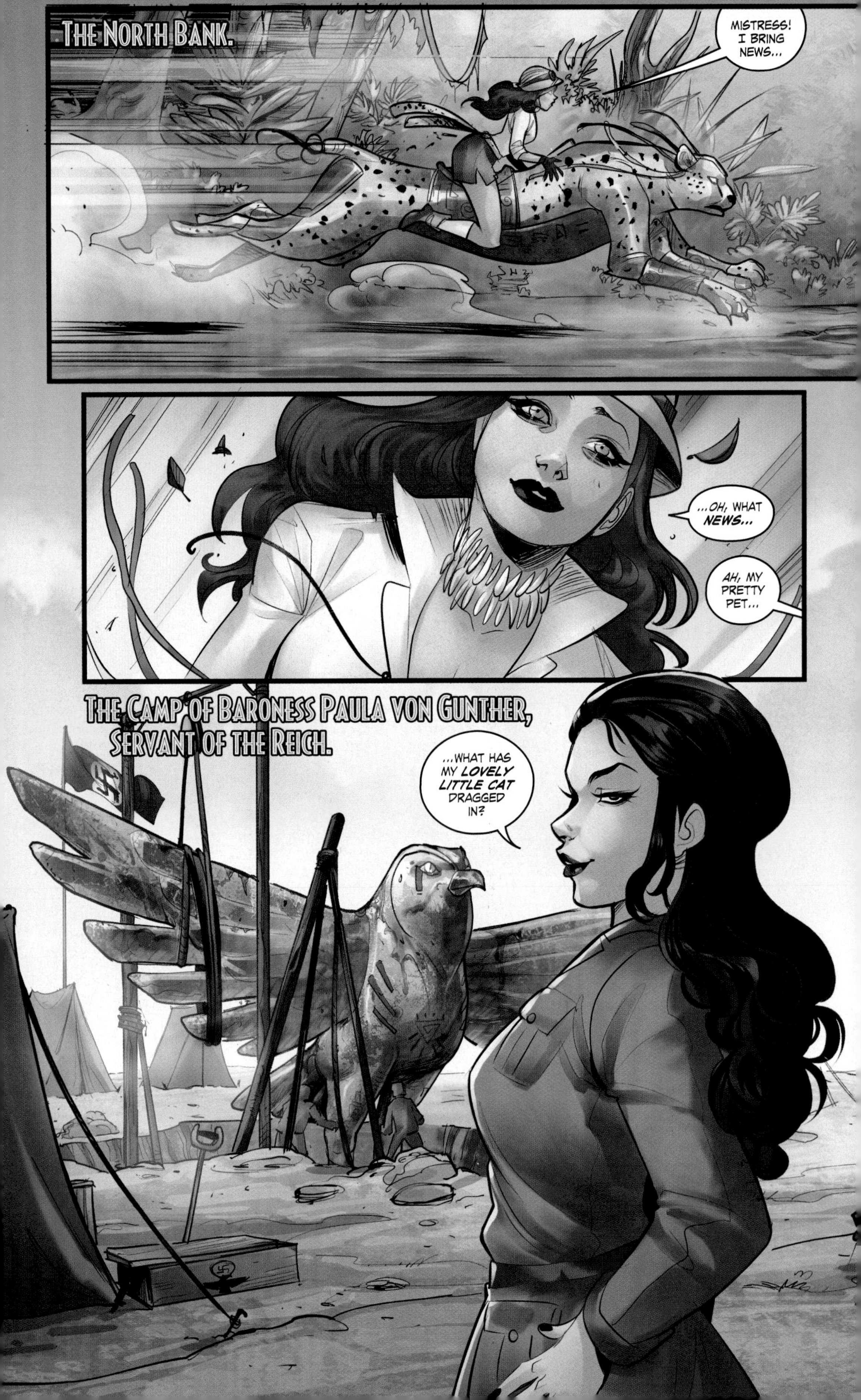
THE NORTH BANK.
MISTRESS! I BRING NEWS...
...OH, WHAT NEWS...
AH, MY PRETTY PET...
THE CAMP OF BARONESS PAULA VON GUNTHER, SERVANT OF THE REICH.
...WHAT HAS MY LOVELY LITTLE CAT DRAGGED IN?

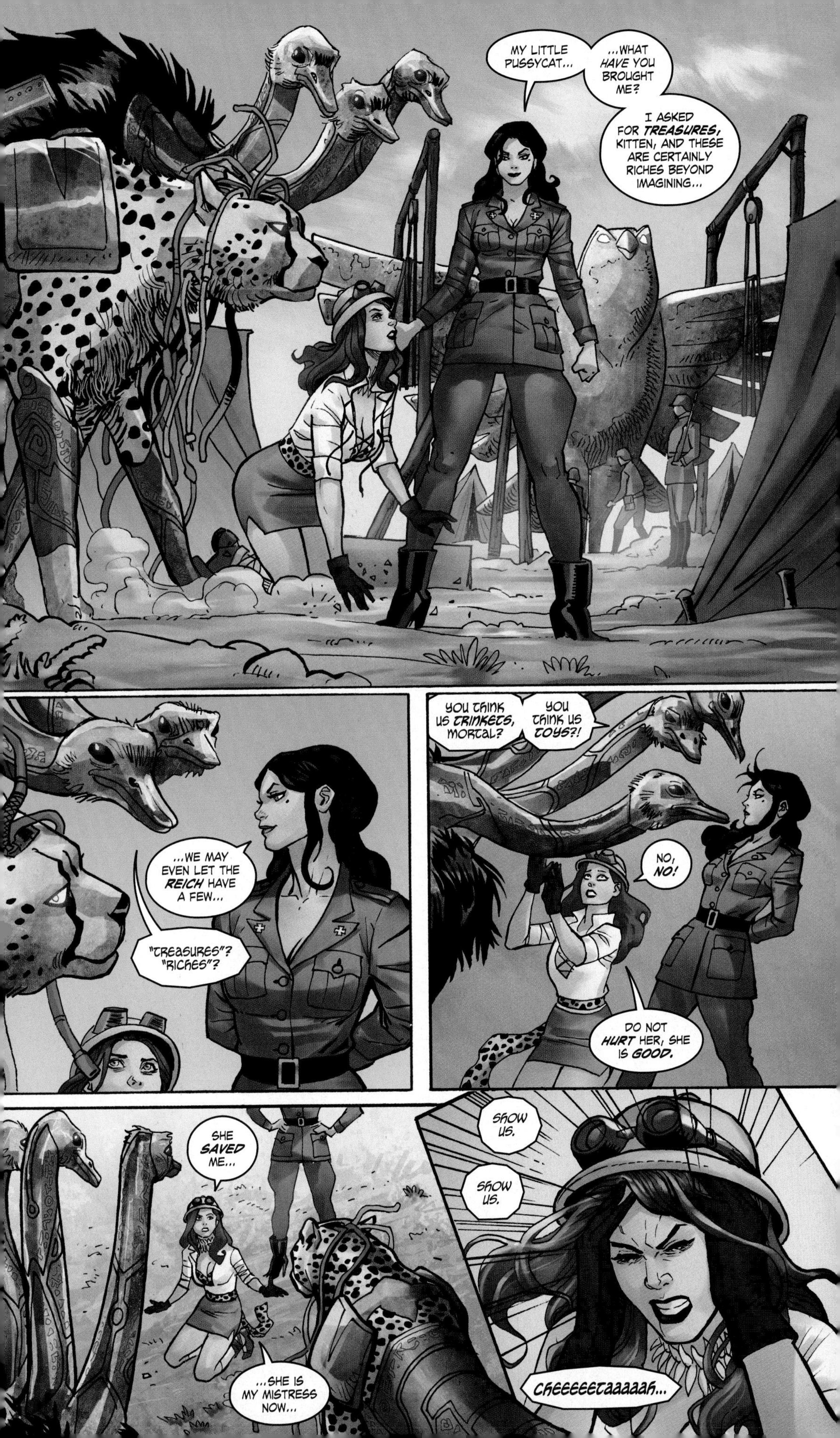
MY LITTLE PUSSYCAT...
...WHAT HAVE YOU BROUGHT ME?
I ASKED FOR TREASURES, KITTEN, AND THESE ARE CERTAINLY RICHES BEYOND IMAGINING...
...WE MAY EVEN LET THE REICH HAVE A FEW...
"TREASURES"? "RICHES"?
YOU THINK US TRINKETS, MORTAL?
YOU THINK US TOYS?!
NO, NO!
DO NOT HURT HER, SHE IS GOOD.
SHE SAVED ME...
...SHE IS MY MISTRESS NOW...
SHOW US.
SHOW US.
CHEEEEETAAAAAH...

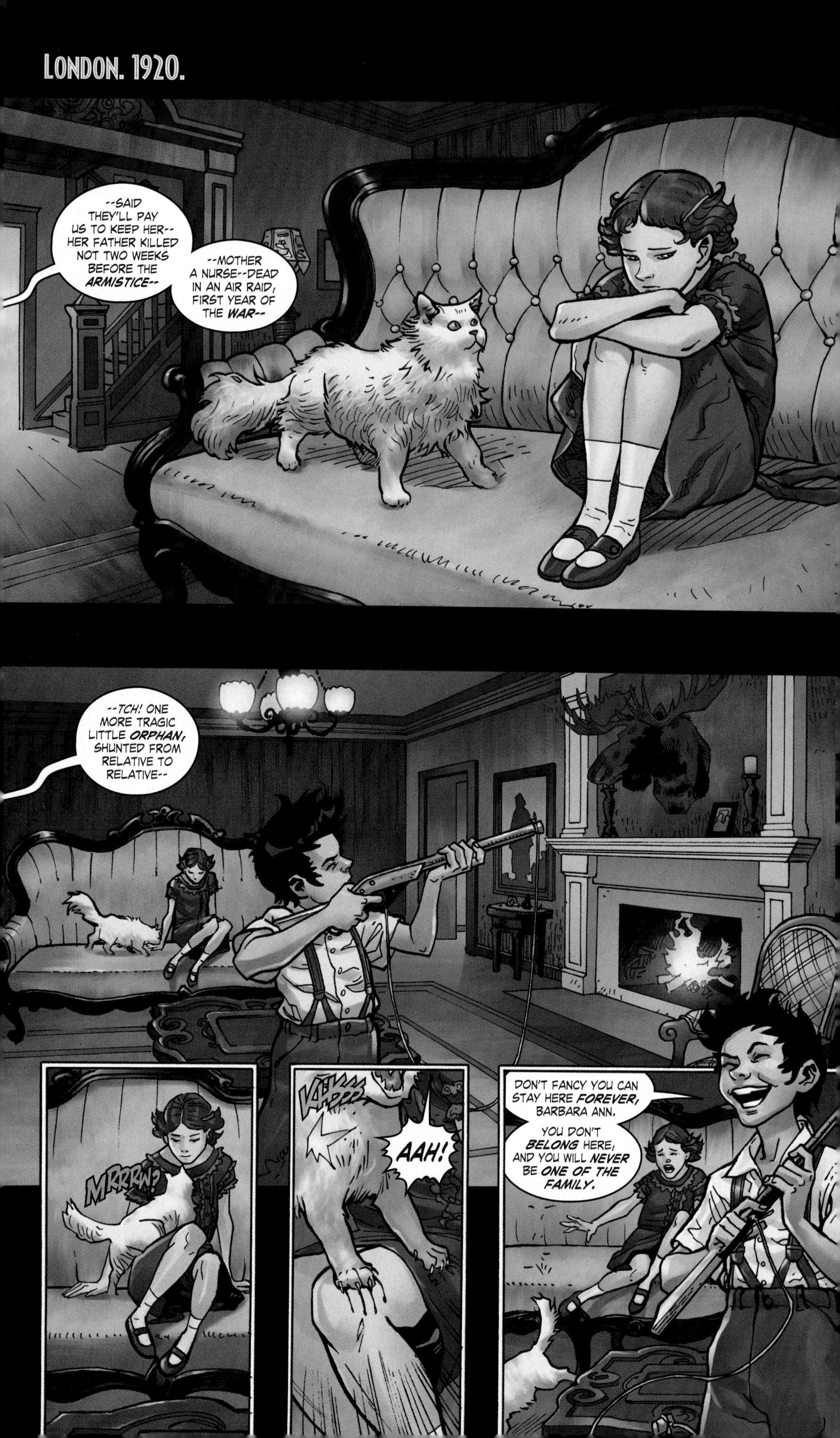
LONDON. 1920.
--SAID THEY'LL PAY US TO KEEP HER-- HER FATHER KILLED NOT TWO WEEKS BEFORE THE ARMISTICE--
--MOTHER A NURSE--DEAD IN AN AIR RAID, FIRST YEAR OF THE WAR--
--TCH! ONE MORE TRAGIC LITTLE ORPHAN, SHUNTED FROM RELATIVE TO RELATIVE--
MRRRW?
AAH!
DON'T FANCY YOU CAN STAY HERE FOREVER, BARBARA ANN.
YOU DON'T BELONG HERE, AND YOU WILL NEVER BE ONE OF THE FAMILY.

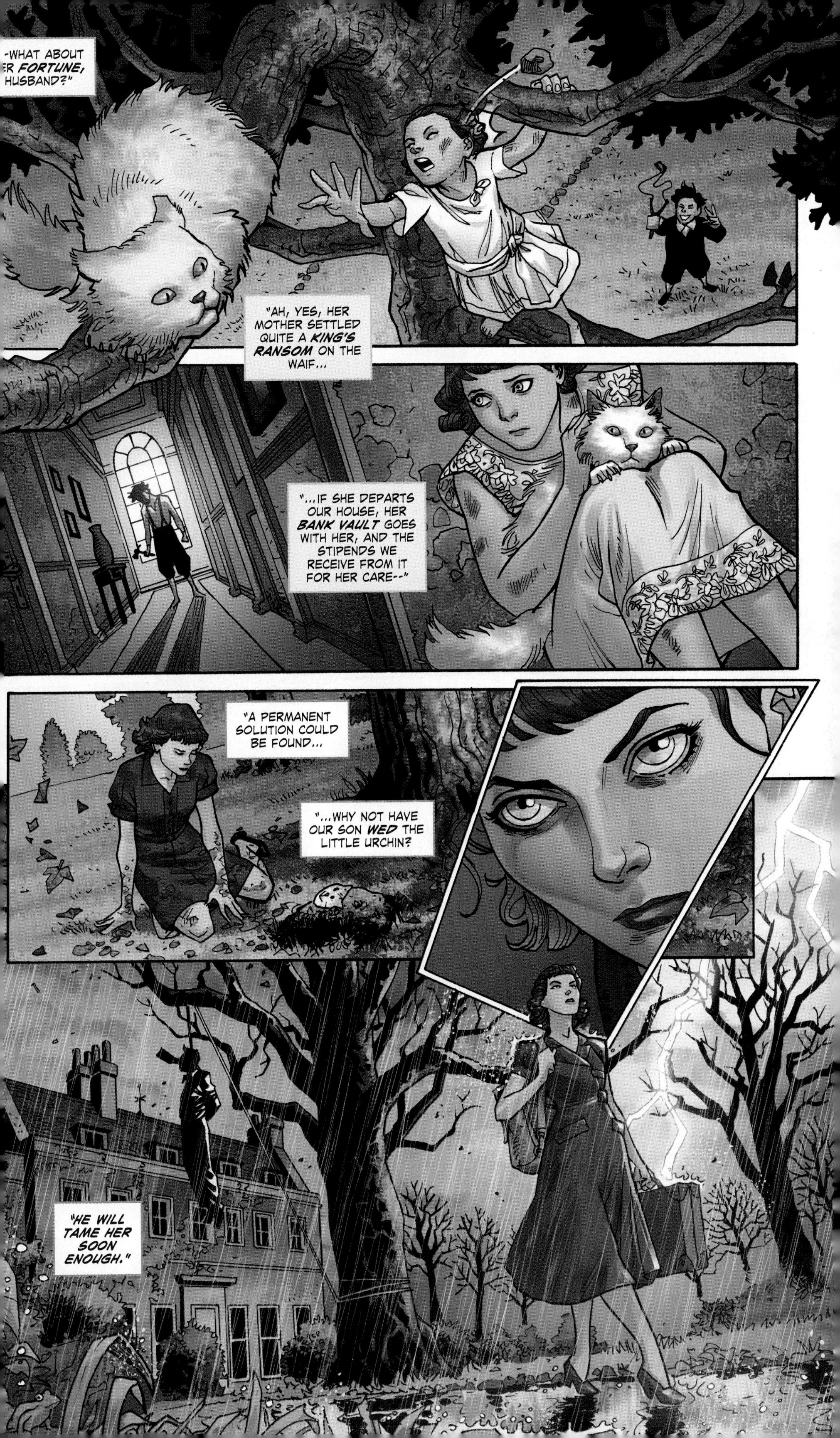
-WHAT ABOUT
ER *FORTUNE,*
HUSBAND?"
"AH, YES, HER MOTHER SETTLED QUITE A *KING'S RANSOM* ON THE WAIF...
"...IF SHE DEPARTS OUR HOUSE, HER *BANK VAULT* GOES WITH HER, AND THE STIPENDS WE RECEIVE FROM IT FOR HER CARE--"
"A PERMANENT SOLUTION COULD BE FOUND...
"...WHY NOT HAVE OUR SON *WED* THE LITTLE URCHIN?
"HE WILL TAME HER SOON ENOUGH."

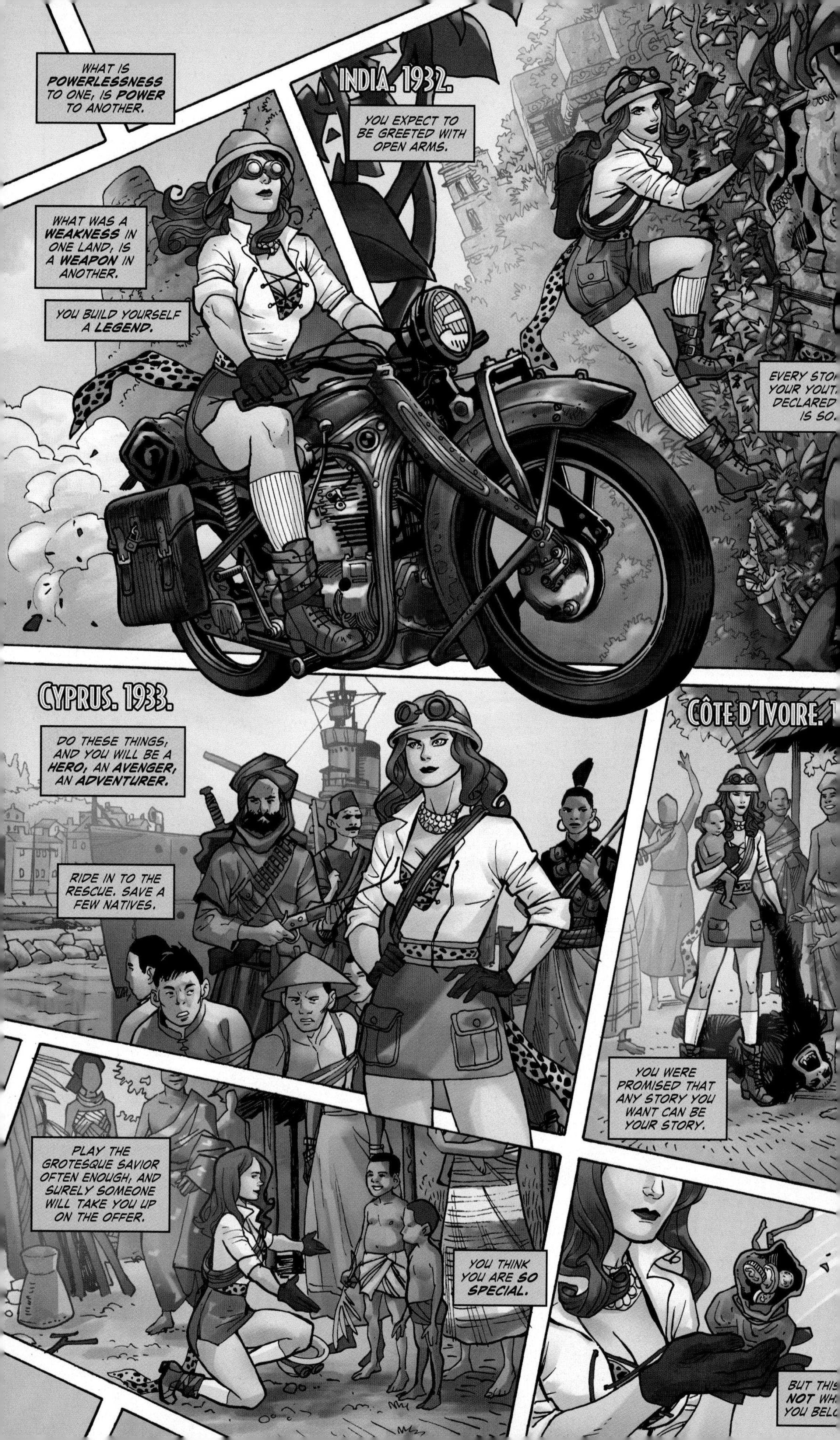

WHAT IS POWERLESSNESS TO ONE, IS POWER TO ANOTHER.
INDIA. 1932.
YOU EXPECT TO BE GREETED WITH OPEN ARMS.
WHAT WAS A WEAKNESS IN ONE LAND, IS A WEAPON IN ANOTHER.
YOU BUILD YOURSELF A LEGEND.
EVERY STO
YOUR YOUT
DECLARED
IS SO.
CYPRUS. 1933.
DO THESE THINGS, AND YOU WILL BE A HERO, AN AVENGER, AN ADVENTURER.
RIDE IN TO THE RESCUE. SAVE A FEW NATIVES.
CÔTE D'IVOIRE.
YOU WERE PROMISED THAT ANY STORY YOU WANT CAN BE YOUR STORY.
PLAY THE GROTESQUE SAVIOR OFTEN ENOUGH, AND SURELY SOMEONE WILL TAKE YOU UP ON THE OFFER.
YOU THINK YOU ARE SO SPECIAL.
BUT THIS
NOT WH
YOU BEL

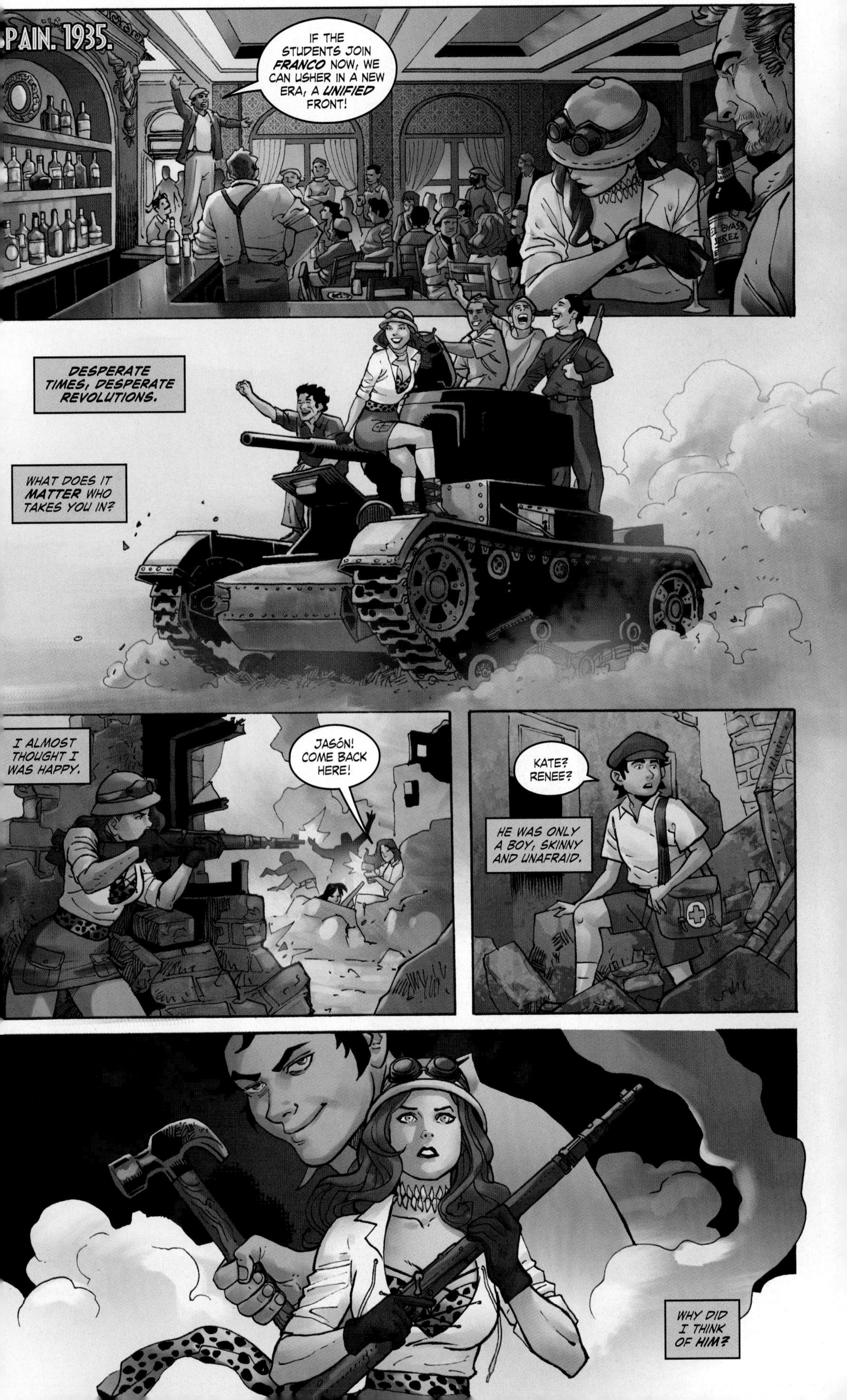
PAIN. 1935.
IF THE STUDENTS JOIN FRANCO NOW, WE CAN USHER IN A NEW ERA, A UNIFIED FRONT!
DESPERATE TIMES, DESPERATE REVOLUTIONS.
WHAT DOES IT MATTER WHO TAKES YOU IN?
I ALMOST THOUGHT I WAS HAPPY.
JASÓN! COME BACK HERE!
KATE? RENEE?
HE WAS ONLY A BOY, SKINNY AND UNAFRAID.
WHY DID I THINK OF HIM?

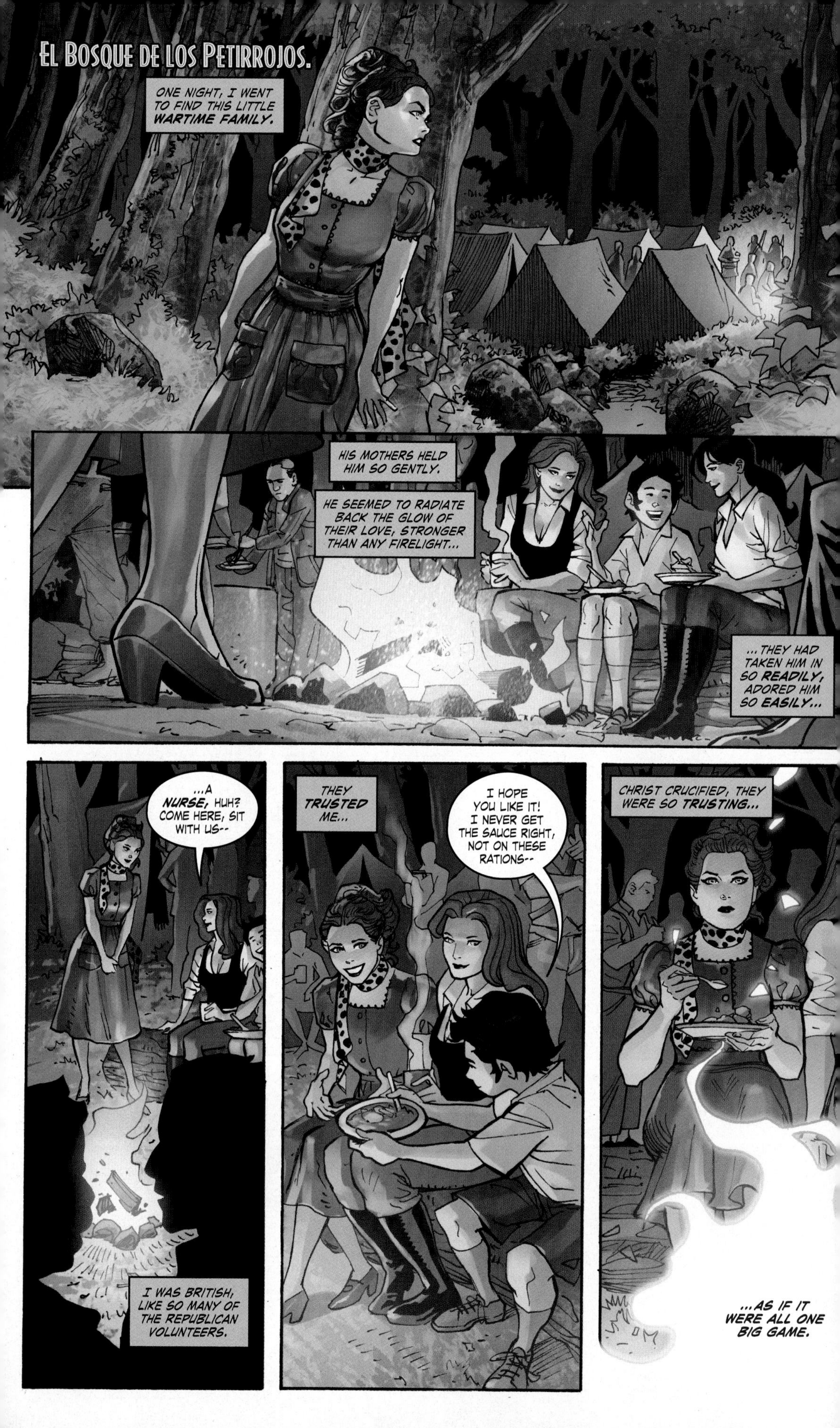
El Bosque de los Petirrojos.
ONE NIGHT, I WENT TO FIND THIS LITTLE WARTIME FAMILY.
HIS MOTHERS HELD HIM SO GENTLY.
HE SEEMED TO RADIATE BACK THE GLOW OF THEIR LOVE, STRONGER THAN ANY FIRELIGHT...
...THEY HAD TAKEN HIM IN SO READILY, ADORED HIM SO EASILY...
...A NURSE, HUH? COME HERE, SIT WITH US--
I WAS BRITISH, LIKE SO MANY OF THE REPUBLICAN VOLUNTEERS.
THEY TRUSTED ME...
I HOPE YOU LIKE IT! I NEVER GET THE SAUCE RIGHT, NOT ON THESE RATIONS--
CHRIST CRUCIFIED, THEY WERE SO TRUSTING...
...AS IF IT WERE ALL ONE BIG GAME.

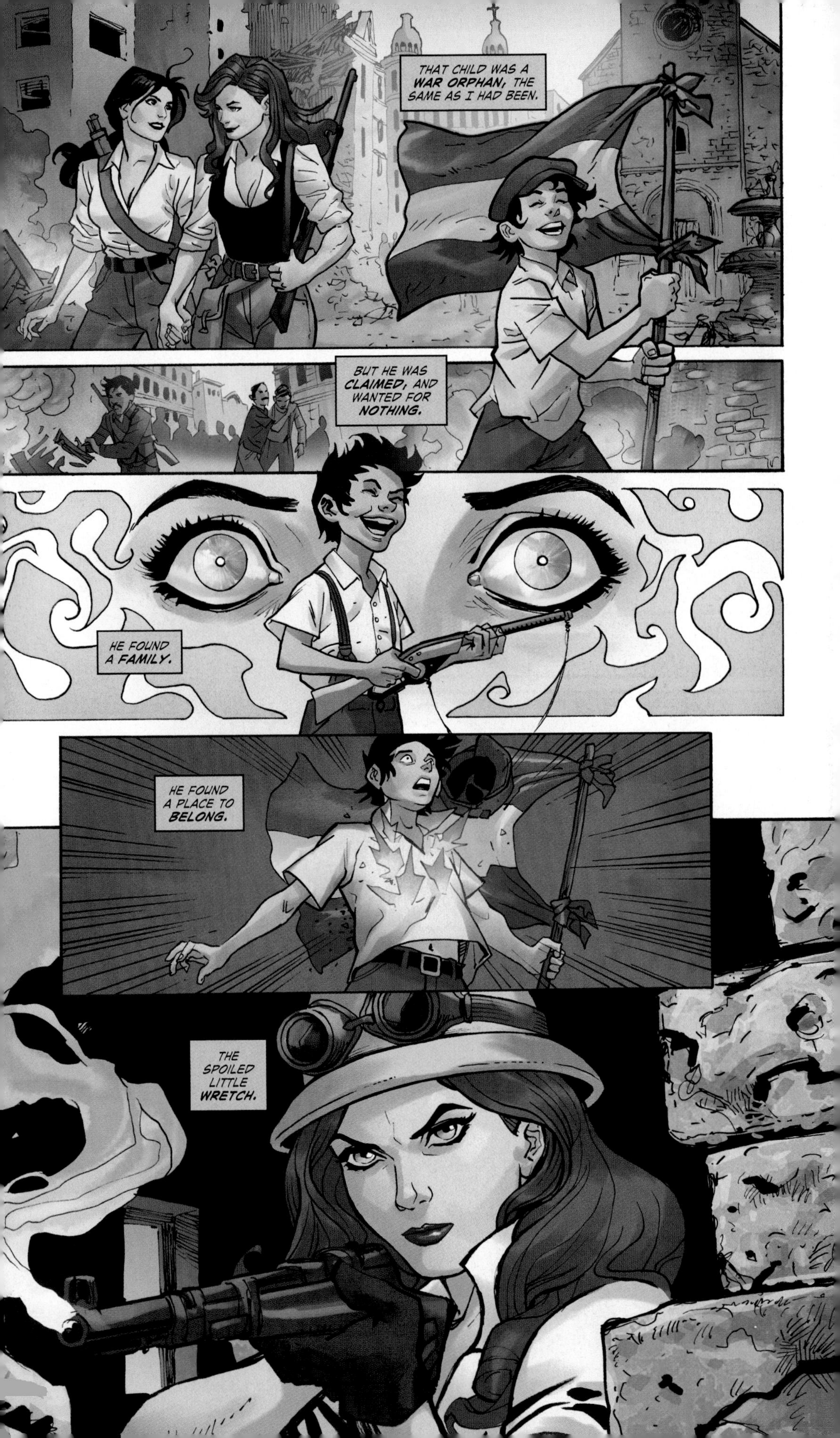

THAT CHILD WAS A WAR ORPHAN, THE SAME AS I HAD BEEN.
BUT HE WAS CLAIMED, AND WANTED FOR NOTHING.
HE FOUND A FAMILY.
HE FOUND A PLACE TO BELONG.
THE SPOILED LITTLE WRETCH.

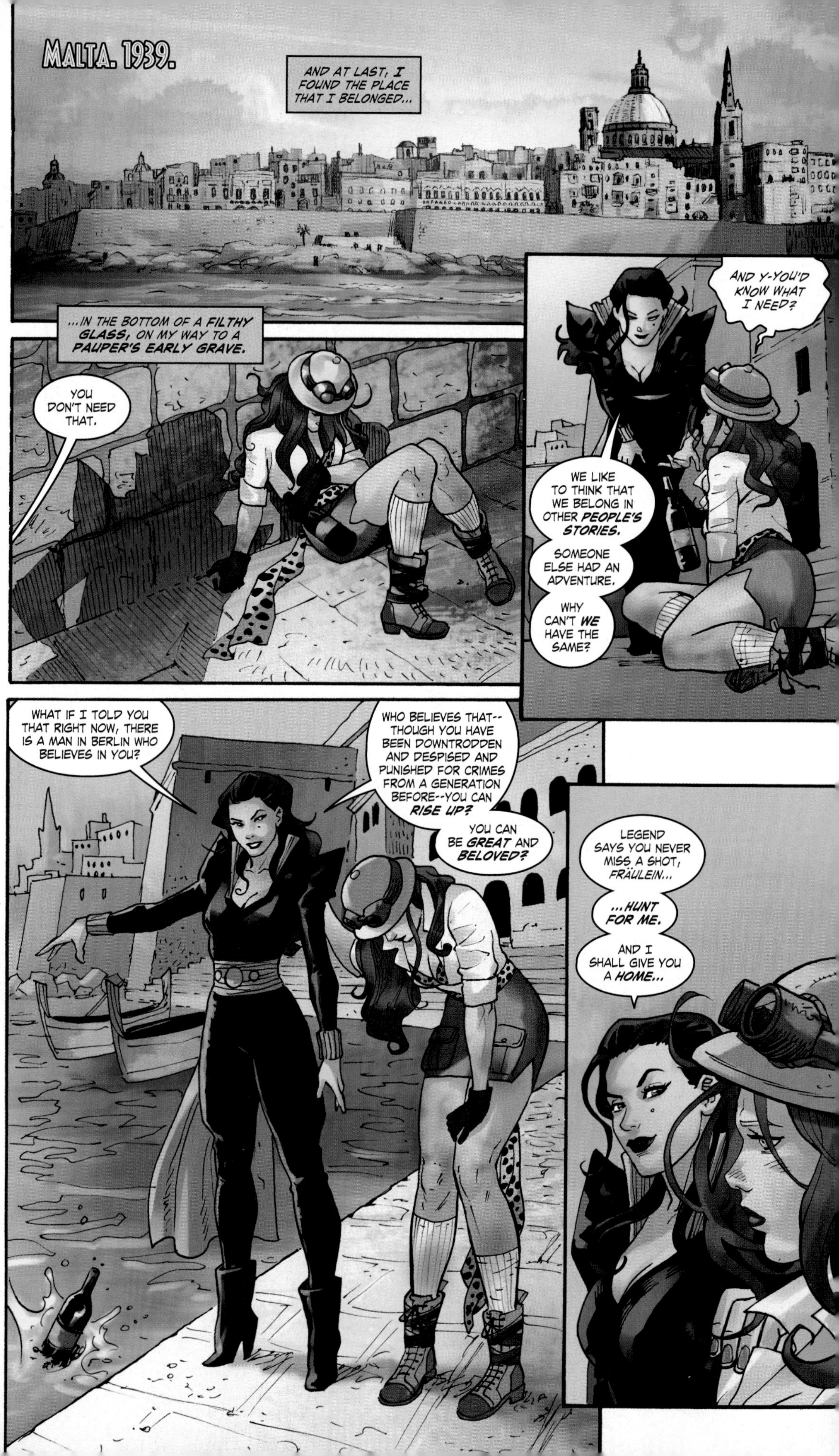
MALTA. 1939.
AND AT LAST, I FOUND THE PLACE THAT I BELONGED...
...IN THE BOTTOM OF A FILTHY GLASS, ON MY WAY TO A PAUPER'S EARLY GRAVE.
YOU DON'T NEED THAT.
AND Y-YOU'D KNOW WHAT I NEED?
WE LIKE TO THINK THAT WE BELONG IN OTHER PEOPLE'S STORIES.
SOMEONE ELSE HAD AN ADVENTURE.
WHY CAN'T WE HAVE THE SAME?
WHAT IF I TOLD YOU THAT RIGHT NOW, THERE IS A MAN IN BERLIN WHO BELIEVES IN YOU?
WHO BELIEVES THAT--THOUGH YOU HAVE BEEN DOWNTRODDEN AND DESPISED AND PUNISHED FOR CRIMES FROM A GENERATION BEFORE--YOU CAN RISE UP?
YOU CAN BE GREAT AND BELOVED?
LEGEND SAYS YOU NEVER MISS A SHOT, FRÄULEIN...
...HUNT FOR ME.
AND I SHALL GIVE YOU A HOME...

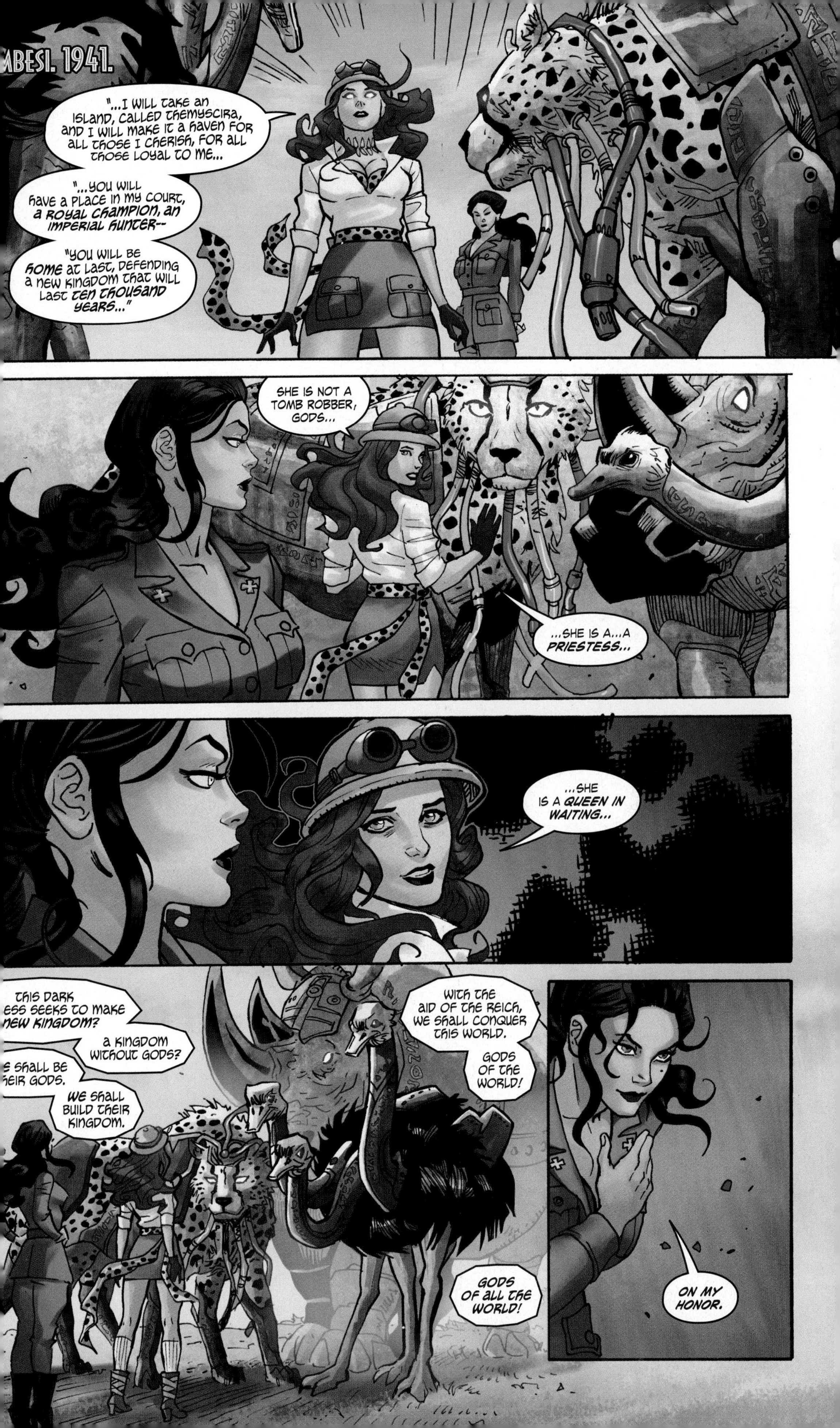

MBESI. 1941.
"...I WILL TAKE AN ISLAND, CALLED THEMYSCIRA, AND I WILL MAKE IT A HAVEN FOR ALL THOSE I CHERISH, FOR ALL THOSE LOYAL TO ME...
"...YOU WILL HAVE A PLACE IN MY COURT, A ROYAL CHAMPION, AN IMPERIAL HUNTER--
"YOU WILL BE HOME AT LAST, DEFENDING A NEW KINGDOM THAT WILL LAST TEN THOUSAND YEARS..."
SHE IS NOT A TOMB ROBBER, GODS...
...SHE IS A...A PRIESTESS...
...SHE IS A QUEEN IN WAITING...
THIS DARK ESS SEEKS TO MAKE NEW KINGDOM?
A KINGDOM WITHOUT GODS?
E SHALL BE EIR GODS.
WE SHALL BUILD THEIR KINGDOM.
WITH THE AID OF THE REICH, WE SHALL CONQUER THIS WORLD.
GODS OF THE WORLD!
GODS OF ALL THE WORLD!
ON MY HONOR.

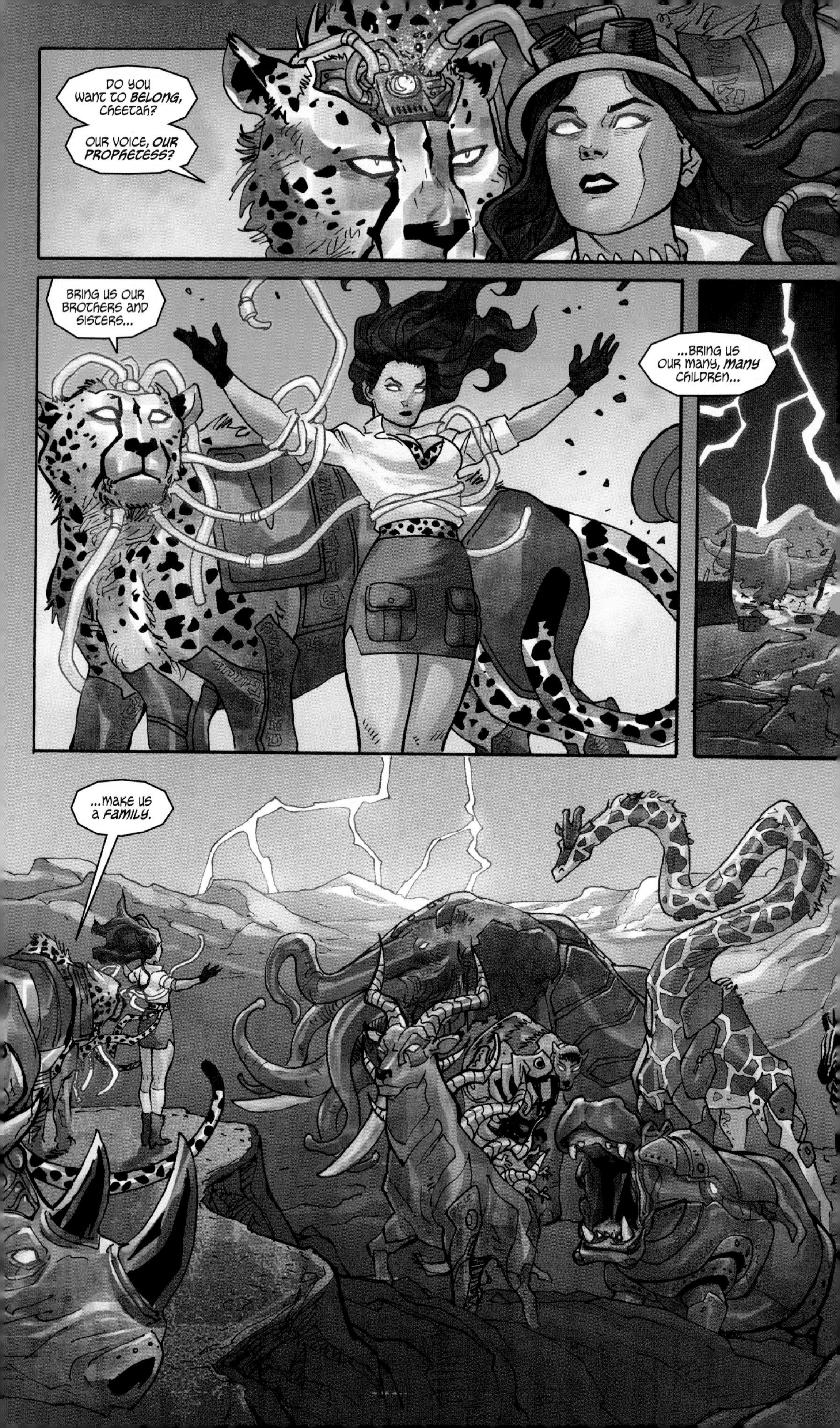
DO YOU WANT TO BELONG, CHEETAH?
OUR VOICE, OUR PROPHETESS?
BRING US OUR BROTHERS AND SISTERS...
...BRING US OUR MANY, MANY CHILDREN...
...MAKE US A FAMILY.

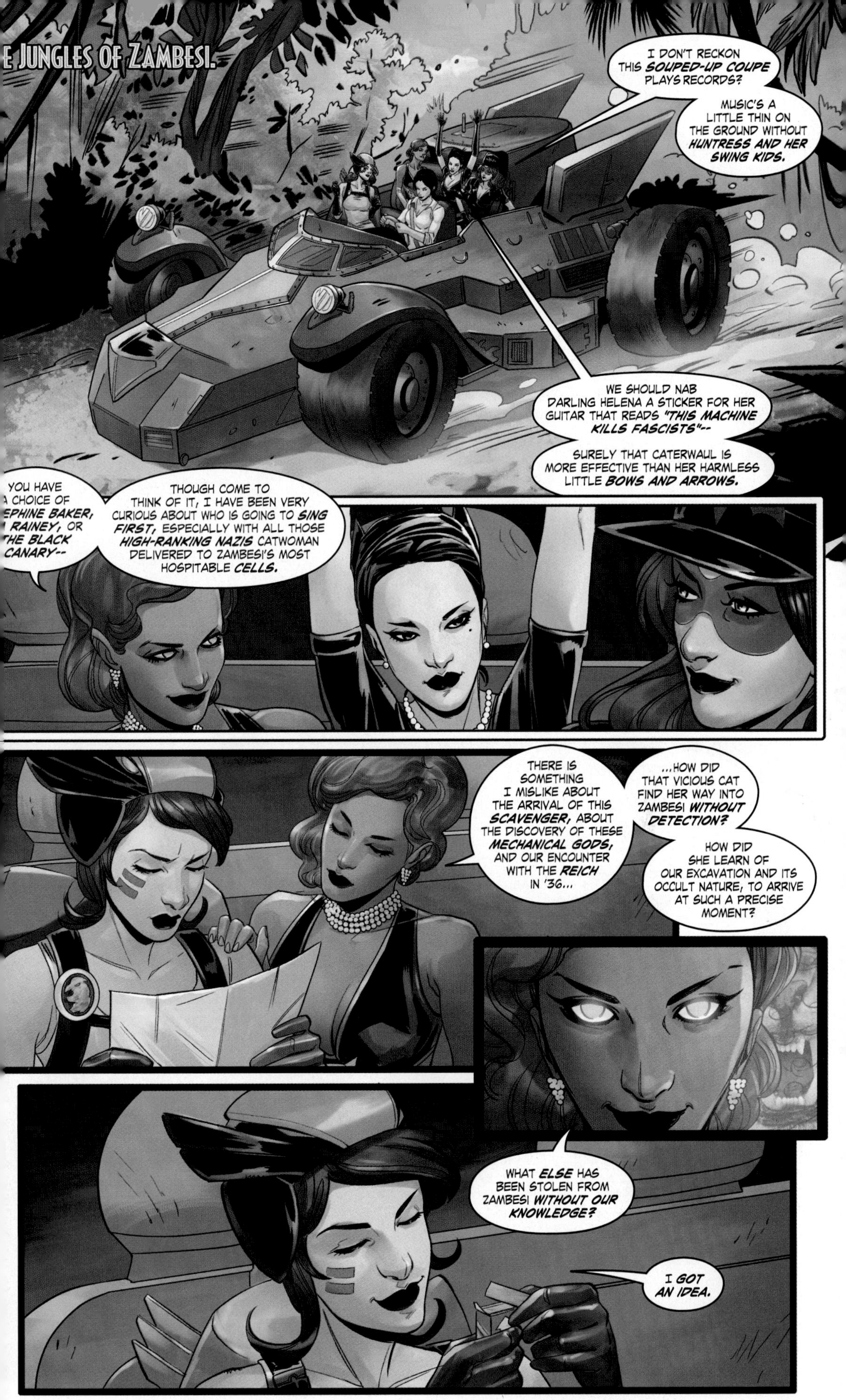
E JUNGLES OF ZAMBESI.
I DON'T RECKON THIS SOUPED-UP COUPE PLAYS RECORDS?
MUSIC'S A LITTLE THIN ON THE GROUND WITHOUT HUNTRESS AND HER SWING KIDS.
WE SHOULD NAB DARLING HELENA A STICKER FOR HER GUITAR THAT READS "THIS MACHINE KILLS FASCISTS"--
SURELY THAT CATERWAUL IS MORE EFFECTIVE THAN HER HARMLESS LITTLE BOWS AND ARROWS.
YOU HAVE A CHOICE OF EPHINE BAKER, RAINEY, OR THE BLACK CANARY--
THOUGH COME TO THINK OF IT, I HAVE BEEN VERY CURIOUS ABOUT WHO IS GOING TO SING FIRST, ESPECIALLY WITH ALL THOSE HIGH-RANKING NAZIS CATWOMAN DELIVERED TO ZAMBESI'S MOST HOSPITABLE CELLS.
THERE IS SOMETHING I MISLIKE ABOUT THE ARRIVAL OF THIS SCAVENGER, ABOUT THE DISCOVERY OF THESE MECHANICAL GODS, AND OUR ENCOUNTER WITH THE REICH IN '36...
...HOW DID THAT VICIOUS CAT FIND HER WAY INTO ZAMBESI WITHOUT DETECTION?
HOW DID SHE LEARN OF OUR EXCAVATION AND ITS OCCULT NATURE, TO ARRIVE AT SUCH A PRECISE MOMENT?
WHAT ELSE HAS BEEN STOLEN FROM ZAMBESI WITHOUT OUR KNOWLEDGE?
I GOT AN IDEA.

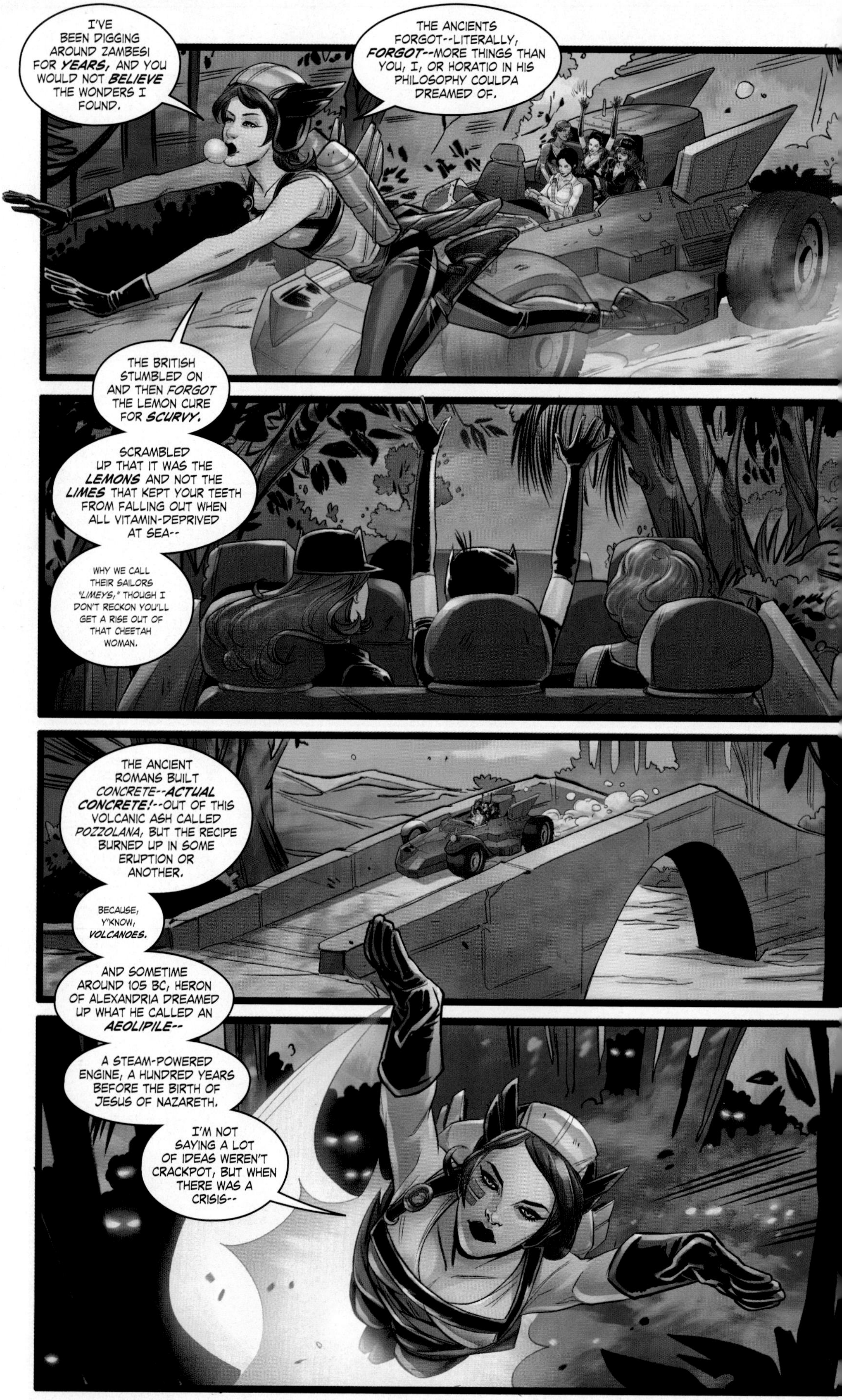
I'VE BEEN DIGGING AROUND ZAMBESI FOR YEARS, AND YOU WOULD NOT BELIEVE THE WONDERS I FOUND.
THE ANCIENTS FORGOT--LITERALLY, FORGOT--MORE THINGS THAN YOU, I, OR HORATIO IN HIS PHILOSOPHY COULDA DREAMED OF.
THE BRITISH STUMBLED ON AND THEN FORGOT THE LEMON CURE FOR SCURVY.
SCRAMBLED UP THAT IT WAS THE LEMONS AND NOT THE LIMES THAT KEPT YOUR TEETH FROM FALLING OUT WHEN ALL VITAMIN-DEPRIVED AT SEA--
WHY WE CALL THEIR SAILORS "LIMEYS," THOUGH I DON'T RECKON YOU'LL GET A RISE OUT OF THAT CHEETAH WOMAN.
THE ANCIENT ROMANS BUILT CONCRETE--ACTUAL CONCRETE!--OUT OF THIS VOLCANIC ASH CALLED POZZOLANA, BUT THE RECIPE BURNED UP IN SOME ERUPTION OR ANOTHER.
BECAUSE, Y'KNOW, VOLCANOES.
AND SOMETIME AROUND 105 BC, HERON OF ALEXANDRIA DREAMED UP WHAT HE CALLED AN AEOLIPILE--
A STEAM-POWERED ENGINE, A HUNDRED YEARS BEFORE THE BIRTH OF JESUS OF NAZARETH.
I'M NOT SAYING A LOT OF IDEAS WEREN'T CRACKPOT, BUT WHEN THERE WAS A CRISIS--

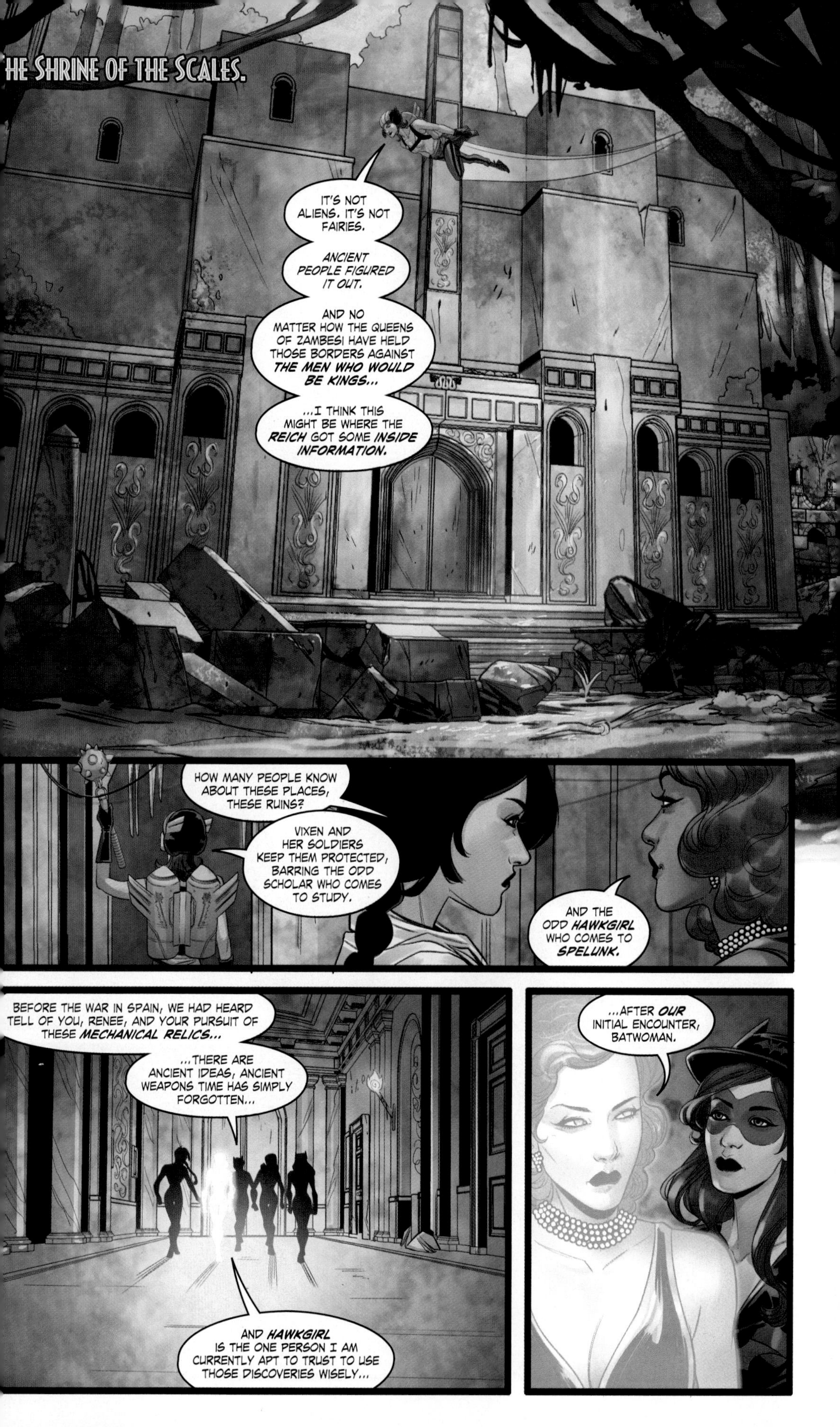
HE SHRINE OF THE SCALES.
IT'S NOT ALIENS. IT'S NOT FAIRIES.
ANCIENT PEOPLE FIGURED IT OUT.
AND NO MATTER HOW THE QUEENS OF ZAMBESI HAVE HELD THOSE BORDERS AGAINST THE MEN WHO WOULD BE KINGS...
...I THINK THIS MIGHT BE WHERE THE REICH GOT SOME INSIDE INFORMATION.
HOW MANY PEOPLE KNOW ABOUT THESE PLACES, THESE RUINS?
VIXEN AND HER SOLDIERS KEEP THEM PROTECTED, BARRING THE ODD SCHOLAR WHO COMES TO STUDY.
AND THE ODD HAWKGIRL WHO COMES TO SPELUNK.
BEFORE THE WAR IN SPAIN, WE HAD HEARD TELL OF YOU, RENEE, AND YOUR PURSUIT OF THESE MECHANICAL RELICS...
...THERE ARE ANCIENT IDEAS, ANCIENT WEAPONS TIME HAS SIMPLY FORGOTTEN...
AND HAWKGIRL IS THE ONE PERSON I AM CURRENTLY APT TO TRUST TO USE THOSE DISCOVERIES WISELY...
...AFTER OUR INITIAL ENCOUNTER, BATWOMAN.

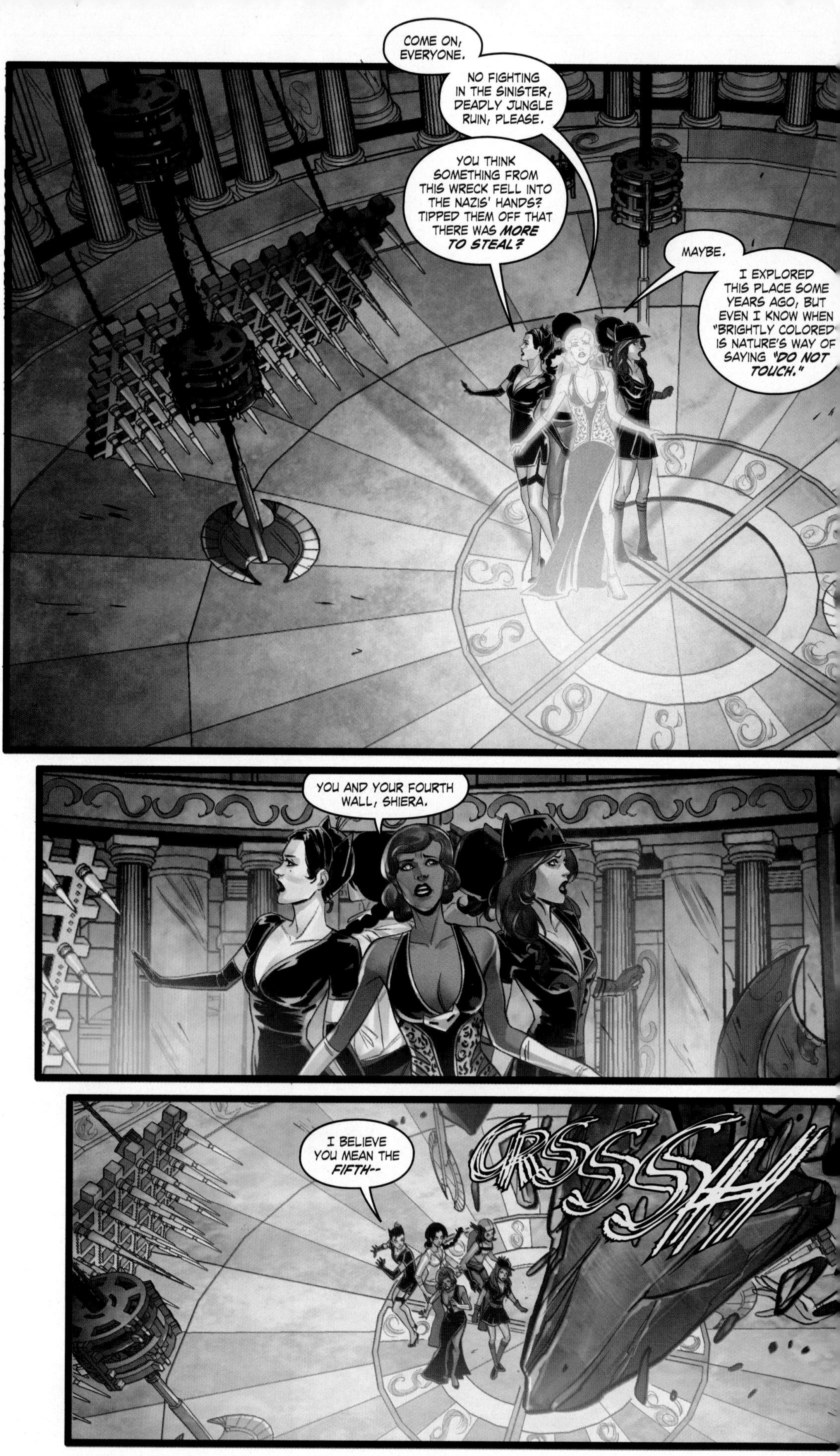
COME ON, EVERYONE.
NO FIGHTING IN THE SINISTER, DEADLY JUNGLE RUIN, PLEASE.
YOU THINK SOMETHING FROM THIS WRECK FELL INTO THE NAZIS' HANDS? TIPPED THEM OFF THAT THERE WAS *MORE TO STEAL?*
MAYBE.
I EXPLORED THIS PLACE SOME YEARS AGO, BUT EVEN I KNOW WHEN "BRIGHTLY COLORED IS NATURE'S WAY OF SAYING *"DO NOT TOUCH."*
YOU AND YOUR FOURTH WALL, SHIERA.
I BELIEVE YOU MEAN THE *FIFTH--*
CRSSSSH

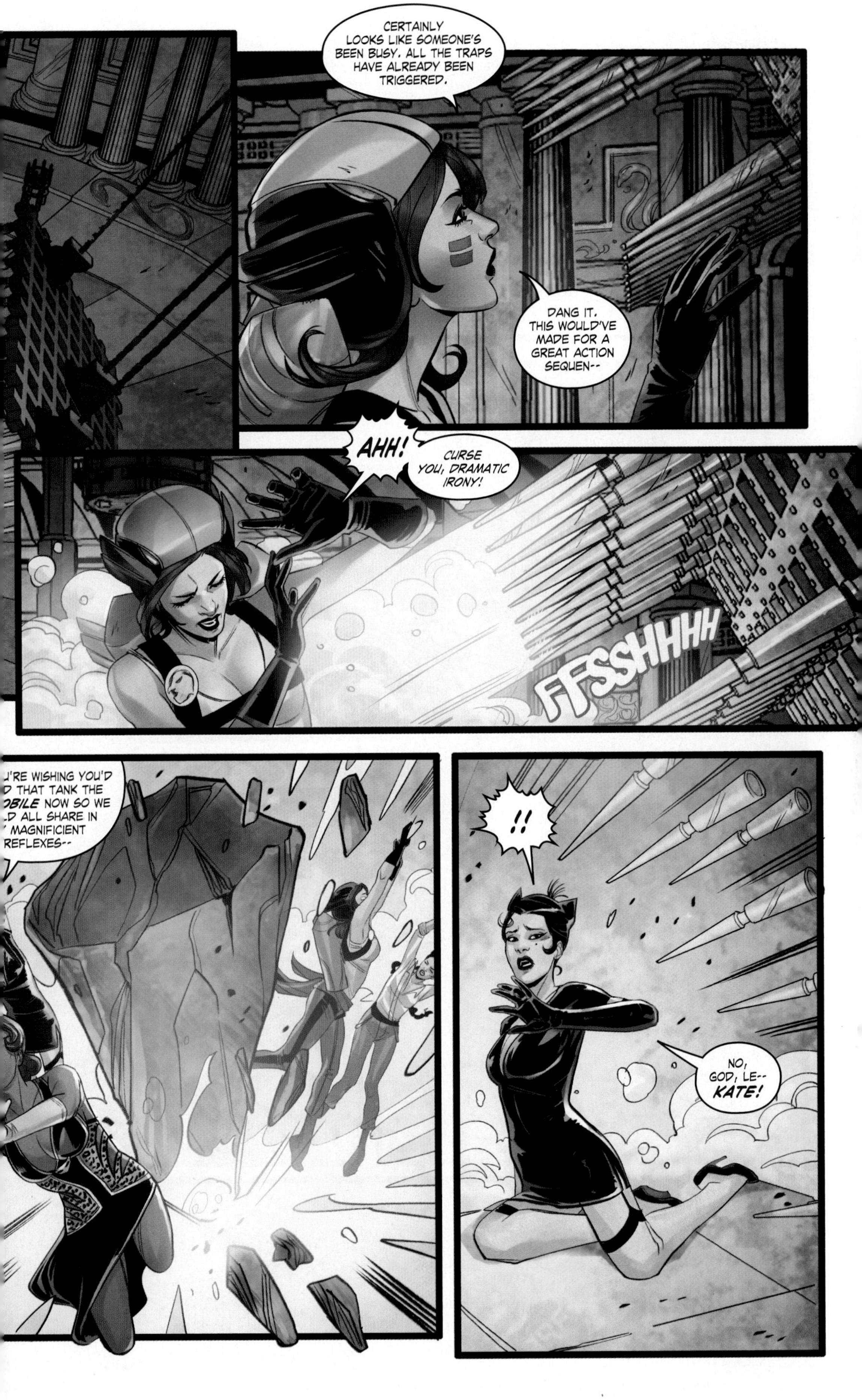

CERTAINLY LOOKS LIKE SOMEONE'S BEEN BUSY. ALL THE TRAPS HAVE ALREADY BEEN TRIGGERED.
DANG IT. THIS WOULD'VE MADE FOR A GREAT ACTION SEQUEN--
AHH!
CURSE YOU, DRAMATIC IRONY!
FFSSHHHH
'RE WISHING YOU'D D THAT TANK THE *OBILE* NOW SO WE D ALL SHARE IN MAGNIFICIENT REFLEXES--
!!
NO, GOD, LE-- *KATE!*

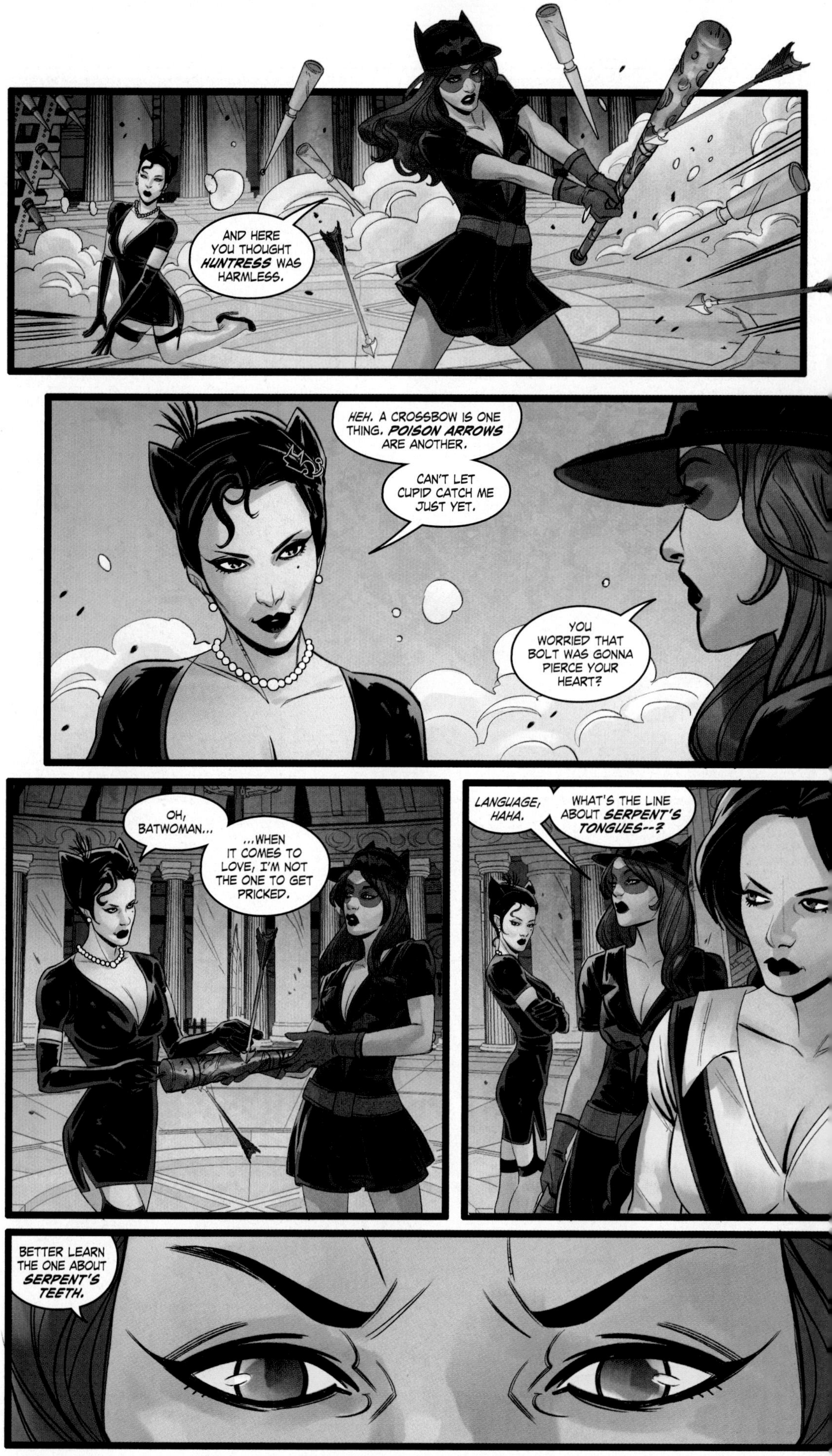
AND HERE YOU THOUGHT HUNTRESS WAS HARMLESS.
HEH. A CROSSBOW IS ONE THING. POISON ARROWS ARE ANOTHER.
CAN'T LET CUPID CATCH ME JUST YET.
YOU WORRIED THAT BOLT WAS GONNA PIERCE YOUR HEART?
OH, BATWOMAN...
...WHEN IT COMES TO LOVE, I'M NOT THE ONE TO GET PRICKED.
LANGUAGE, HAHA.
WHAT'S THE LINE ABOUT SERPENT'S TONGUES--?
BETTER LEARN THE ONE ABOUT SERPENT'S TEETH.

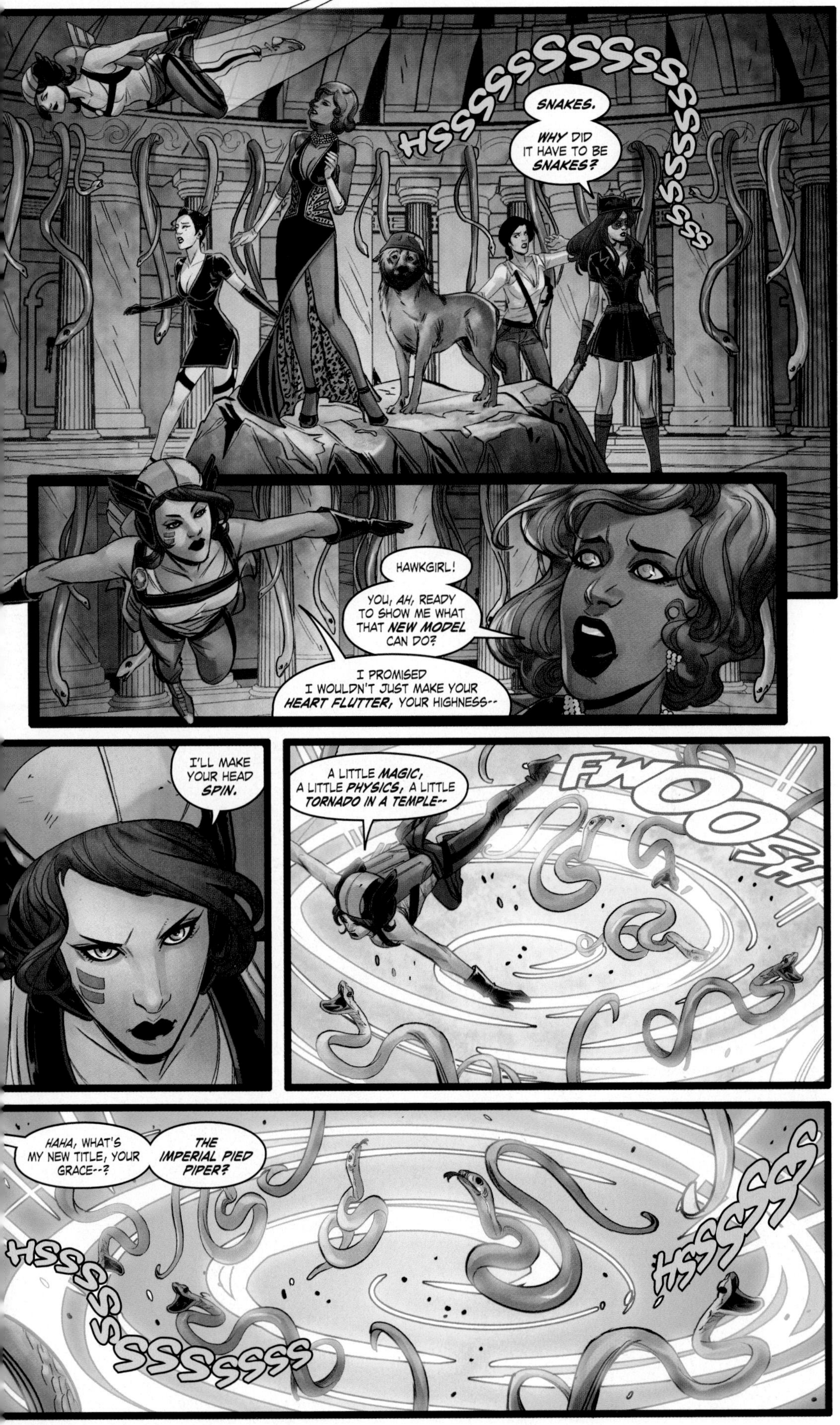
HSSSSSSSSSSSSSSSSSS
SNAKES.
WHY DID IT HAVE TO BE SNAKES?
HAWKGIRL!
YOU, AH, READY TO SHOW ME WHAT THAT NEW MODEL CAN DO?
I PROMISED I WOULDN'T JUST MAKE YOUR HEART FLUTTER, YOUR HIGHNESS--
I'LL MAKE YOUR HEAD SPIN.
A LITTLE MAGIC, A LITTLE PHYSICS, A LITTLE TORNADO IN A TEMPLE--
FWOOOSH
HAHA, WHAT'S MY NEW TITLE, YOUR GRACE--?
THE IMPERIAL PIED PIPER?
HSSSSSSSSSSSS
HSSSSH

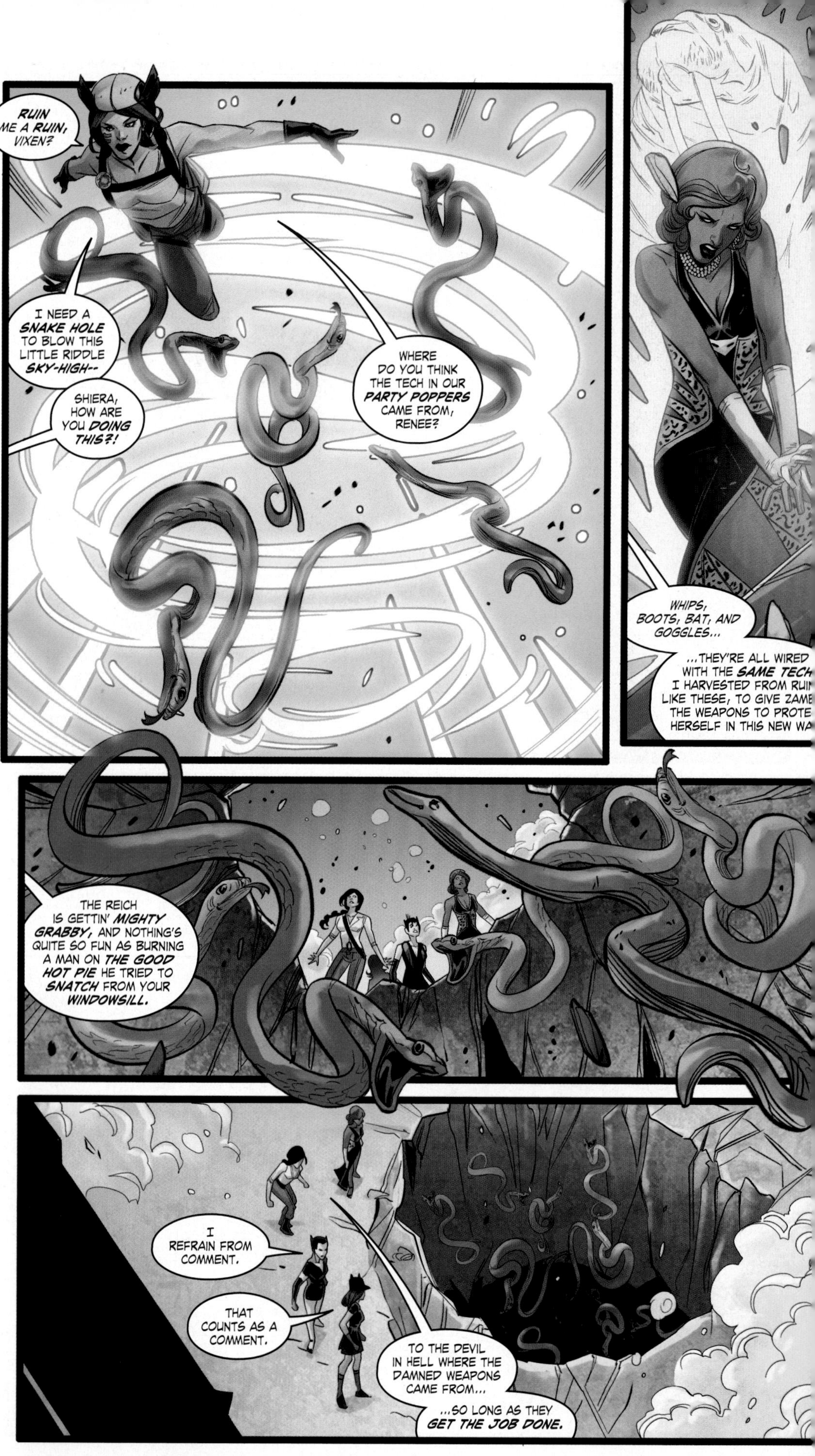
RUIN ME A RUIN, VIXEN?
I NEED A SNAKE HOLE TO BLOW THIS LITTLE RIDDLE SKY-HIGH--
SHIERA, HOW ARE YOU DOING THIS?!
WHERE DO YOU THINK THE TECH IN OUR PARTY POPPERS CAME FROM, RENEE?
WHIPS, BOOTS, BAT, AND GOGGLES...
...THEY'RE ALL WIRED WITH THE SAME TECH I HARVESTED FROM RUI LIKE THESE, TO GIVE ZAME THE WEAPONS TO PROTE HERSELF IN THIS NEW WA
THE REICH IS GETTIN' MIGHTY GRABBY, AND NOTHING'S QUITE SO FUN AS BURNING A MAN ON THE GOOD HOT PIE HE TRIED TO SNATCH FROM YOUR WINDOWSILL.
I REFRAIN FROM COMMENT.
THAT COUNTS AS A COMMENT.
TO THE DEVIL IN HELL WHERE THE DAMNED WEAPONS CAME FROM...
...SO LONG AS THEY GET THE JOB DONE.

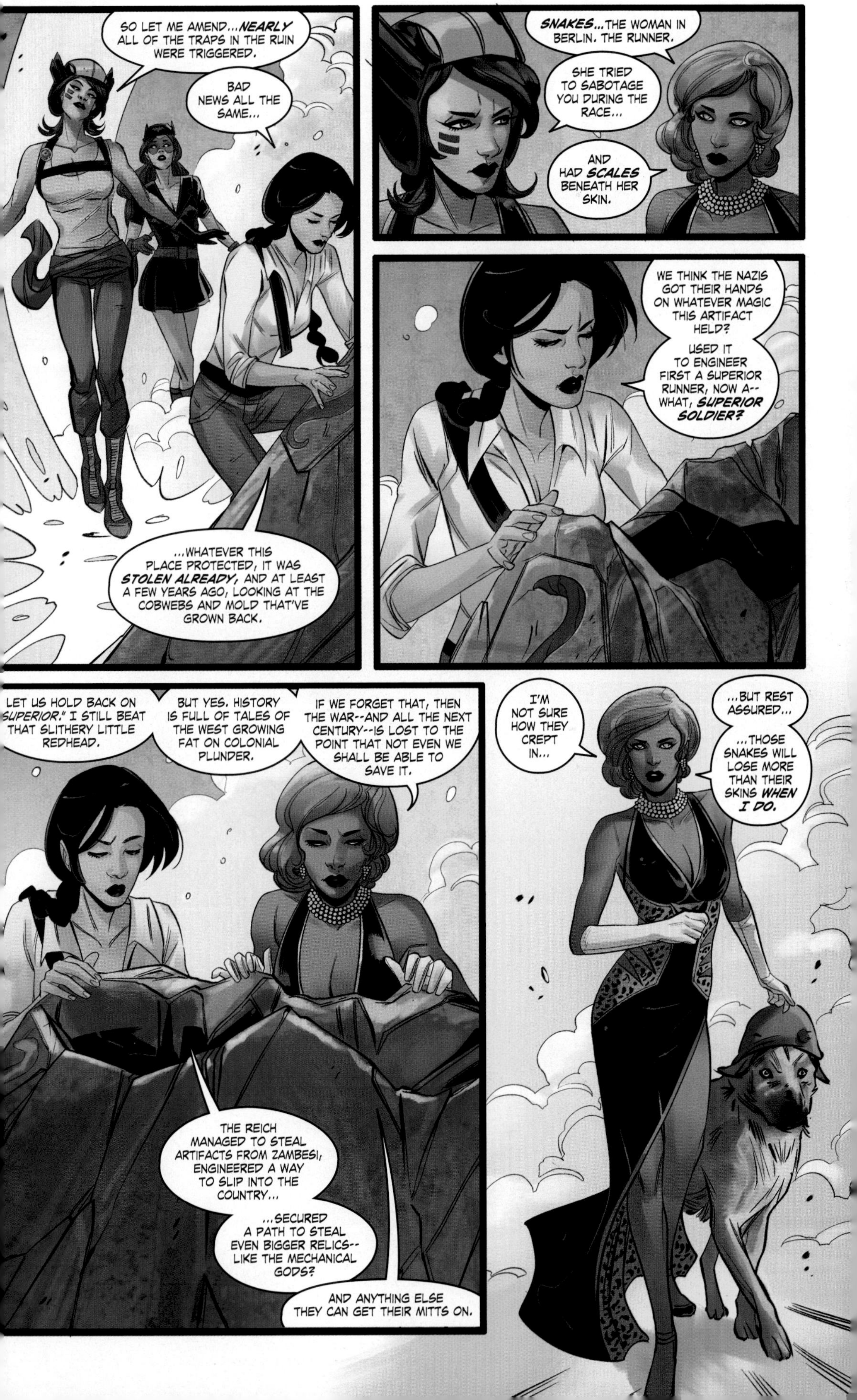
SO LET ME AMEND...NEARLY ALL OF THE TRAPS IN THE RUIN WERE TRIGGERED.
BAD NEWS ALL THE SAME...
...WHATEVER THIS PLACE PROTECTED, IT WAS STOLEN ALREADY, AND AT LEAST A FEW YEARS AGO, LOOKING AT THE COBWEBS AND MOLD THAT'VE GROWN BACK.
SNAKES...THE WOMAN IN BERLIN. THE RUNNER.
SHE TRIED TO SABOTAGE YOU DURING THE RACE...
AND HAD SCALES BENEATH HER SKIN.
WE THINK THE NAZIS GOT THEIR HANDS ON WHATEVER MAGIC THIS ARTIFACT HELD?
USED IT TO ENGINEER FIRST A SUPERIOR RUNNER, NOW A--WHAT, SUPERIOR SOLDIER?
LET US HOLD BACK ON "SUPERIOR." I STILL BEAT THAT SLITHERY LITTLE REDHEAD.
BUT YES. HISTORY IS FULL OF TALES OF THE WEST GROWING FAT ON COLONIAL PLUNDER.
IF WE FORGET THAT, THEN THE WAR--AND ALL THE NEXT CENTURY--IS LOST TO THE POINT THAT NOT EVEN WE SHALL BE ABLE TO SAVE IT.
THE REICH MANAGED TO STEAL ARTIFACTS FROM ZAMBESI, ENGINEERED A WAY TO SLIP INTO THE COUNTRY...
...SECURED A PATH TO STEAL EVEN BIGGER RELICS--LIKE THE MECHANICAL GODS?
AND ANYTHING ELSE THEY CAN GET THEIR MITTS ON.
I'M NOT SURE HOW THEY CREPT IN...
...BUT REST ASSURED...
...THOSE SNAKES WILL LOSE MORE THAN THEIR SKINS WHEN I DO.

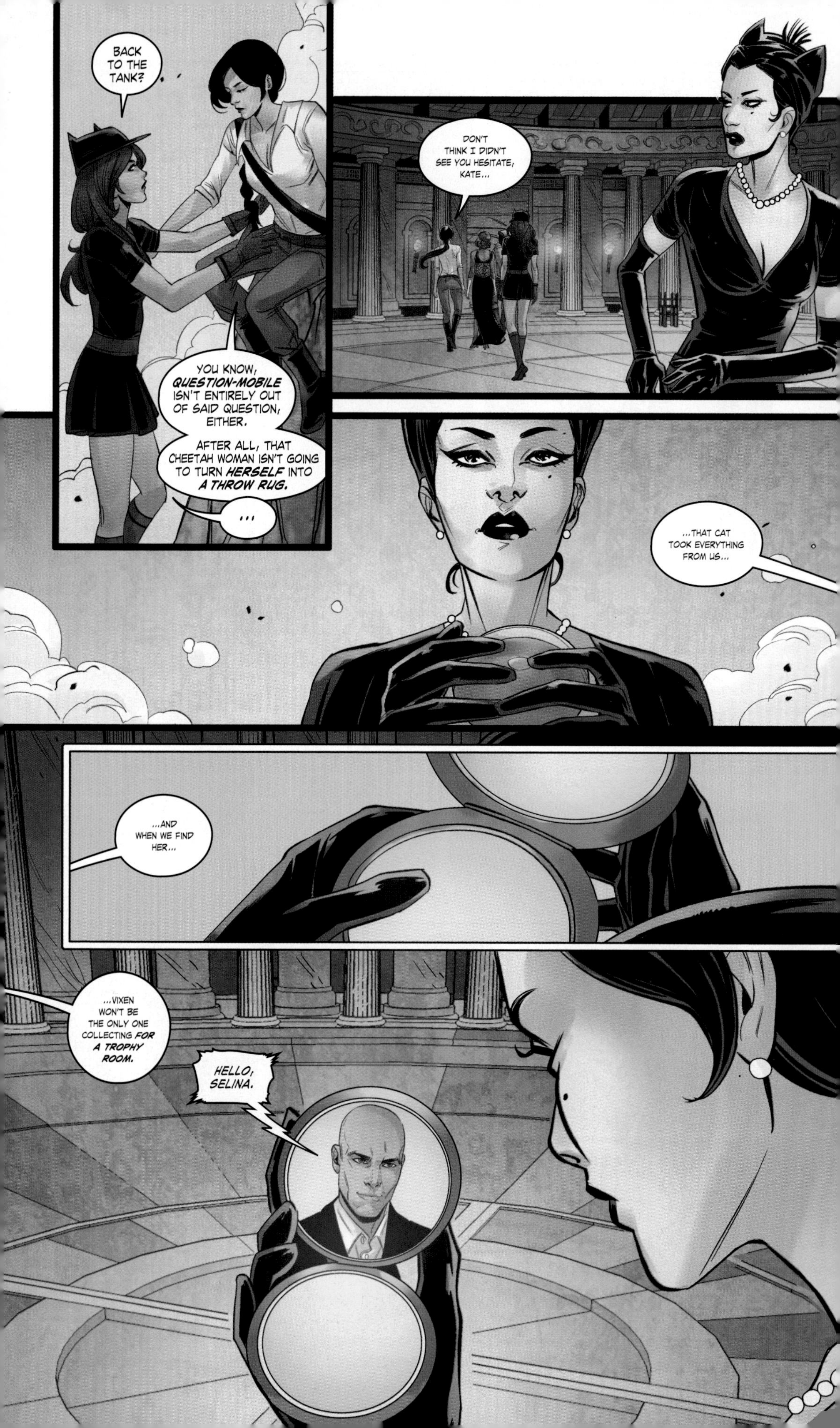
BACK TO THE TANK?
YOU KNOW, QUESTION-MOBILE ISN'T ENTIRELY OUT OF SAID QUESTION, EITHER.
AFTER ALL, THAT CHEETAH WOMAN ISN'T GOING TO TURN HERSELF INTO A THROW RUG.
...
DON'T THINK I DIDN'T SEE YOU HESITATE, KATE...
...THAT CAT TOOK EVERYTHING FROM US...
...AND WHEN WE FIND HER...
...VIXEN WON'T BE THE ONLY ONE COLLECTING FOR A TROPHY ROOM.
HELLO, SELINA.

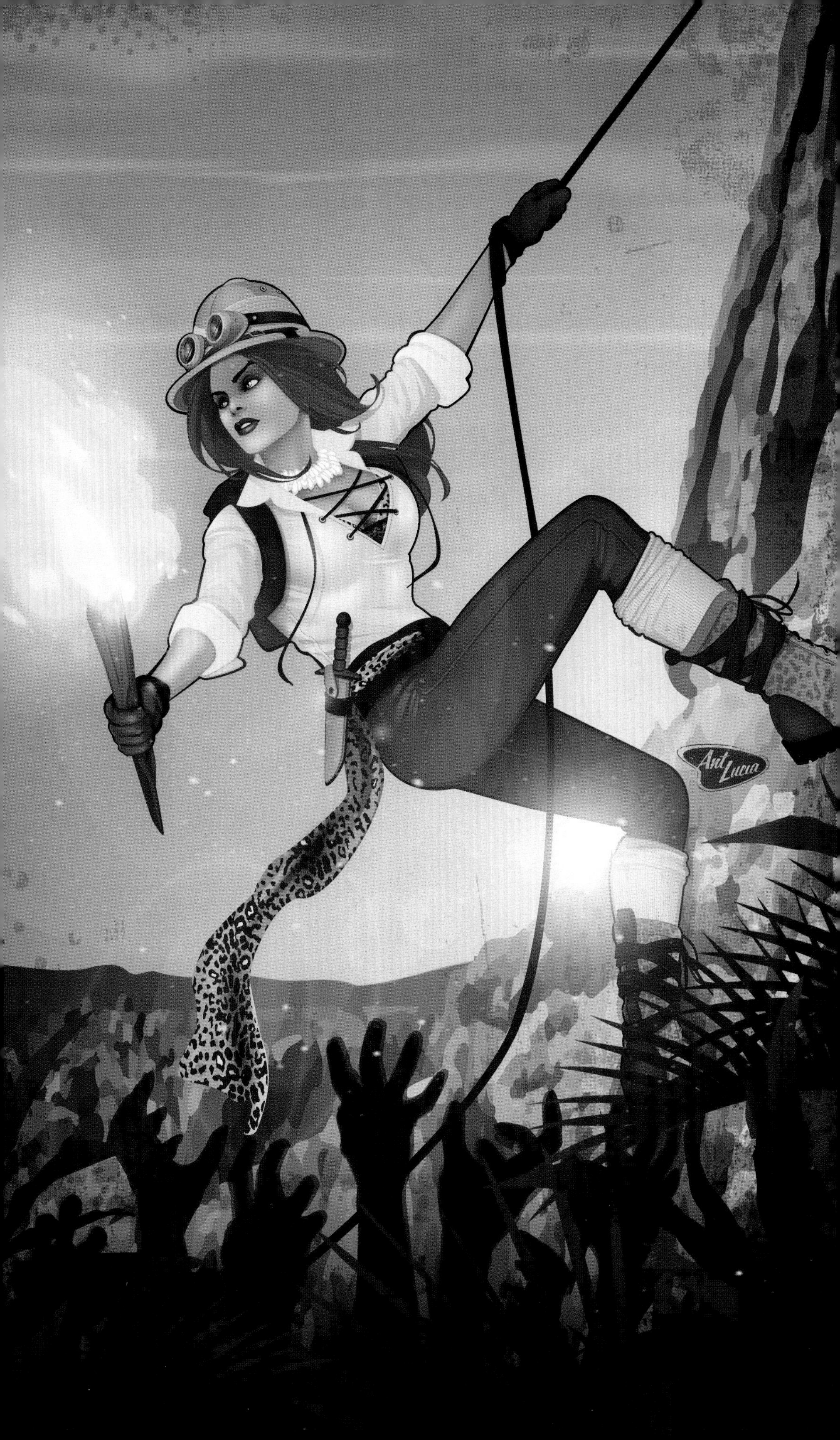
Ant Lucia

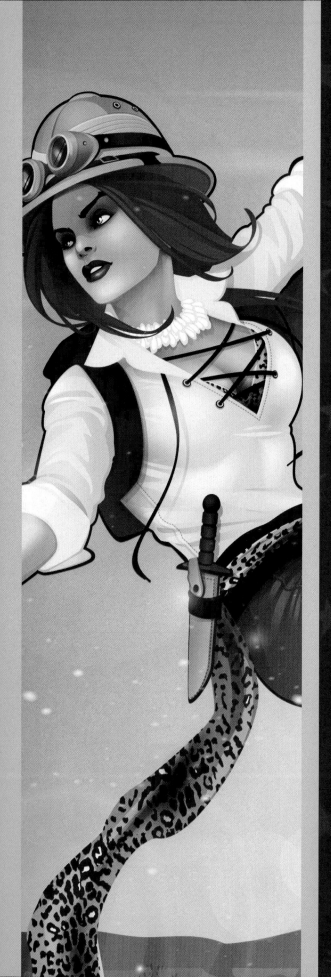

MECHANICAL GODS

MARGUERITE BENNETT
Writer

MIRKA ANDOLFO
PASQUALE QUALANO
RICHARD ORTIZ
Artists

J. NANJAN
Colorist

Cover by
ANT LUCIA

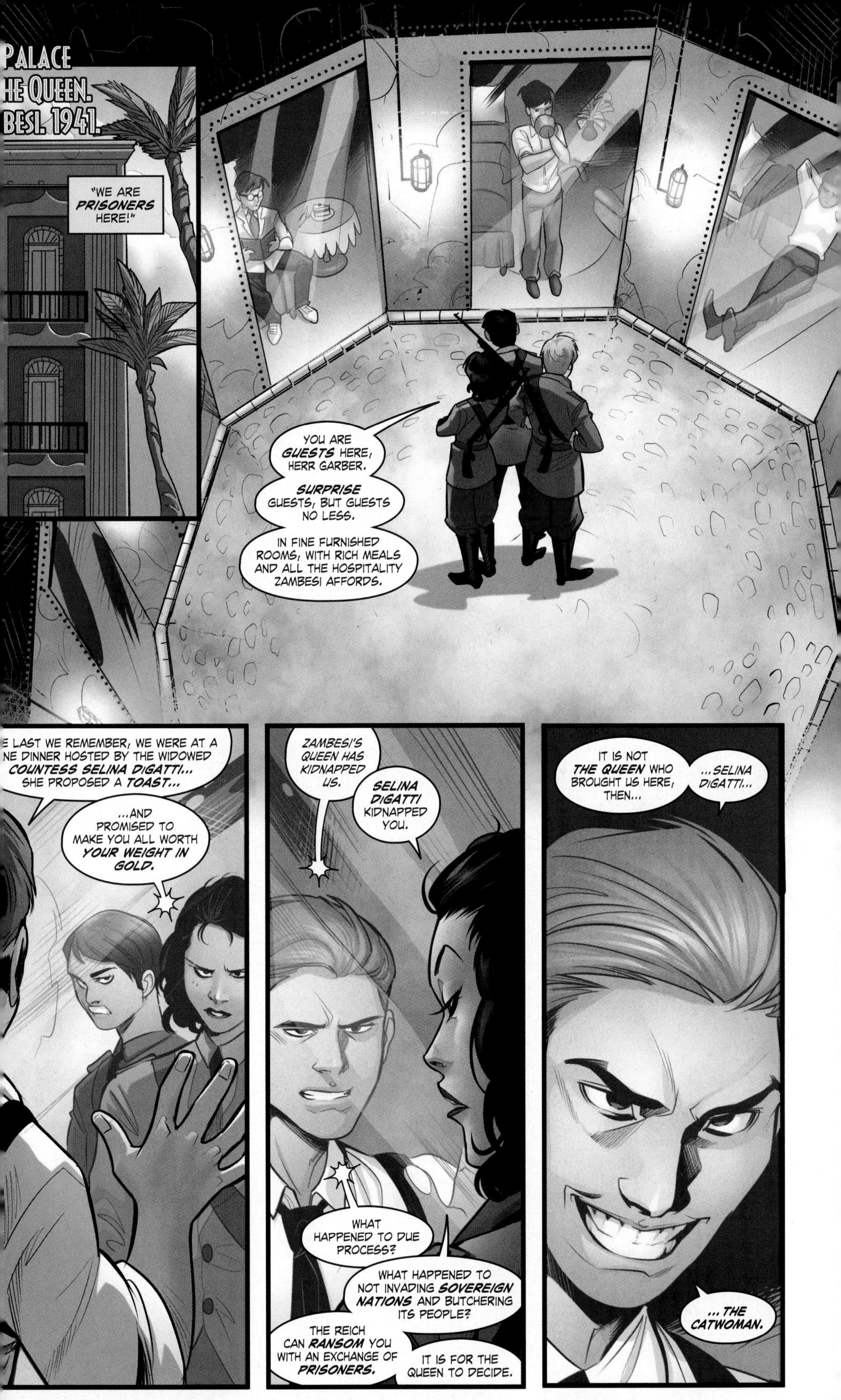
PALACE
HE QUEEN.
BESI. 1941.
"WE ARE PRISONERS HERE!"
YOU ARE GUESTS HERE, HERR GARBER.
SURPRISE GUESTS, BUT GUESTS NO LESS.
IN FINE FURNISHED ROOMS, WITH RICH MEALS AND ALL THE HOSPITALITY ZAMBESI AFFORDS.
E LAST WE REMEMBER, WE WERE AT A NE DINNER HOSTED BY THE WIDOWED COUNTESS SELINA DIGATTI... SHE PROPOSED A TOAST...
...AND PROMISED TO MAKE YOU ALL WORTH YOUR WEIGHT IN GOLD.
ZAMBESI'S QUEEN HAS KIDNAPPED US.
SELINA DIGATTI KIDNAPPED YOU.
WHAT HAPPENED TO DUE PROCESS?
WHAT HAPPENED TO NOT INVADING SOVEREIGN NATIONS AND BUTCHERING ITS PEOPLE?
THE REICH CAN RANSOM YOU WITH AN EXCHANGE OF PRISONERS.
IT IS FOR THE QUEEN TO DECIDE.
IT IS NOT THE QUEEN WHO BROUGHT US HERE, THEN...
...SELINA DIGATTI...
...THE CATWOMAN.

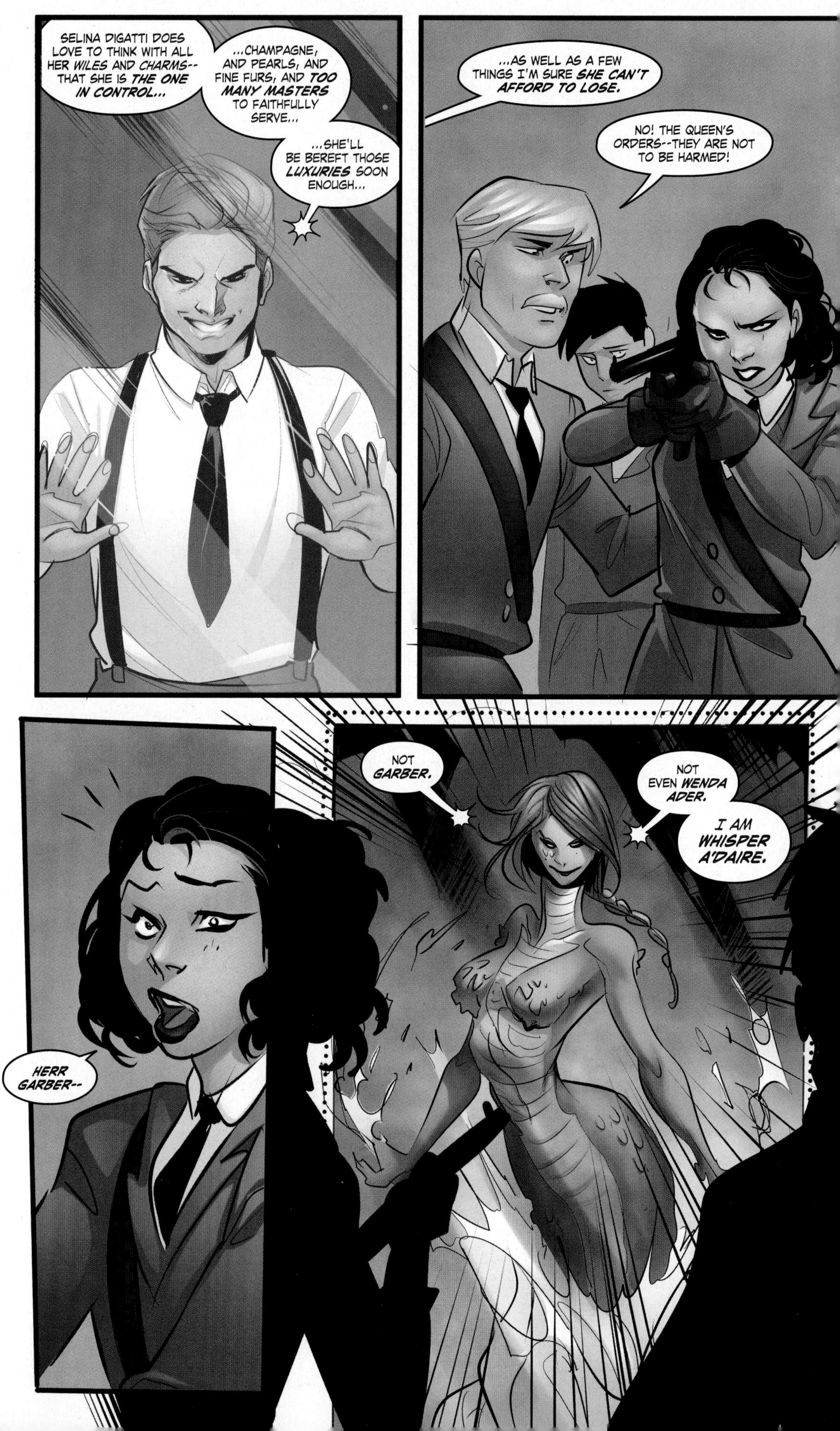
SELINA DIGATTI DOES LOVE TO THINK WITH ALL HER WILES AND CHARMS--THAT SHE IS THE ONE IN CONTROL...
...CHAMPAGNE, AND PEARLS, AND FINE FURS, AND TOO MANY MASTERS TO FAITHFULLY SERVE...
...SHE'LL BE BEREFT THOSE LUXURIES SOON ENOUGH...
...AS WELL AS A FEW THINGS I'M SURE SHE CAN'T AFFORD TO LOSE.
NO! THE QUEEN'S ORDERS--THEY ARE NOT TO BE HARMED!
HERR GARBER--
NOT GARBER.
NOT EVEN WENDA ADER.
I AM WHISPER A'DAIRE.

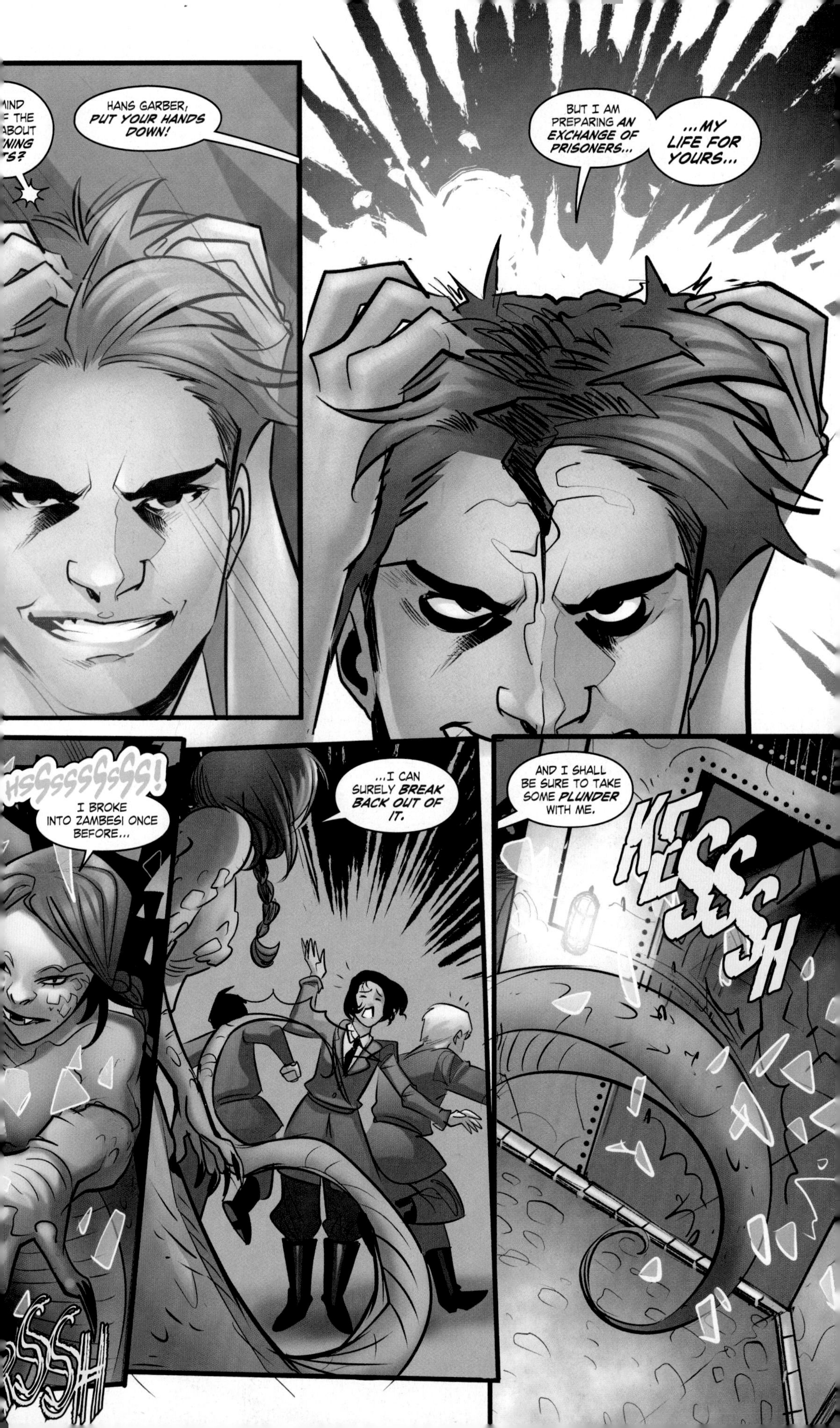

HANS GARBER, *PUT YOUR HANDS DOWN!*
BUT I AM PREPARING *AN EXCHANGE OF PRISONERS...*
...MY LIFE FOR YOURS...
I BROKE INTO ZAMBESI ONCE BEFORE...
...I CAN SURELY *BREAK BACK OUT OF IT.*
AND I SHALL BE SURE TO TAKE SOME *PLUNDER* WITH ME.

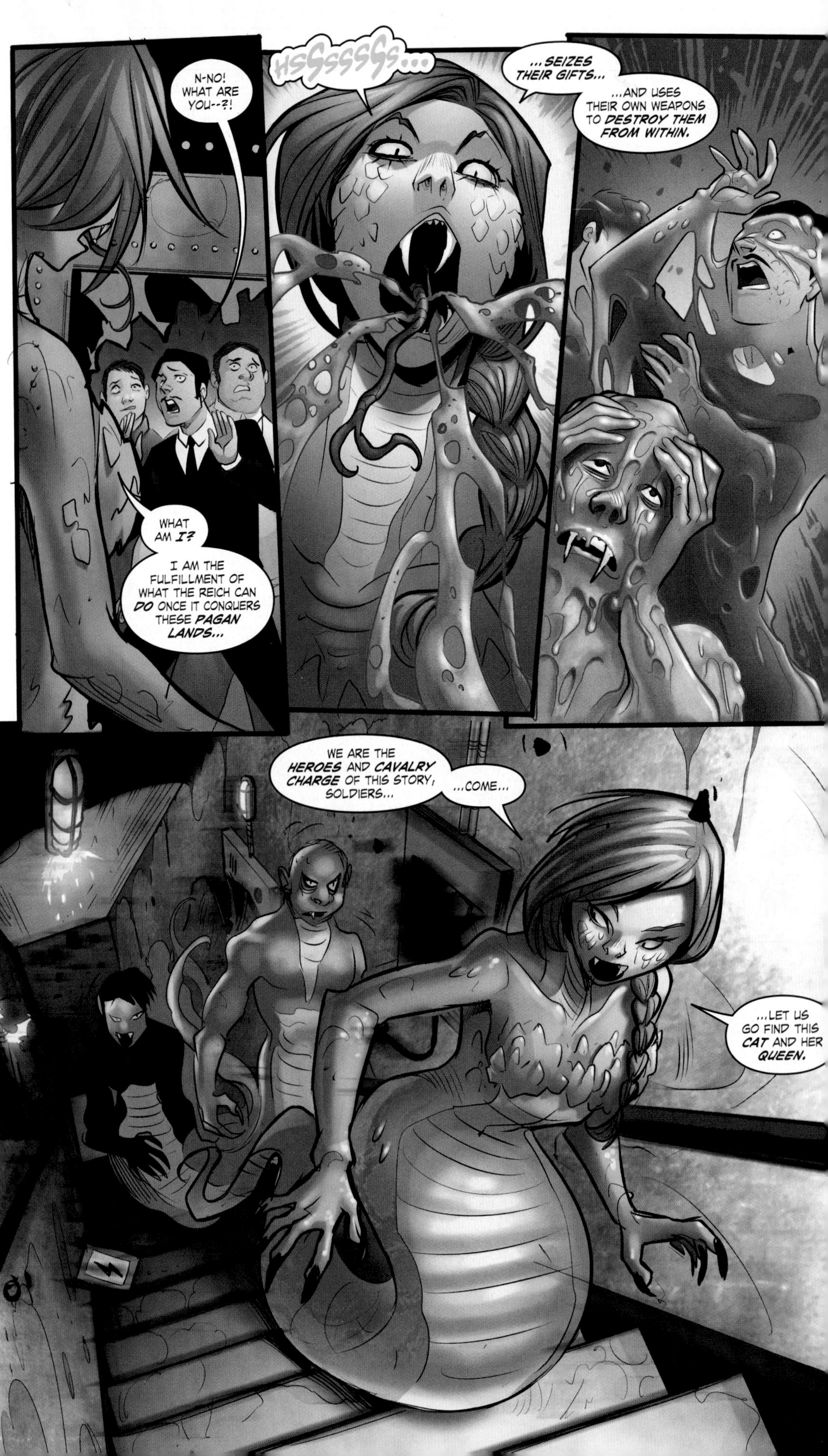
N-NO! WHAT ARE YOU--?!
WHAT AM I?
I AM THE FULFILLMENT OF WHAT THE REICH CAN DO ONCE IT CONQUERS THESE PAGAN LANDS...
HSSSSSSS...
...SEIZES THEIR GIFTS...
...AND USES THEIR OWN WEAPONS TO DESTROY THEM FROM WITHIN.
WE ARE THE HEROES AND CAVALRY CHARGE OF THIS STORY, SOLDIERS...
...COME...
...LET US GO FIND THIS CAT AND HER QUEEN.

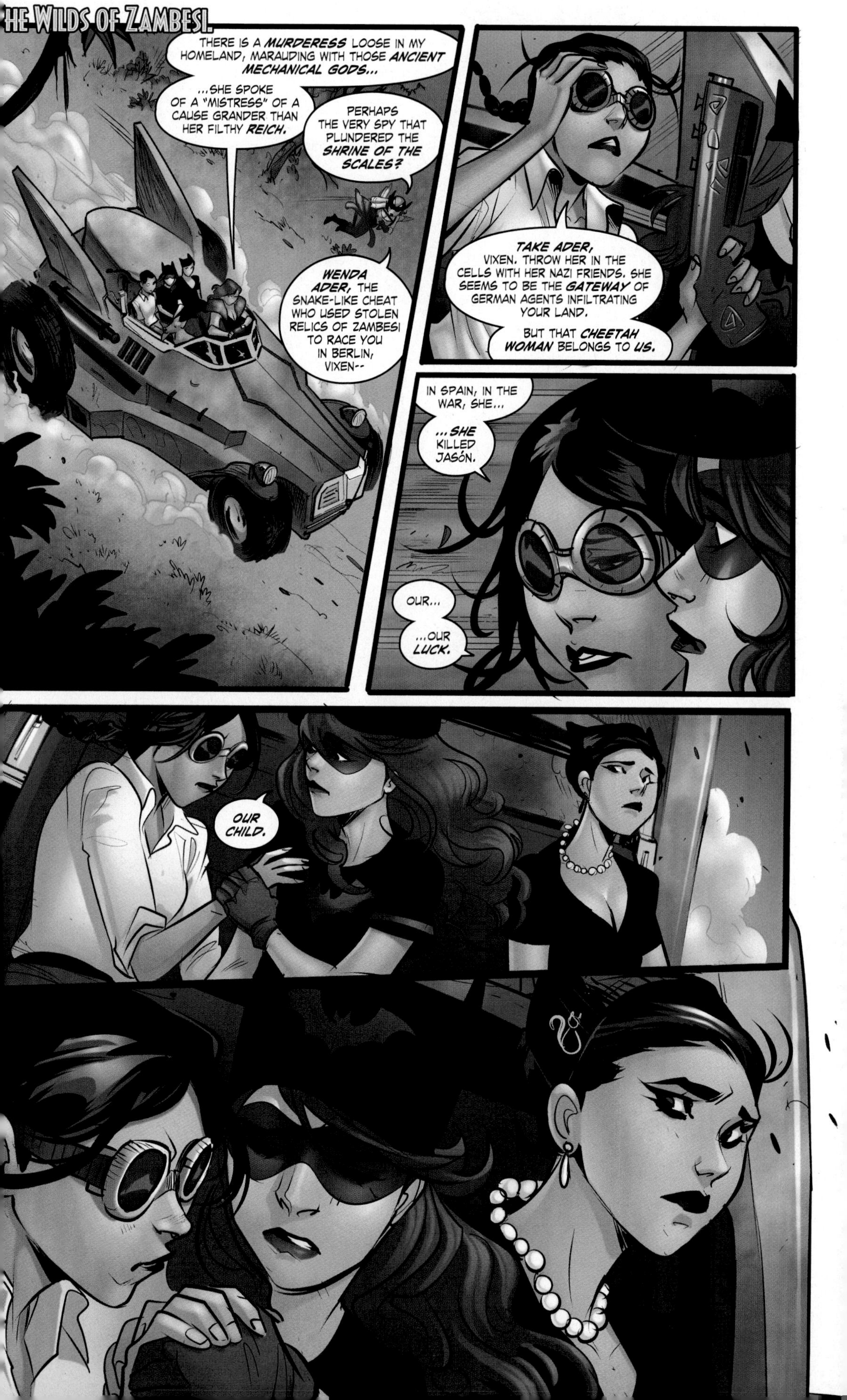

THE WILDS OF ZAMBESI.
THERE IS A MURDERESS LOOSE IN MY HOMELAND, MARAUDING WITH THOSE ANCIENT MECHANICAL GODS...
...SHE SPOKE OF A "MISTRESS" OF A CAUSE GRANDER THAN HER FILTHY REICH.
PERHAPS THE VERY SPY THAT PLUNDERED THE SHRINE OF THE SCALES?
WENDA ADER, THE SNAKE-LIKE CHEAT WHO USED STOLEN RELICS OF ZAMBESI TO RACE YOU IN BERLIN, VIXEN--
TAKE ADER, VIXEN. THROW HER IN THE CELLS WITH HER NAZI FRIENDS. SHE SEEMS TO BE THE GATEWAY OF GERMAN AGENTS INFILTRATING YOUR LAND.
BUT THAT CHEETAH WOMAN BELONGS TO US.
IN SPAIN, IN THE WAR, SHE...
...SHE KILLED JASÓN.
OUR...
...OUR LUCK.
OUR CHILD.

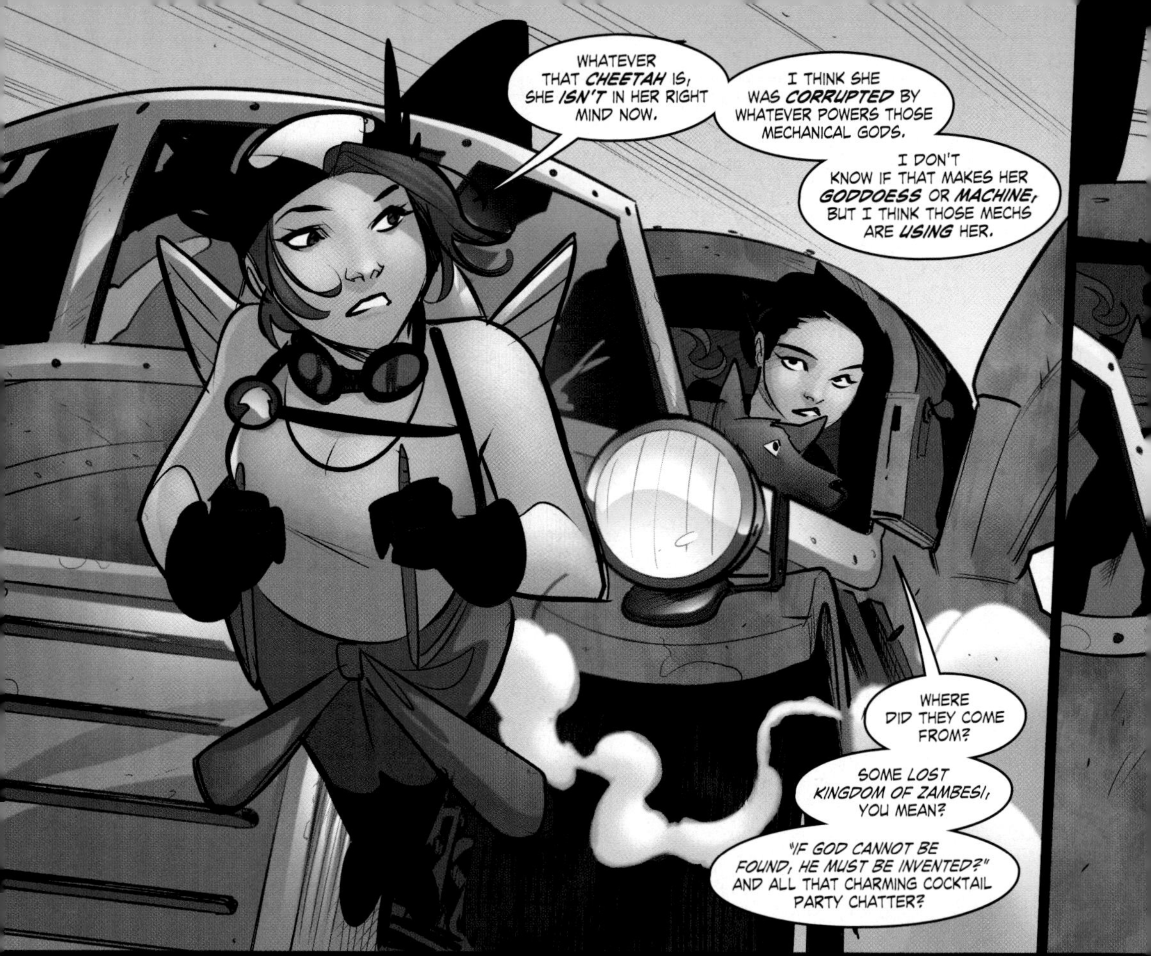
WHATEVER THAT CHEETAH IS, SHE ISN'T IN HER RIGHT MIND NOW.
I THINK SHE WAS CORRUPTED BY WHATEVER POWERS THOSE MECHANICAL GODS.
I DON'T KNOW IF THAT MAKES HER GODDOESS OR MACHINE, BUT I THINK THOSE MECHS ARE USING HER.
WHERE DID THEY COME FROM?
SOME LOST KINGDOM OF ZAMBESI, YOU MEAN?
"IF GOD CANNOT BE FOUND, HE MUST BE INVENTED?" AND ALL THAT CHARMING COCKTAIL PARTY CHATTER?

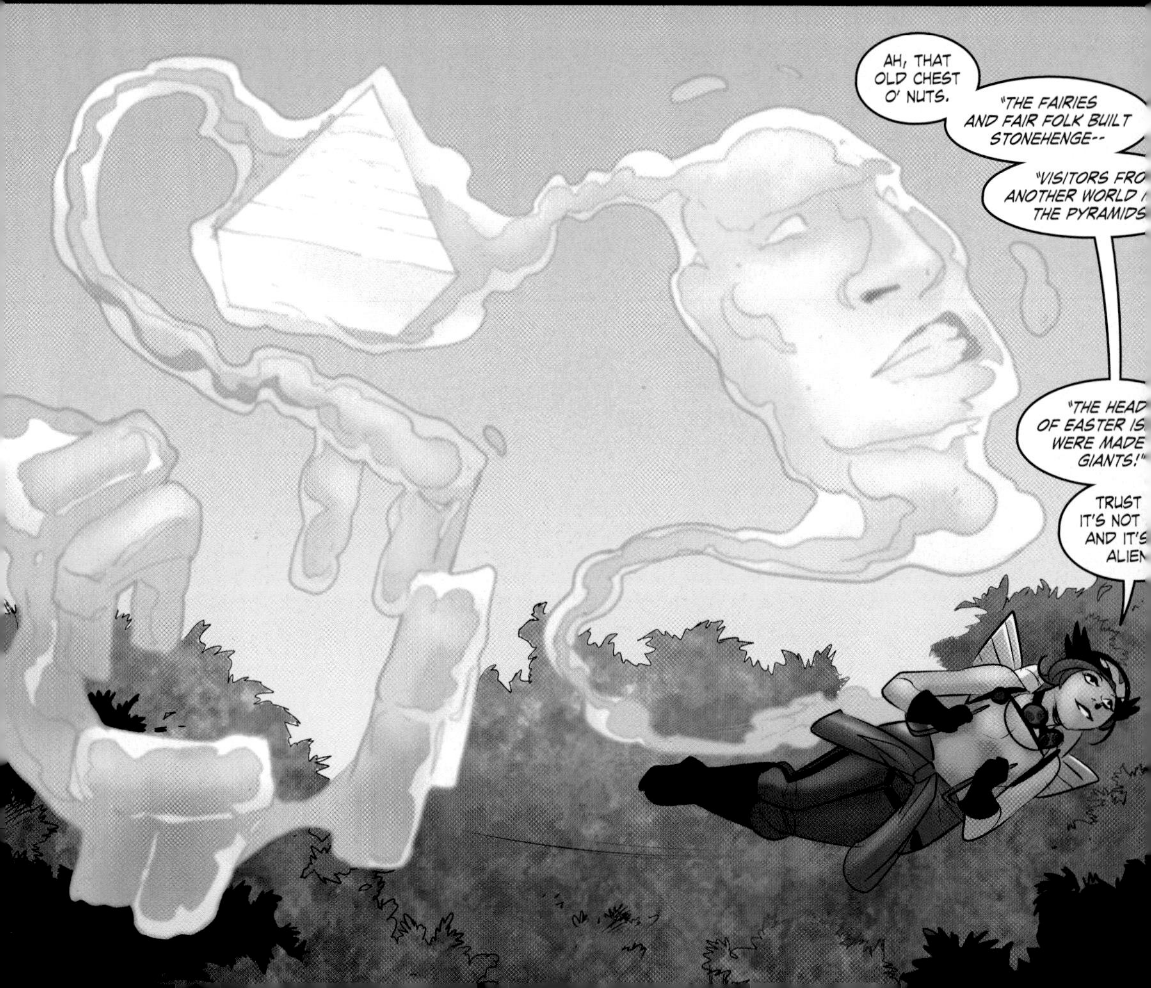
AH, THAT OLD CHEST O' NUTS.
"THE FAIRIES AND FAIR FOLK BUILT STONEHENGE--
"VISITORS FRO ANOTHER WORLD THE PYRAMIDS
"THE HEAD OF EASTER IS WERE MADE GIANTS!"
TRUST IT'S NOT AND IT'S ALIEN

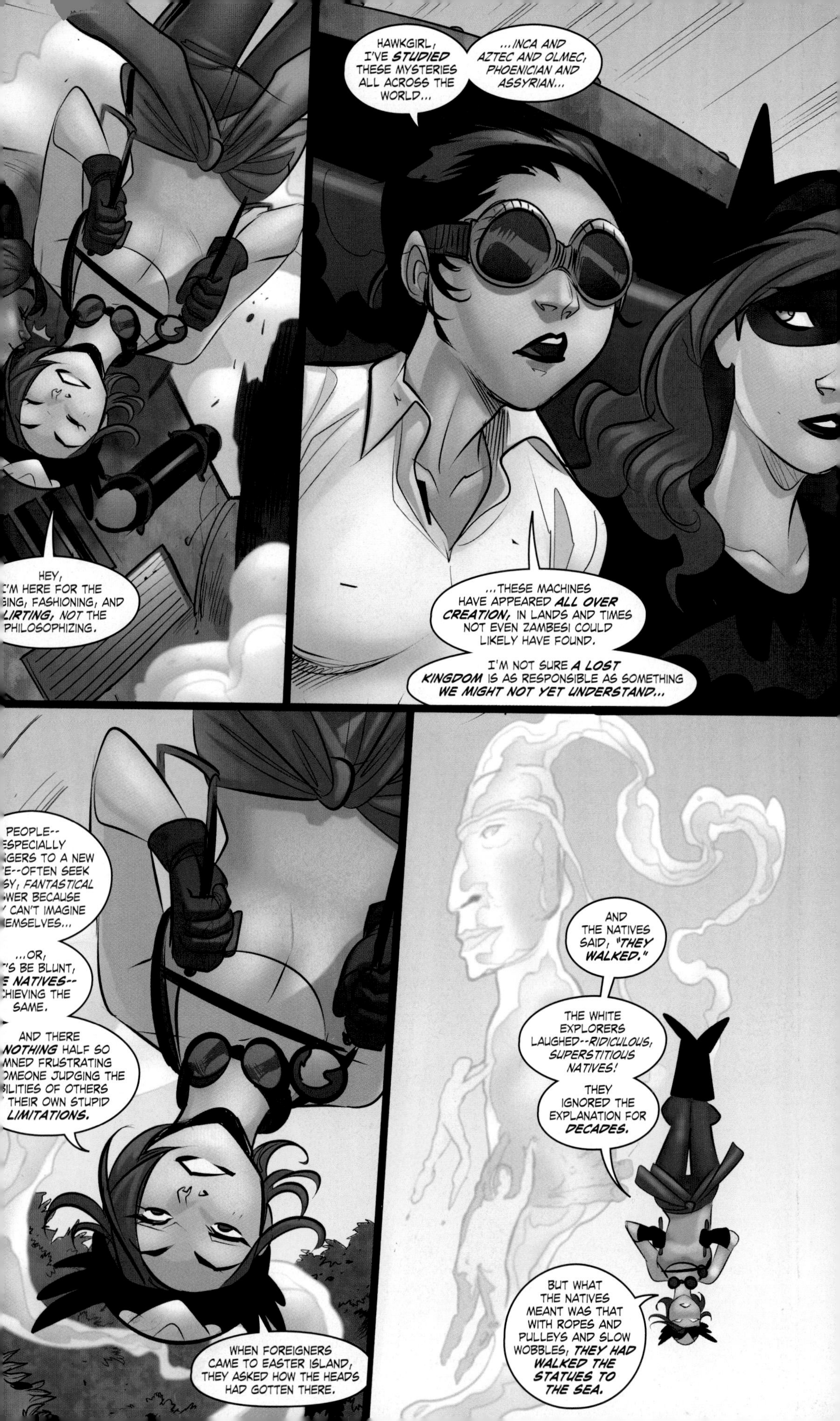

HAWKGIRL, I'VE STUDIED THESE MYSTERIES ALL ACROSS THE WORLD...
...INCA AND AZTEC AND OLMEC, PHOENICIAN AND ASSYRIAN...
HEY, I'M HERE FOR THE GING, FASHIONING, AND LIRTING, NOT THE PHILOSOPHIZING.
...THESE MACHINES HAVE APPEARED ALL OVER CREATION, IN LANDS AND TIMES NOT EVEN ZAMBESI COULD LIKELY HAVE FOUND.
I'M NOT SURE A LOST KINGDOM IS AS RESPONSIBLE AS SOMETHING WE MIGHT NOT YET UNDERSTAND...
PEOPLE-- ESPECIALLY GERS TO A NEW E--OFTEN SEEK SY, FANTASTICAL WER BECAUSE CAN'T IMAGINE EMSELVES...
...OR, 'S BE BLUNT, E NATIVES-- CHIEVING THE SAME.
AND THERE NOTHING HALF SO MNED FRUSTRATING OMEONE JUDGING THE BILITIES OF OTHERS THEIR OWN STUPID LIMITATIONS.
WHEN FOREIGNERS CAME TO EASTER ISLAND, THEY ASKED HOW THE HEADS HAD GOTTEN THERE.
AND THE NATIVES SAID, "THEY WALKED."
THE WHITE EXPLORERS LAUGHED--RIDICULOUS, SUPERSTITIOUS NATIVES!
THEY IGNORED THE EXPLANATION FOR DECADES.
BUT WHAT THE NATIVES MEANT WAS THAT WITH ROPES AND PULLEYS AND SLOW WOBBLES, THEY HAD WALKED THE STATUES TO THE SEA.

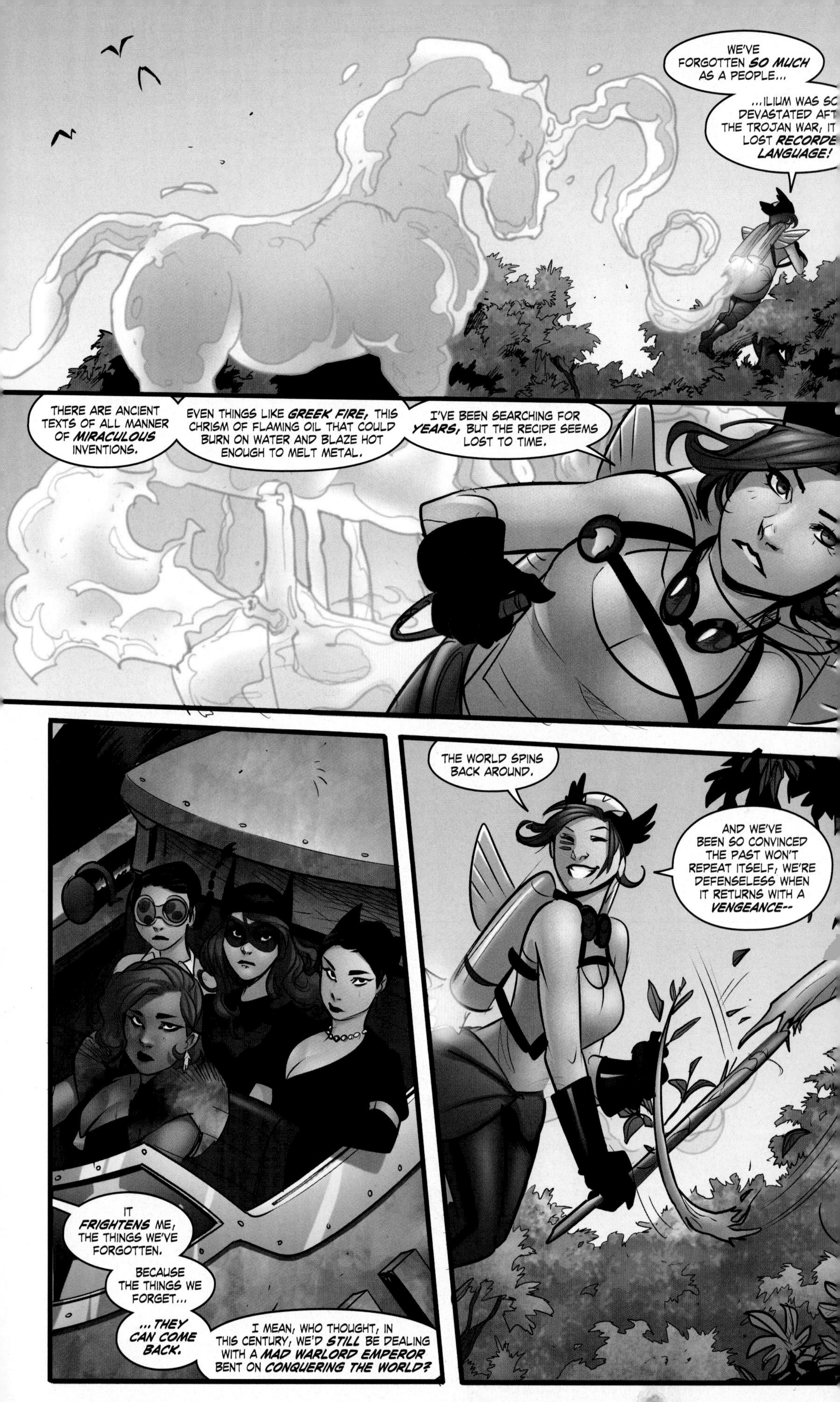
WE'VE FORGOTTEN SO MUCH AS A PEOPLE...
...ILIUM WAS SO DEVASTATED AFT THE TROJAN WAR, IT LOST RECORDE LANGUAGE!
THERE ARE ANCIENT TEXTS OF ALL MANNER OF MIRACULOUS INVENTIONS.
EVEN THINGS LIKE GREEK FIRE, THIS CHRISM OF FLAMING OIL THAT COULD BURN ON WATER AND BLAZE HOT ENOUGH TO MELT METAL.
I'VE BEEN SEARCHING FOR YEARS, BUT THE RECIPE SEEMS LOST TO TIME.
IT FRIGHTENS ME, THE THINGS WE'VE FORGOTTEN.
BECAUSE THE THINGS WE FORGET...
...THEY CAN COME BACK.
I MEAN, WHO THOUGHT, IN THIS CENTURY, WE'D STILL BE DEALING WITH A MAD WARLORD EMPEROR BENT ON CONQUERING THE WORLD?
THE WORLD SPINS BACK AROUND.
AND WE'VE BEEN SO CONVINCED THE PAST WON'T REPEAT ITSELF, WE'RE DEFENSELESS WHEN IT RETURNS WITH A VENGEANCE--

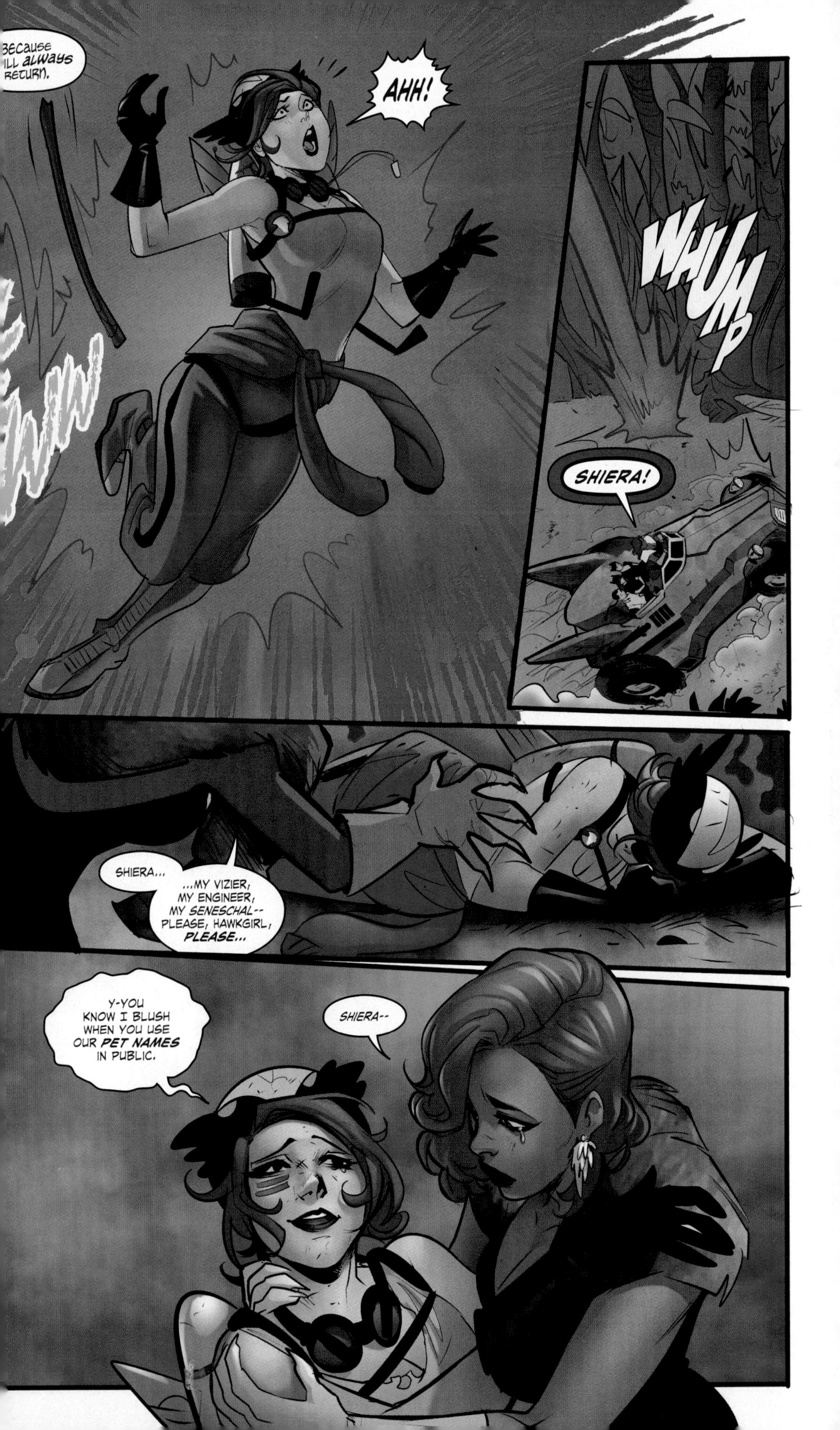

BECAUSE
...ILL *ALWAYS* RETURN.
AHH!
WHUMP
SHIERA!
SHIERA...
...MY VIZIER, MY ENGINEER, MY *SENESCHAL*-- PLEASE, HAWKGIRL, ***PLEASE...***
Y-YOU KNOW I BLUSH WHEN YOU USE OUR ***PET NAMES*** IN PUBLIC.
SHIERA--

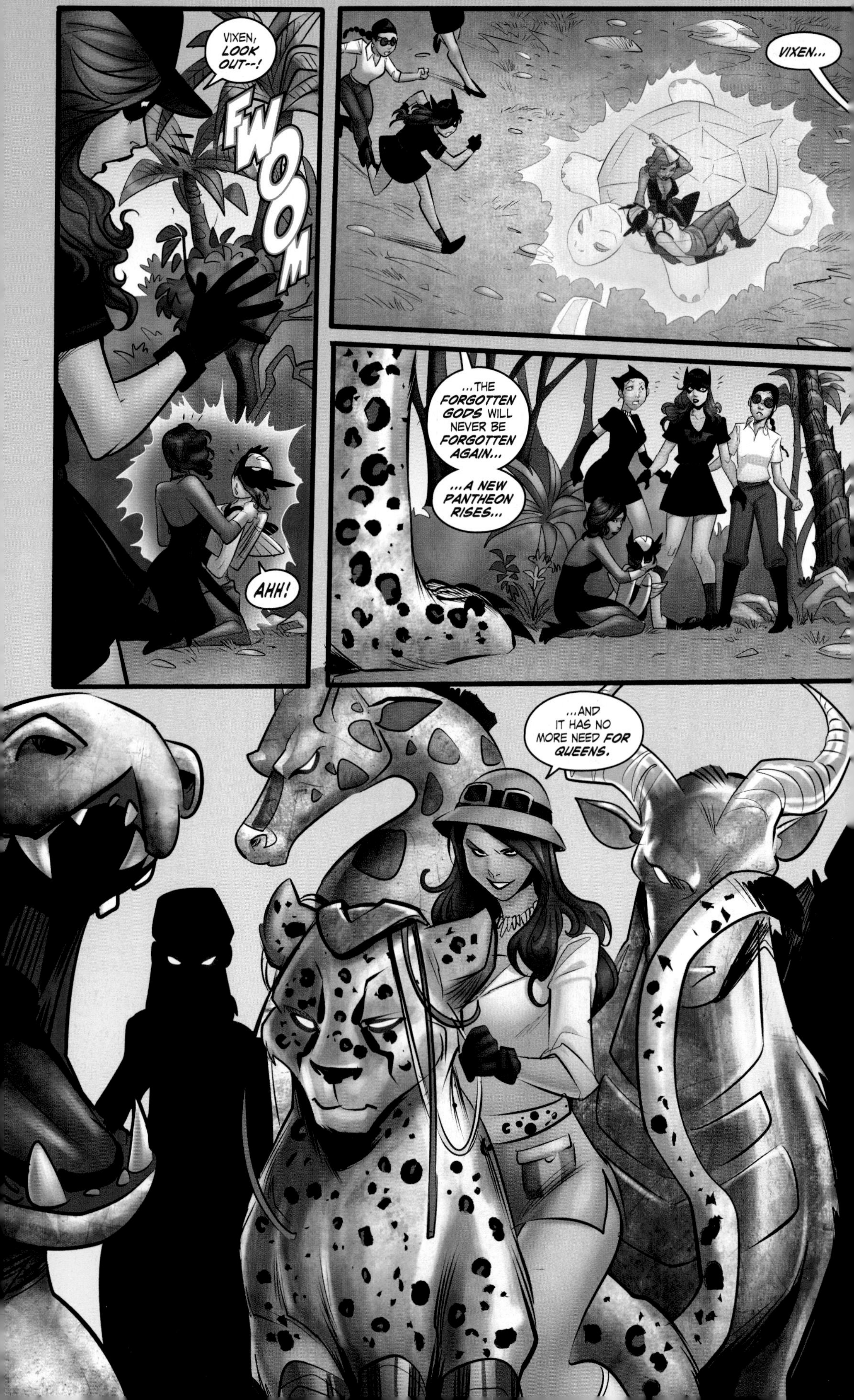
VIXEN, LOOK OUT--!
FWOOOM
AHH!
VIXEN...
...THE FORGOTTEN GODS WILL NEVER BE FORGOTTEN AGAIN...
...A NEW PANTHEON RISES...
...AND IT HAS NO MORE NEED FOR QUEENS.

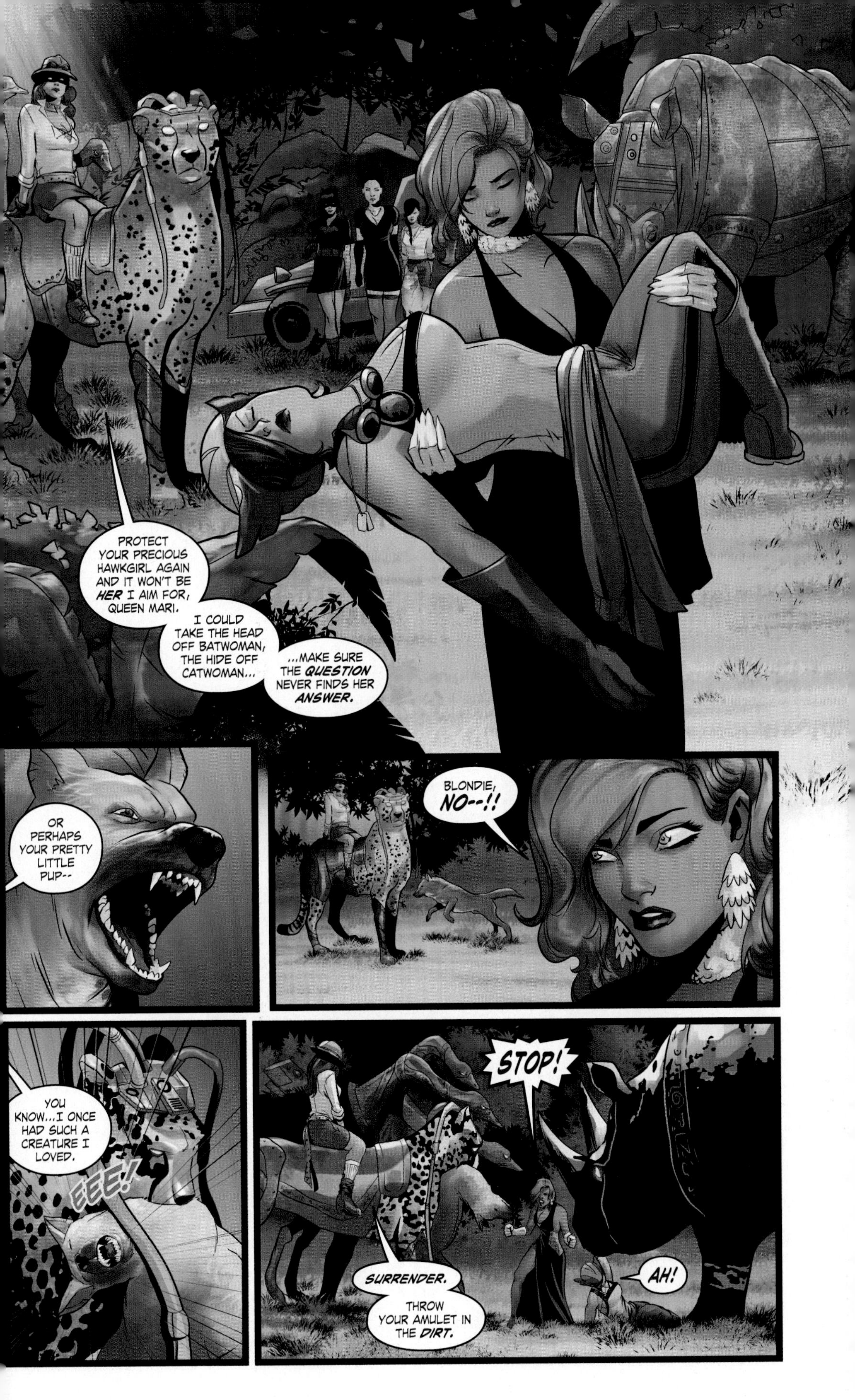
PROTECT YOUR PRECIOUS HAWKGIRL AGAIN AND IT WON'T BE HER I AIM FOR, QUEEN MARI.
I COULD TAKE THE HEAD OFF BATWOMAN, THE HIDE OFF CATWOMAN...
...MAKE SURE THE QUESTION NEVER FINDS HER ANSWER.
OR PERHAPS YOUR PRETTY LITTLE PUP--
BLONDIE, NO--!!
YOU KNOW...I ONCE HAD SUCH A CREATURE I LOVED.
EEE!
STOP!
SURRENDER.
THROW YOUR AMULET IN THE DIRT.
AH!

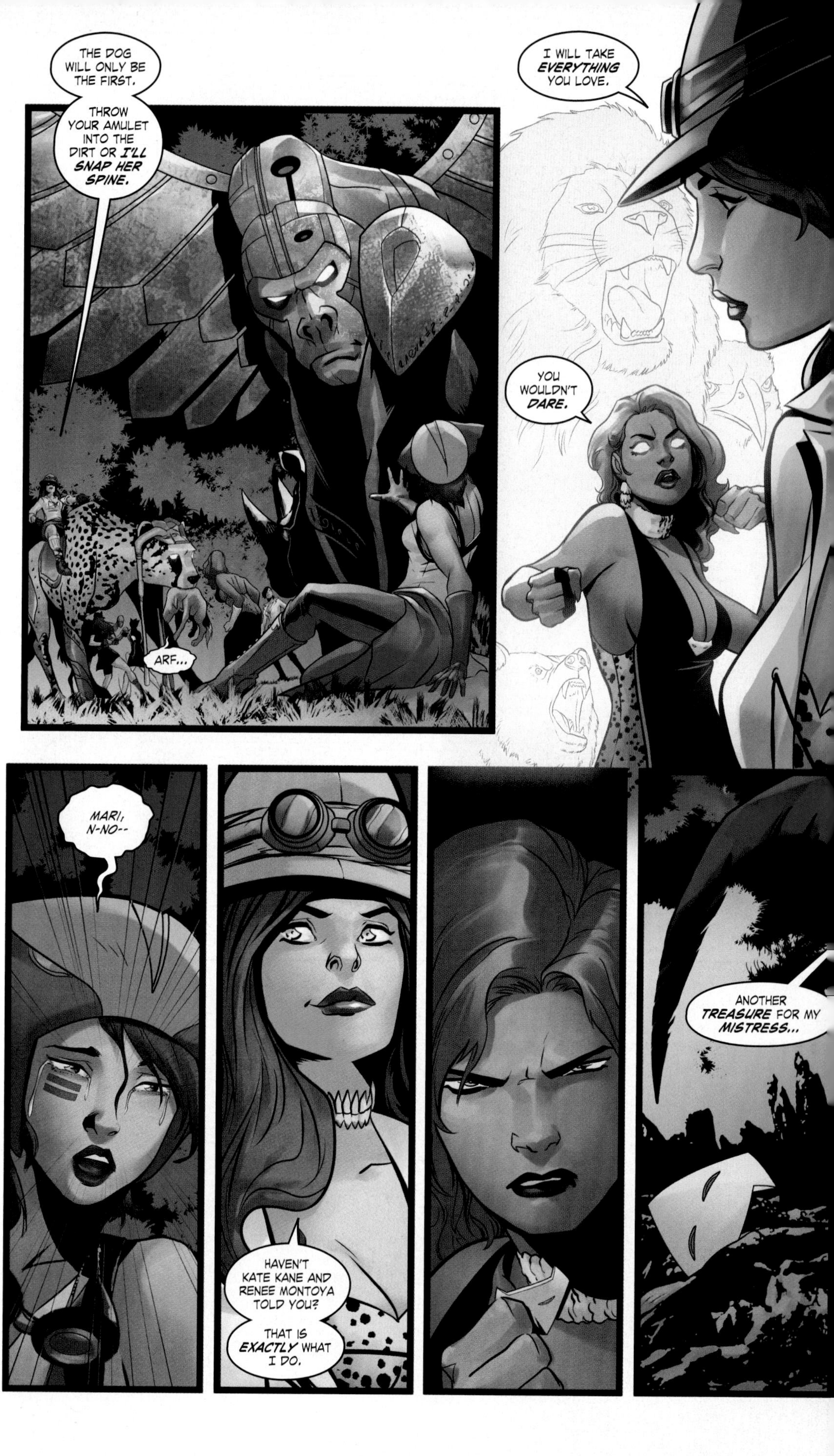
THE DOG WILL ONLY BE THE FIRST.
THROW YOUR AMULET INTO THE DIRT OR I'LL SNAP HER SPINE.
ARF...
I WILL TAKE EVERYTHING YOU LOVE.
YOU WOULDN'T DARE.
MARI, N-NO--
HAVEN'T KATE KANE AND RENEE MONTOYA TOLD YOU?
THAT IS EXACTLY WHAT I DO.
ANOTHER TREASURE FOR MY MISTRESS...

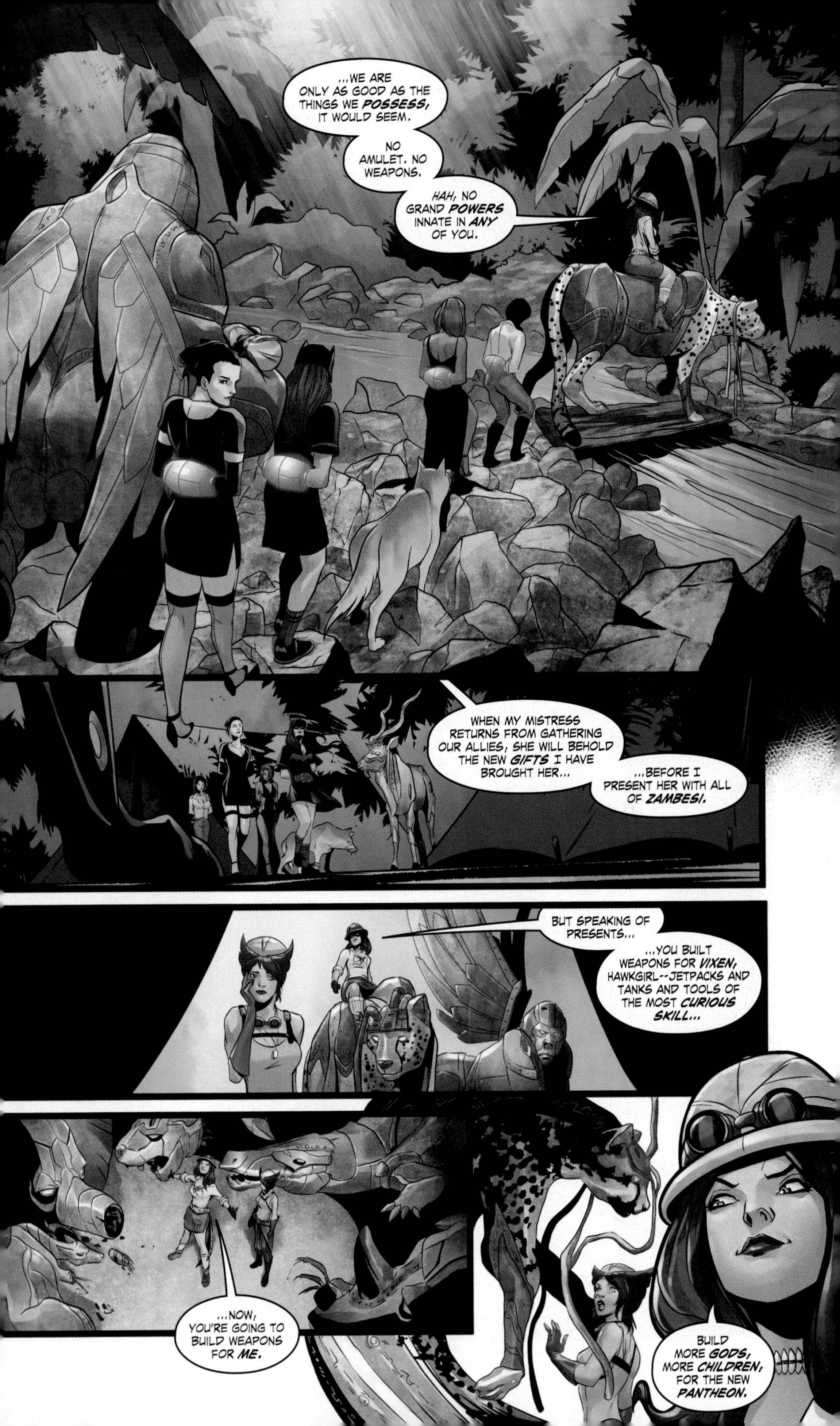
...WE ARE ONLY AS GOOD AS THE THINGS WE POSSESS, IT WOULD SEEM.
NO AMULET. NO WEAPONS.
HAH, NO GRAND POWERS INNATE IN ANY OF YOU.
WHEN MY MISTRESS RETURNS FROM GATHERING OUR ALLIES, SHE WILL BEHOLD THE NEW GIFTS I HAVE BROUGHT HER...
...BEFORE I PRESENT HER WITH ALL OF ZAMBESI.
BUT SPEAKING OF PRESENTS...
...YOU BUILT WEAPONS FOR VIXEN, HAWKGIRL--JETPACKS AND TANKS AND TOOLS OF THE MOST CURIOUS SKILL...
...NOW, YOU'RE GOING TO BUILD WEAPONS FOR ME.
BUILD MORE GODS, MORE CHILDREN, FOR THE NEW PANTHEON.

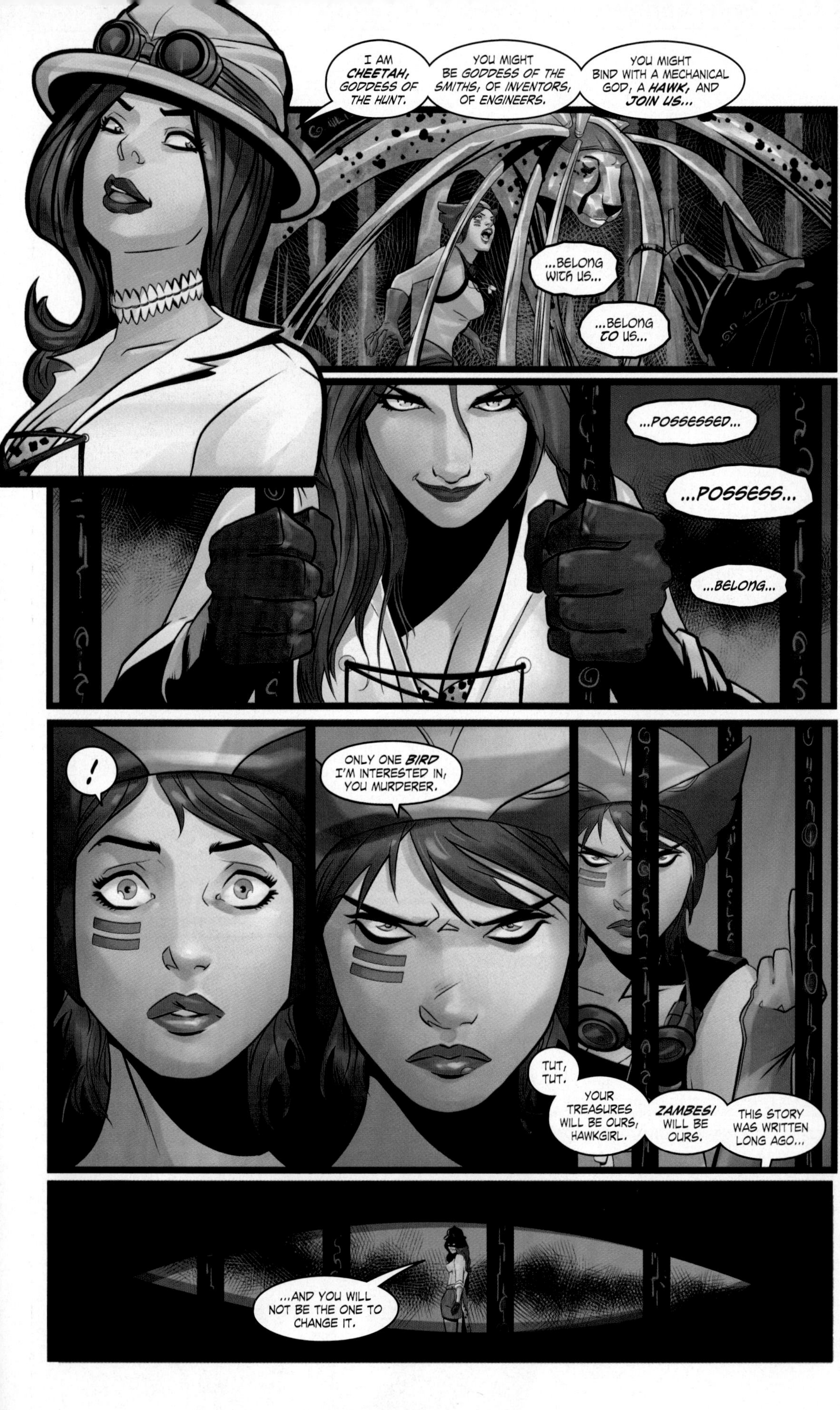
I AM CHEETAH, GODDESS OF THE HUNT.
YOU MIGHT BE GODDESS OF THE SMITHS, OF INVENTORS, OF ENGINEERS.
YOU MIGHT BIND WITH A MECHANICAL GOD, A HAWK, AND JOIN US...
...BELONG WITH US...
...BELONG TO US...
...POSSESSED...
...POSSESS...
...BELONG...
!
ONLY ONE BIRD I'M INTERESTED IN, YOU MURDERER.
TUT, TUT.
YOUR TREASURES WILL BE OURS, HAWKGIRL.
ZAMBESI WILL BE OURS.
THIS STORY WAS WRITTEN LONG AGO...
...AND YOU WILL NOT BE THE ONE TO CHANGE IT.

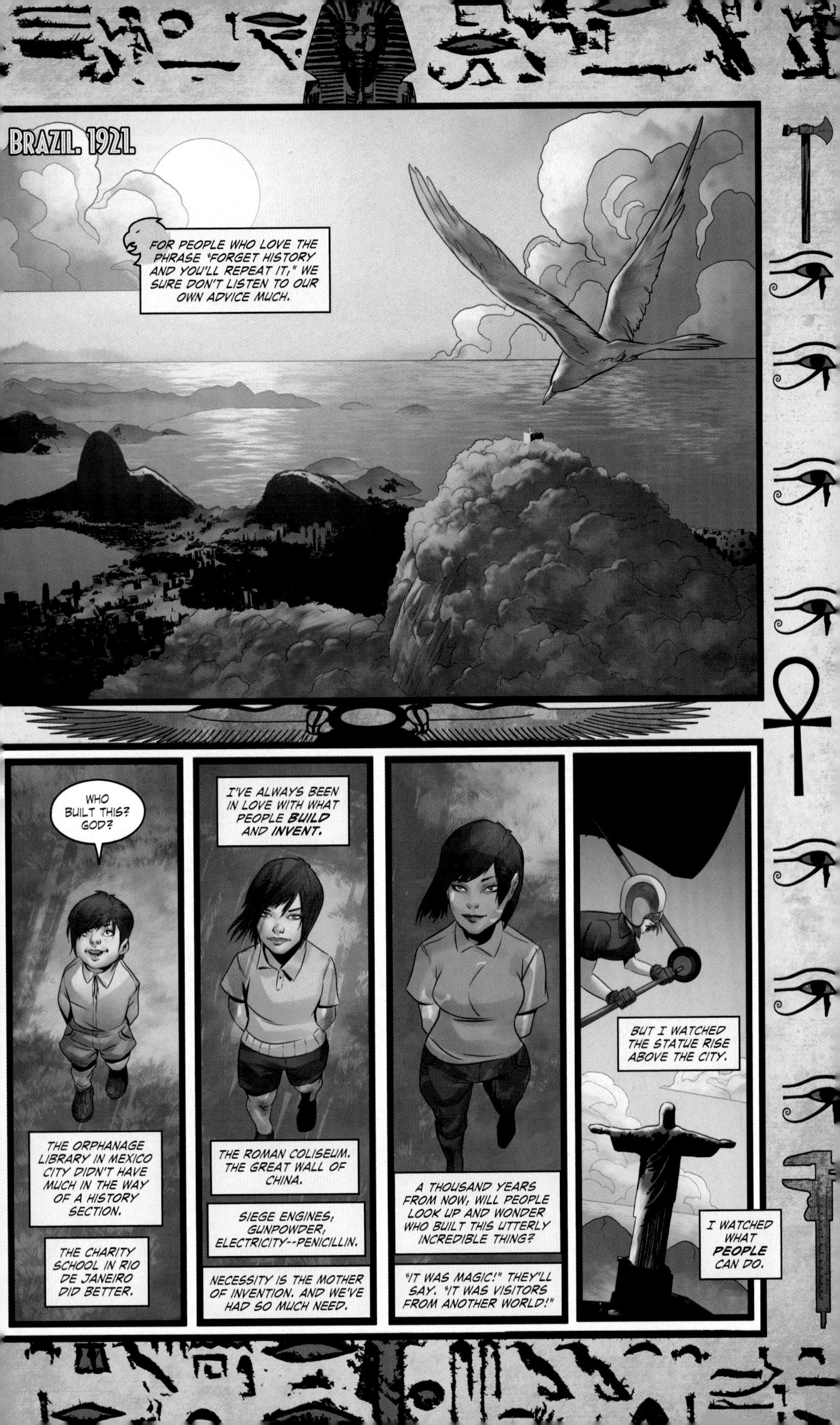

BRAZIL. 1921.
FOR PEOPLE WHO LOVE THE PHRASE "FORGET HISTORY AND YOU'LL REPEAT IT," WE SURE DON'T LISTEN TO OUR OWN ADVICE MUCH.
WHO BUILT THIS? GOD?
THE ORPHANAGE LIBRARY IN MEXICO CITY DIDN'T HAVE MUCH IN THE WAY OF A HISTORY SECTION.
THE CHARITY SCHOOL IN RIO DE JANEIRO DID BETTER.
I'VE ALWAYS BEEN IN LOVE WITH WHAT PEOPLE **BUILD** AND **INVENT.**
THE ROMAN COLISEUM. THE GREAT WALL OF CHINA.
SIEGE ENGINES, GUNPOWDER, ELECTRICITY--PENICILLIN.
NECESSITY IS THE MOTHER OF INVENTION. AND WE'VE HAD SO MUCH NEED.
A THOUSAND YEARS FROM NOW, WILL PEOPLE LOOK UP AND WONDER WHO BUILT THIS UTTERLY INCREDIBLE THING?
"IT WAS MAGIC!" THEY'LL SAY. "IT WAS VISITORS FROM ANOTHER WORLD!"
BUT I WATCHED THE STATUE RISE ABOVE THE CITY.
I WATCHED WHAT **PEOPLE** CAN DO.

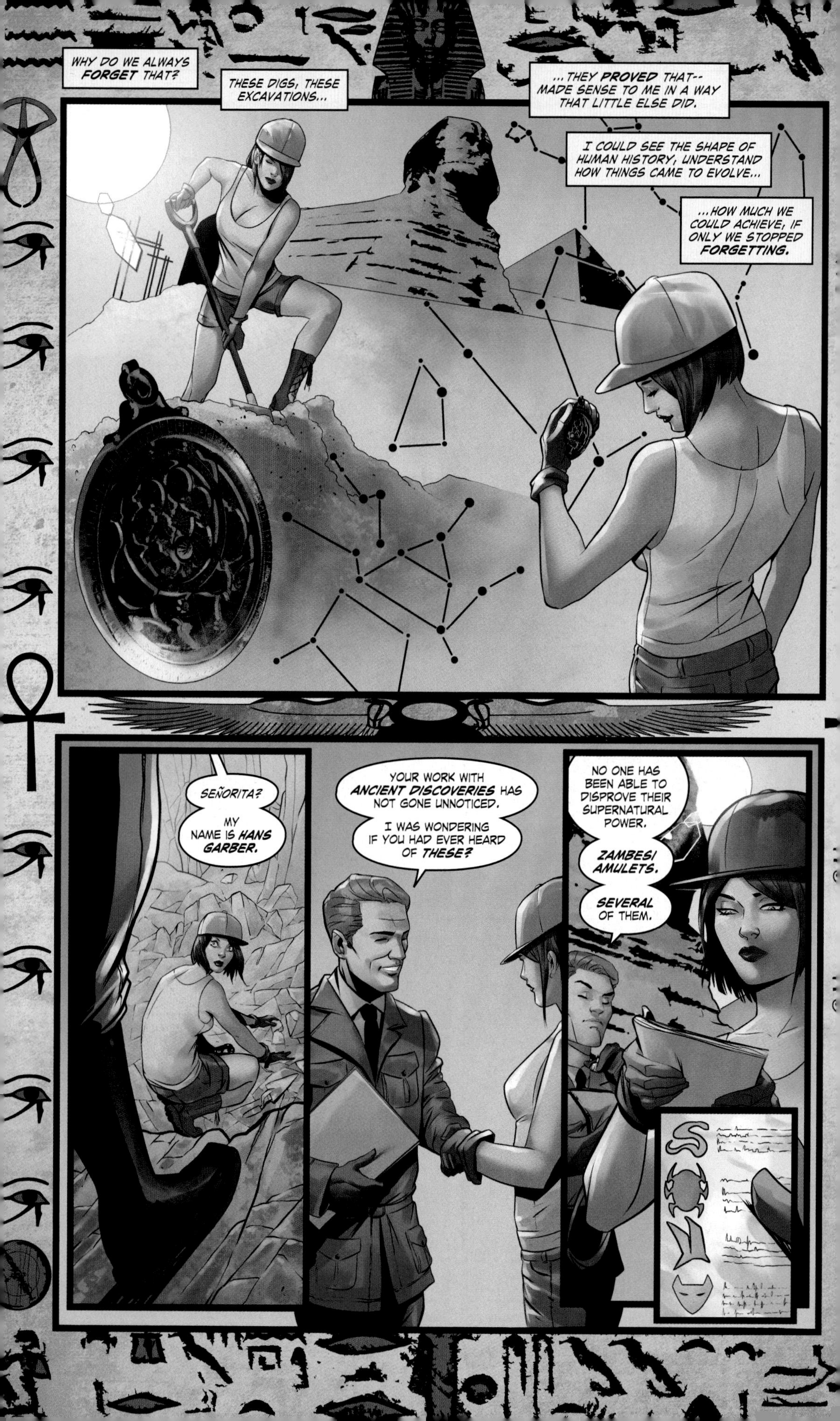

WHY DO WE ALWAYS FORGET THAT?
THESE DIGS, THESE EXCAVATIONS...
...THEY PROVED THAT-- MADE SENSE TO ME IN A WAY THAT LITTLE ELSE DID.
I COULD SEE THE SHAPE OF HUMAN HISTORY, UNDERSTAND HOW THINGS CAME TO EVOLVE...
...HOW MUCH WE COULD ACHIEVE, IF ONLY WE STOPPED FORGETTING.
SEÑORITA?
MY NAME IS HANS GARBER.
YOUR WORK WITH ANCIENT DISCOVERIES HAS NOT GONE UNNOTICED.
I WAS WONDERING IF YOU HAD EVER HEARD OF THESE?
NO ONE HAS BEEN ABLE TO DISPROVE THEIR SUPERNATURAL POWER.
ZAMBESI AMULETS.
SEVERAL OF THEM.

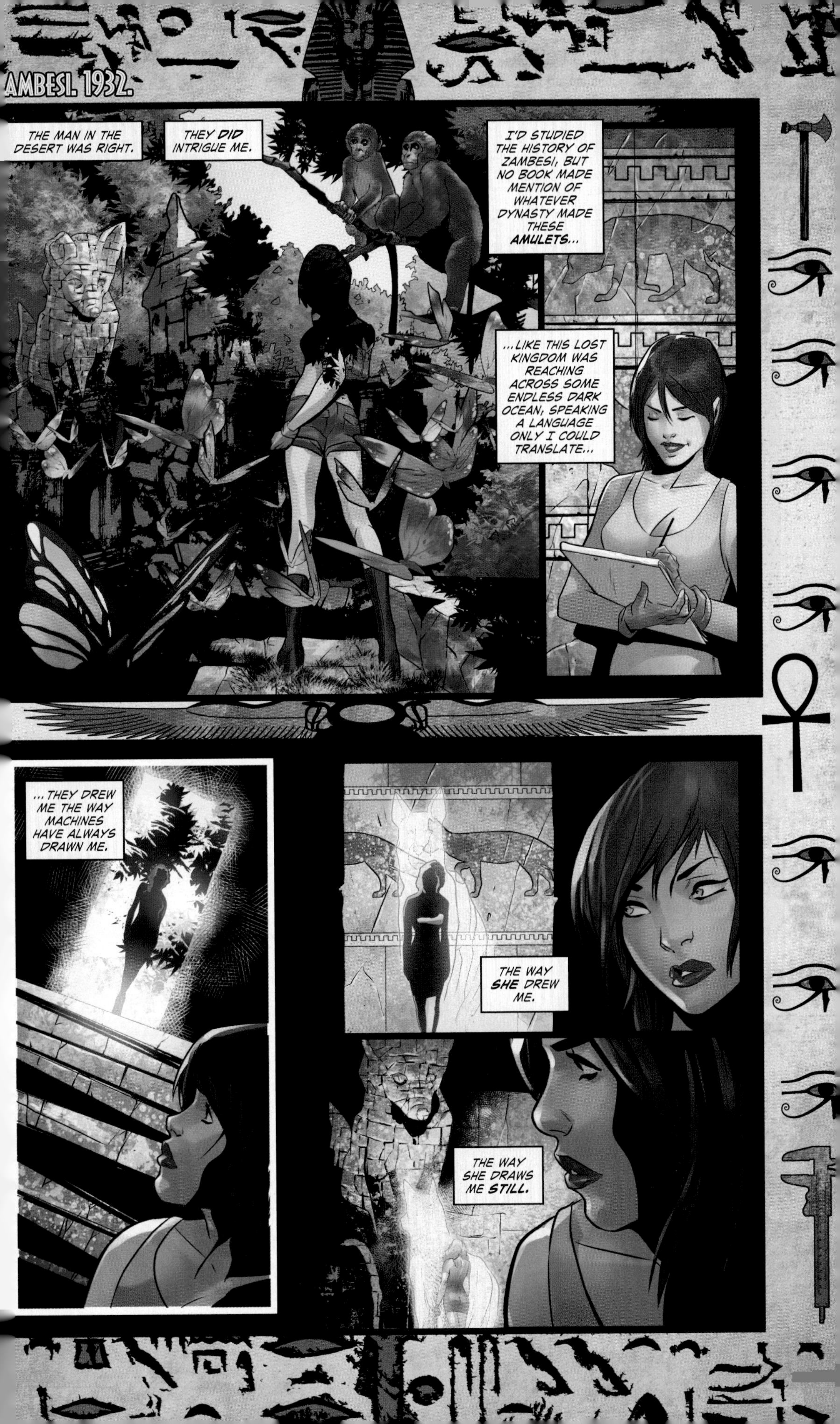
AMBESI. 1932.
THE MAN IN THE DESERT WAS RIGHT.
THEY DID INTRIGUE ME.
I'D STUDIED THE HISTORY OF ZAMBESI, BUT NO BOOK MADE MENTION OF WHATEVER DYNASTY MADE THESE AMULETS...
...LIKE THIS LOST KINGDOM WAS REACHING ACROSS SOME ENDLESS DARK OCEAN, SPEAKING A LANGUAGE ONLY I COULD TRANSLATE...
...THEY DREW ME THE WAY MACHINES HAVE ALWAYS DRAWN ME.
THE WAY SHE DREW ME.
THE WAY SHE DRAWS ME STILL.

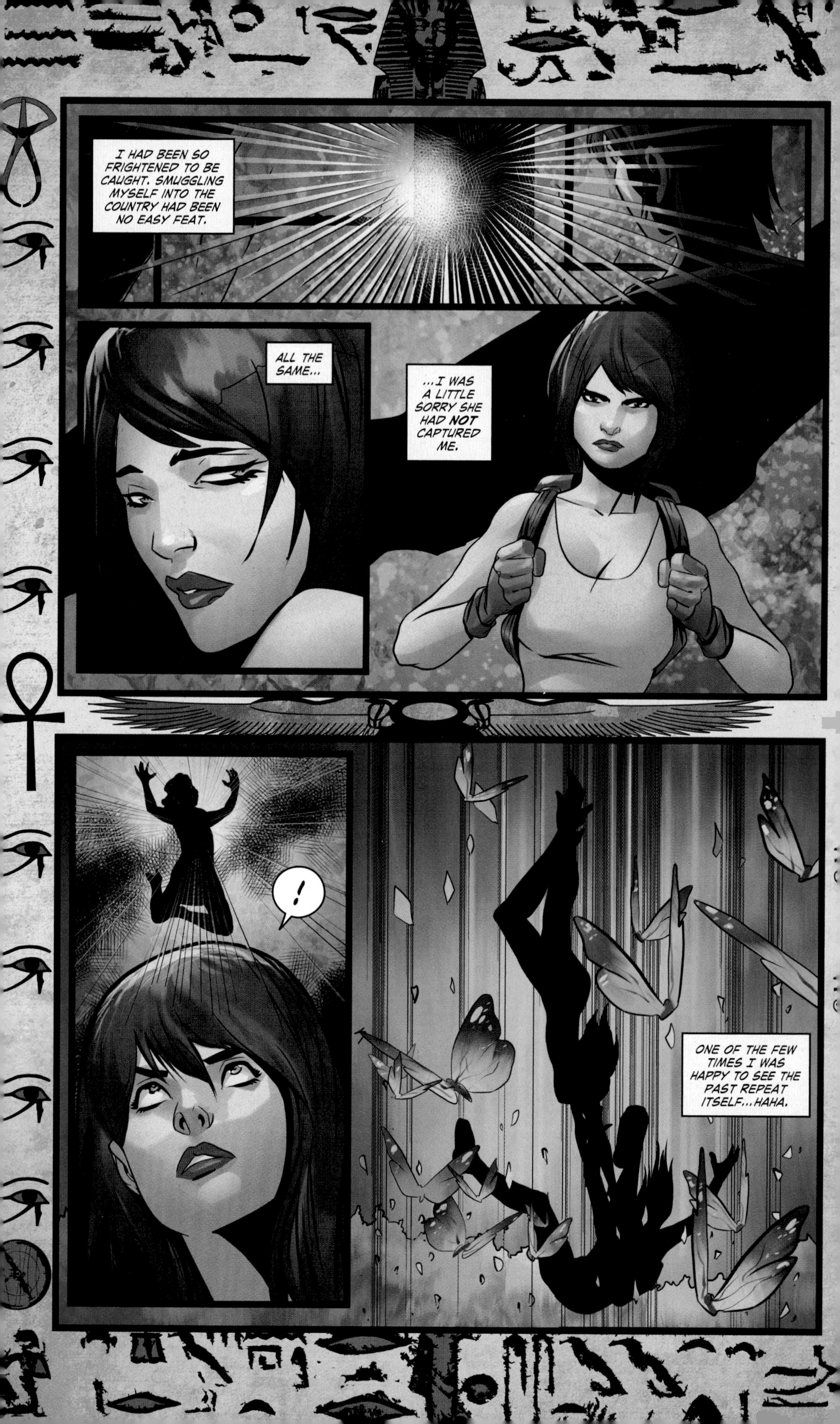
I HAD BEEN SO FRIGHTENED TO BE CAUGHT. SMUGGLING MYSELF INTO THE COUNTRY HAD BEEN NO EASY FEAT.
ALL THE SAME...
...I WAS A LITTLE SORRY SHE HAD NOT CAPTURED ME.
!
ONE OF THE FEW TIMES I WAS HAPPY TO SEE THE PAST REPEAT ITSELF...HAHA.

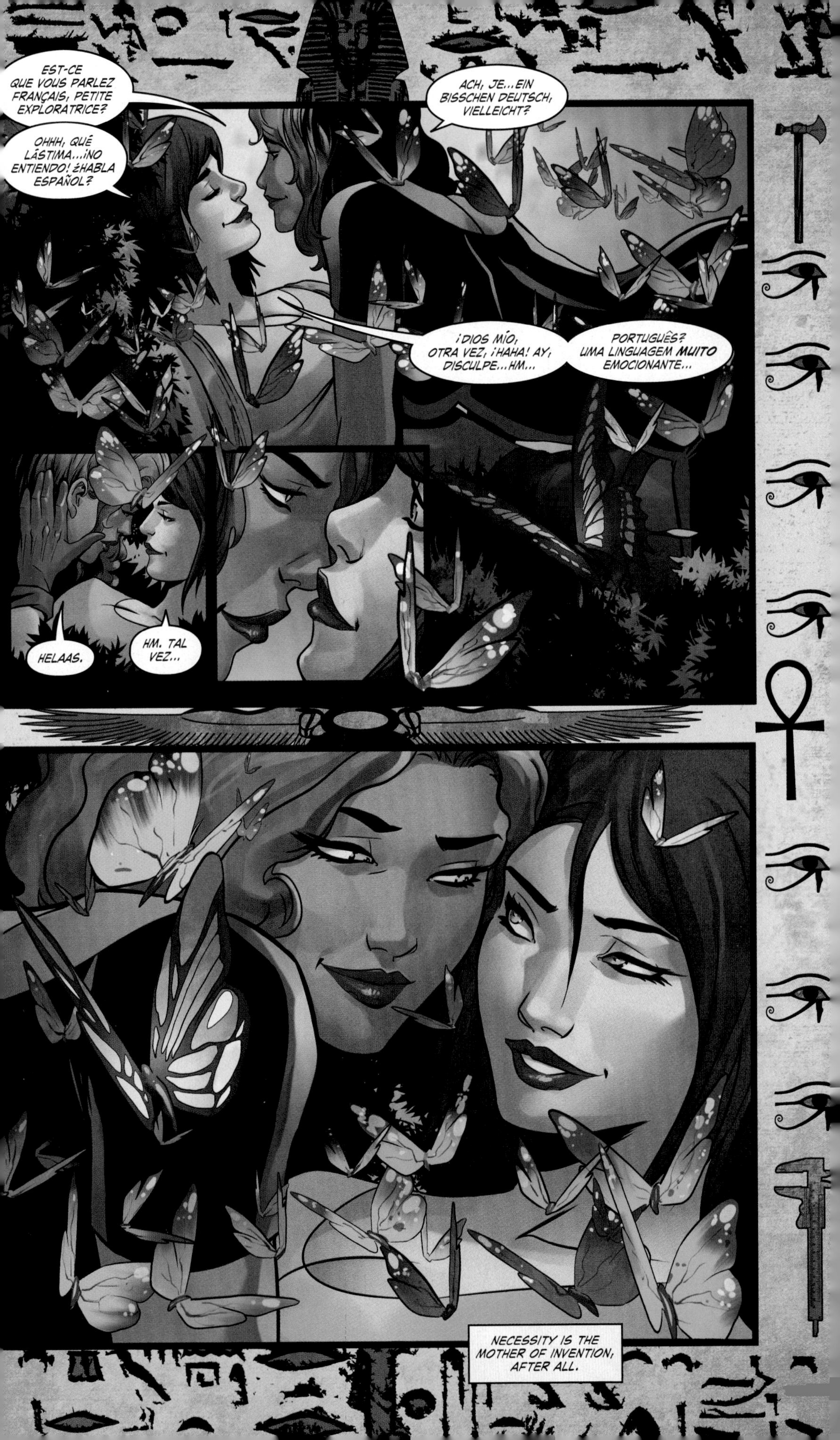

EST-CE QUE VOUS PARLEZ FRANÇAIS, PETITE EXPLORATRICE?
ACH, JE...EIN BISSCHEN DEUTSCH, VIELLEICHT?
OHHH, QUÉ LÁSTIMA...¡NO ENTIENDO! ¿HABLA ESPAÑOL?
¡DIOS MÍO, OTRA VEZ, ¡HAHA! AY, DISCULPE...HM...
PORTUGUÊS? UMA LINGUAGEM MUITO EMOCIONANTE...
HELAAS.
HM. TAL VEZ...
NECESSITY IS THE MOTHER OF INVENTION, AFTER ALL.

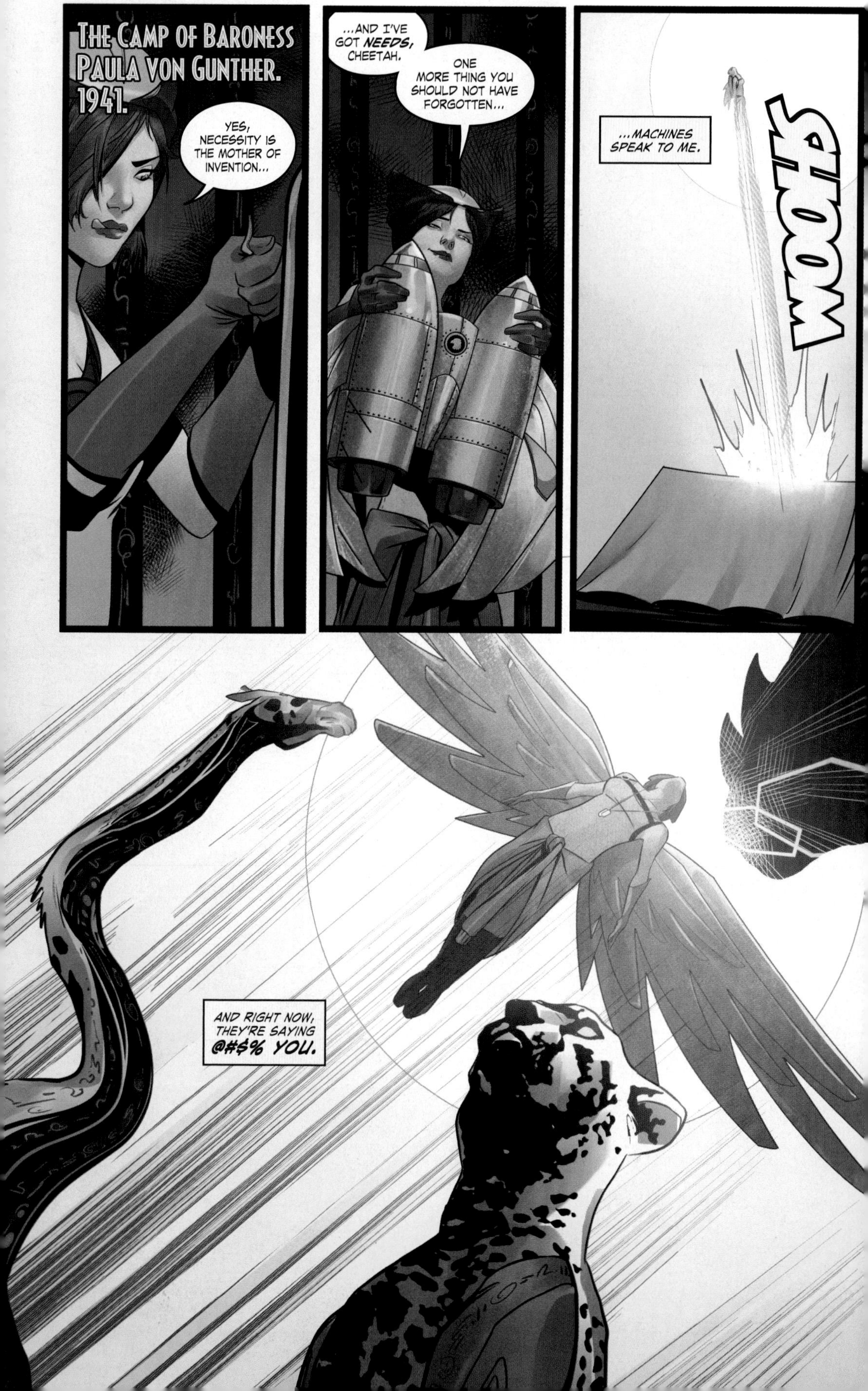

THE CAMP OF BARONESS PAULA VON GUNTHER. 1941.
YES, NECESSITY IS THE MOTHER OF INVENTION...
...AND I'VE GOT NEEDS, CHEETAH.
ONE MORE THING YOU SHOULD NOT HAVE FORGOTTEN...
...MACHINES SPEAK TO ME.
WOOSH
AND RIGHT NOW, THEY'RE SAYING @#$% YOU.

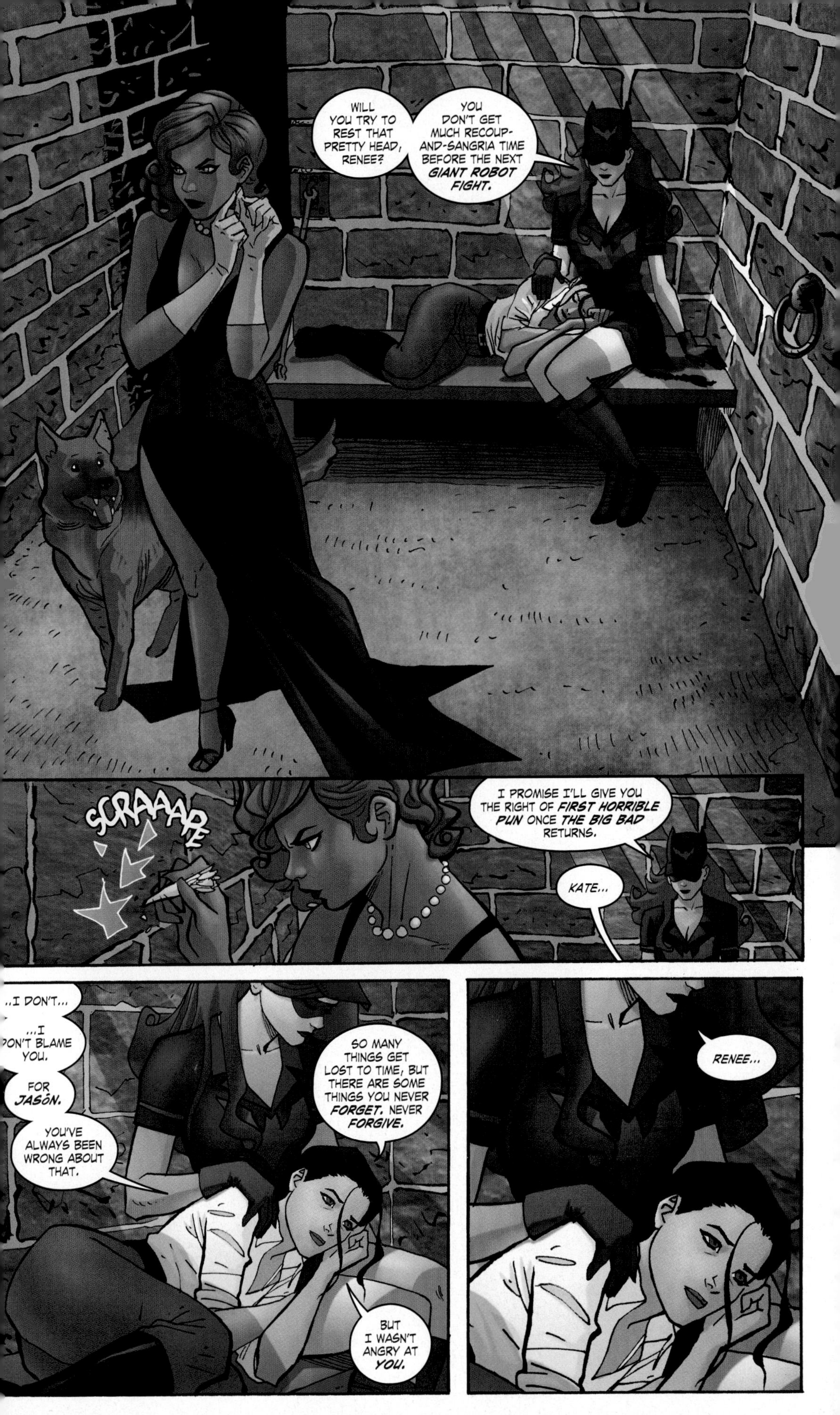
WILL YOU TRY TO REST THAT PRETTY HEAD, RENEE?
YOU DON'T GET MUCH RECOUP-AND-SANGRIA TIME BEFORE THE NEXT GIANT ROBOT FIGHT.
SCRAAAPE
I PROMISE I'LL GIVE YOU THE RIGHT OF FIRST HORRIBLE PUN ONCE THE BIG BAD RETURNS.
KATE...
...I DON'T...
...I DON'T BLAME YOU.
FOR JASÓN.
YOU'VE ALWAYS BEEN WRONG ABOUT THAT.
SO MANY THINGS GET LOST TO TIME, BUT THERE ARE SOME THINGS YOU NEVER FORGET. NEVER FORGIVE.
BUT I WASN'T ANGRY AT YOU.
RENEE...

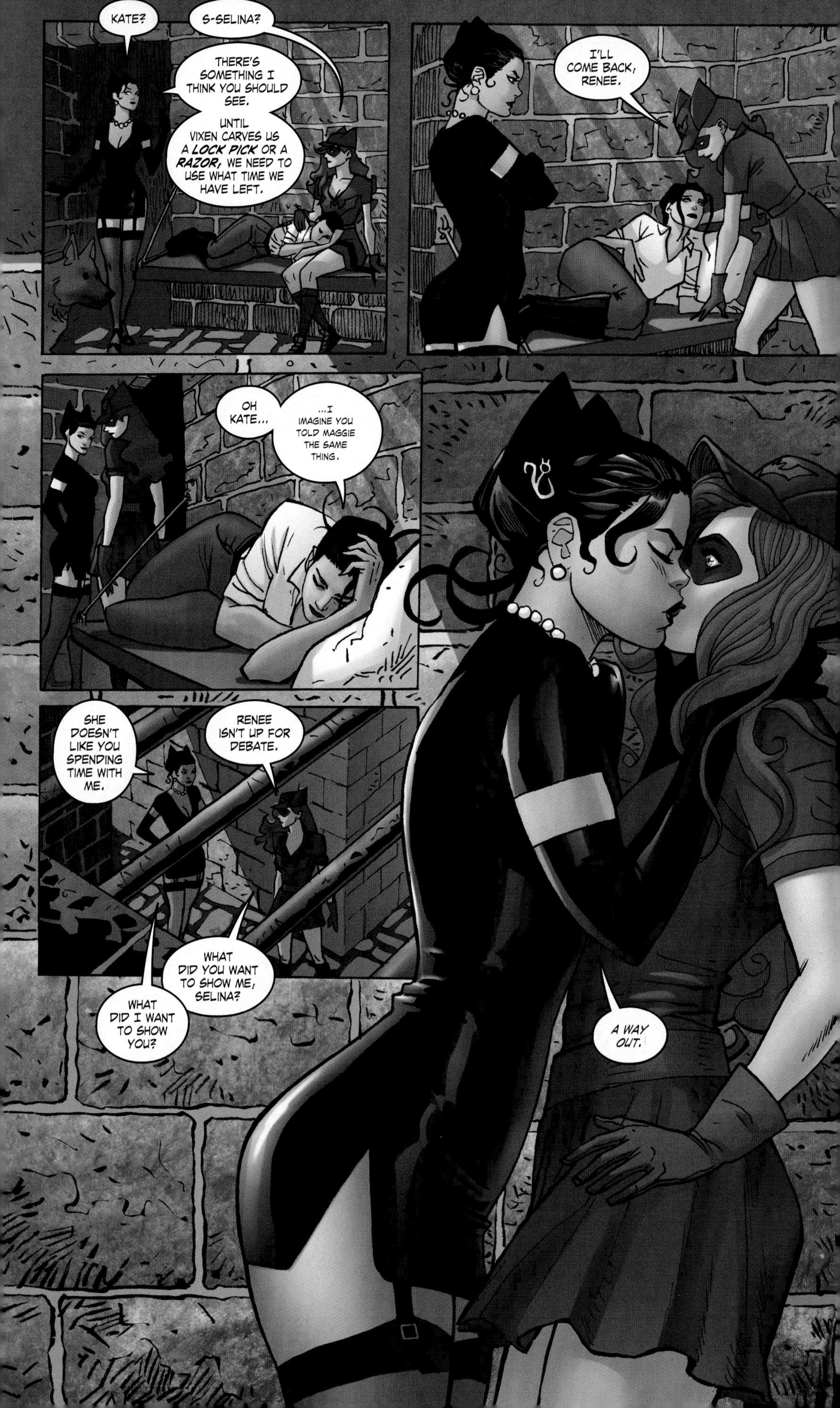
KATE?
S-SELINA?
THERE'S SOMETHING I THINK YOU SHOULD SEE.
UNTIL VIXEN CARVES US A LOCK PICK OR A RAZOR, WE NEED TO USE WHAT TIME WE HAVE LEFT.
I'LL COME BACK, RENEE.
OH KATE...
...I IMAGINE YOU TOLD MAGGIE THE SAME THING.
SHE DOESN'T LIKE YOU SPENDING TIME WITH ME.
RENEE ISN'T UP FOR DEBATE.
WHAT DID YOU WANT TO SHOW ME, SELINA?
WHAT DID I WANT TO SHOW YOU?
A WAY OUT.

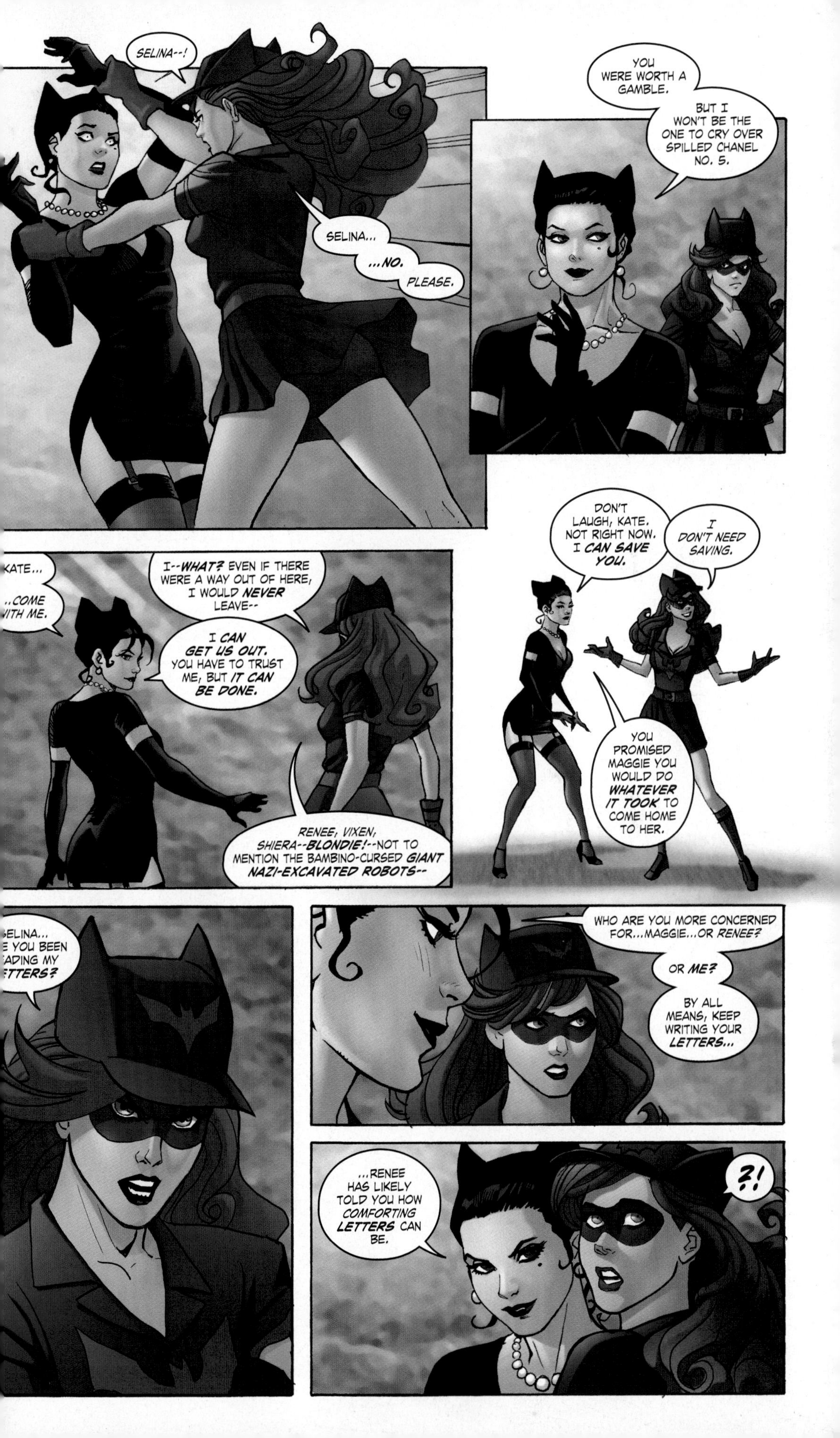
SELINA--!
SELINA... ...NO. PLEASE.
YOU WERE WORTH A GAMBLE.
BUT I WON'T BE THE ONE TO CRY OVER SPILLED CHANEL NO. 5.
KATE... ...COME WITH ME.
I--WHAT? EVEN IF THERE WERE A WAY OUT OF HERE, I WOULD NEVER LEAVE--
I CAN GET US OUT. YOU HAVE TO TRUST ME, BUT IT CAN BE DONE.
RENEE, VIXEN, SHIERA--BLONDIE!--NOT TO MENTION THE BAMBINO-CURSED GIANT NAZI-EXCAVATED ROBOTS--
DON'T LAUGH, KATE. NOT RIGHT NOW. I CAN SAVE YOU.
I DON'T NEED SAVING.
YOU PROMISED MAGGIE YOU WOULD DO WHATEVER IT TOOK TO COME HOME TO HER.
SELINA...
WHO ARE YOU MORE CONCERNED FOR...MAGGIE...OR RENEE?
OR ME?
BY ALL MEANS, KEEP WRITING YOUR LETTERS...
...RENEE HAS LIKELY TOLD YOU HOW COMFORTING LETTERS CAN BE.
?!

CRASSH!

HAWKGIRL!

OH DEAR, WERE YOU CRAZY KIDS HAVING A MOMENT?

I DETECT SOME TENSION IN THE AIR THAT ISN'T THE ADRENALINE RUSH FROM BUILDING MYSELF *AN ICARUS STARTER PACK* OUT OF THE *SPARE GOD PARTS.*

SHIERA?!

WE'RE GOING TO HAVE TO PROMOTE ME, YOUR WICKEDNESS.

CHIEF OF ALL RESCUE MISSIONS AND BACK-TALKING THE ENEMY, AT *MINIMUM.*

CHEETAH IS HELL--OR HEAVE[N] OR *UNDETERMINE[D] ASTRAL-PLANE-OF-NEW-PANTHEON'S-C[?]* DETERMINED TO B[E] MORE GODS FO[R] THE BARONESS' ARMY.

THE BARONESS WANT[S] *CONQUEST--*

AND WE WILL NEVER LET THAT HAPPEN TO ZAMBESI, NOR ANY OTHER NATION TO WHICH SHE TURNS HER EYE.

CHEETA[H] WANTS US FO[R] GODS? WANT[S] *POSSESS[?]*

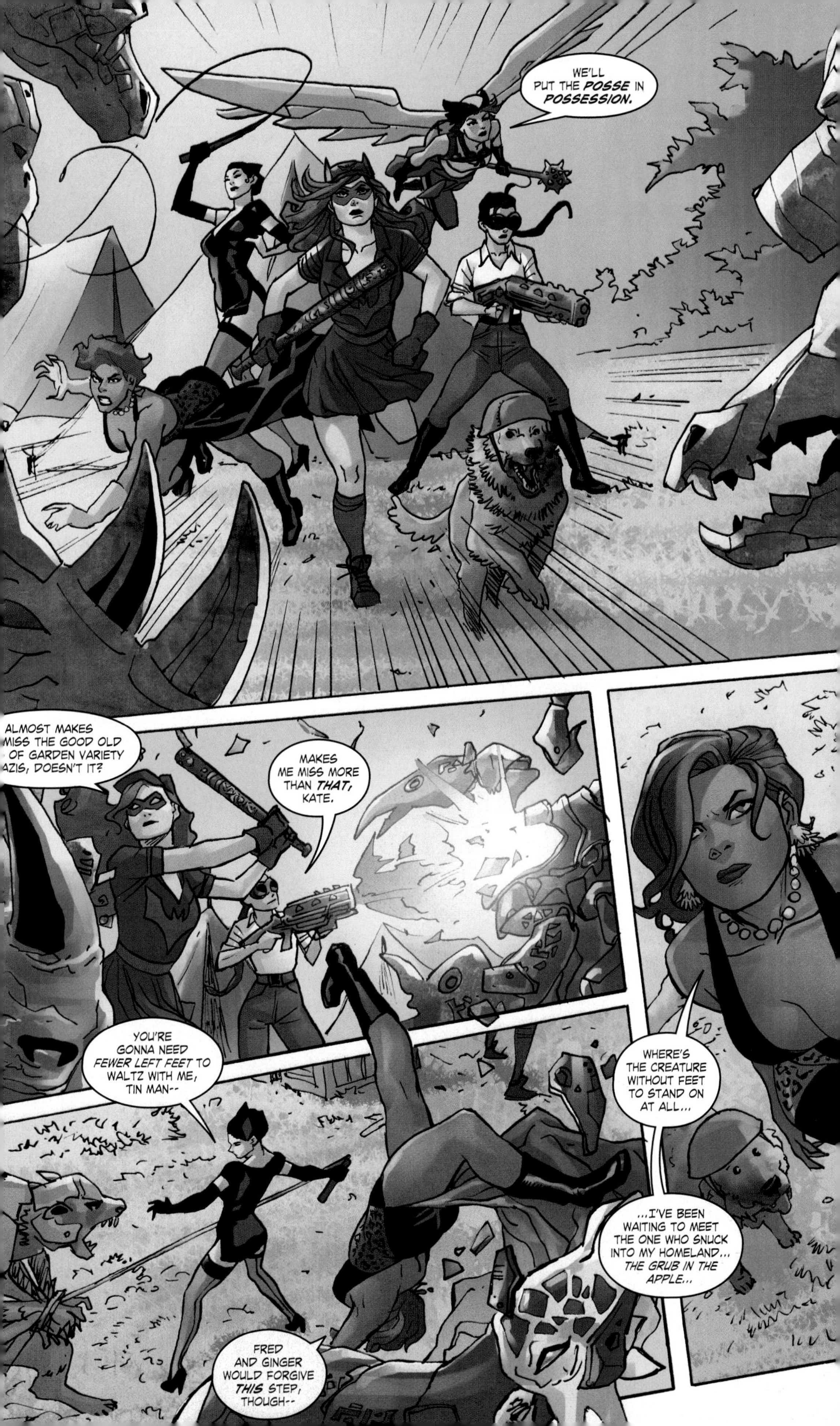
WE'LL PUT THE POSSE IN POSSESSION.
ALMOST MAKES MISS THE GOOD OLD OF GARDEN VARIETY AZIS, DOESN'T IT?
MAKES ME MISS MORE THAN THAT, KATE.
YOU'RE GONNA NEED FEWER LEFT FEET TO WALTZ WITH ME, TIN MAN--
FRED AND GINGER WOULD FORGIVE THIS STEP, THOUGH--
WHERE'S THE CREATURE WITHOUT FEET TO STAND ON AT ALL...
...I'VE BEEN WAITING TO MEET THE ONE WHO SNUCK INTO MY HOMELAND... THE GRUB IN THE APPLE...

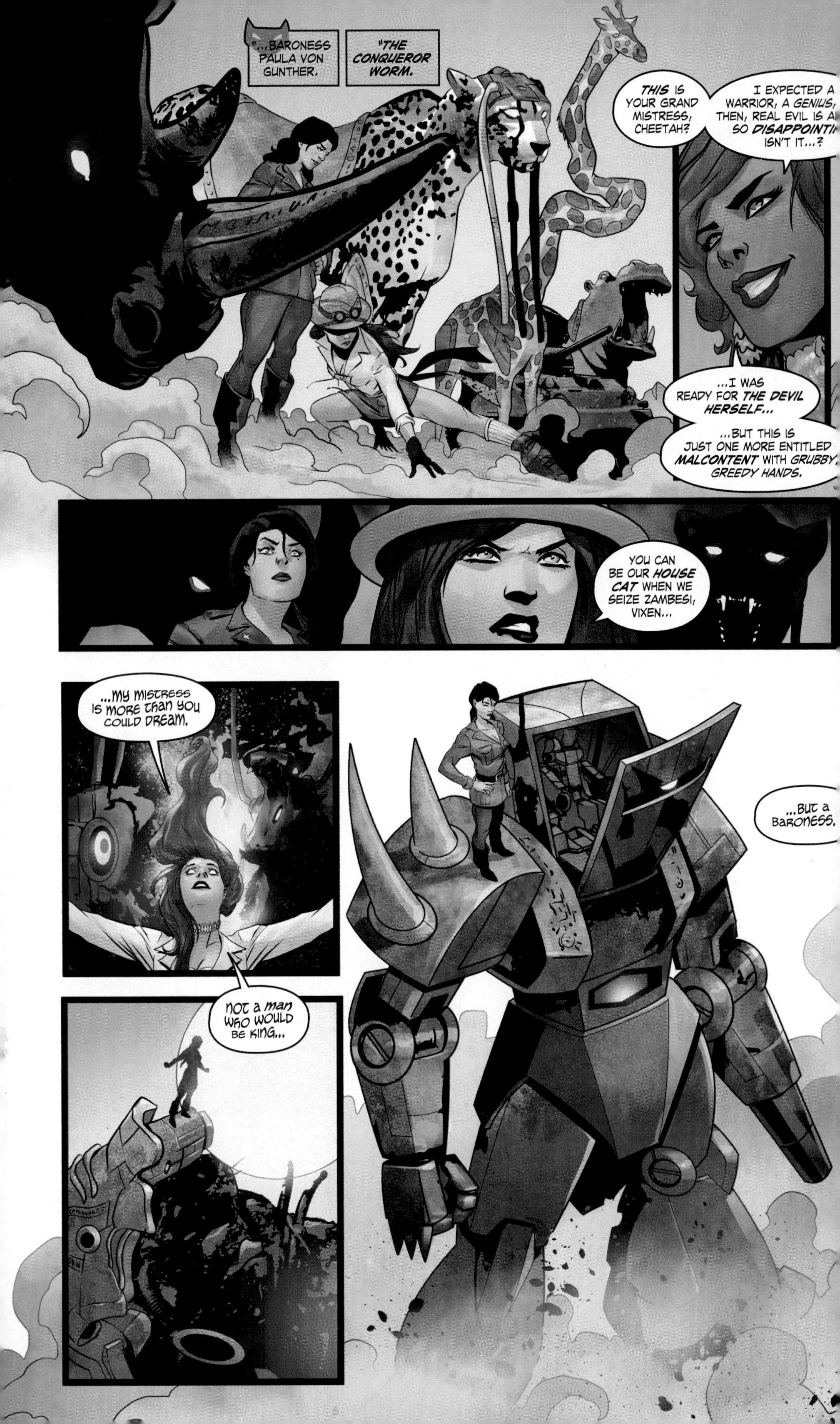
"...BARONESS PAULA VON GUNTHER.
"THE CONQUEROR WORM.
THIS IS YOUR GRAND MISTRESS, CHEETAH?
I EXPECTED A WARRIOR, A GENIUS, THEN, REAL EVIL IS A SO DISAPPOINTI ISN'T IT...?
...I WAS READY FOR THE DEVIL HERSELF...
...BUT THIS IS JUST ONE MORE ENTITLED MALCONTENT WITH GRUBBY, GREEDY HANDS.
YOU CAN BE OUR HOUSE CAT WHEN WE SEIZE ZAMBESI, VIXEN...
...MY MISTRESS IS MORE THAN YOU COULD DREAM.
NOT A MAN WHO WOULD BE KING...
...BUT A BARONESS.

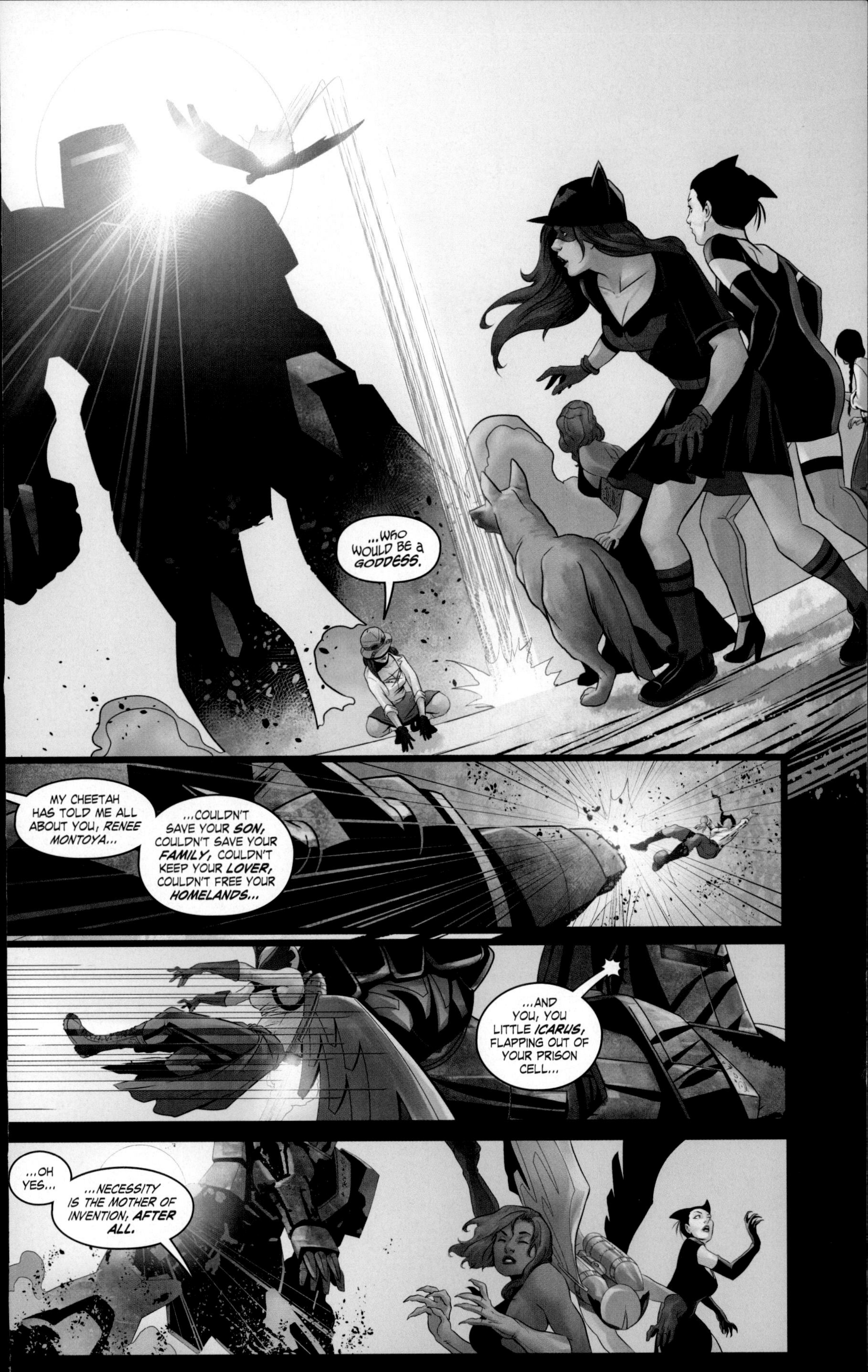

...WHO WOULD BE A GODDESS.
MY CHEETAH HAS TOLD ME ALL ABOUT YOU, RENEE MONTOYA...
...COULDN'T SAVE YOUR SON, COULDN'T SAVE YOUR FAMILY, COULDN'T KEEP YOUR LOVER, COULDN'T FREE YOUR HOMELANDS...
...AND YOU, YOU LITTLE ICARUS, FLAPPING OUT OF YOUR PRISON CELL...
...OH YES...
...NECESSITY IS THE MOTHER OF INVENTION, AFTER ALL.

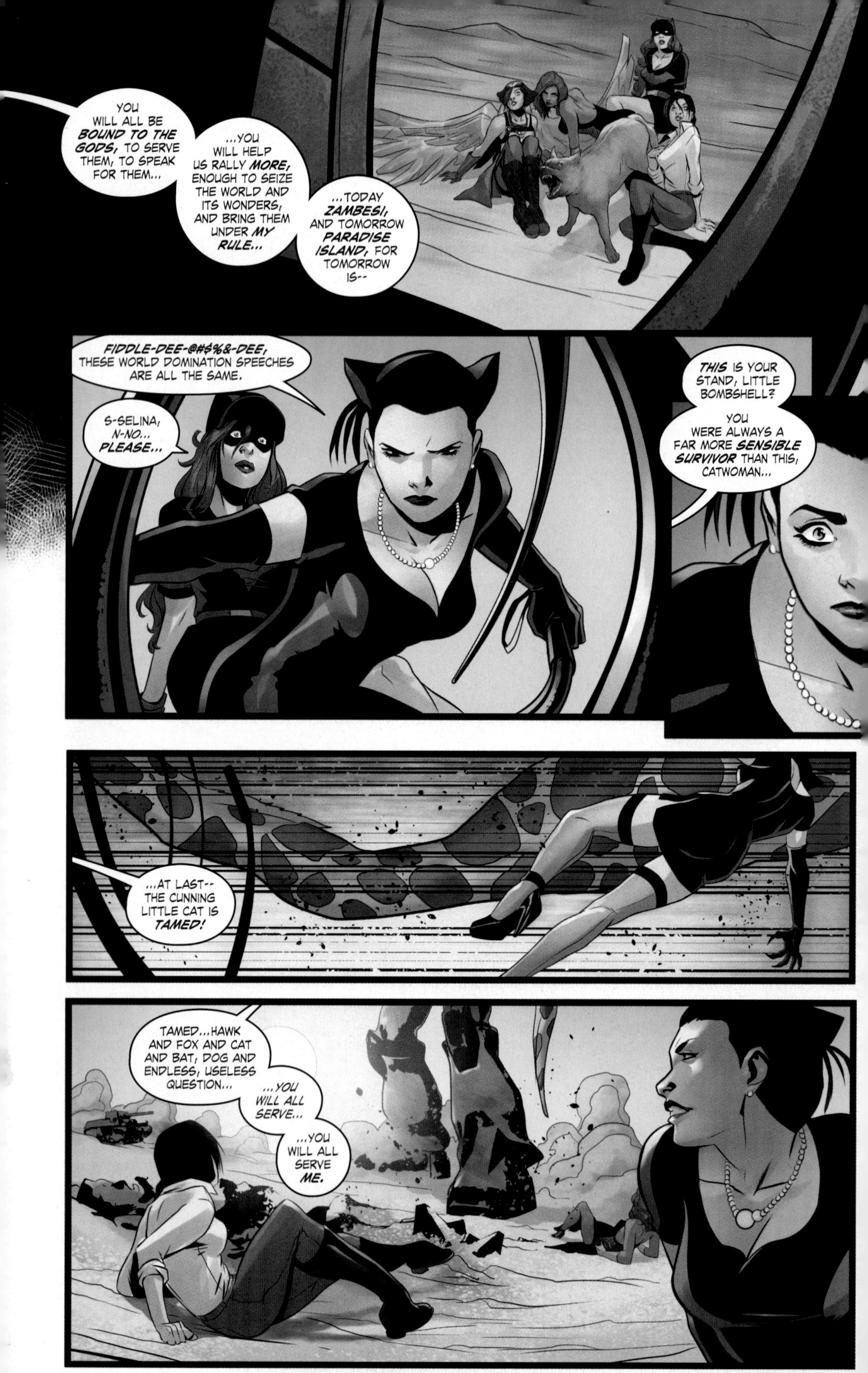
YOU WILL ALL BE BOUND TO THE GODS, TO SERVE THEM, TO SPEAK FOR THEM...
...YOU WILL HELP US RALLY MORE, ENOUGH TO SEIZE THE WORLD AND ITS WONDERS, AND BRING THEM UNDER MY RULE...
...TODAY ZAMBESI, AND TOMORROW PARADISE ISLAND, FOR TOMORROW IS--
FIDDLE-DEE-@#$%&-DEE, THESE WORLD DOMINATION SPEECHES ARE ALL THE SAME.
S-SELINA, N-NO... PLEASE...
THIS IS YOUR STAND, LITTLE BOMBSHELL?
YOU WERE ALWAYS A FAR MORE SENSIBLE SURVIVOR THAN THIS, CATWOMAN...
...AT LAST-- THE CUNNING LITTLE CAT IS TAMED!
TAMED...HAWK AND FOX AND CAT AND BAT, DOG AND ENDLESS, USELESS QUESTION...
...YOU WILL ALL SERVE...
...YOU WILL ALL SERVE ME.

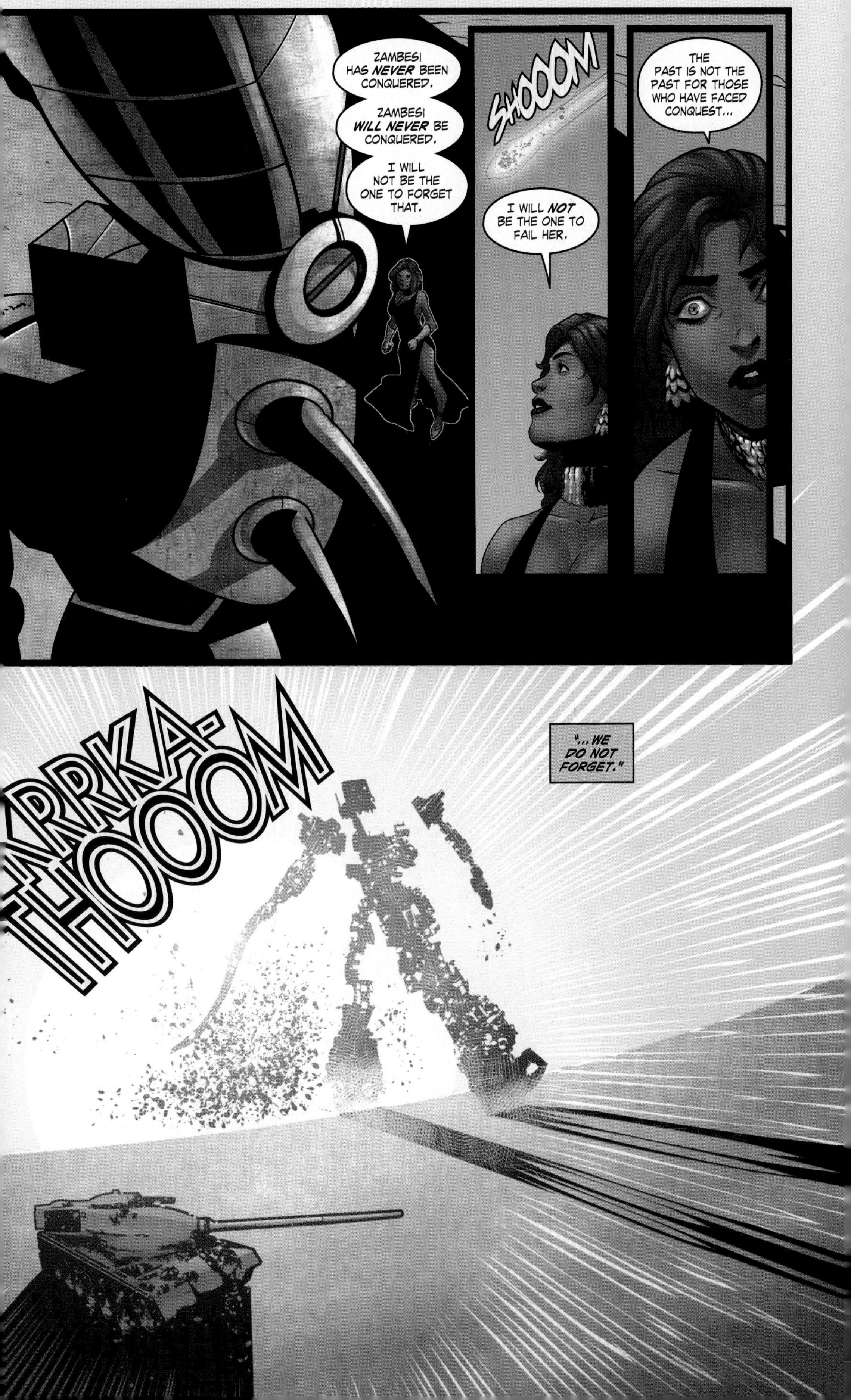
ZAMBESI HAS **NEVER** BEEN CONQUERED.
ZAMBESI **WILL NEVER** BE CONQUERED.
I WILL NOT BE THE ONE TO FORGET THAT.
SHOOOM
I WILL **NOT** BE THE ONE TO FAIL HER.
THE PAST IS NOT THE PAST FOR THOSE WHO HAVE FACED CONQUEST...
KRRKA-THOOOM
"...WE DO NOT FORGET."

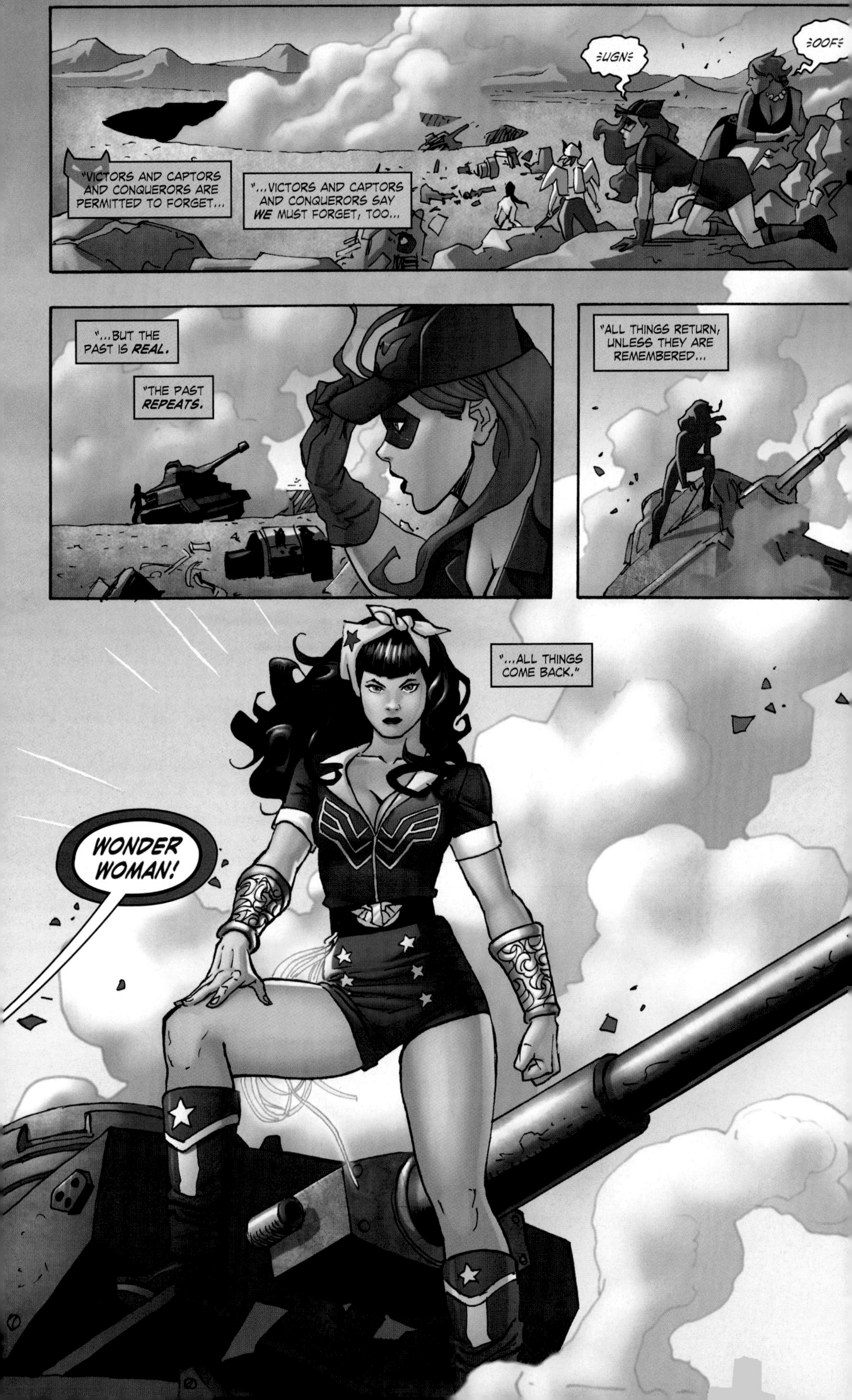
UGN
OOF
"VICTORS AND CAPTORS AND CONQUERORS ARE PERMITTED TO FORGET...
"...VICTORS AND CAPTORS AND CONQUERORS SAY WE MUST FORGET, TOO...
"...BUT THE PAST IS REAL.
"THE PAST REPEATS.
"ALL THINGS RETURN, UNLESS THEY ARE REMEMBERED...
"...ALL THINGS COME BACK."
WONDER WOMAN!

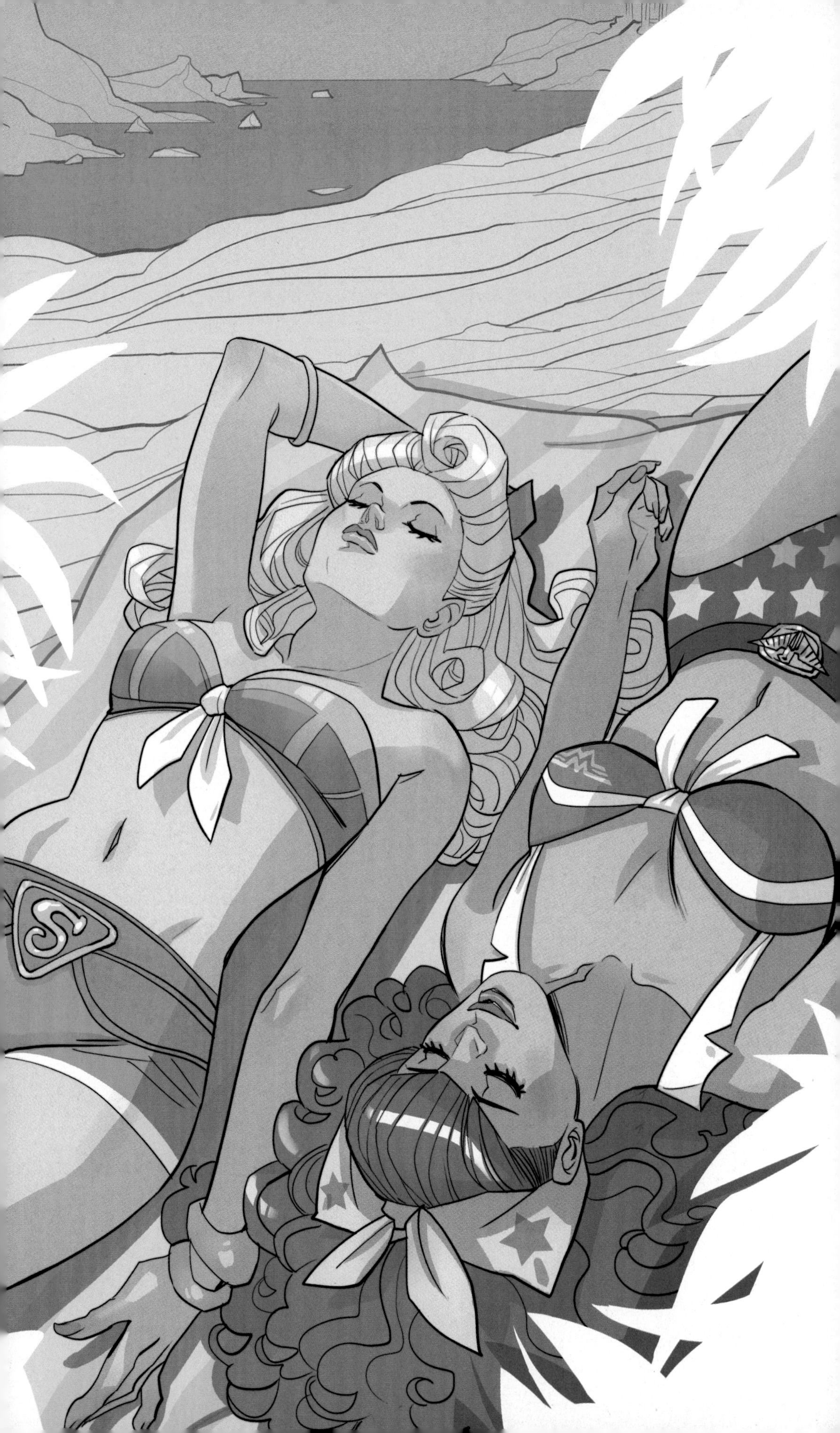

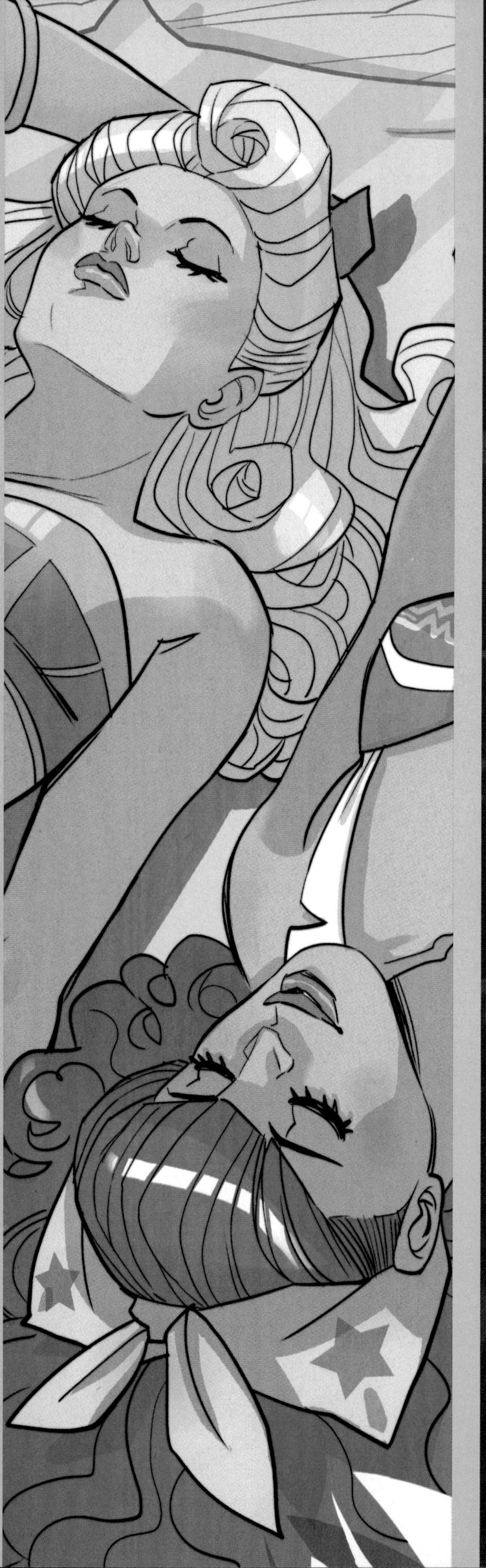

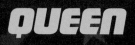

QUEEN

MARGUERITE BENNETT
Writer

MATÍAS BERGARA
LAURA BRAGA
MIRKA ANDOLFO
Artists

J. NANJAN
Colorist

Cover by
MARGUERITE SAUVAGE

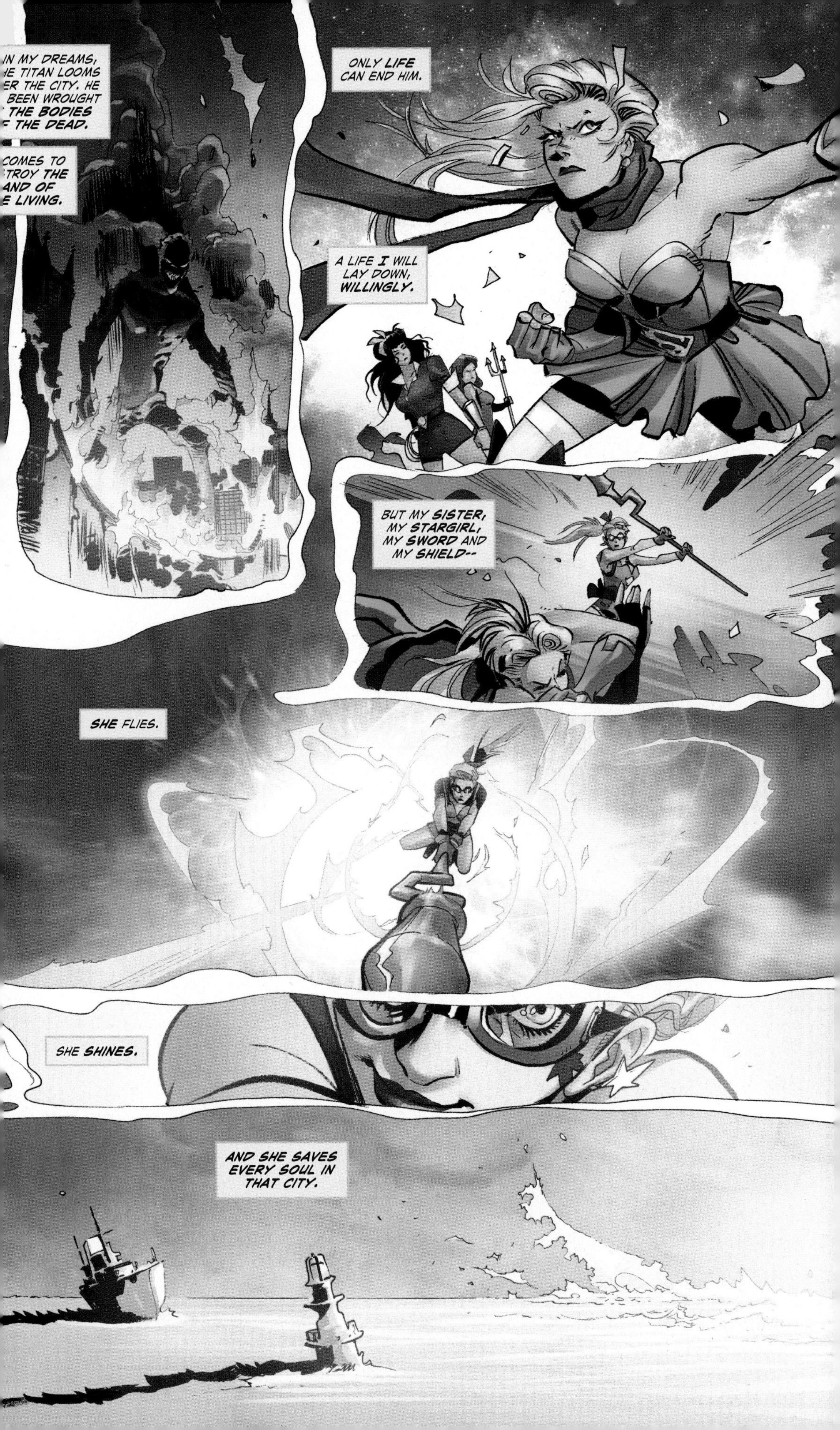
IN MY DREAMS, HE TITAN LOOMS ER THE CITY. HE BEEN WROUGHT THE BODIES F THE DEAD.
COMES TO TROY THE AND OF E LIVING.
ONLY LIFE CAN END HIM.
A LIFE I WILL LAY DOWN, WILLINGLY.
BUT MY SISTER, MY STARGIRL, MY SWORD AND MY SHIELD--
SHE FLIES.
SHE SHINES.
AND SHE SAVES EVERY SOUL IN THAT CITY.

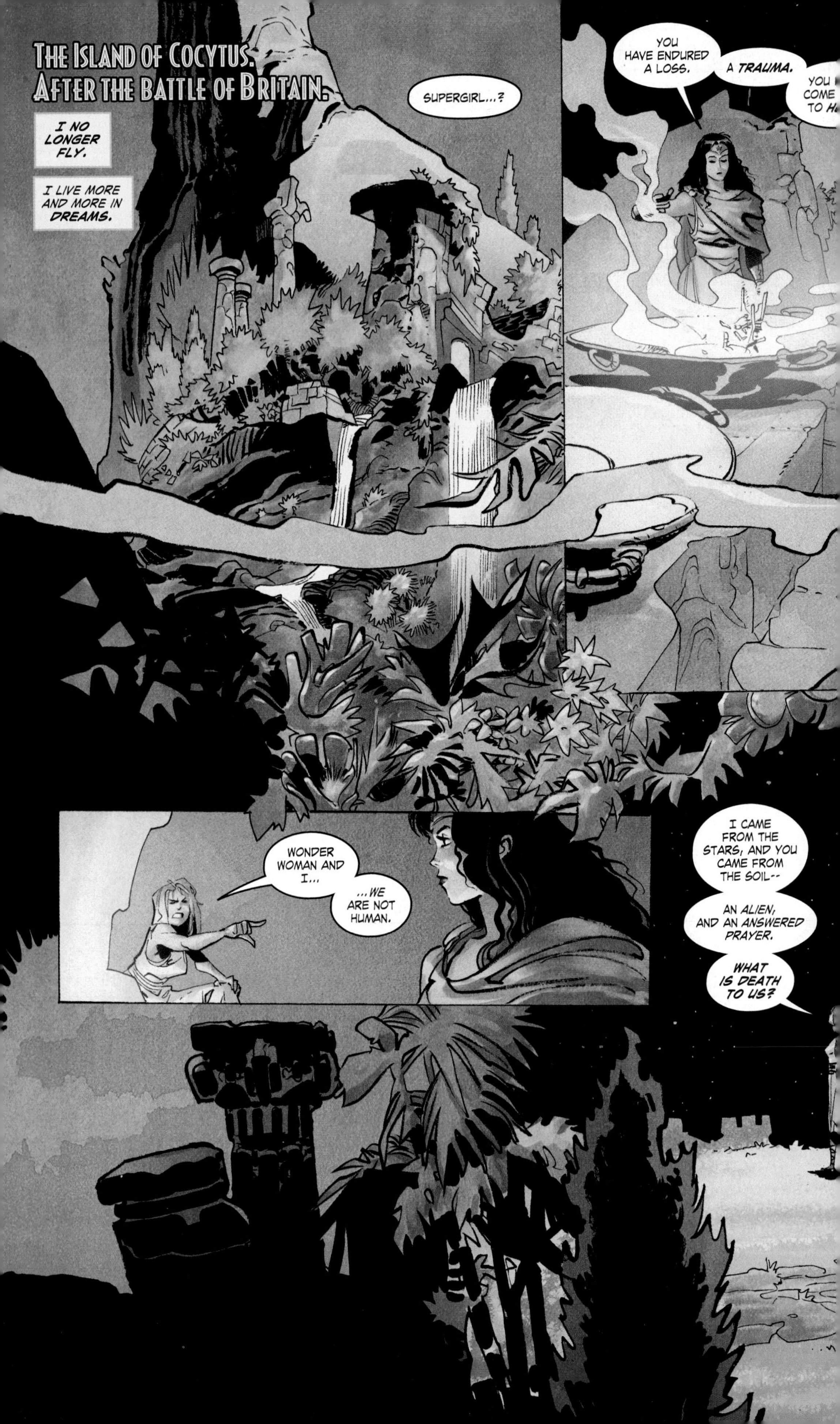
The Island of Cocytus.
After the battle of Britain.
I NO LONGER FLY.
I LIVE MORE AND MORE IN DREAMS.
SUPERGIRL...?
YOU HAVE ENDURED A LOSS.
A TRAUMA.
WONDER WOMAN AND I...
...WE ARE NOT HUMAN.
I CAME FROM THE STARS, AND YOU CAME FROM THE SOIL--
AN ALIEN, AND AN ANSWERED PRAYER.
WHAT IS DEATH TO US?

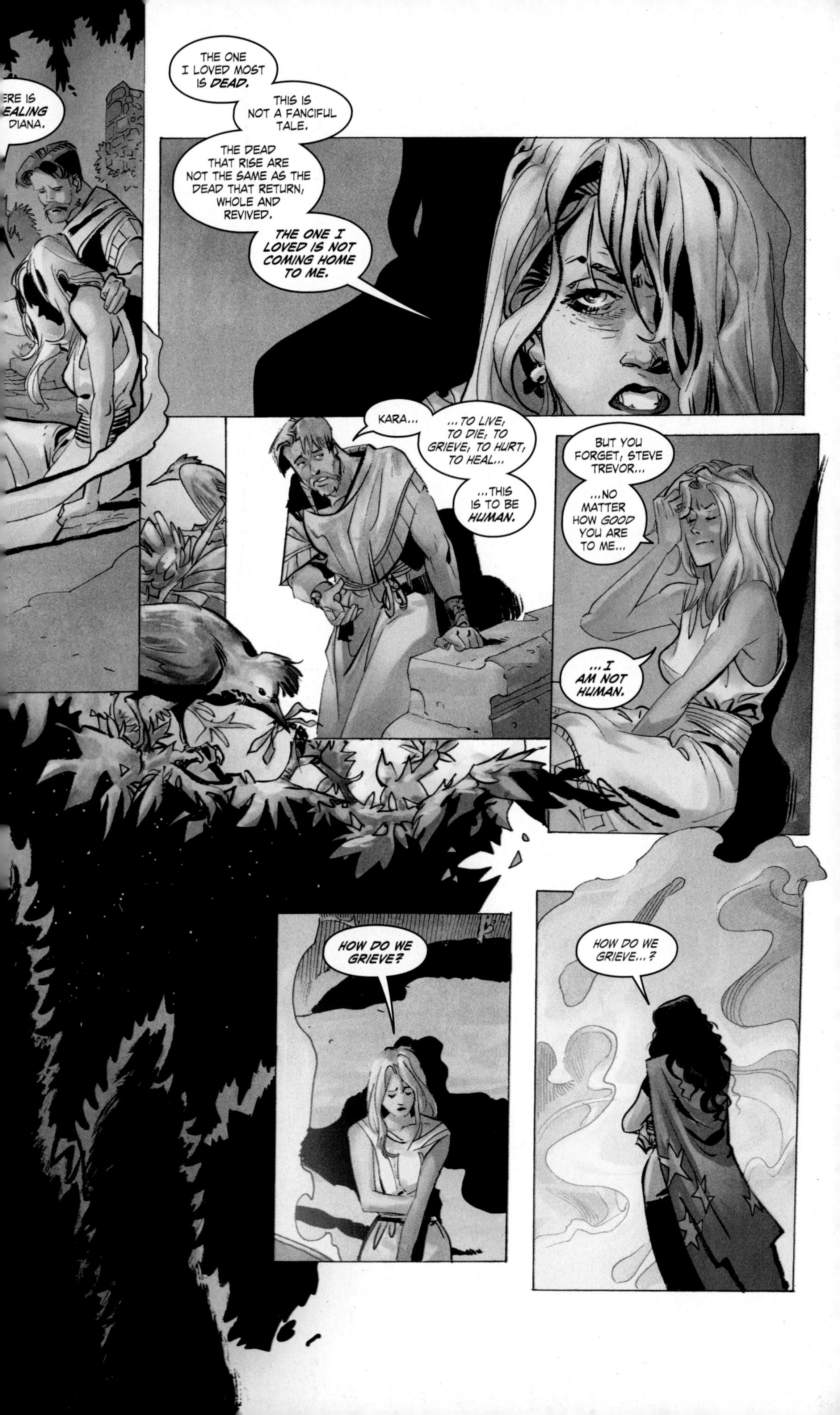

ERE IS EALING DIANA.
THE ONE I LOVED MOST IS DEAD.
THIS IS NOT A FANCIFUL TALE.
THE DEAD THAT RISE ARE NOT THE SAME AS THE DEAD THAT RETURN, WHOLE AND REVIVED.
THE ONE I LOVED IS NOT COMING HOME TO ME.
KARA...
...TO LIVE, TO DIE, TO GRIEVE, TO HURT, TO HEAL...
...THIS IS TO BE HUMAN.
BUT YOU FORGET, STEVE TREVOR...
...NO MATTER HOW GOOD YOU ARE TO ME...
...I AM NOT HUMAN.
HOW DO WE GRIEVE?
HOW DO WE GRIEVE...?

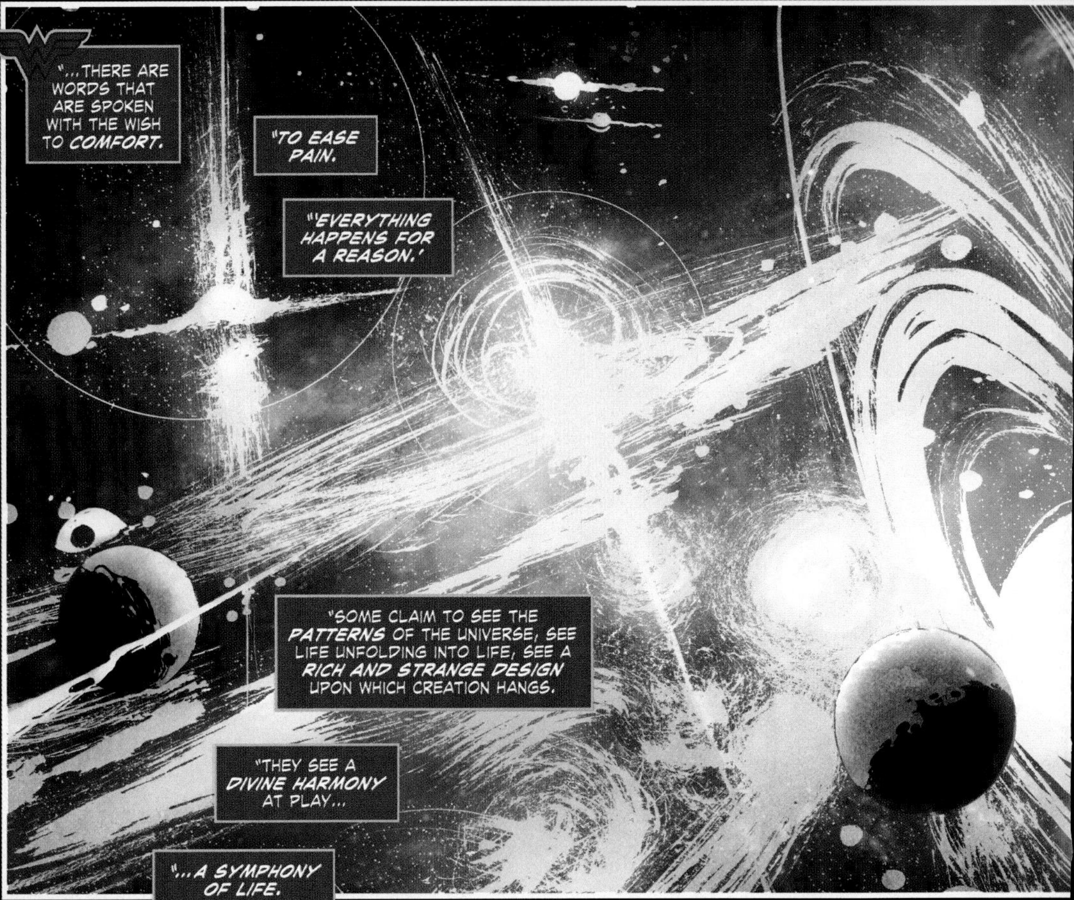
"...THERE ARE WORDS THAT ARE SPOKEN WITH THE WISH TO COMFORT.
"TO EASE PAIN.
"'EVERYTHING HAPPENS FOR A REASON.'
"SOME CLAIM TO SEE THE PATTERNS OF THE UNIVERSE, SEE LIFE UNFOLDING INTO LIFE, SEE A RICH AND STRANGE DESIGN UPON WHICH CREATION HANGS.
"THEY SEE A DIVINE HARMONY AT PLAY...
"...A SYMPHONY OF LIFE.

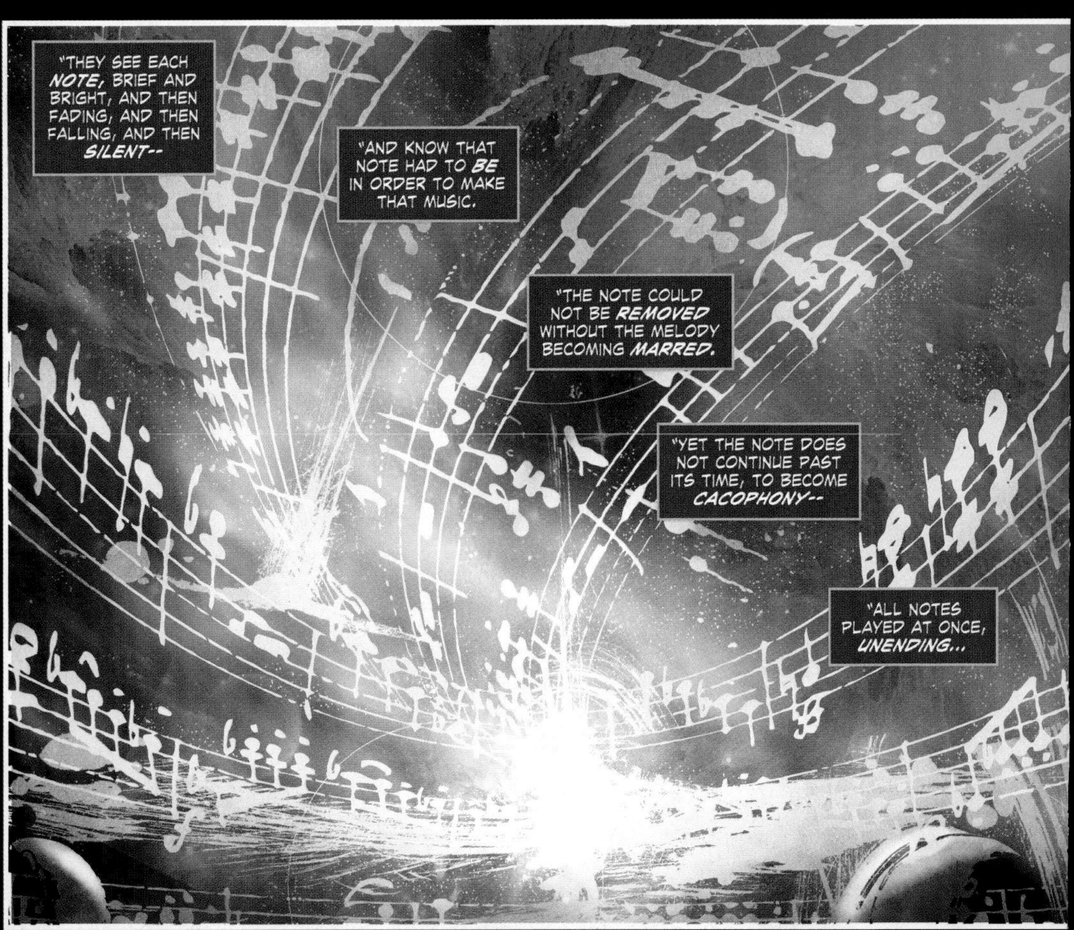
"THEY SEE EACH NOTE, BRIEF AND BRIGHT, AND THEN FADING, AND THEN FALLING, AND THEN SILENT--
"AND KNOW THAT NOTE HAD TO BE IN ORDER TO MAKE THAT MUSIC.
"THE NOTE COULD NOT BE REMOVED WITHOUT THE MELODY BECOMING MARRED.
"YET THE NOTE DOES NOT CONTINUE PAST ITS TIME, TO BECOME CACOPHONY--
"ALL NOTES PLAYED AT ONCE, UNENDING...

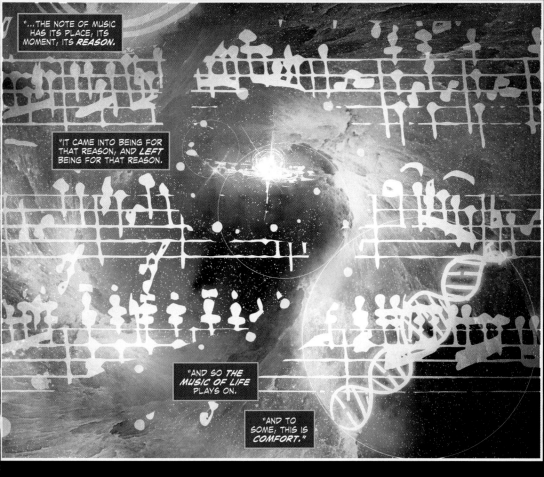

"...THE NOTE OF MUSIC HAS ITS PLACE, ITS MOMENT, ITS *REASON*.

"IT CAME INTO BEING FOR THAT REASON, AND *LEFT* BEING FOR THAT REASON.

"AND SO *THE MUSIC OF LIFE* PLAYS ON.

"AND TO SOME, THIS IS *COMFORT*."

BUT NOT TO YOU.

I DO NOT KNOW THE NATURE OF THE UNIVERSE.

I DO NOT *PRESUME* TO KNOW...

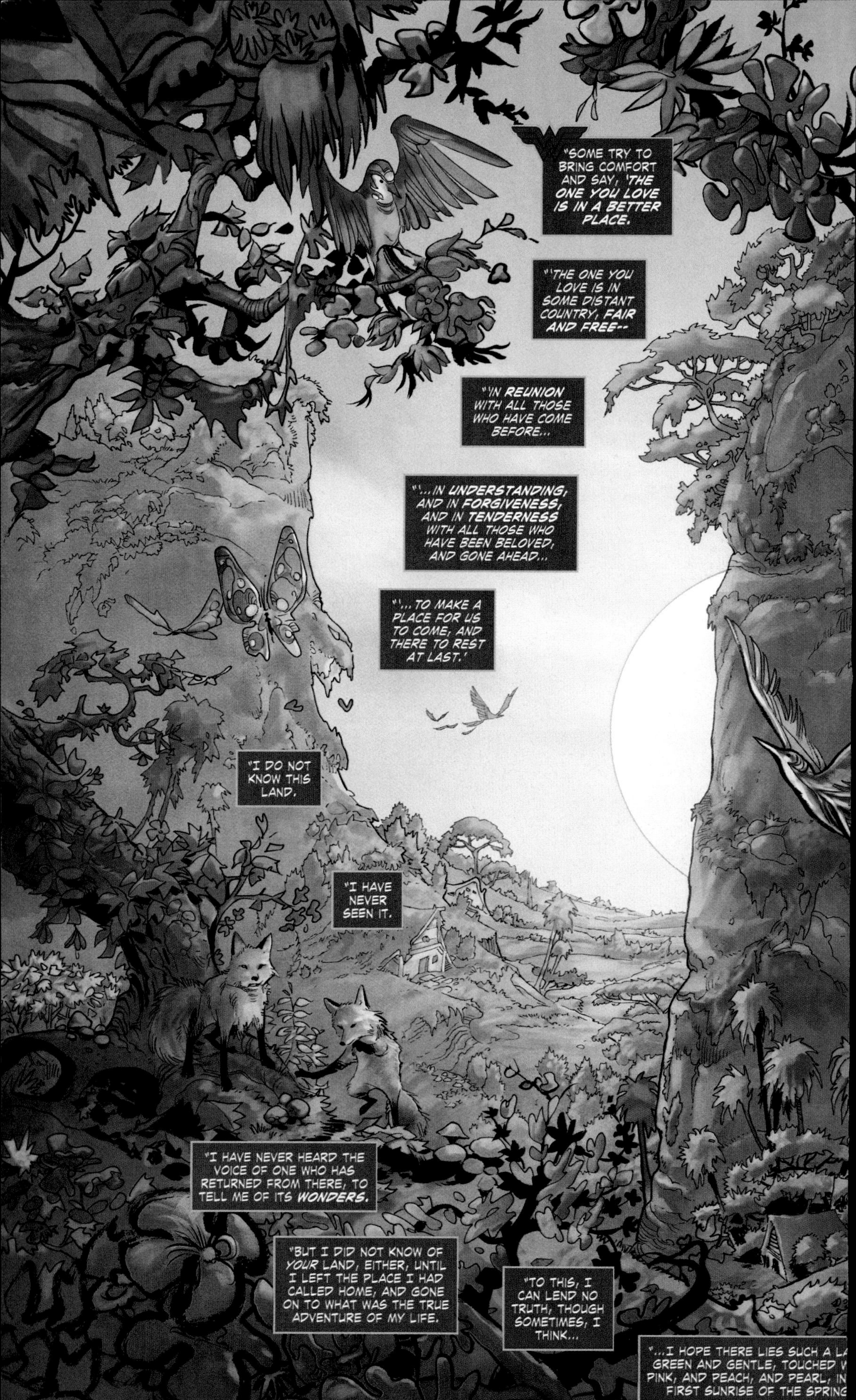
"SOME TRY TO BRING COMFORT AND SAY, 'THE ONE YOU LOVE IS IN A BETTER PLACE.
"'THE ONE YOU LOVE IS IN SOME DISTANT COUNTRY, FAIR AND FREE--
"'IN REUNION WITH ALL THOSE WHO HAVE COME BEFORE...
"'...IN UNDERSTANDING, AND IN FORGIVENESS, AND IN TENDERNESS WITH ALL THOSE WHO HAVE BEEN BELOVED, AND GONE AHEAD...
"'...TO MAKE A PLACE FOR US TO COME, AND THERE TO REST AT LAST.'
"I DO NOT KNOW THIS LAND.
"I HAVE NEVER SEEN IT.
"I HAVE NEVER HEARD THE VOICE OF ONE WHO HAS RETURNED FROM THERE, TO TELL ME OF ITS WONDERS.
"BUT I DID NOT KNOW OF YOUR LAND, EITHER, UNTIL I LEFT THE PLACE I HAD CALLED HOME, AND GONE ON TO WHAT WAS THE TRUE ADVENTURE OF MY LIFE.
"TO THIS, I CAN LEND NO TRUTH, THOUGH SOMETIMES, I THINK...
"...I HOPE THERE LIES SUCH A
GREEN AND GENTLE, TOUCHED
PINK, AND PEACH, AND PEARL,
FIRST SUNRISE OF THE

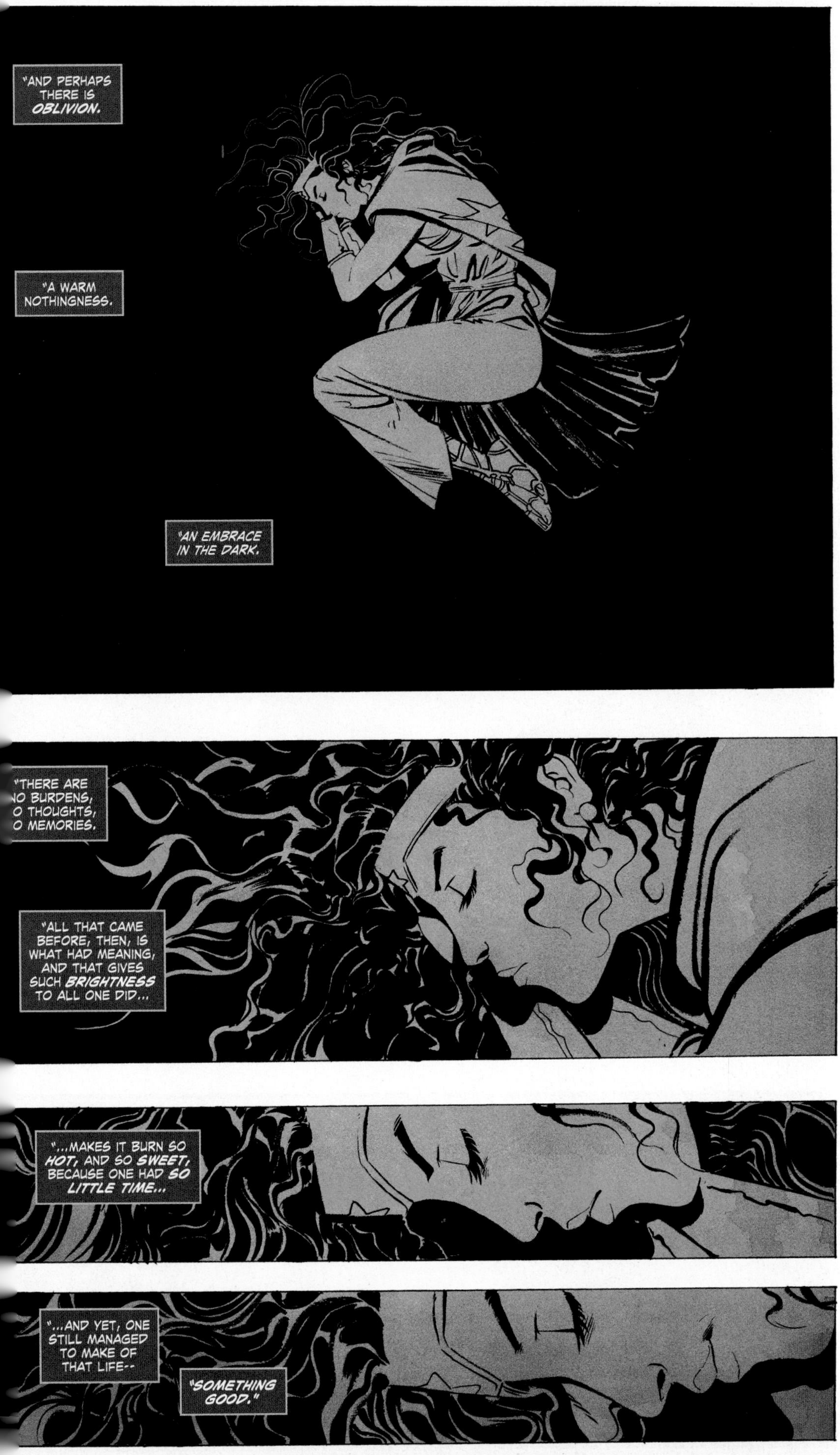
"AND PERHAPS THERE IS OBLIVION.
"A WARM NOTHINGNESS.
"AN EMBRACE IN THE DARK.
"THERE ARE NO BURDENS, O THOUGHTS, O MEMORIES.
"ALL THAT CAME BEFORE, THEN, IS WHAT HAD MEANING, AND THAT GIVES SUCH BRIGHTNESS TO ALL ONE DID...
"...MAKES IT BURN SO HOT, AND SO SWEET, BECAUSE ONE HAD SO LITTLE TIME...
"...AND YET, ONE STILL MANAGED TO MAKE OF THAT LIFE--
"SOMETHING GOOD."

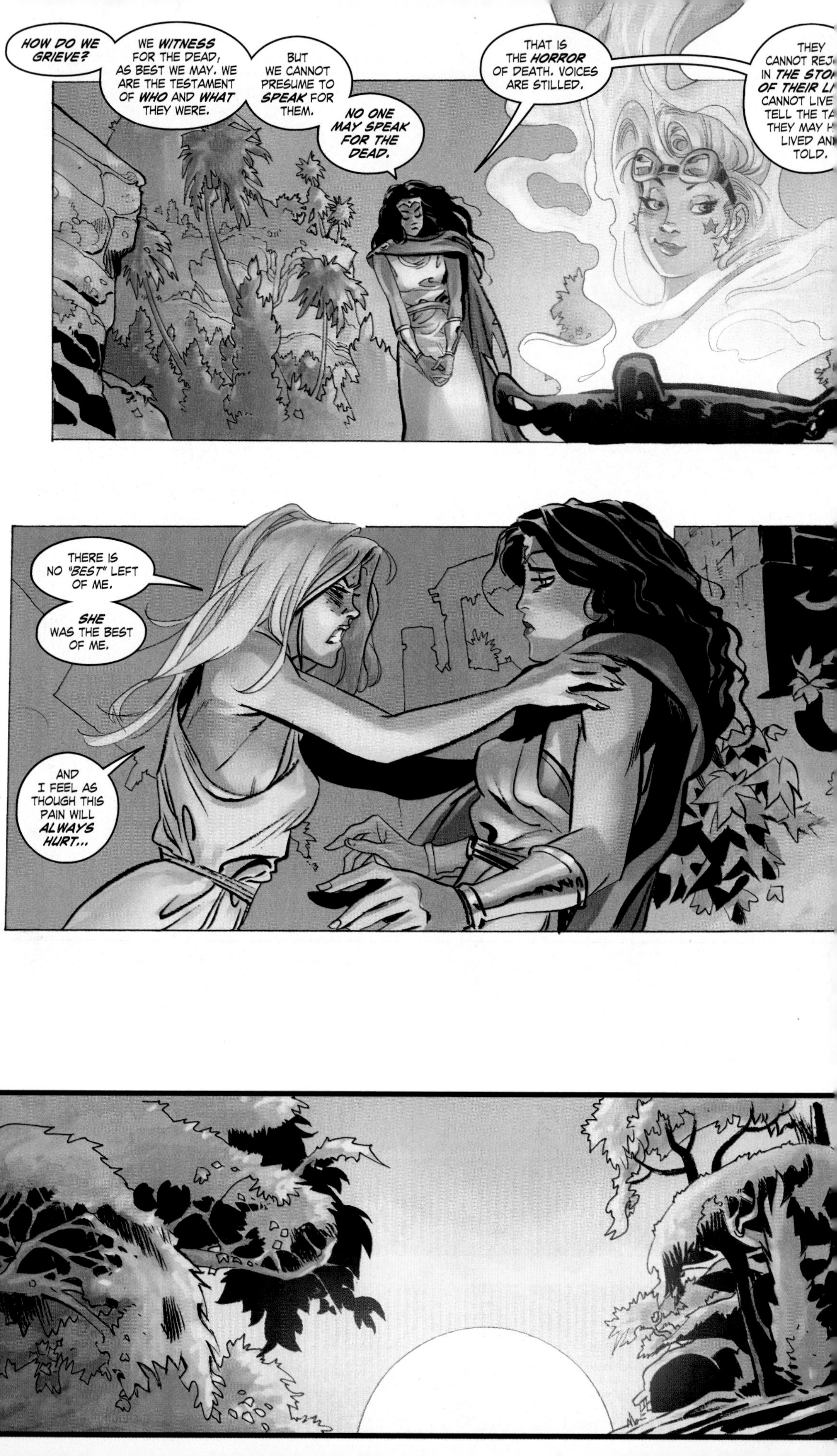

HOW DO WE GRIEVE?
WE WITNESS FOR THE DEAD, AS BEST WE MAY. WE ARE THE TESTAMENT OF WHO AND WHAT THEY WERE.
BUT WE CANNOT PRESUME TO SPEAK FOR THEM.
NO ONE MAY SPEAK FOR THE DEAD.
THAT IS THE HORROR OF DEATH. VOICES ARE STILLED.
THEY CANNOT REJ IN THE STO OF THEIR LI CANNOT LIVE TELL THE TA THEY MAY H LIVED AN TOLD.
THERE IS NO "BEST" LEFT OF ME.
SHE WAS THE BEST OF ME.
AND I FEEL AS THOUGH THIS PAIN WILL ALWAYS HURT...

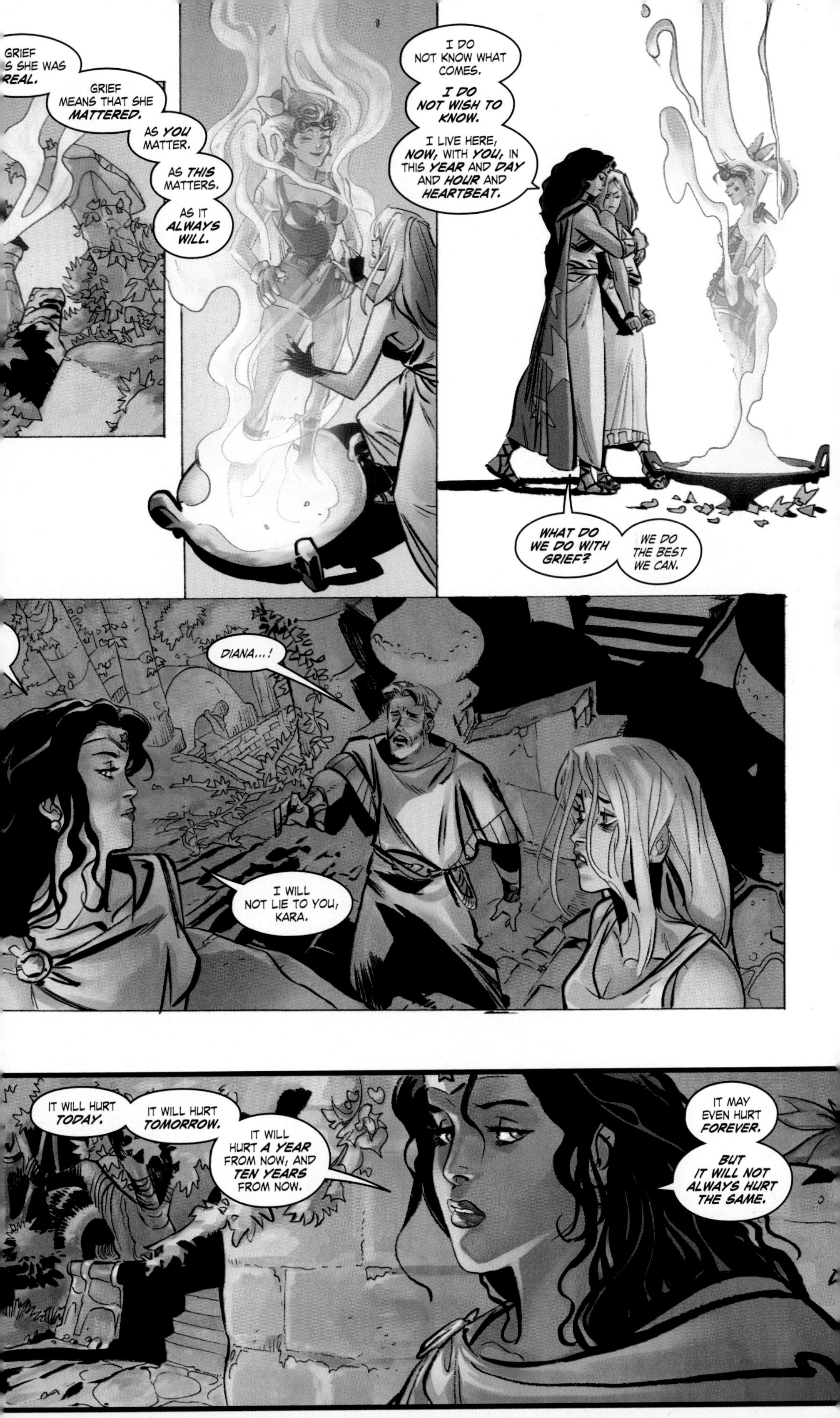
GRIEF
S SHE WAS
REAL.
GRIEF MEANS THAT SHE MATTERED.
AS YOU MATTER.
AS THIS MATTERS.
AS IT ALWAYS WILL.
I DO NOT KNOW WHAT COMES.
I DO NOT WISH TO KNOW.
I LIVE HERE, NOW, WITH YOU, IN THIS YEAR AND DAY AND HOUR AND HEARTBEAT.
WHAT DO WE DO WITH GRIEF?
WE DO THE BEST WE CAN.
DIANA...!
I WILL NOT LIE TO YOU, KARA.
IT WILL HURT TODAY.
IT WILL HURT TOMORROW.
IT WILL HURT A YEAR FROM NOW, AND TEN YEARS FROM NOW.
IT MAY EVEN HURT FOREVER.
BUT IT WILL NOT ALWAYS HURT THE SAME.

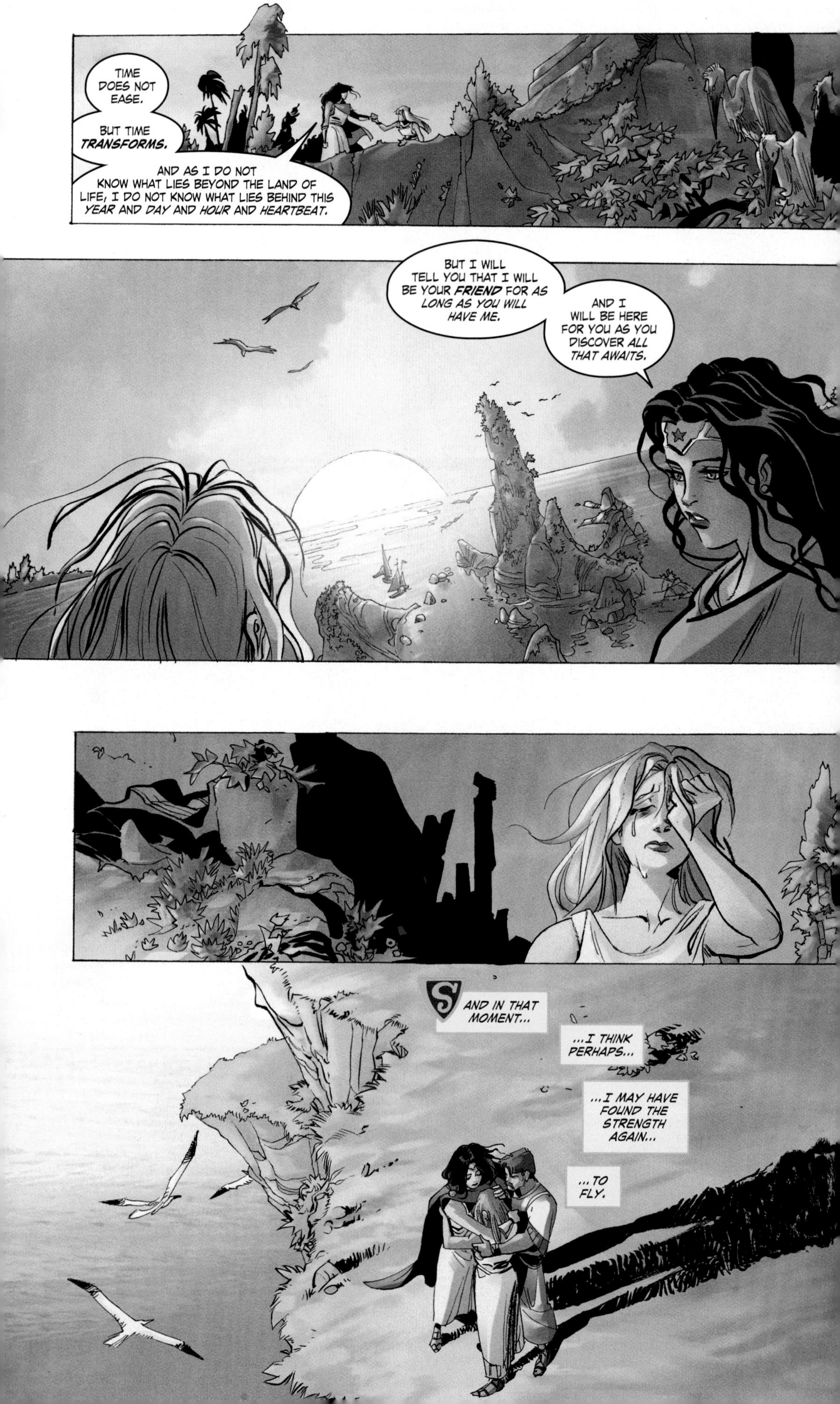
TIME DOES NOT EASE.
BUT TIME TRANSFORMS.
AND AS I DO NOT KNOW WHAT LIES BEYOND THE LAND OF LIFE, I DO NOT KNOW WHAT LIES BEHIND THIS YEAR AND DAY AND HOUR AND HEARTBEAT.
BUT I WILL TELL YOU THAT I WILL BE YOUR FRIEND FOR AS LONG AS YOU WILL HAVE ME.
AND I WILL BE HERE FOR YOU AS YOU DISCOVER ALL THAT AWAITS.
AND IN THAT MOMENT...
...I THINK PERHAPS...
...I MAY HAVE FOUND THE STRENGTH AGAIN...
...TO FLY.

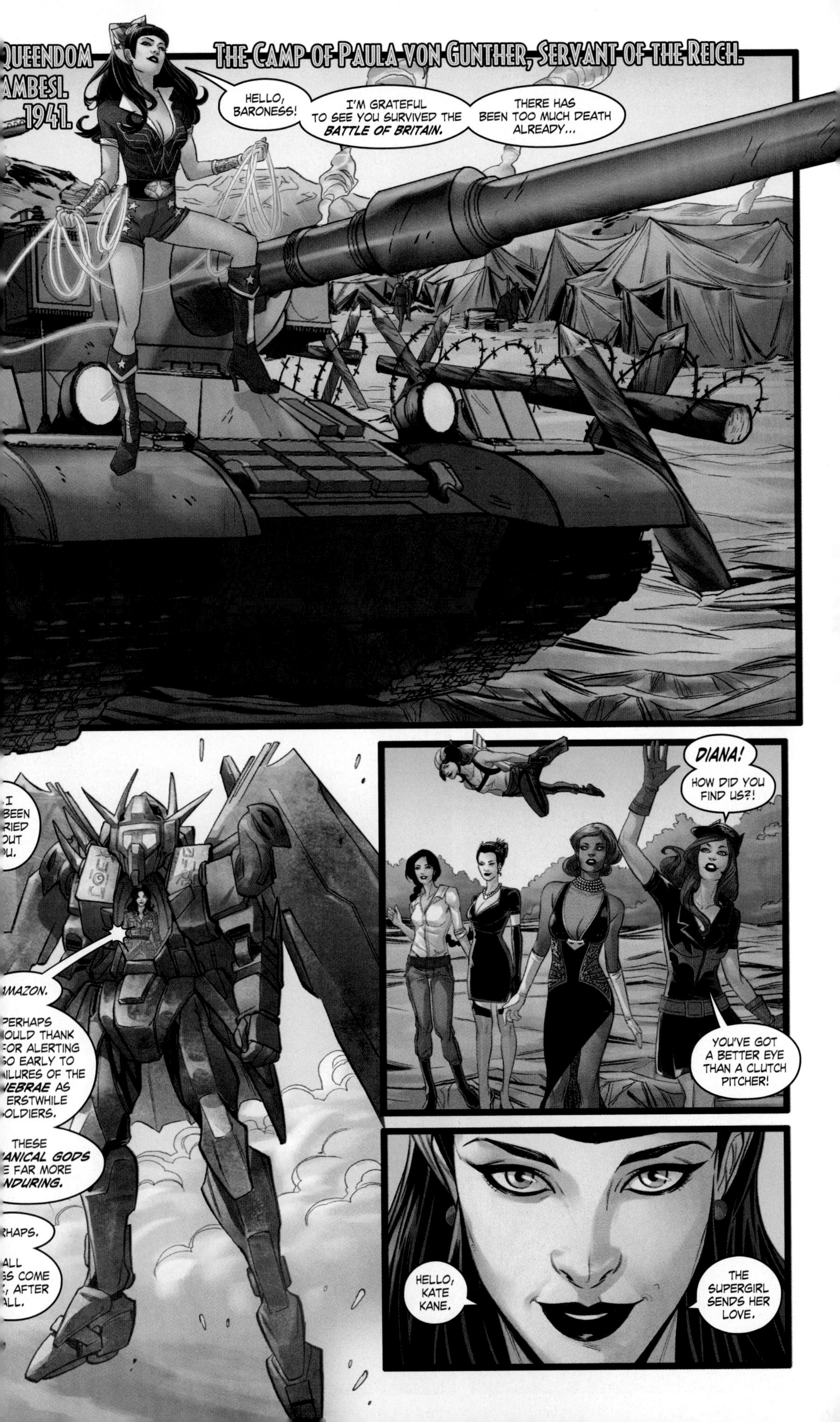

QUEENDOM
AMBESI.
1941.
THE CAMP OF PAULA VON GUNTHER, SERVANT OF THE REICH.
HELLO, BARONESS!
I'M GRATEFUL TO SEE YOU SURVIVED THE BATTLE OF BRITAIN.
THERE HAS BEEN TOO MUCH DEATH ALREADY...
AMAZON.
PERHAPS
OULD THANK
FOR ALERTING
SO EARLY TO
AILURES OF THE
NEBRAE AS
ERSTWHILE
OLDIERS.
THESE
ANICAL GODS
E FAR MORE
NDURING.
RHAPS.
ALL
GS COME
, AFTER
ALL.
DIANA!
HOW DID YOU FIND US?!
YOU'VE GOT A BETTER EYE THAN A CLUTCH PITCHER!
HELLO, KATE KANE.
THE SUPERGIRL SENDS HER LOVE.

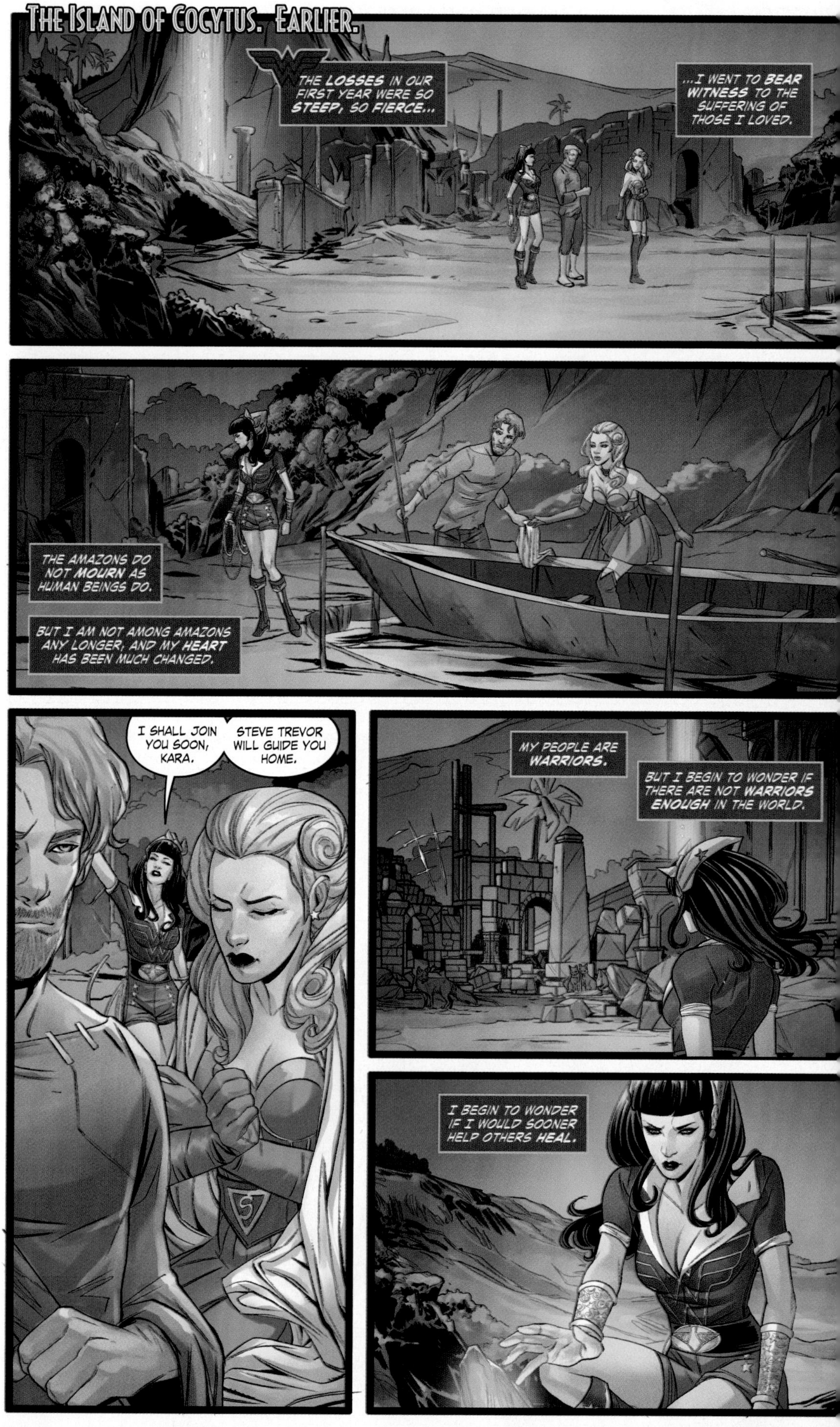

THE ISLAND OF COCYTUS. EARLIER.
THE LOSSES IN OUR FIRST YEAR WERE SO STEEP, SO FIERCE...
...I WENT TO BEAR WITNESS TO THE SUFFERING OF THOSE I LOVED.
THE AMAZONS DO NOT MOURN AS HUMAN BEINGS DO.
BUT I AM NOT AMONG AMAZONS ANY LONGER, AND MY HEART HAS BEEN MUCH CHANGED.
I SHALL JOIN YOU SOON, KARA.
STEVE TREVOR WILL GUIDE YOU HOME.
MY PEOPLE ARE WARRIORS.
BUT I BEGIN TO WONDER IF THERE ARE NOT WARRIORS ENOUGH IN THE WORLD.
I BEGIN TO WONDER IF I WOULD SOONER HELP OTHERS HEAL.

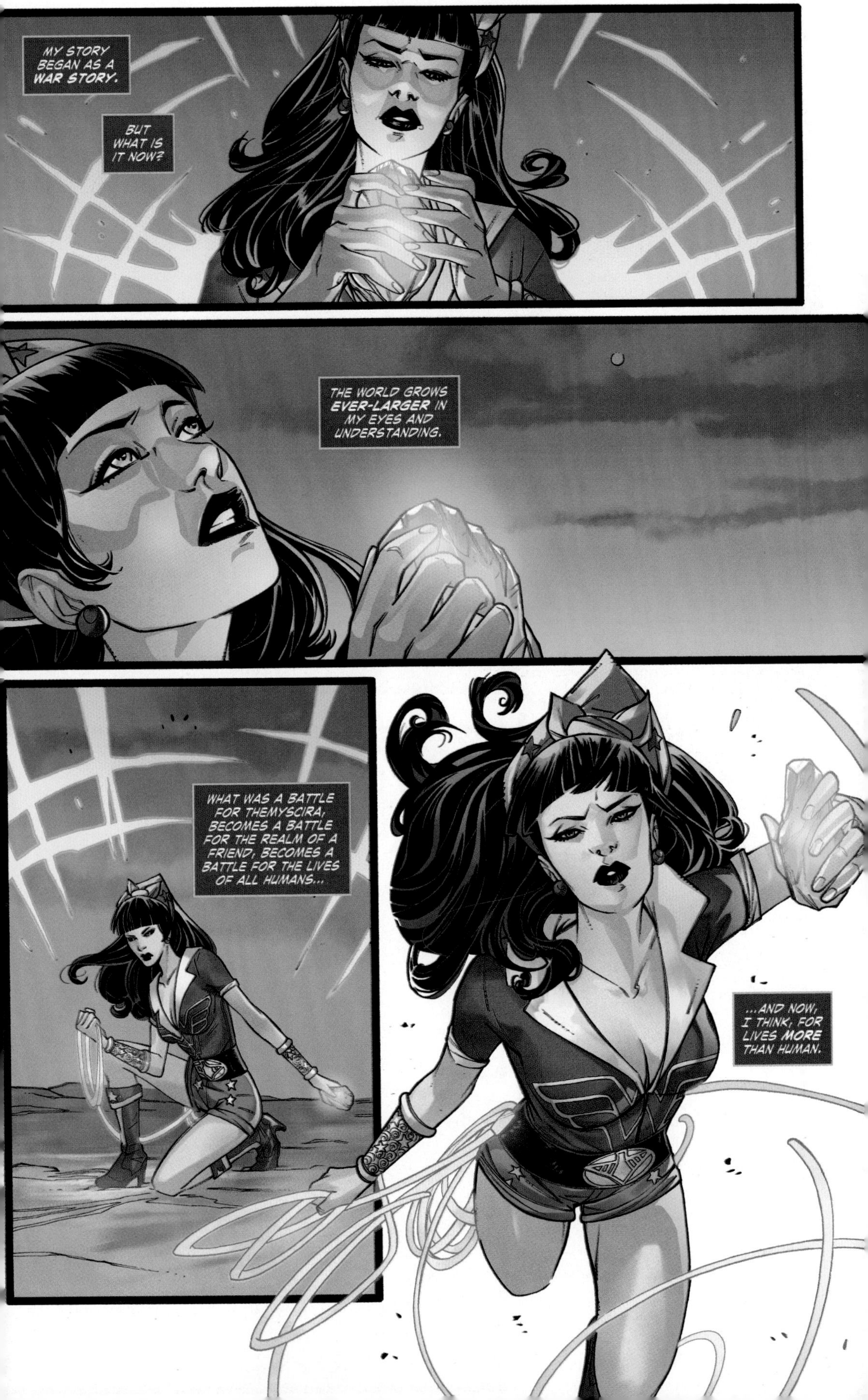
MY STORY BEGAN AS A WAR STORY.
BUT WHAT IS IT NOW?
THE WORLD GROWS EVER-LARGER IN MY EYES AND UNDERSTANDING.
WHAT WAS A BATTLE FOR THEMYSCIRA, BECOMES A BATTLE FOR THE REALM OF A FRIEND, BECOMES A BATTLE FOR THE LIVES OF ALL HUMANS...
...AND NOW, I THINK, FOR LIVES MORE THAN HUMAN.

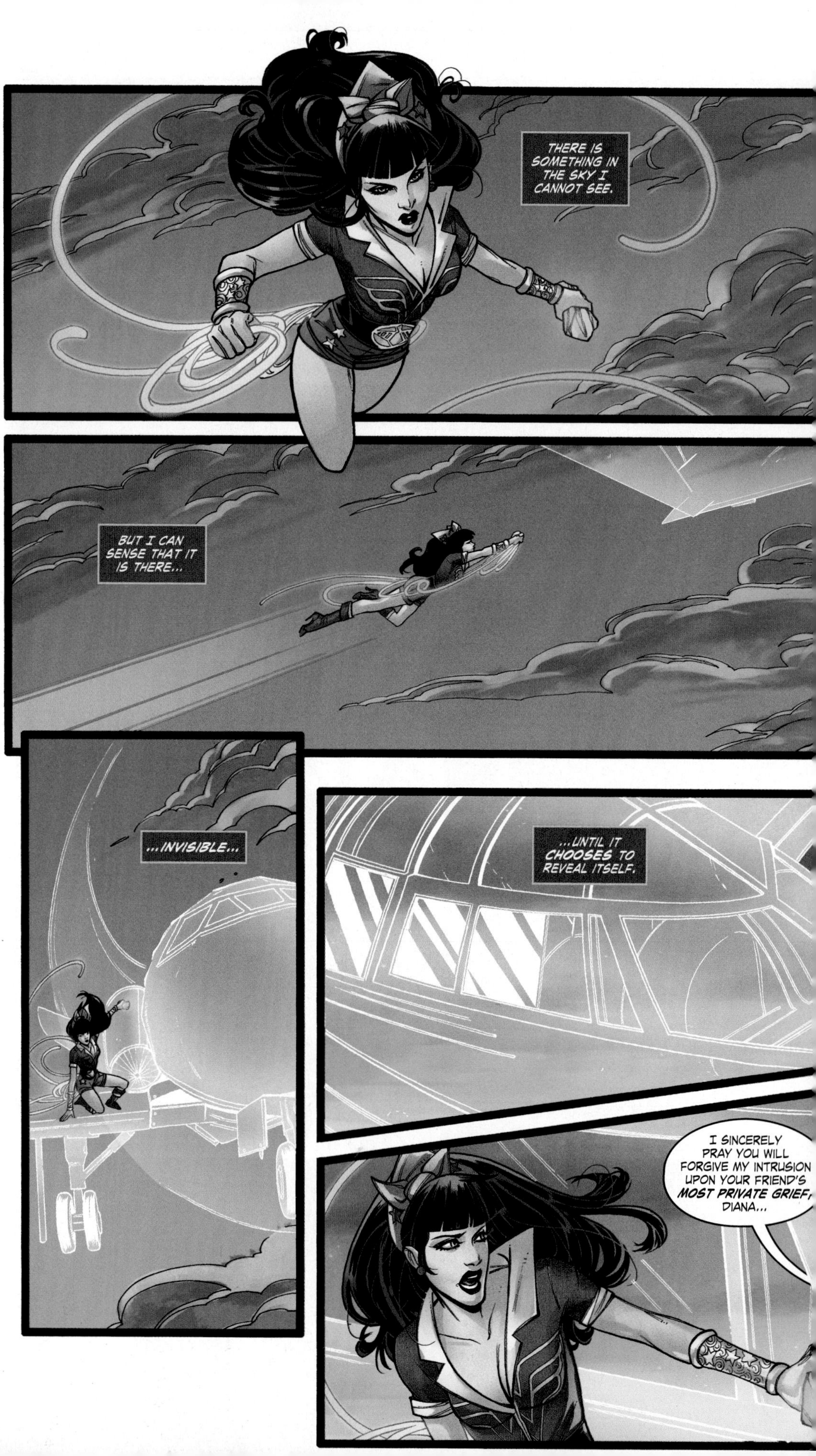
THERE IS SOMETHING IN THE SKY I CANNOT SEE.
BUT I CAN SENSE THAT IT IS THERE...
...INVISIBLE...
...UNTIL IT CHOOSES TO REVEAL ITSELF.
I SINCERELY PRAY YOU WILL FORGIVE MY INTRUSION UPON YOUR FRIEND'S MOST PRIVATE GRIEF, DIANA...

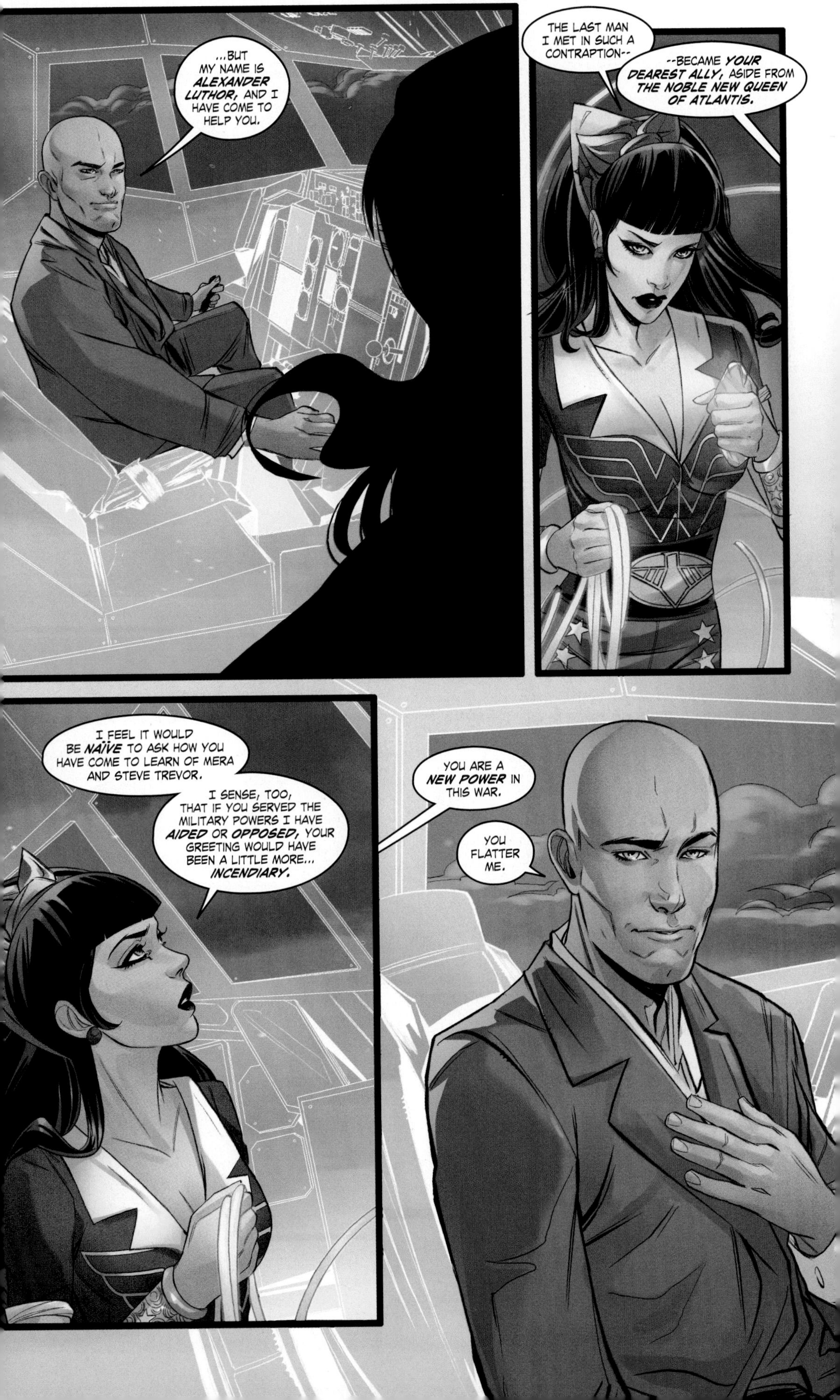
...BUT MY NAME IS ALEXANDER LUTHOR, AND I HAVE COME TO HELP YOU.
THE LAST MAN I MET IN SUCH A CONTRAPTION--
--BECAME YOUR DEAREST ALLY, ASIDE FROM THE NOBLE NEW QUEEN OF ATLANTIS.
I FEEL IT WOULD BE NAÏVE TO ASK HOW YOU HAVE COME TO LEARN OF MERA AND STEVE TREVOR.
I SENSE, TOO, THAT IF YOU SERVED THE MILITARY POWERS I HAVE AIDED OR OPPOSED, YOUR GREETING WOULD HAVE BEEN A LITTLE MORE... INCENDIARY.
YOU ARE A NEW POWER IN THIS WAR.
YOU FLATTER ME.

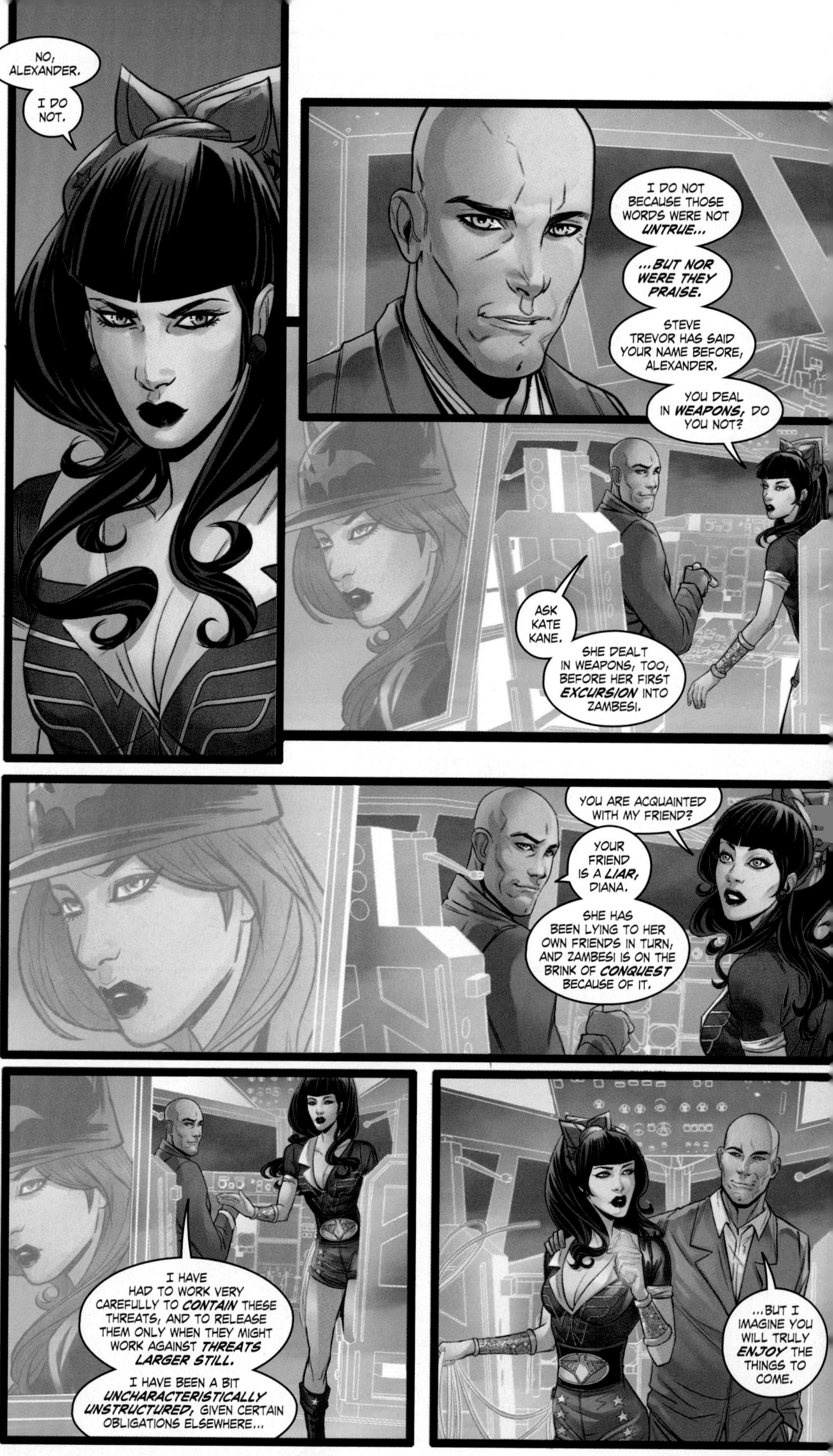
NO, ALEXANDER.
I DO NOT.
I DO NOT BECAUSE THOSE WORDS WERE NOT UNTRUE...
...BUT NOR WERE THEY PRAISE.
STEVE TREVOR HAS SAID YOUR NAME BEFORE, ALEXANDER.
YOU DEAL IN WEAPONS, DO YOU NOT?
ASK KATE KANE.
SHE DEALT IN WEAPONS, TOO, BEFORE HER FIRST EXCURSION INTO ZAMBESI.
YOU ARE ACQUAINTED WITH MY FRIEND?
YOUR FRIEND IS A LIAR, DIANA.
SHE HAS BEEN LYING TO HER OWN FRIENDS IN TURN, AND ZAMBESI IS ON THE BRINK OF CONQUEST BECAUSE OF IT.
I HAVE HAD TO WORK VERY CAREFULLY TO CONTAIN THESE THREATS, AND TO RELEASE THEM ONLY WHEN THEY MIGHT WORK AGAINST THREATS LARGER STILL.
I HAVE BEEN A BIT UNCHARACTERISTICALLY UNSTRUCTURED, GIVEN CERTAIN OBLIGATIONS ELSEWHERE...
...BUT I IMAGINE YOU WILL TRULY ENJOY THE THINGS TO COME.

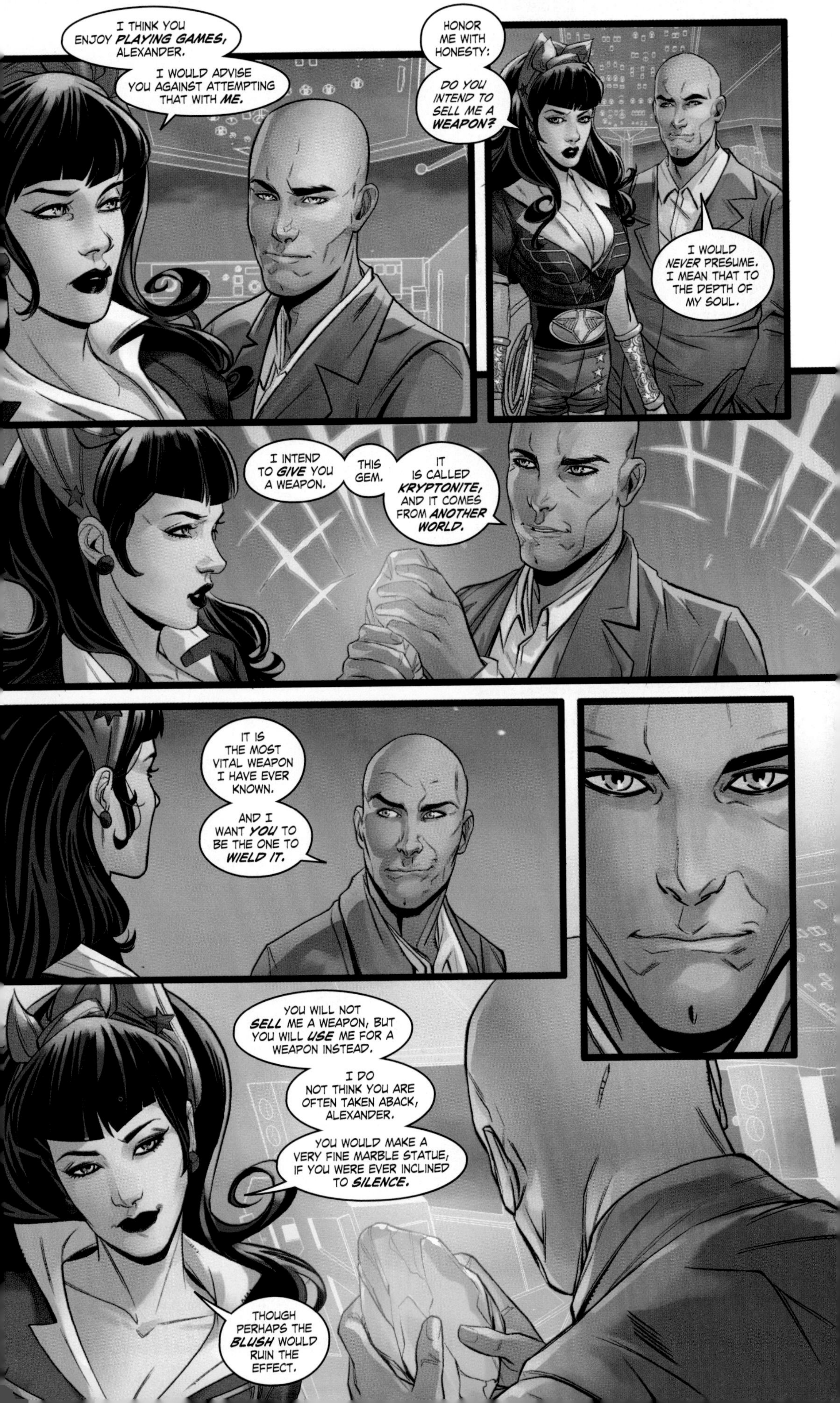
I THINK YOU ENJOY PLAYING GAMES, ALEXANDER.
I WOULD ADVISE YOU AGAINST ATTEMPTING THAT WITH ME.
HONOR ME WITH HONESTY:
DO YOU INTEND TO SELL ME A WEAPON?
I WOULD NEVER PRESUME. I MEAN THAT TO THE DEPTH OF MY SOUL.
I INTEND TO GIVE YOU A WEAPON.
THIS GEM.
IT IS CALLED KRYPTONITE, AND IT COMES FROM ANOTHER WORLD.
IT IS THE MOST VITAL WEAPON I HAVE EVER KNOWN.
AND I WANT YOU TO BE THE ONE TO WIELD IT.
YOU WILL NOT SELL ME A WEAPON, BUT YOU WILL USE ME FOR A WEAPON INSTEAD.
I DO NOT THINK YOU ARE OFTEN TAKEN ABACK, ALEXANDER.
YOU WOULD MAKE A VERY FINE MARBLE STATUE, IF YOU WERE EVER INCLINED TO SILENCE.
THOUGH PERHAPS THE BLUSH WOULD RUIN THE EFFECT.

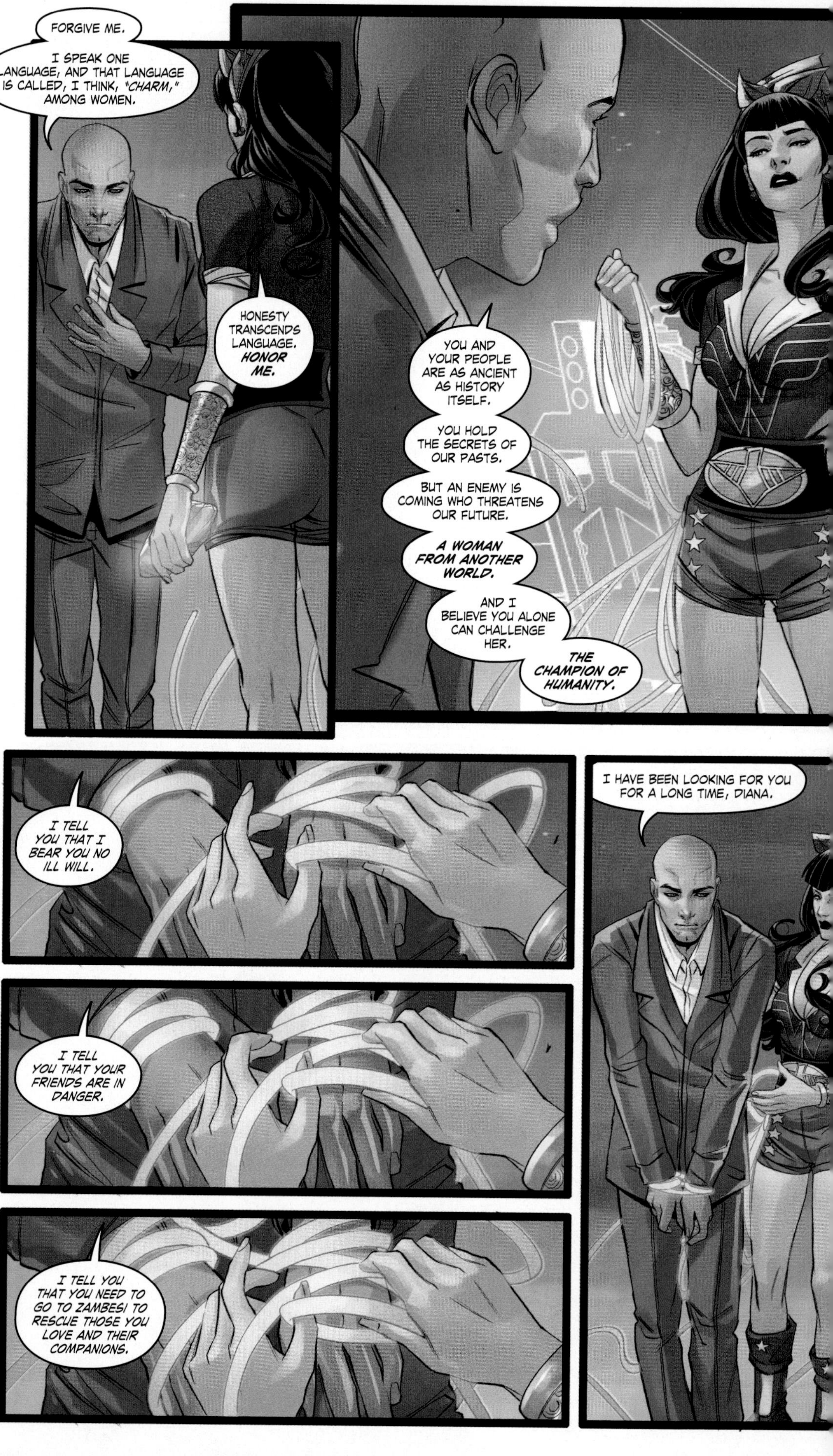
FORGIVE ME.
I SPEAK ONE LANGUAGE, AND THAT LANGUAGE IS CALLED, I THINK, "CHARM," AMONG WOMEN.
HONESTY TRANSCENDS LANGUAGE. HONOR ME.
YOU AND YOUR PEOPLE ARE AS ANCIENT AS HISTORY ITSELF.
YOU HOLD THE SECRETS OF OUR PASTS.
BUT AN ENEMY IS COMING WHO THREATENS OUR FUTURE.
A WOMAN FROM ANOTHER WORLD.
AND I BELIEVE YOU ALONE CAN CHALLENGE HER.
THE CHAMPION OF HUMANITY.
I TELL YOU THAT I BEAR YOU NO ILL WILL.
I TELL YOU THAT YOUR FRIENDS ARE IN DANGER.
I TELL YOU THAT YOU NEED TO GO TO ZAMBESI TO RESCUE THOSE YOU LOVE AND THEIR COMPANIONS.
I HAVE BEEN LOOKING FOR YOU FOR A LONG TIME, DIANA.

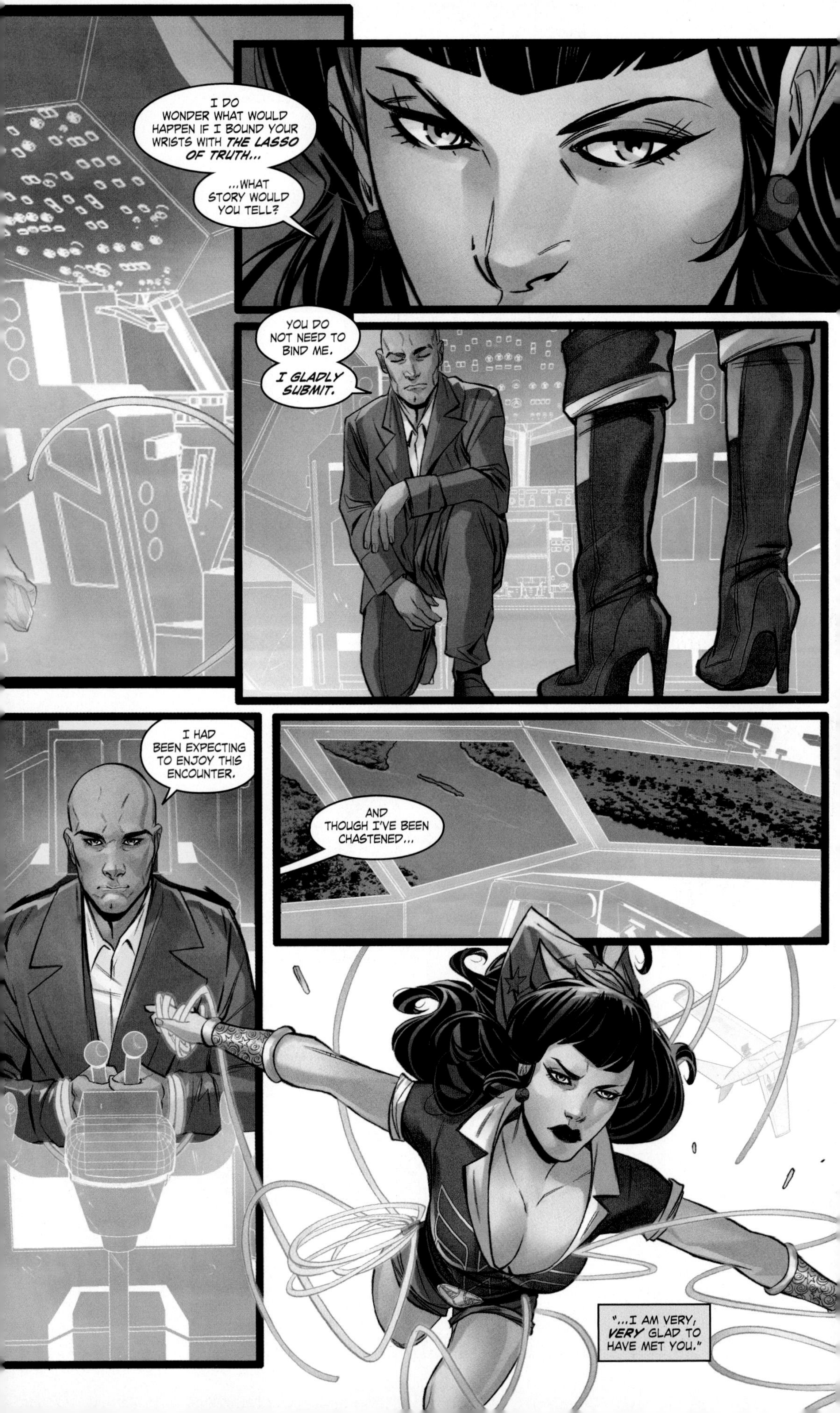

I DO WONDER WHAT WOULD HAPPEN IF I BOUND YOUR WRISTS WITH ***THE LASSO OF TRUTH...***
...WHAT STORY WOULD YOU TELL?
YOU DO NOT NEED TO BIND ME.
I GLADLY SUBMIT.
I HAD BEEN EXPECTING TO ENJOY THIS ENCOUNTER.
AND THOUGH I'VE BEEN CHASTENED...
"...I AM VERY, ***VERY*** GLAD TO HAVE MET YOU."

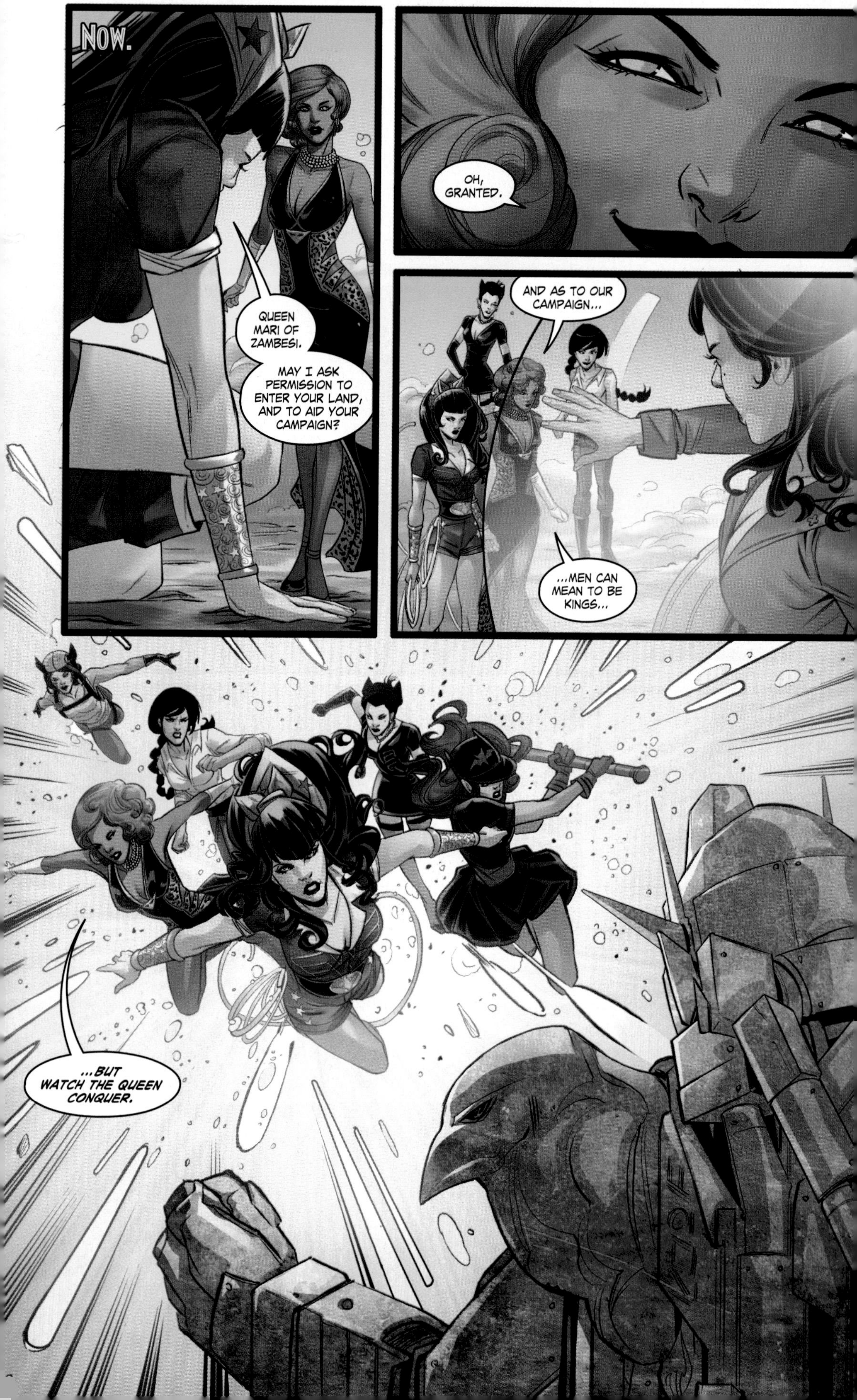
NOW.
QUEEN MARI OF ZAMBESI.
MAY I ASK PERMISSION TO ENTER YOUR LAND, AND TO AID YOUR CAMPAIGN?
OH, GRANTED.
AND AS TO OUR CAMPAIGN...
...MEN CAN MEAN TO BE KINGS...
...BUT WATCH THE QUEEN CONQUER.

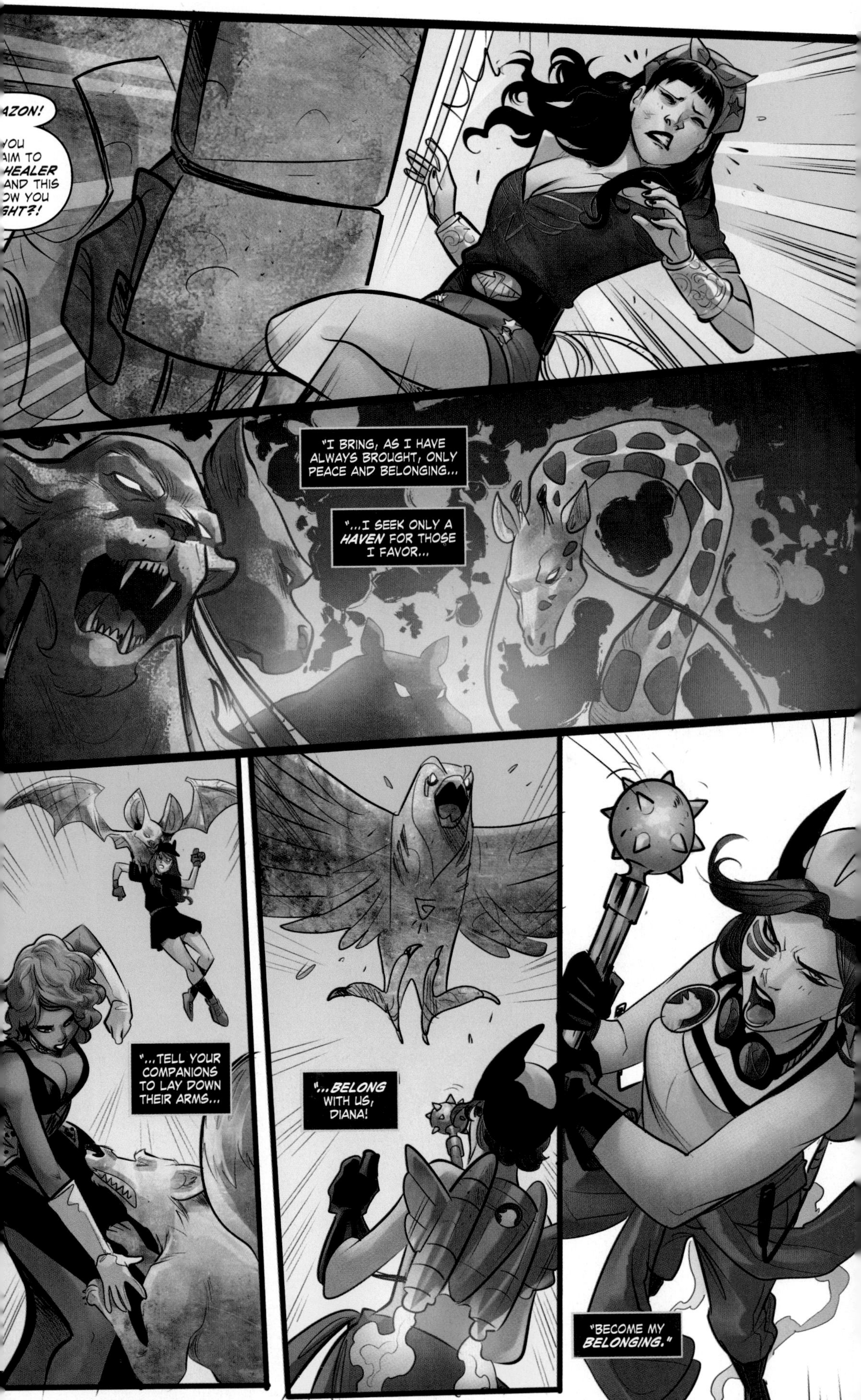

AZON!
YOU
AIM TO
HEALER
AND THIS
OW YOU
GHT?!
"I BRING, AS I HAVE ALWAYS BROUGHT, ONLY PEACE AND BELONGING...
"...I SEEK ONLY A HAVEN FOR THOSE I FAVOR...
"...TELL YOUR COMPANIONS TO LAY DOWN THEIR ARMS...
"...BELONG WITH US, DIANA!
"BECOME MY BELONGING."

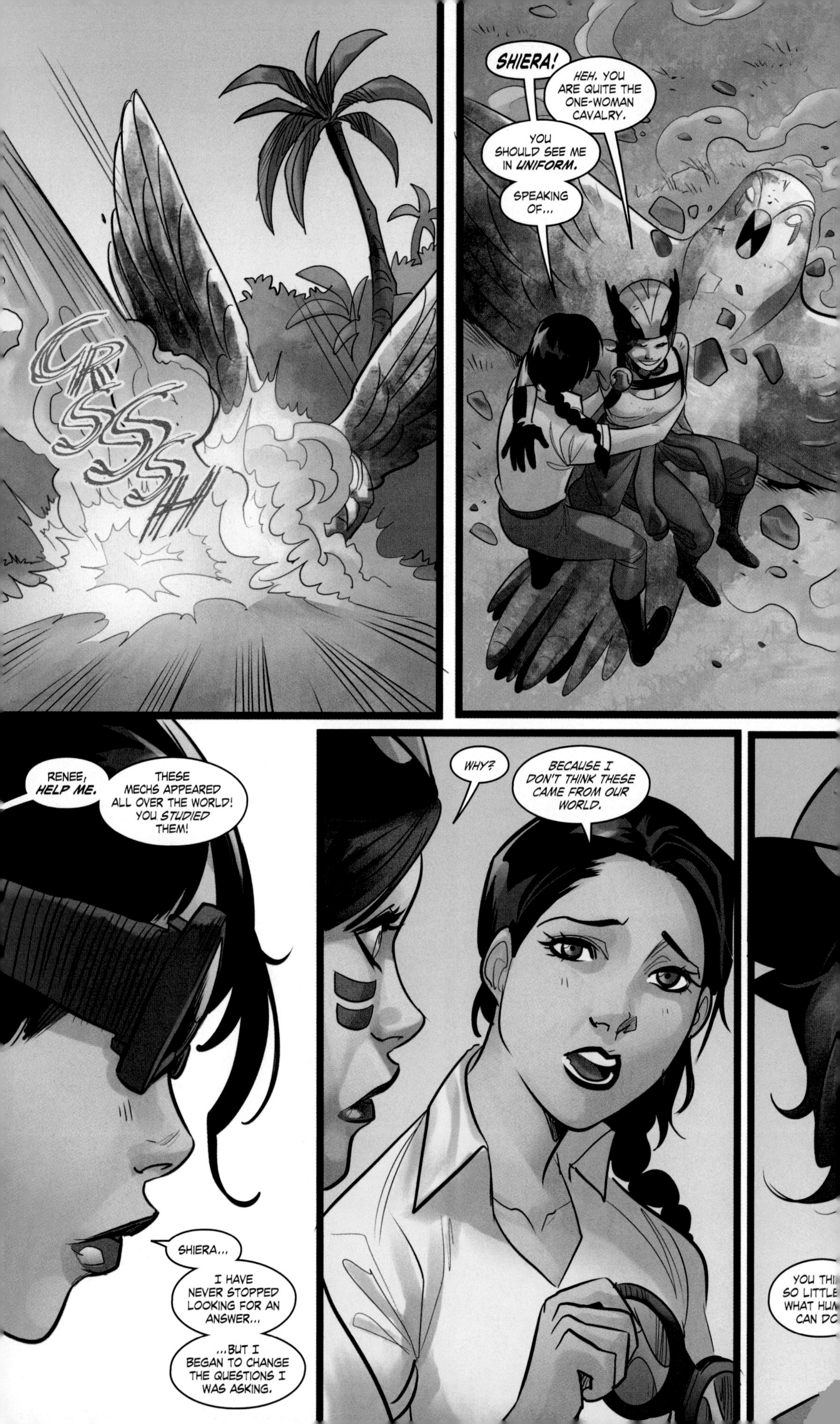
GRSSSSH
SHIERA!
HEH. YOU ARE QUITE THE ONE-WOMAN CAVALRY.
YOU SHOULD SEE ME IN UNIFORM.
SPEAKING OF...
RENEE, HELP ME.
THESE MECHS APPEARED ALL OVER THE WORLD! YOU STUDIED THEM!
SHIERA...
I HAVE NEVER STOPPED LOOKING FOR AN ANSWER...
...BUT I BEGAN TO CHANGE THE QUESTIONS I WAS ASKING.
WHY?
BECAUSE I DON'T THINK THESE CAME FROM OUR WORLD.

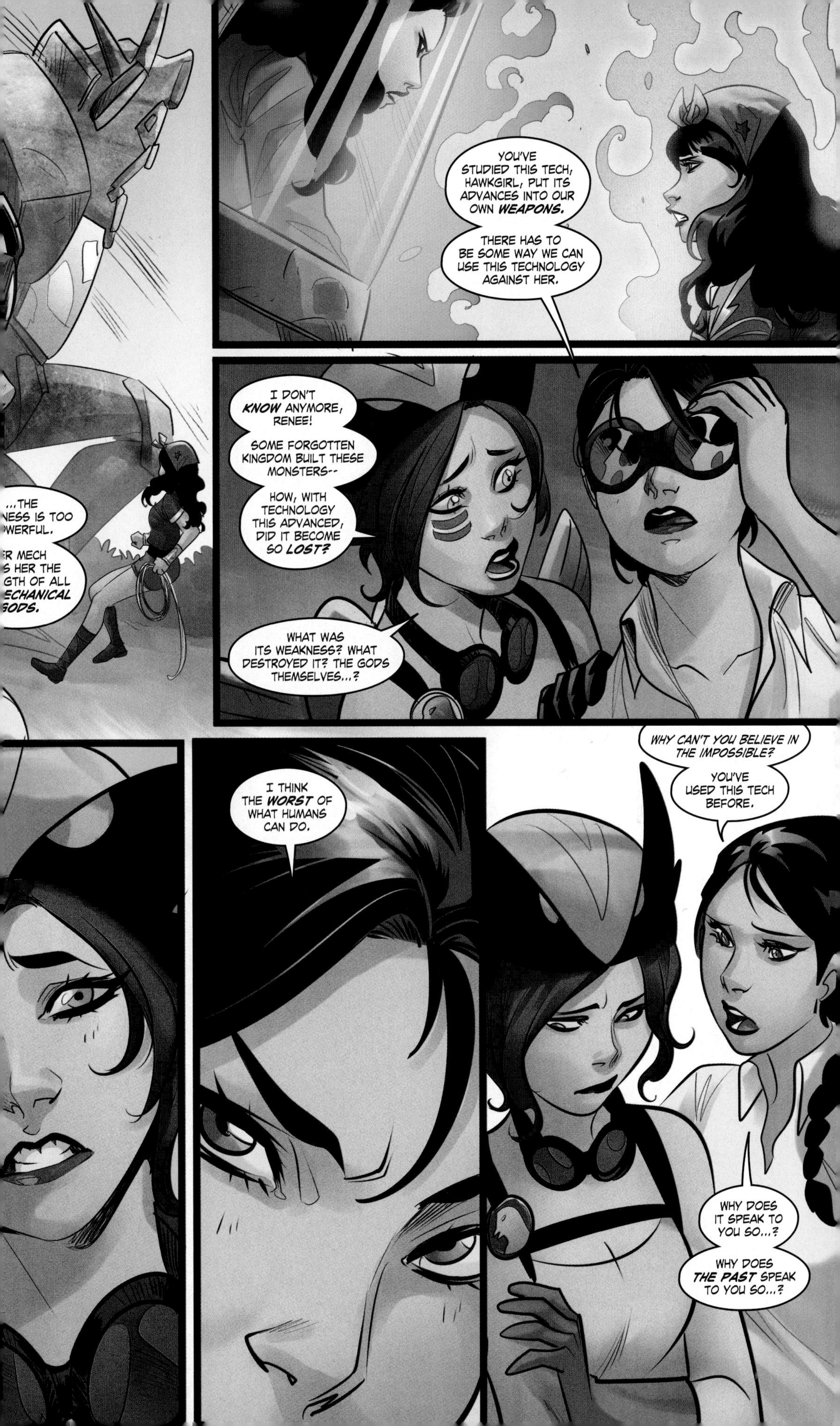
YOU'VE STUDIED THIS TECH, HAWKGIRL, PUT ITS ADVANCES INTO OUR OWN WEAPONS.
THERE HAS TO BE SOME WAY WE CAN USE THIS TECHNOLOGY AGAINST HER.
...THE NESS IS TOO POWERFUL.
ER MECH S HER THE GTH OF ALL ECHANICAL GODS.
I DON'T KNOW ANYMORE, RENEE!
SOME FORGOTTEN KINGDOM BUILT THESE MONSTERS--
HOW, WITH TECHNOLOGY THIS ADVANCED, DID IT BECOME SO LOST?
WHAT WAS ITS WEAKNESS? WHAT DESTROYED IT? THE GODS THEMSELVES...?
I THINK THE WORST OF WHAT HUMANS CAN DO.
WHY CAN'T YOU BELIEVE IN THE IMPOSSIBLE?
YOU'VE USED THIS TECH BEFORE.
WHY DOES IT SPEAK TO YOU SO...?
WHY DOES THE PAST SPEAK TO YOU SO...?

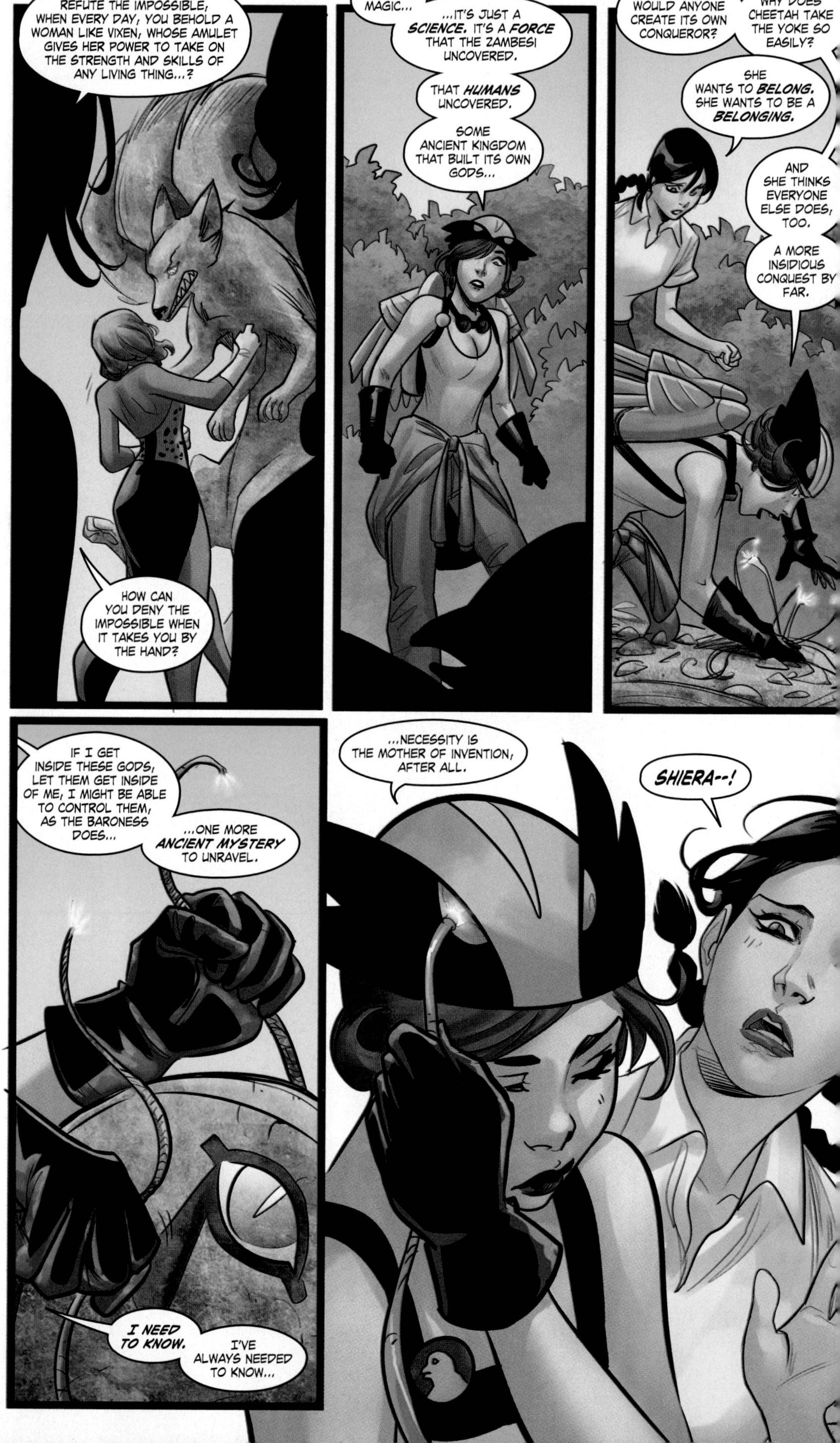
WHY DO YOU REFUTE THE IMPOSSIBLE, WHEN EVERY DAY, YOU BEHOLD A WOMAN LIKE VIXEN, WHOSE AMULET GIVES HER POWER TO TAKE ON THE STRENGTH AND SKILLS OF ANY LIVING THING...?
HOW CAN YOU DENY THE IMPOSSIBLE WHEN IT TAKES YOU BY THE HAND?
VIXEN'S MAGIC...
...IT'S JUST A **SCIENCE.** IT'S A **FORCE** THAT THE ZAMBESI UNCOVERED.
THAT **HUMANS** UNCOVERED.
SOME ANCIENT KINGDOM THAT BUILT ITS OWN GODS...
...BUT WHY WOULD ANYONE CREATE ITS OWN CONQUEROR?
WHY DOES CHEETAH TAKE THE YOKE SO EASILY?
SHE WANTS TO **BELONG.** SHE WANTS TO BE A **BELONGING.**
AND SHE THINKS EVERYONE ELSE DOES, TOO.
A MORE INSIDIOUS CONQUEST BY FAR.
IF I GET INSIDE THESE GODS, LET THEM GET INSIDE OF ME, I MIGHT BE ABLE TO CONTROL THEM, AS THE BARONESS DOES...
...ONE MORE **ANCIENT MYSTERY** TO UNRAVEL.
I NEED TO KNOW.
I'VE ALWAYS NEEDED TO KNOW...
...NECESSITY IS THE MOTHER OF INVENTION, AFTER ALL.
SHIERA--!

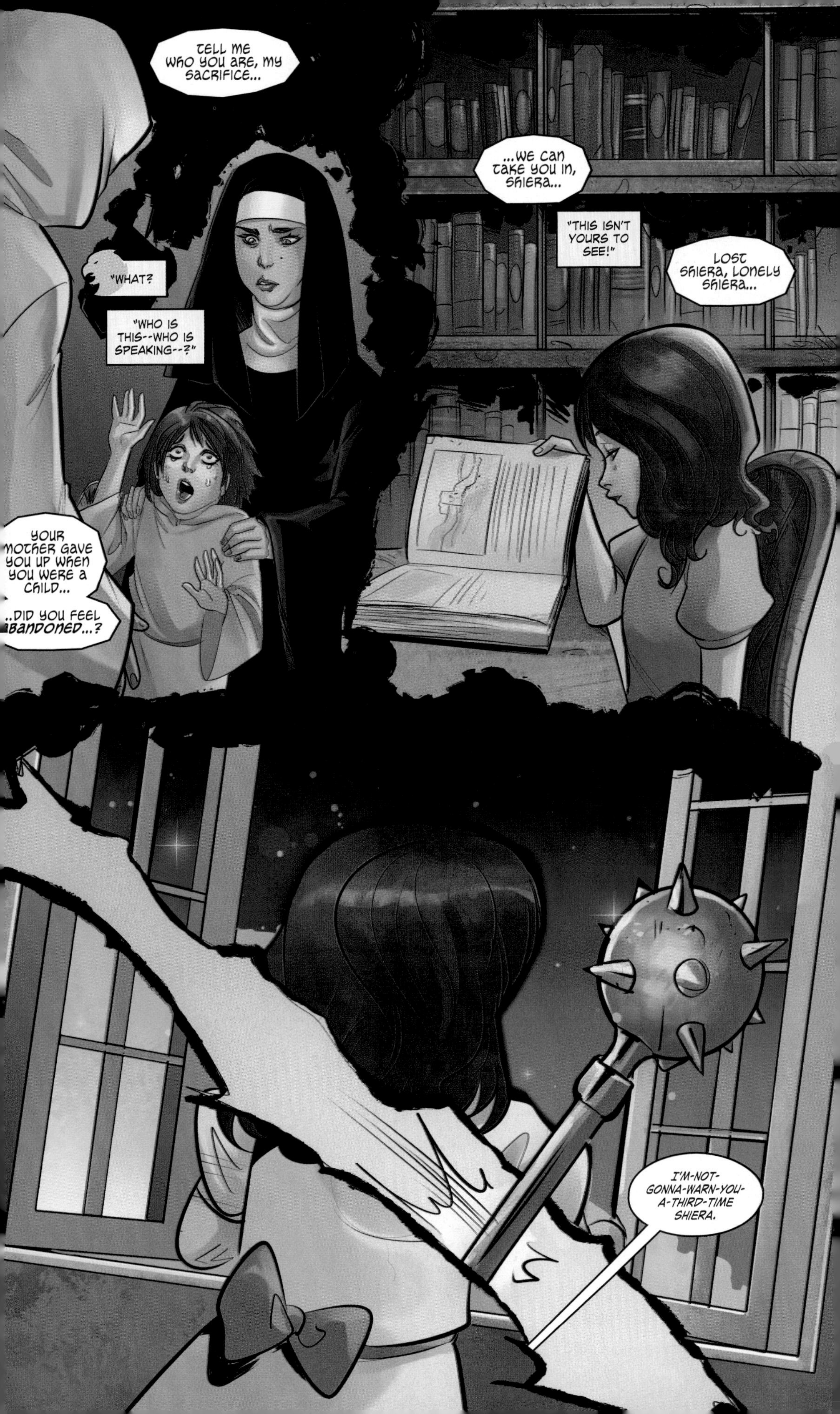
TELL ME WHO YOU ARE, MY SACRIFICE...
"WHAT?
"WHO IS THIS--WHO IS SPEAKING--?"
...WE CAN TAKE YOU IN, SHIERA...
"THIS ISN'T YOURS TO SEE!"
LOST SHIERA, LONELY SHIERA...
YOUR MOTHER GAVE YOU UP WHEN YOU WERE A CHILD...
..DID YOU FEEL ABANDONED...?
I'M-NOT-GONNA-WARN-YOU-A-THIRD-TIME SHIERA.

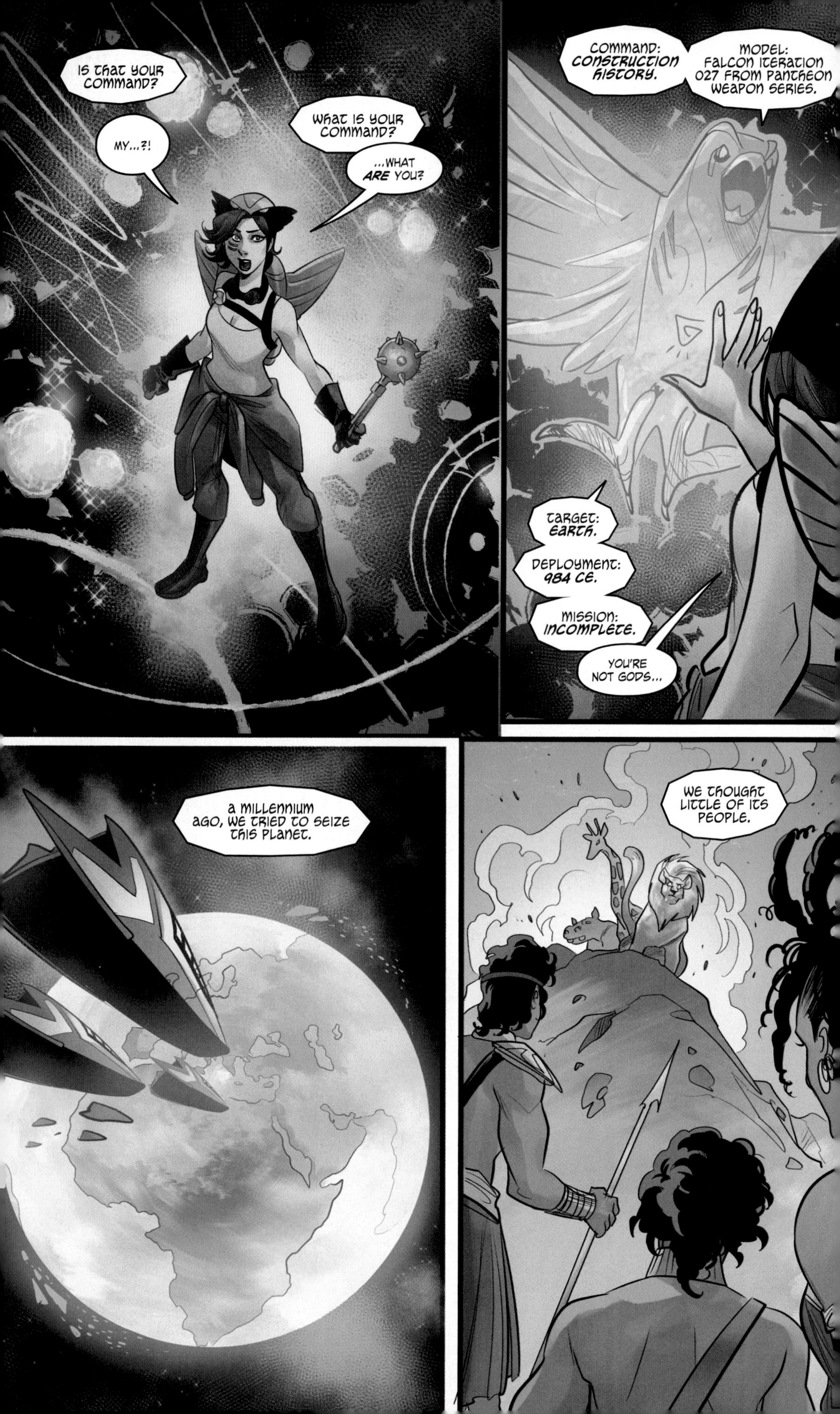
IS THAT YOUR COMMAND?
MY...?!
WHAT IS YOUR COMMAND?
...WHAT ARE YOU?
COMMAND: CONSTRUCTION HISTORY.
MODEL: FALCON ITERATION 027 FROM PANTHEON WEAPON SERIES.
TARGET: EARTH.
DEPLOYMENT: 984 CE.
MISSION: INCOMPLETE.
YOU'RE NOT GODS...
A MILLENNIUM AGO, WE TRIED TO SEIZE THIS PLANET.
WE THOUGHT LITTLE OF ITS PEOPLE.

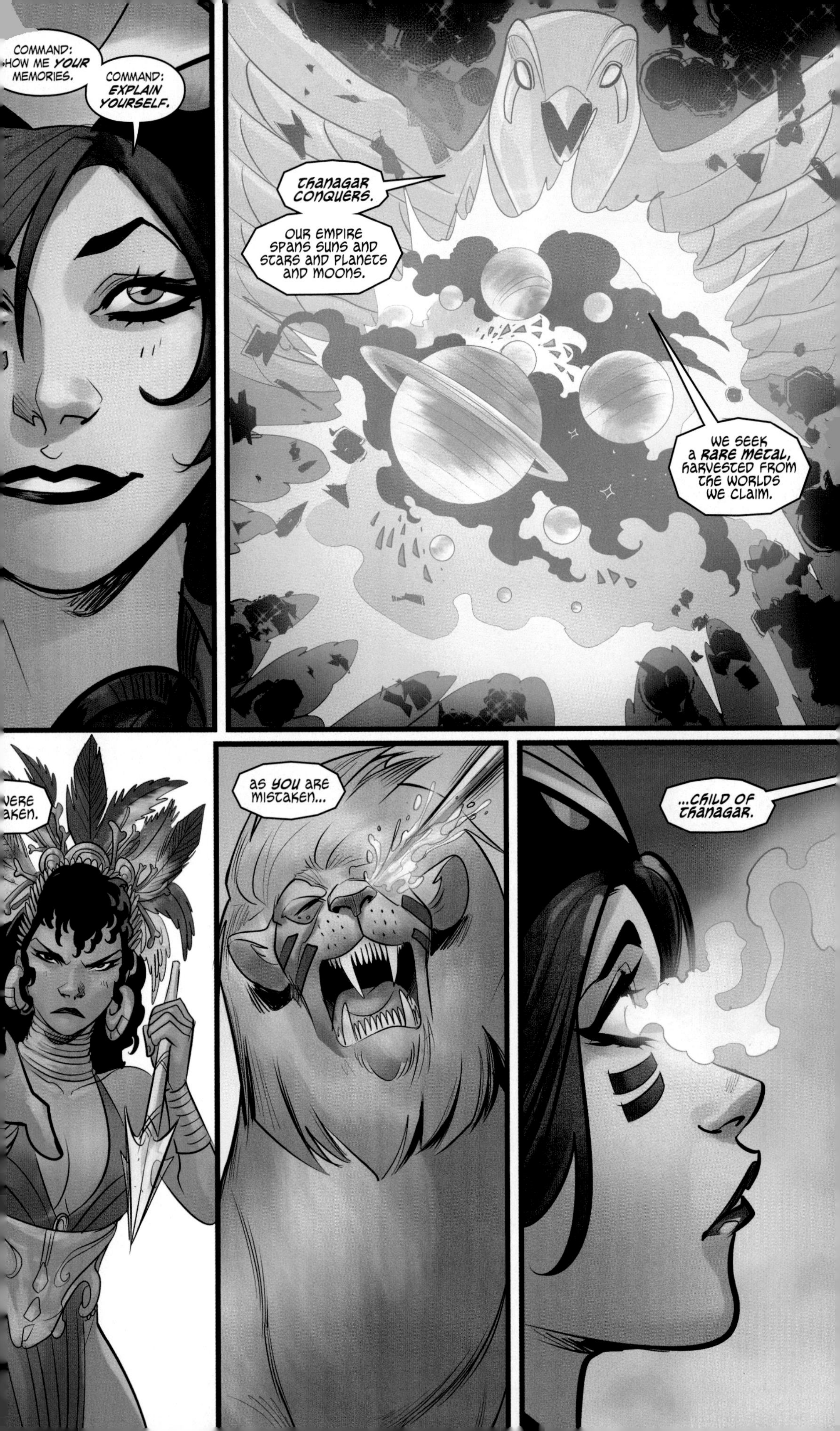
COMMAND: SHOW ME YOUR MEMORIES.
COMMAND: EXPLAIN YOURSELF.
THANAGAR CONQUERS.
OUR EMPIRE SPANS SUNS AND STARS AND PLANETS AND MOONS.
WE SEEK A RARE METAL, HARVESTED FROM THE WORLDS WE CLAIM.
AS YOU ARE MISTAKEN...
...CHILD OF THANAGAR.

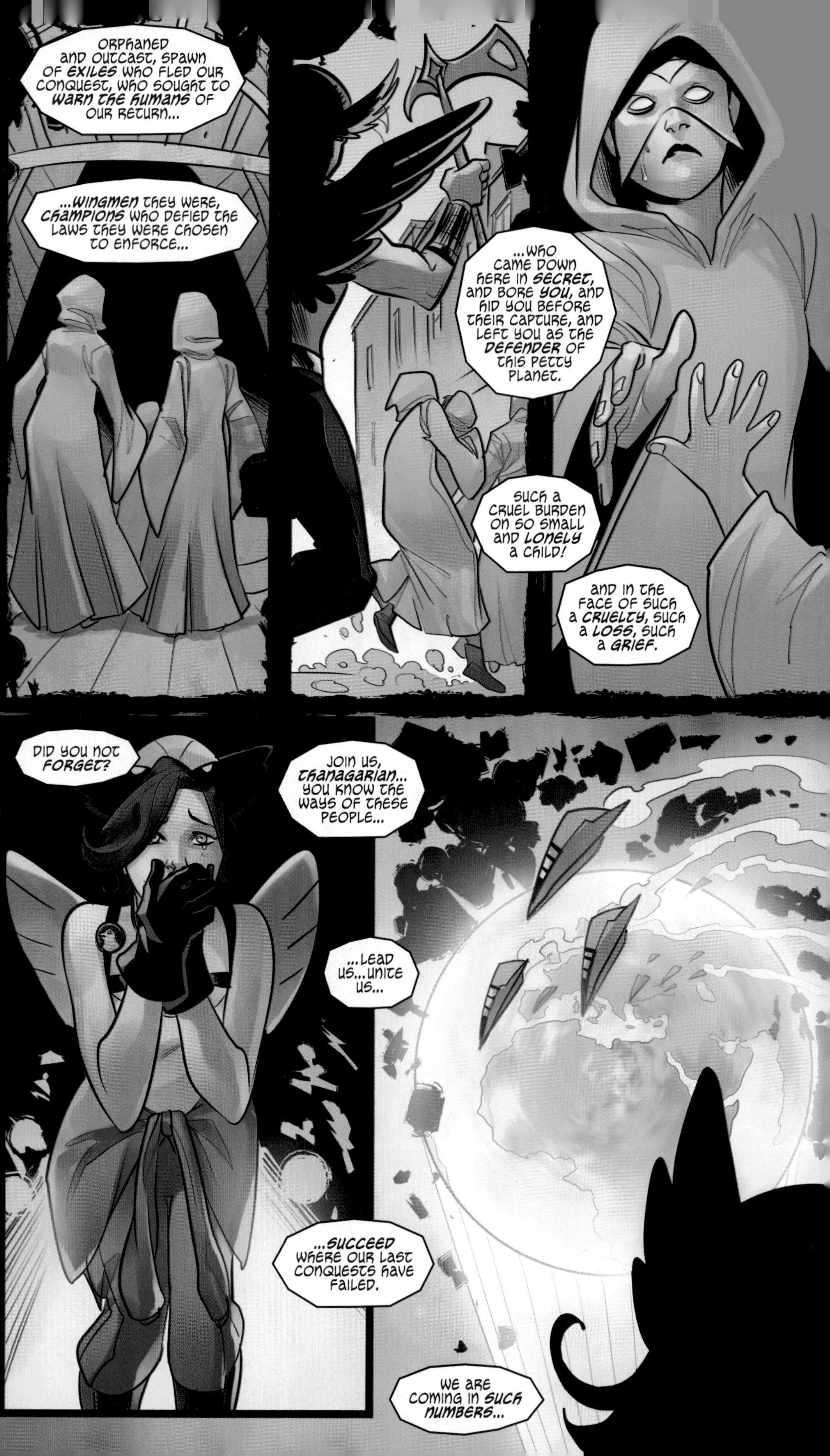
ORPHANED AND OUTCAST, SPAWN OF EXILES WHO FLED OUR CONQUEST, WHO SOUGHT TO WARN THE HUMANS OF OUR RETURN...
...WINGMEN THEY WERE, CHAMPIONS WHO DEFIED THE LAWS THEY WERE CHOSEN TO ENFORCE...
...WHO CAME DOWN HERE IN SECRET, AND BORE YOU, AND HID YOU BEFORE THEIR CAPTURE, AND LEFT YOU AS THE DEFENDER OF THIS PETTY PLANET.
SUCH A CRUEL BURDEN ON SO SMALL AND LONELY A CHILD!
AND IN THE FACE OF SUCH A CRUELTY, SUCH A LOSS, SUCH A GRIEF.
DID YOU NOT FORGET?
JOIN US, THANAGARIAN... YOU KNOW THE WAYS OF THESE PEOPLE...
...LEAD US...UNITE US...
...SUCCEED WHERE OUR LAST CONQUESTS HAVE FAILED.
WE ARE COMING IN SUCH NUMBERS...

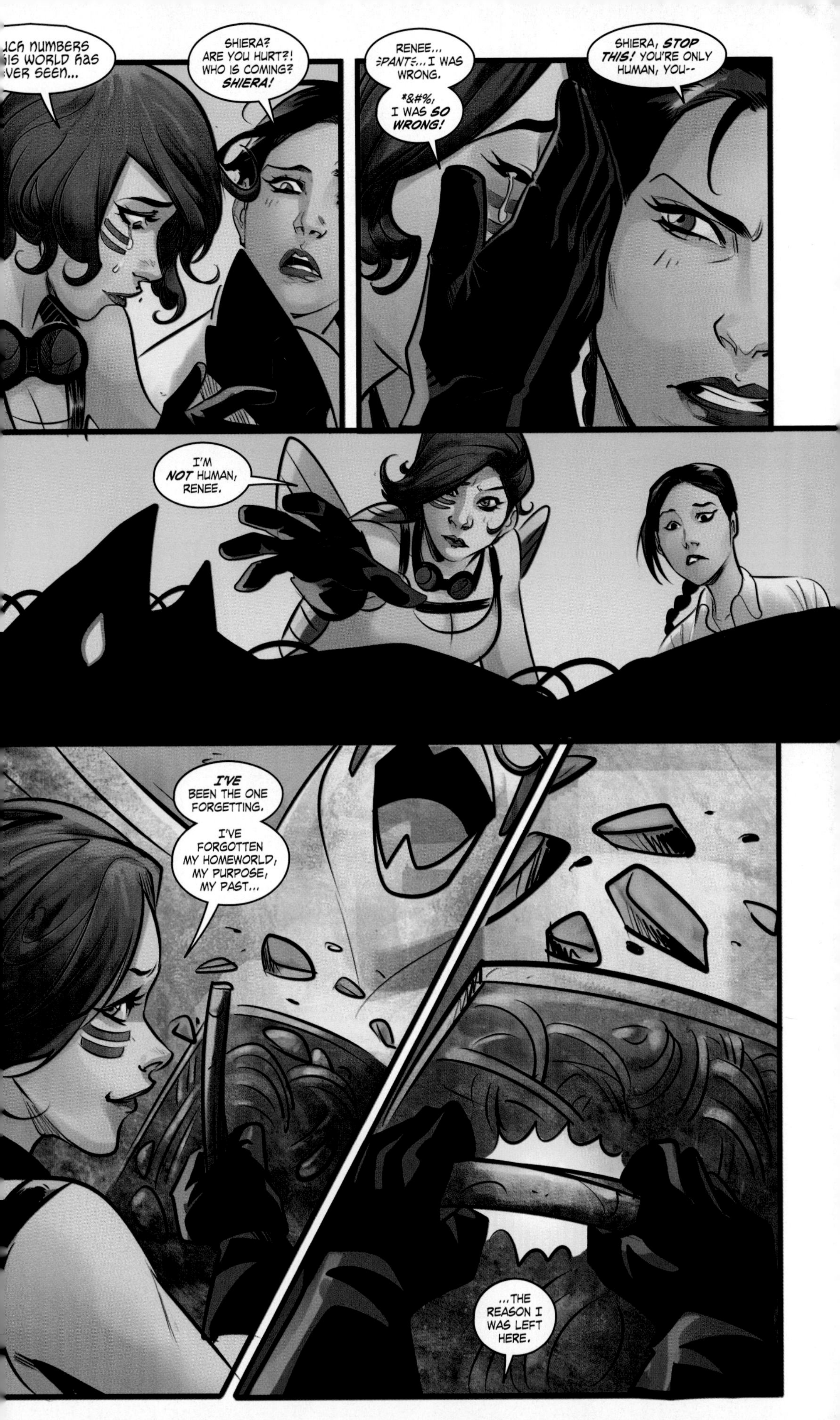

...UCH NUMBERS
...IS WORLD HAS
...VER SEEN...
SHIERA? ARE YOU HURT?! WHO IS COMING? SHIERA!
RENEE... PANT... I WAS WRONG.
*&#%, I WAS SO WRONG!
SHIERA, STOP THIS! YOU'RE ONLY HUMAN, YOU--
I'M NOT HUMAN, RENEE.
I'VE BEEN THE ONE FORGETTING.
I'VE FORGOTTEN MY HOMEWORLD, MY PURPOSE, MY PAST...
...THE REASON I WAS LEFT HERE.

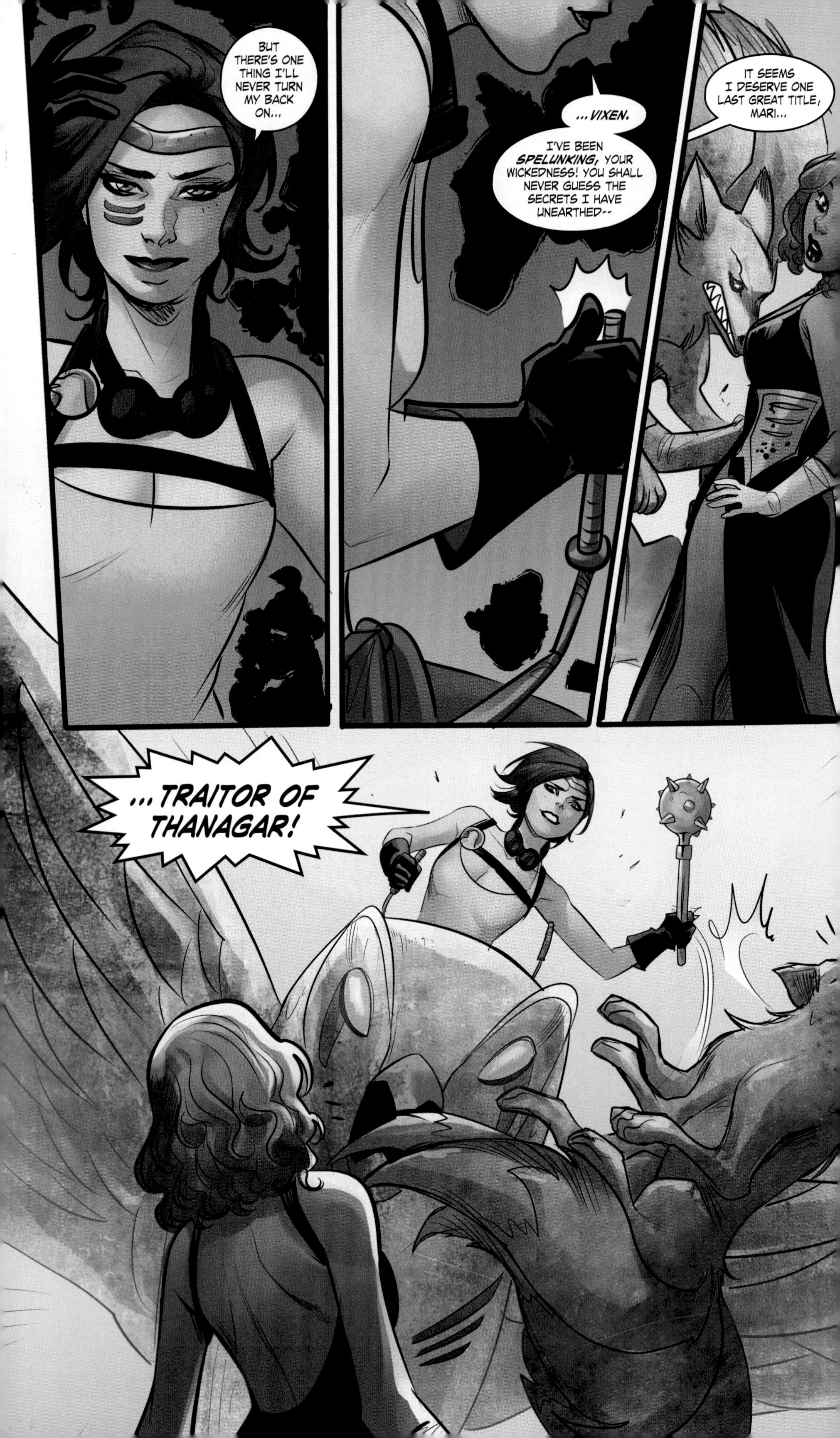
BUT THERE'S ONE THING I'LL NEVER TURN MY BACK ON...
...VIXEN.
I'VE BEEN SPELUNKING, YOUR WICKEDNESS! YOU SHALL NEVER GUESS THE SECRETS I HAVE UNEARTHED--
IT SEEMS I DESERVE ONE LAST GREAT TITLE, MARI...
...TRAITOR OF THANAGAR!

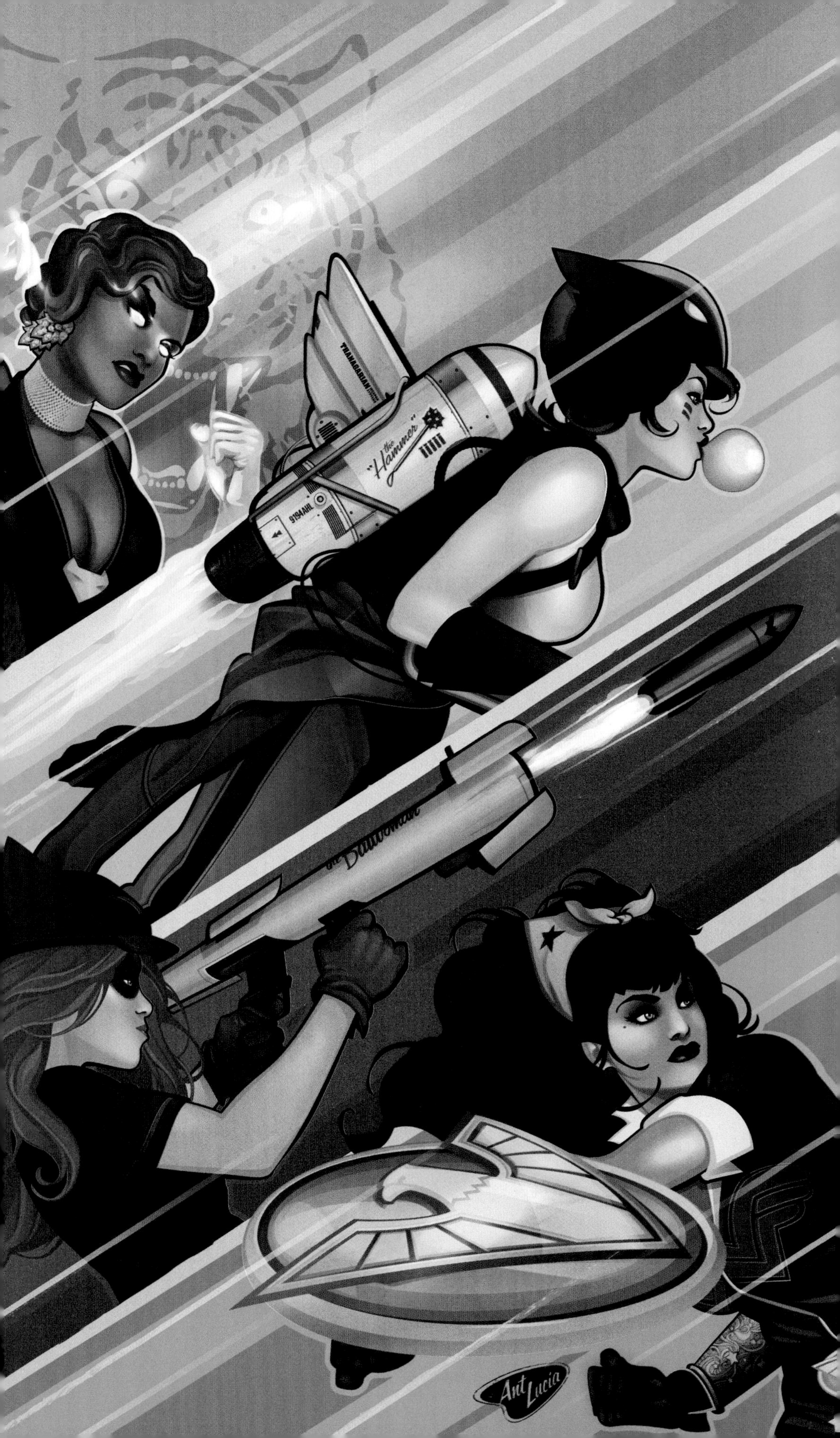

the "Hammer"
9194AHL
Ant Lucia

WHAT'S PAST IS PROLOGUE

MARGUERITE BENNETT
Writer

RICHARD ORTIZ
LAURA BRAGA
Artists

J. NANJAN
Colorist

Cover by
ANT LUCIA

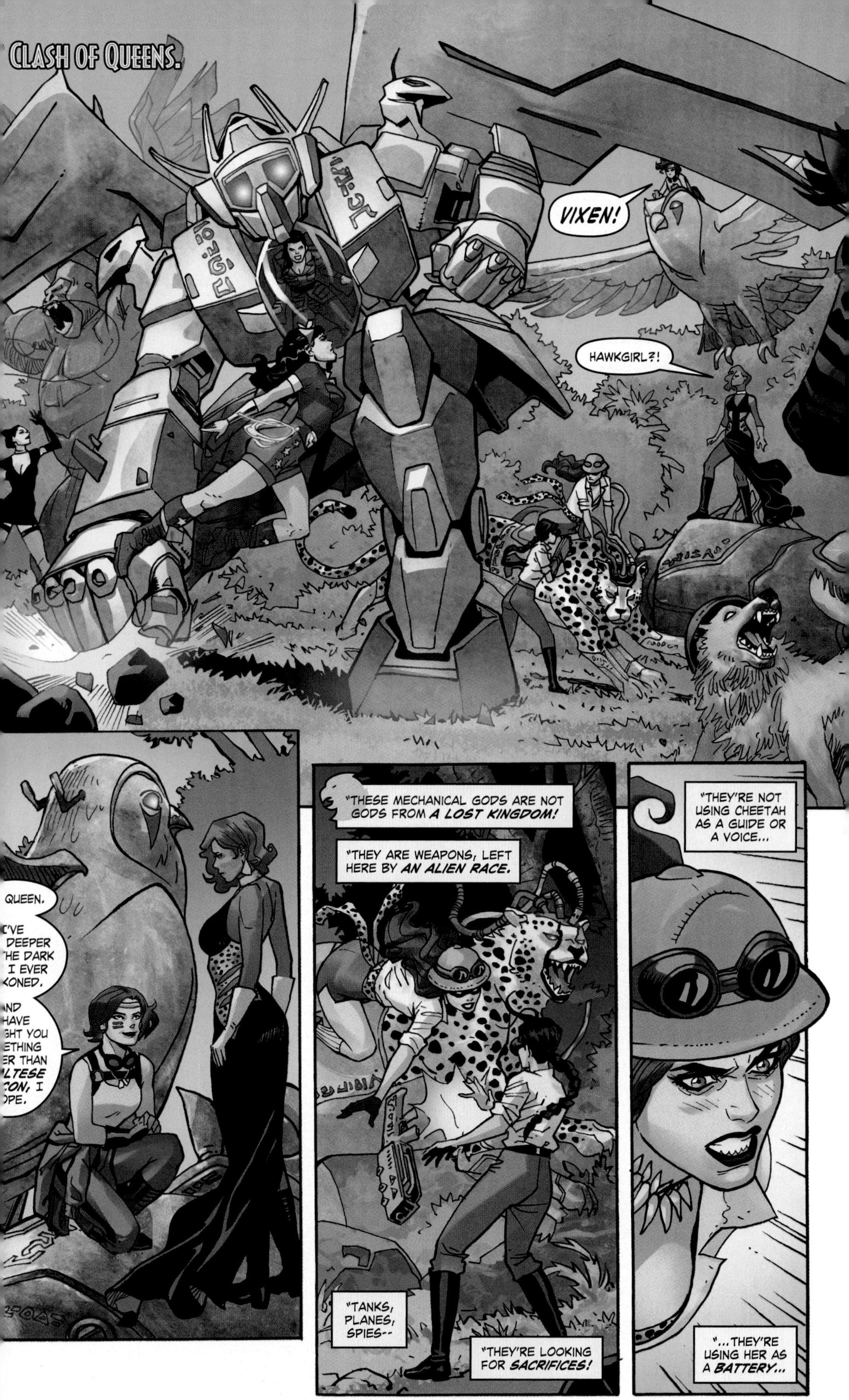

CLASH OF QUEENS.
VIXEN!
HAWKGIRL?!
QUEEN.
'VE DEEPER THE DARK I EVER KONED.
ND HAVE GHT YOU ETHING ER THAN LTESE CON, I OPE.
"THESE MECHANICAL GODS ARE NOT GODS FROM A LOST KINGDOM!
"THEY ARE WEAPONS, LEFT HERE BY AN ALIEN RACE.
"TANKS, PLANES, SPIES--
"THEY'RE LOOKING FOR SACRIFICES!
"THEY'RE NOT USING CHEETAH AS A GUIDE OR A VOICE...
"...THEY'RE USING HER AS A BATTERY...

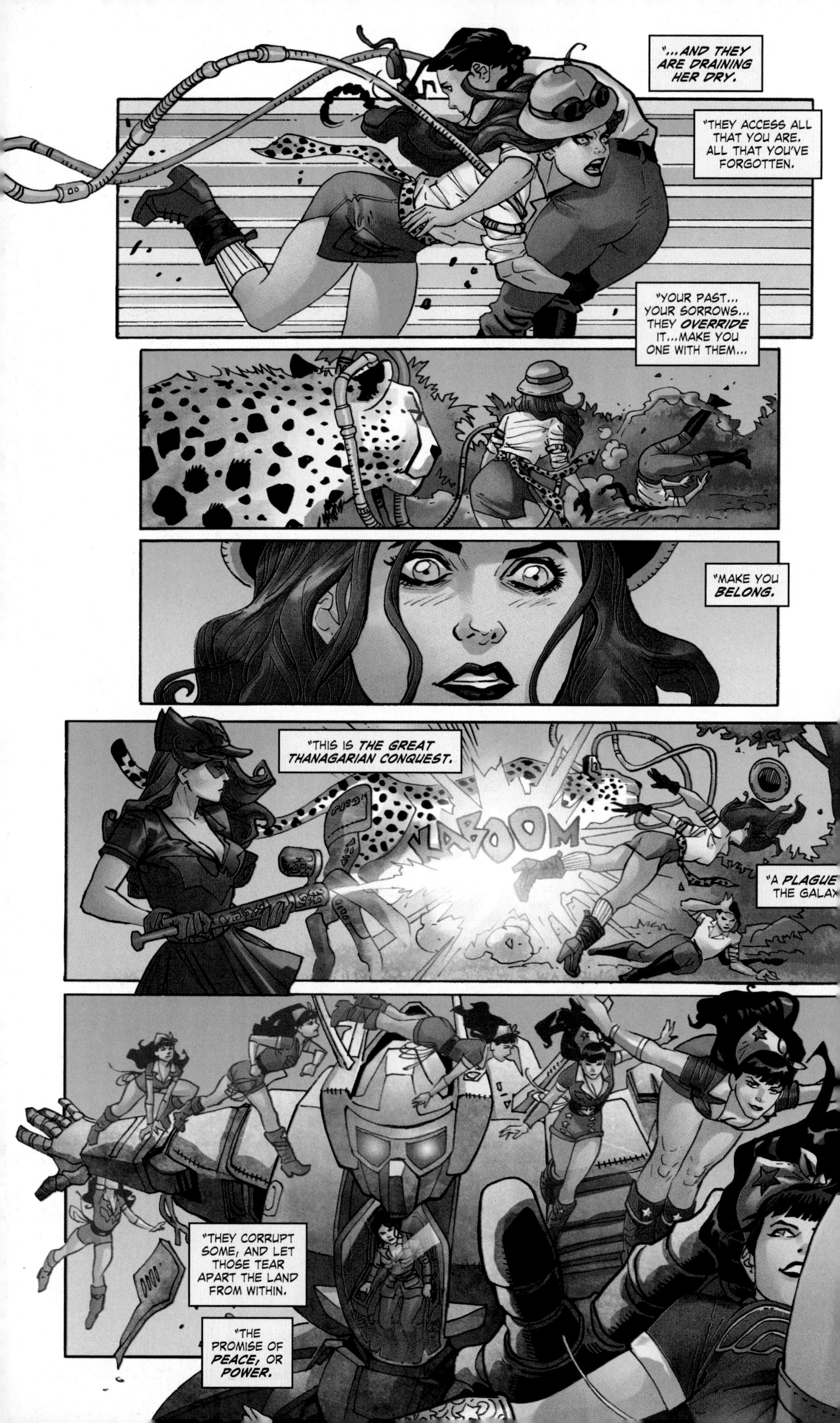
"...AND THEY ARE DRAINING HER DRY.
"THEY ACCESS ALL THAT YOU ARE. ALL THAT YOU'VE FORGOTTEN.
"YOUR PAST... YOUR SORROWS... THEY OVERRIDE IT...MAKE YOU ONE WITH THEM...
"MAKE YOU BELONG.
"THIS IS THE GREAT THANAGARIAN CONQUEST.
KABOOM
"THEY CORRUPT SOME, AND LET THOSE TEAR APART THE LAND FROM WITHIN.
"THE PROMISE OF PEACE, OR POWER.

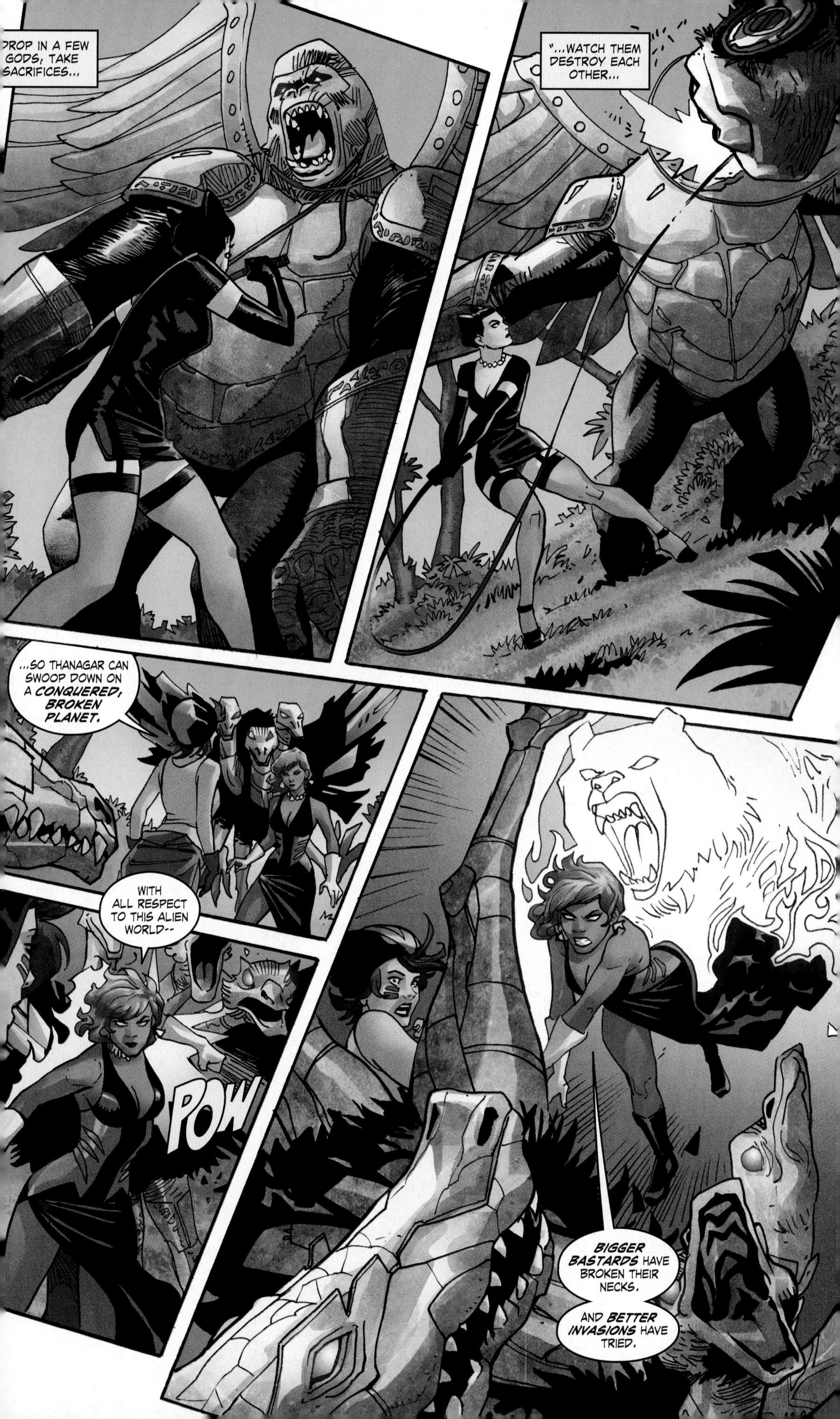
DROP IN A FEW GODS, TAKE SACRIFICES...
"...WATCH THEM DESTROY EACH OTHER...
...SO THANAGAR CAN SWOOP DOWN ON A CONQUERED, BROKEN PLANET.
WITH ALL RESPECT TO THIS ALIEN WORLD--
POW
BIGGER BASTARDS HAVE BROKEN THEIR NECKS.
AND BETTER INVASIONS HAVE TRIED.

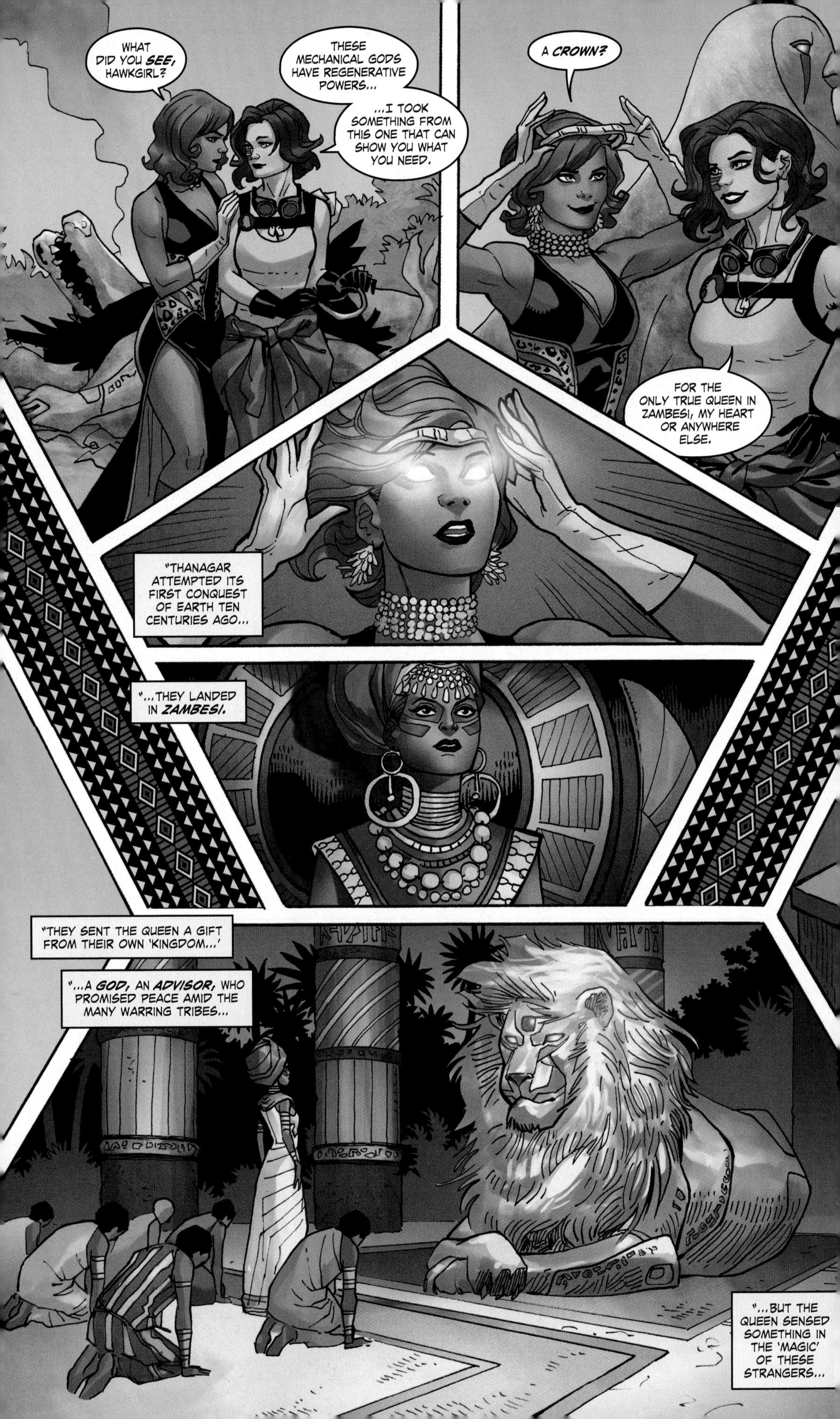
WHAT DID YOU SEE, HAWKGIRL?
THESE MECHANICAL GODS HAVE REGENERATIVE POWERS...
...I TOOK SOMETHING FROM THIS ONE THAT CAN SHOW YOU WHAT YOU NEED.
A CROWN?
FOR THE ONLY TRUE QUEEN IN ZAMBESI, MY HEART OR ANYWHERE ELSE.
"THANAGAR ATTEMPTED ITS FIRST CONQUEST OF EARTH TEN CENTURIES AGO...
"...THEY LANDED IN ZAMBESI.
"THEY SENT THE QUEEN A GIFT FROM THEIR OWN 'KINGDOM...'
"...A GOD, AN ADVISOR, WHO PROMISED PEACE AMID THE MANY WARRING TRIBES...
"...BUT THE QUEEN SENSED SOMETHING IN THE 'MAGIC' OF THESE STRANGERS...

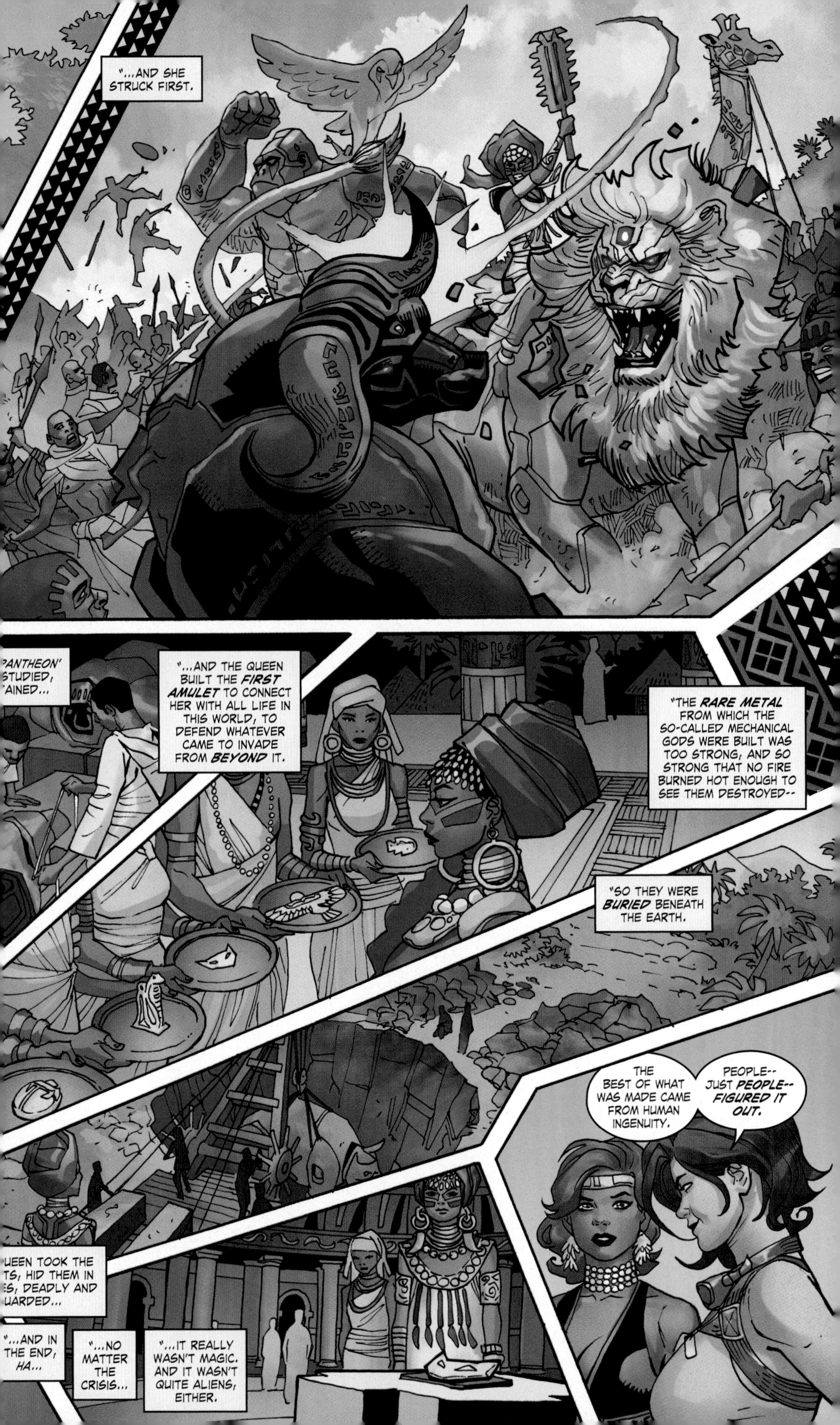
"...AND SHE STRUCK FIRST.
PANTHEON' STUDIED, TAINED...
"...AND THE QUEEN BUILT THE FIRST AMULET TO CONNECT HER WITH ALL LIFE IN THIS WORLD, TO DEFEND WHATEVER CAME TO INVADE FROM BEYOND IT.
"THE RARE METAL FROM WHICH THE SO-CALLED MECHANICAL GODS WERE BUILT WAS TOO STRONG, AND SO STRONG THAT NO FIRE BURNED HOT ENOUGH TO SEE THEM DESTROYED--
"SO THEY WERE BURIED BENEATH THE EARTH.
UEEN TOOK THE TS, HID THEM IN ES, DEADLY AND UARDED...
"...AND IN THE END, HA...
"...NO MATTER THE CRISIS...
"...IT REALLY WASN'T MAGIC. AND IT WASN'T QUITE ALIENS, EITHER.
THE BEST OF WHAT WAS MADE CAME FROM HUMAN INGENUITY.
PEOPLE-- JUST PEOPLE-- FIGURED IT OUT.

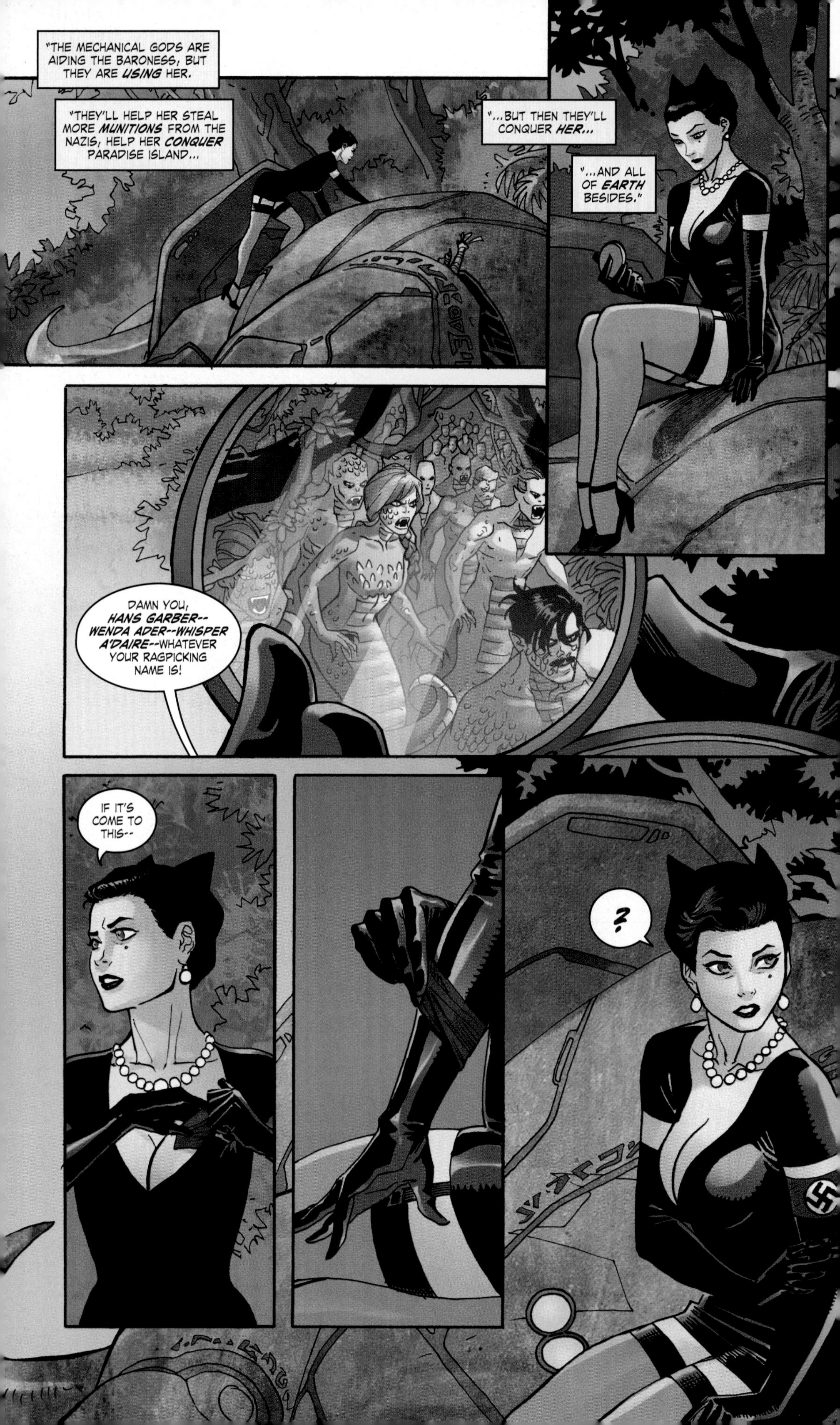
"THE MECHANICAL GODS ARE AIDING THE BARONESS, BUT THEY ARE *USING* HER.
"THEY'LL HELP HER STEAL MORE *MUNITIONS* FROM THE NAZIS, HELP HER *CONQUER* PARADISE ISLAND...
"...BUT THEN THEY'LL CONQUER *HER*...
"...AND ALL OF *EARTH* BESIDES."
DAMN YOU, *HANS GARBER-- WENDA ADER--WHISPER A'DAIRE*--WHATEVER YOUR RAGPICKING NAME IS!
IF IT'S COME TO THIS--
?

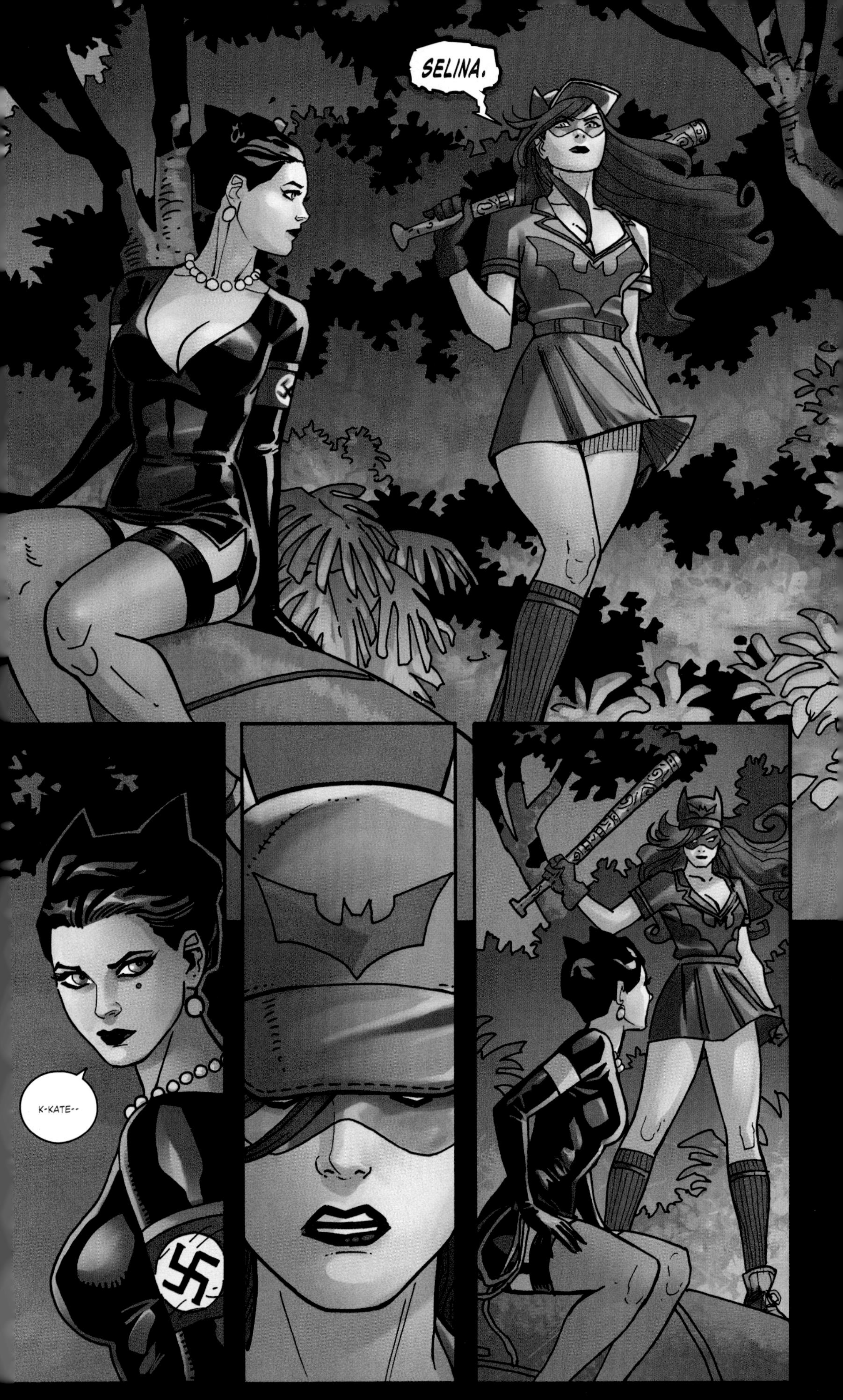
SELINA.
K-KATE--

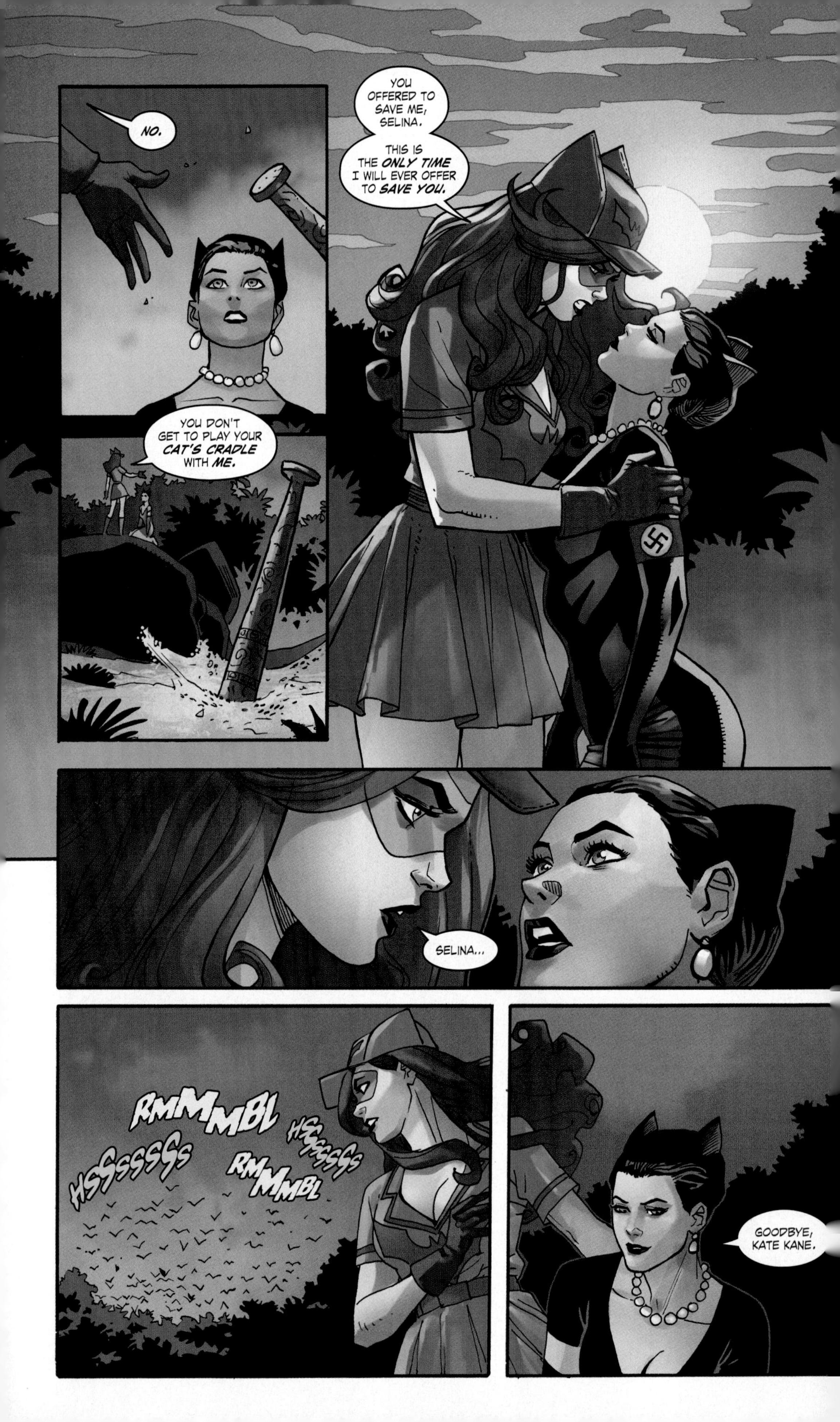
NO.
YOU OFFERED TO SAVE ME, SELINA.
THIS IS THE ONLY TIME I WILL EVER OFFER TO SAVE YOU.
YOU DON'T GET TO PLAY YOUR CAT'S CRADLE WITH ME.
SELINA...
RMMMBL
HSSSSSSS
HSSSSSS
RMMMBL
GOODBYE, KATE KANE.

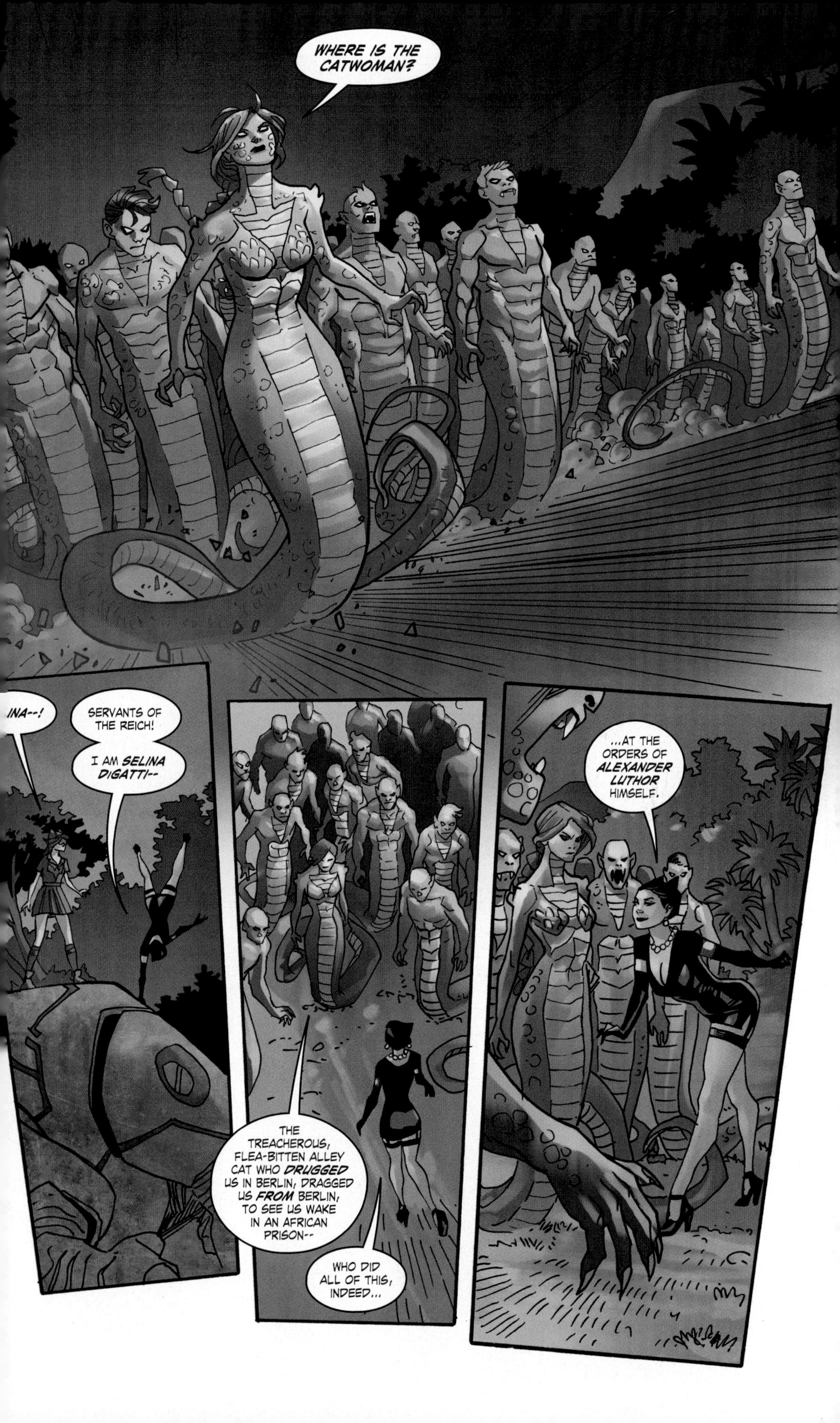
WHERE IS THE CATWOMAN?
INA--!
SERVANTS OF THE REICH!
I AM SELINA DIGATTI--
THE TREACHEROUS, FLEA-BITTEN ALLEY CAT WHO DRUGGED US IN BERLIN, DRAGGED US FROM BERLIN, TO SEE US WAKE IN AN AFRICAN PRISON--
WHO DID ALL OF THIS, INDEED...
...AT THE ORDERS OF ALEXANDER LUTHOR HIMSELF.

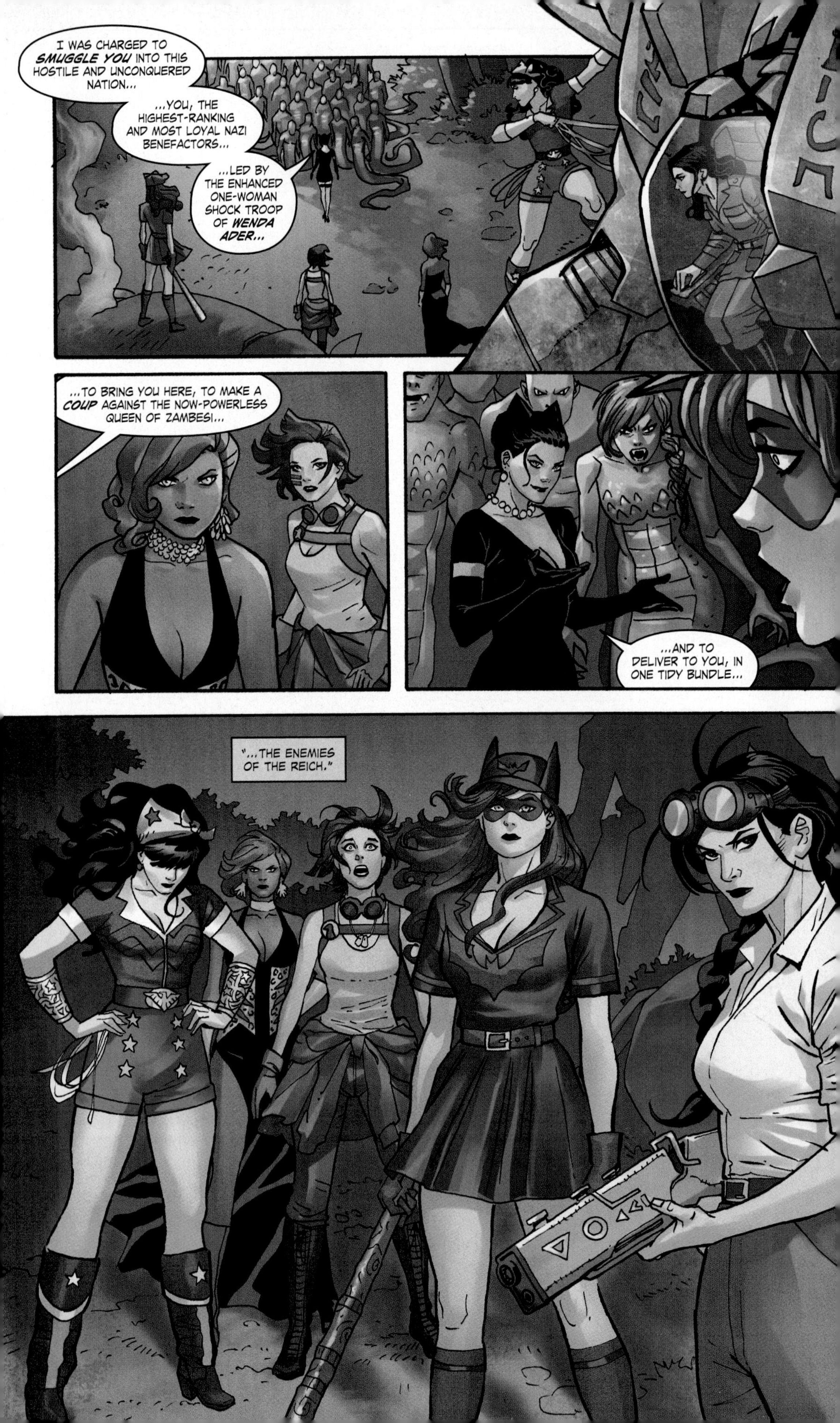
I WAS CHARGED TO SMUGGLE YOU INTO THIS HOSTILE AND UNCONQUERED NATION...
...YOU, THE HIGHEST-RANKING AND MOST LOYAL NAZI BENEFACTORS...
...LED BY THE ENHANCED ONE-WOMAN SHOCK TROOP OF WENDA ADER...
...TO BRING YOU HERE, TO MAKE A COUP AGAINST THE NOW-POWERLESS QUEEN OF ZAMBESI...
...AND TO DELIVER TO YOU, IN ONE TIDY BUNDLE...
"...THE ENEMIES OF THE REICH."

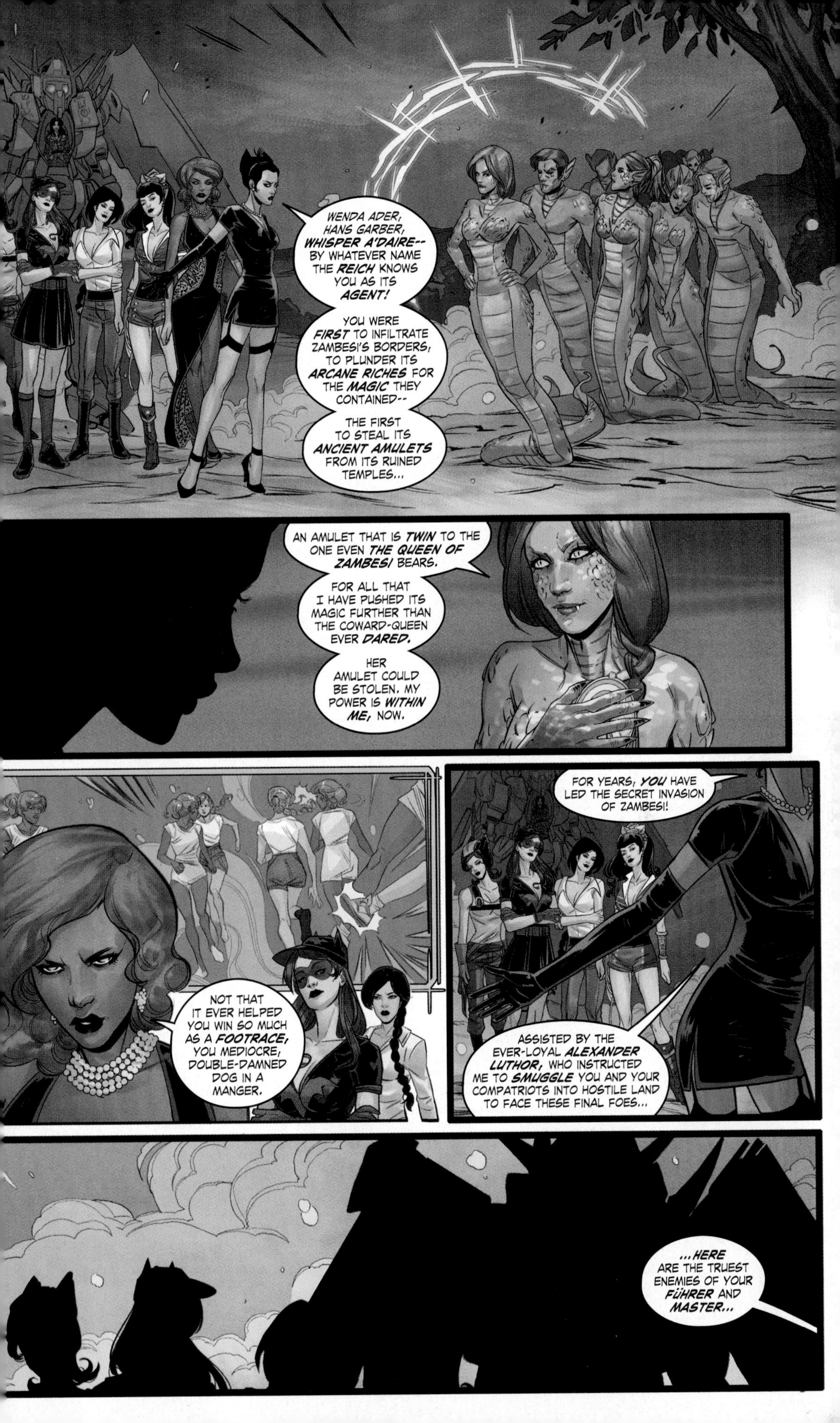
WENDA ADER, HANS GARBER, WHISPER A'DAIRE-- BY WHATEVER NAME THE REICH KNOWS YOU AS ITS AGENT!
YOU WERE FIRST TO INFILTRATE ZAMBESI'S BORDERS, TO PLUNDER ITS ARCANE RICHES FOR THE MAGIC THEY CONTAINED--
THE FIRST TO STEAL ITS ANCIENT AMULETS FROM ITS RUINED TEMPLES...
AN AMULET THAT IS TWIN TO THE ONE EVEN THE QUEEN OF ZAMBESI BEARS.
FOR ALL THAT I HAVE PUSHED ITS MAGIC FURTHER THAN THE COWARD-QUEEN EVER DARED.
HER AMULET COULD BE STOLEN. MY POWER IS WITHIN ME, NOW.
NOT THAT IT EVER HELPED YOU WIN SO MUCH AS A FOOTRACE, YOU MEDIOCRE, DOUBLE-DAMNED DOG IN A MANGER.
FOR YEARS, YOU HAVE LED THE SECRET INVASION OF ZAMBESI!
ASSISTED BY THE EVER-LOYAL ALEXANDER LUTHOR, WHO INSTRUCTED ME TO SMUGGLE YOU AND YOUR COMPATRIOTS INTO HOSTILE LAND TO FACE THESE FINAL FOES...
...HERE ARE THE TRUEST ENEMIES OF YOUR FÜHRER AND MASTER...

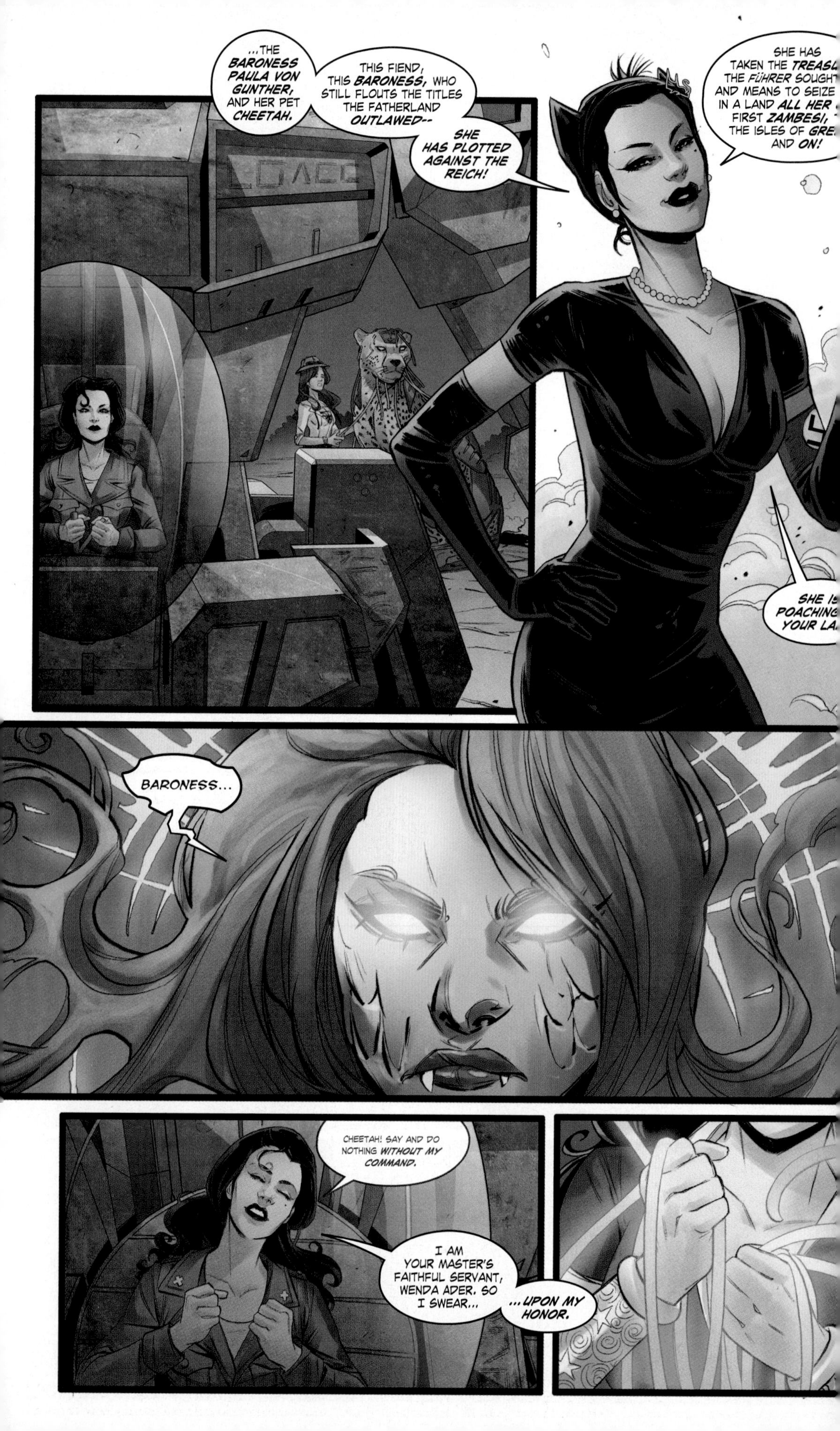
...THE BARONESS PAULA VON GUNTHER, AND HER PET CHEETAH.
THIS FIEND, THIS BARONESS, WHO STILL FLOUTS THE TITLES THE FATHERLAND OUTLAWED--
SHE HAS PLOTTED AGAINST THE REICH!
SHE HAS TAKEN THE TREAS THE FÜHRER SOUGHT AND MEANS TO SEIZE IN A LAND ALL HER FIRST ZAMBESI, THE ISLES OF GRE AND ON!
SHE IS POACHING YOUR LA
BARONESS...
CHEETAH! SAY AND DO NOTHING WITHOUT MY COMMAND.
I AM YOUR MASTER'S FAITHFUL SERVANT, WENDA ADER. SO I SWEAR...
...UPON MY HONOR.

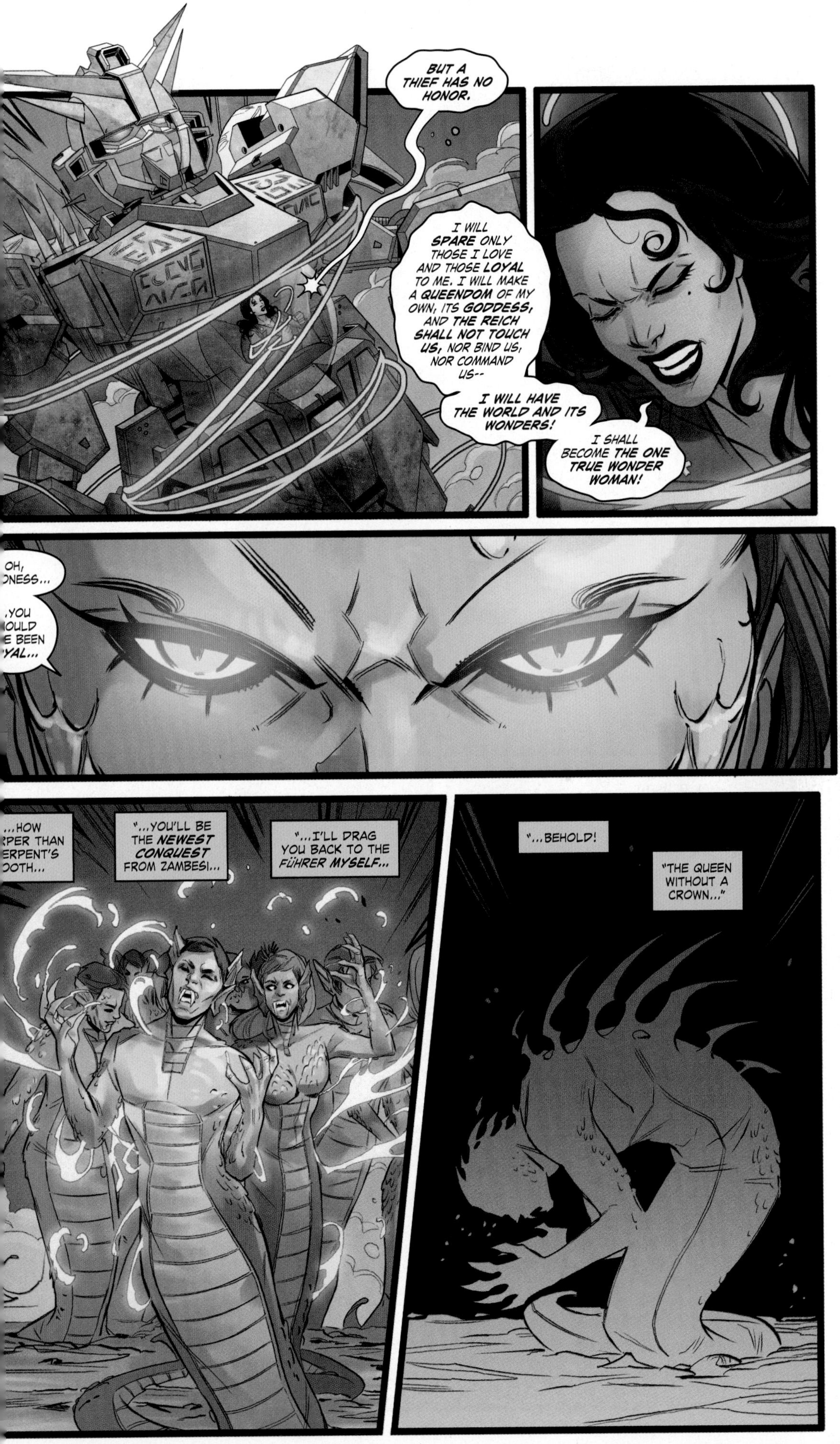
BUT A THIEF HAS NO HONOR.
I WILL SPARE ONLY THOSE I LOVE AND THOSE LOYAL TO ME. I WILL MAKE A QUEENDOM OF MY OWN, ITS GODDESS, AND THE REICH SHALL NOT TOUCH US, NOR BIND US, NOR COMMAND US--
I WILL HAVE THE WORLD AND ITS WONDERS!
I SHALL BECOME THE ONE TRUE WONDER WOMAN!
OH, ONESS...
...YOU OULD E BEEN YAL...
...HOW RPER THAN ERPENT'S OOTH...
"...YOU'LL BE THE NEWEST CONQUEST FROM ZAMBESI...
"...I'LL DRAG YOU BACK TO THE FÜHRER MYSELF...
"...BEHOLD!
"THE QUEEN WITHOUT A CROWN..."

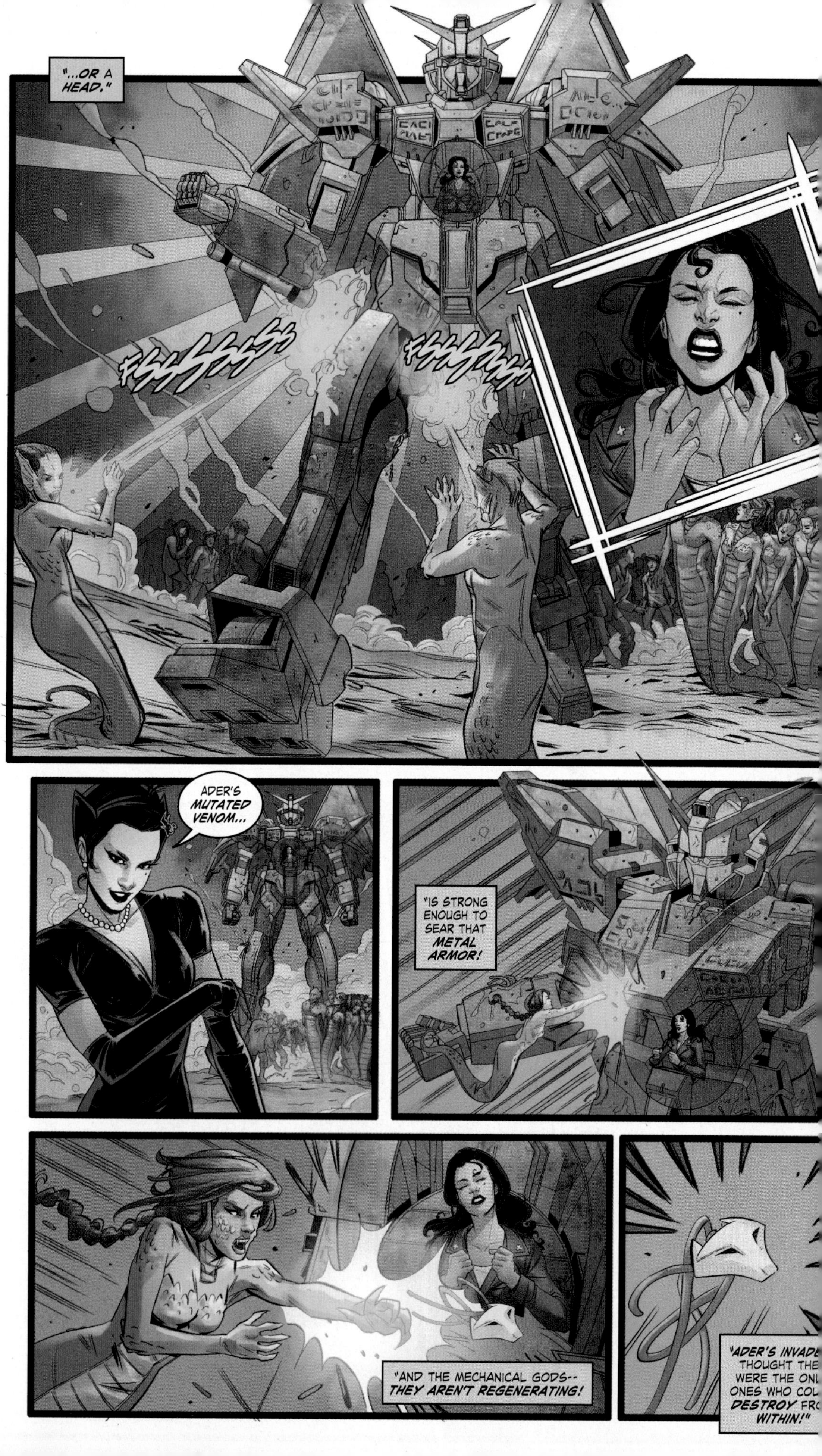
"...OR A HEAD."
FSSSSSSSS
FSSSSSSSS
ADER'S MUTATED VENOM...
"IS STRONG ENOUGH TO SEAR THAT METAL ARMOR!
"AND THE MECHANICAL GODS-- THEY AREN'T REGENERATING!

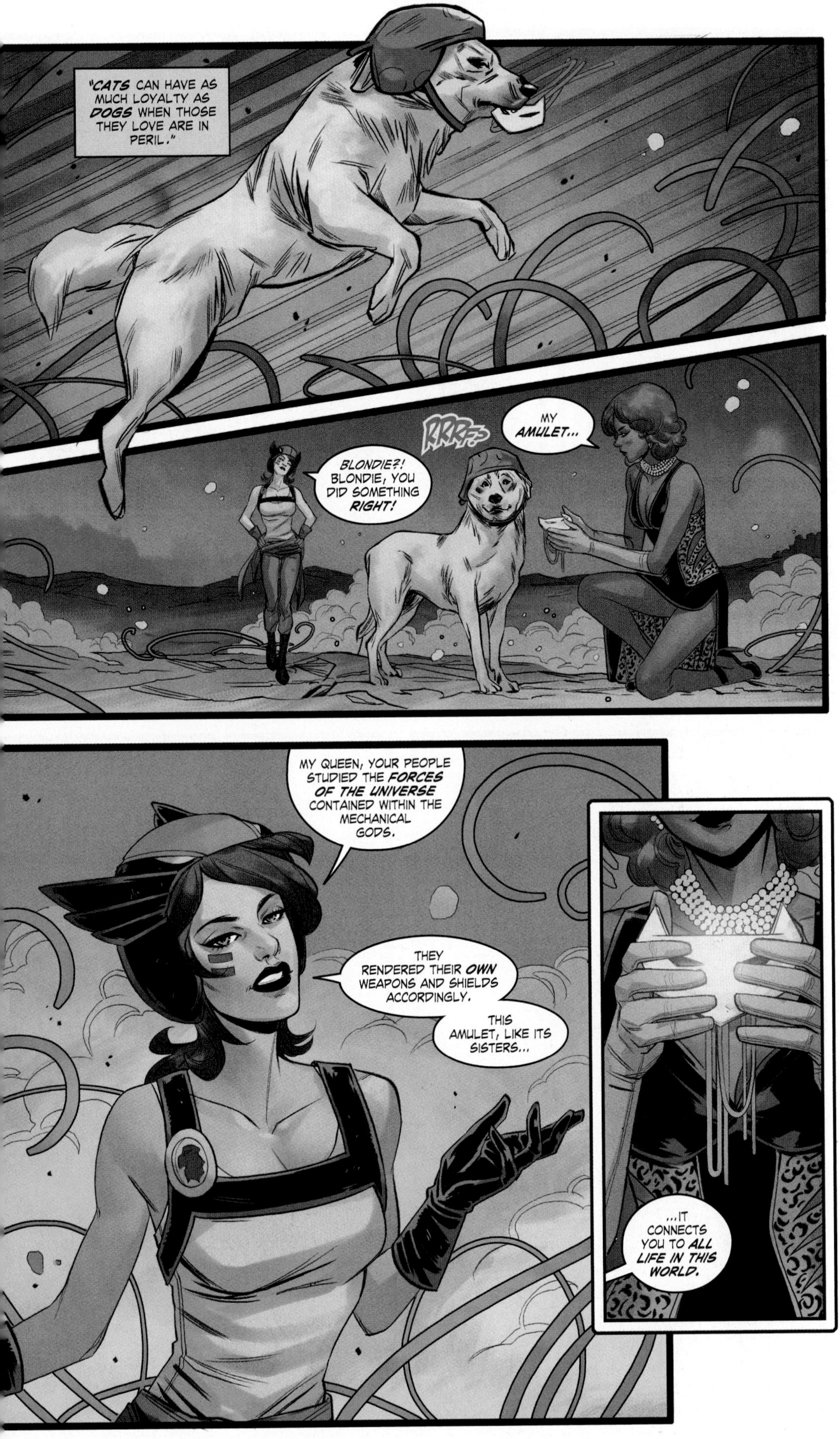
"CATS CAN HAVE AS MUCH LOYALTY AS DOGS WHEN THOSE THEY LOVE ARE IN PERIL."
RRRF?
MY AMULET...
BLONDIE?! BLONDIE, YOU DID SOMETHING RIGHT!
MY QUEEN, YOUR PEOPLE STUDIED THE FORCES OF THE UNIVERSE CONTAINED WITHIN THE MECHANICAL GODS.
THEY RENDERED THEIR OWN WEAPONS AND SHIELDS ACCORDINGLY.
THIS AMULET, LIKE ITS SISTERS...
...IT CONNECTS YOU TO ALL LIFE IN THIS WORLD.

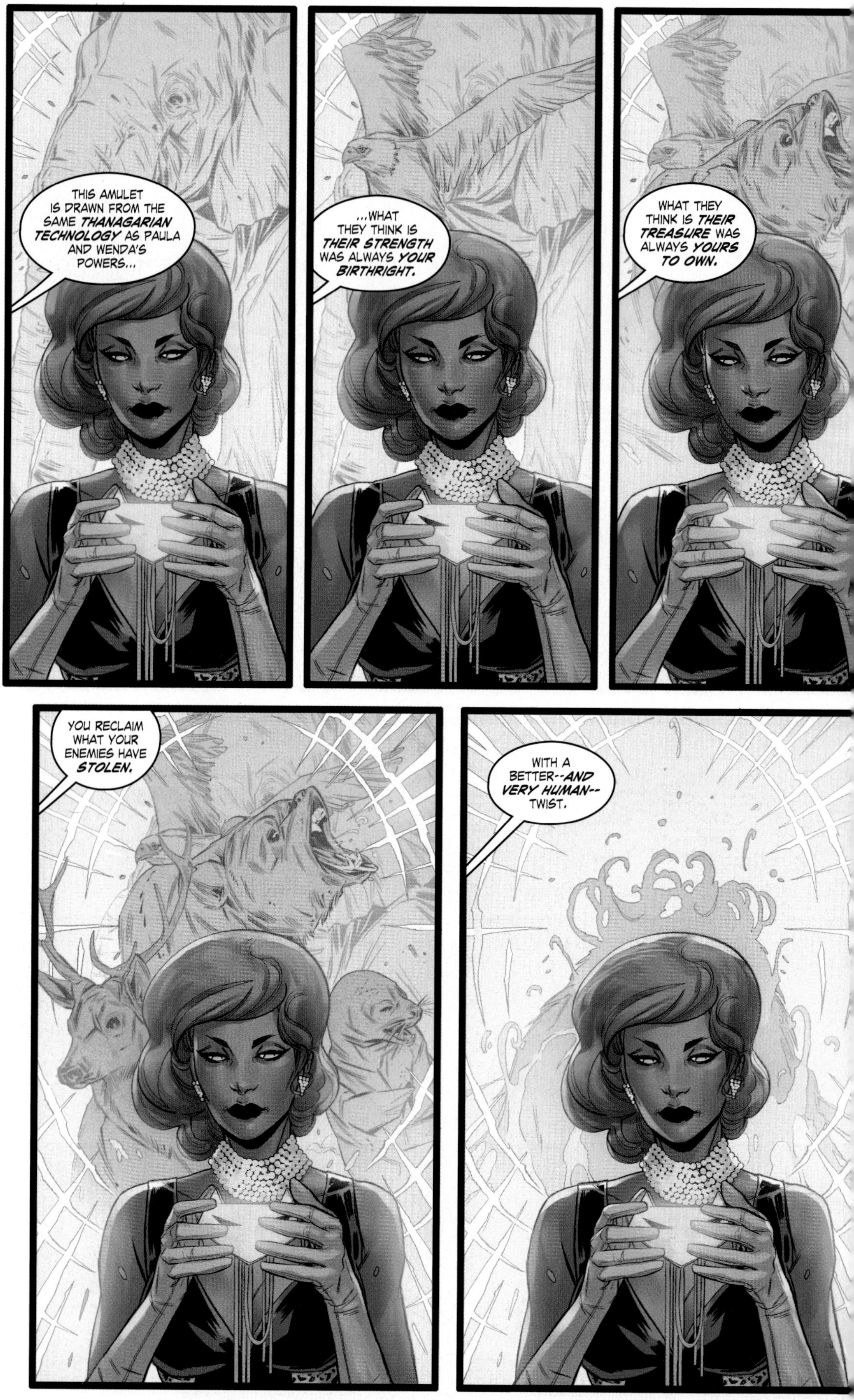
THIS AMULET IS DRAWN FROM THE SAME THANAGARIAN TECHNOLOGY AS PAULA AND WENDA'S POWERS...
...WHAT THEY THINK IS THEIR STRENGTH WAS ALWAYS YOUR BIRTHRIGHT.
WHAT THEY THINK IS THEIR TREASURE WAS ALWAYS YOURS TO OWN.
YOU RECLAIM WHAT YOUR ENEMIES HAVE STOLEN.
WITH A BETTER--AND VERY HUMAN--TWIST.

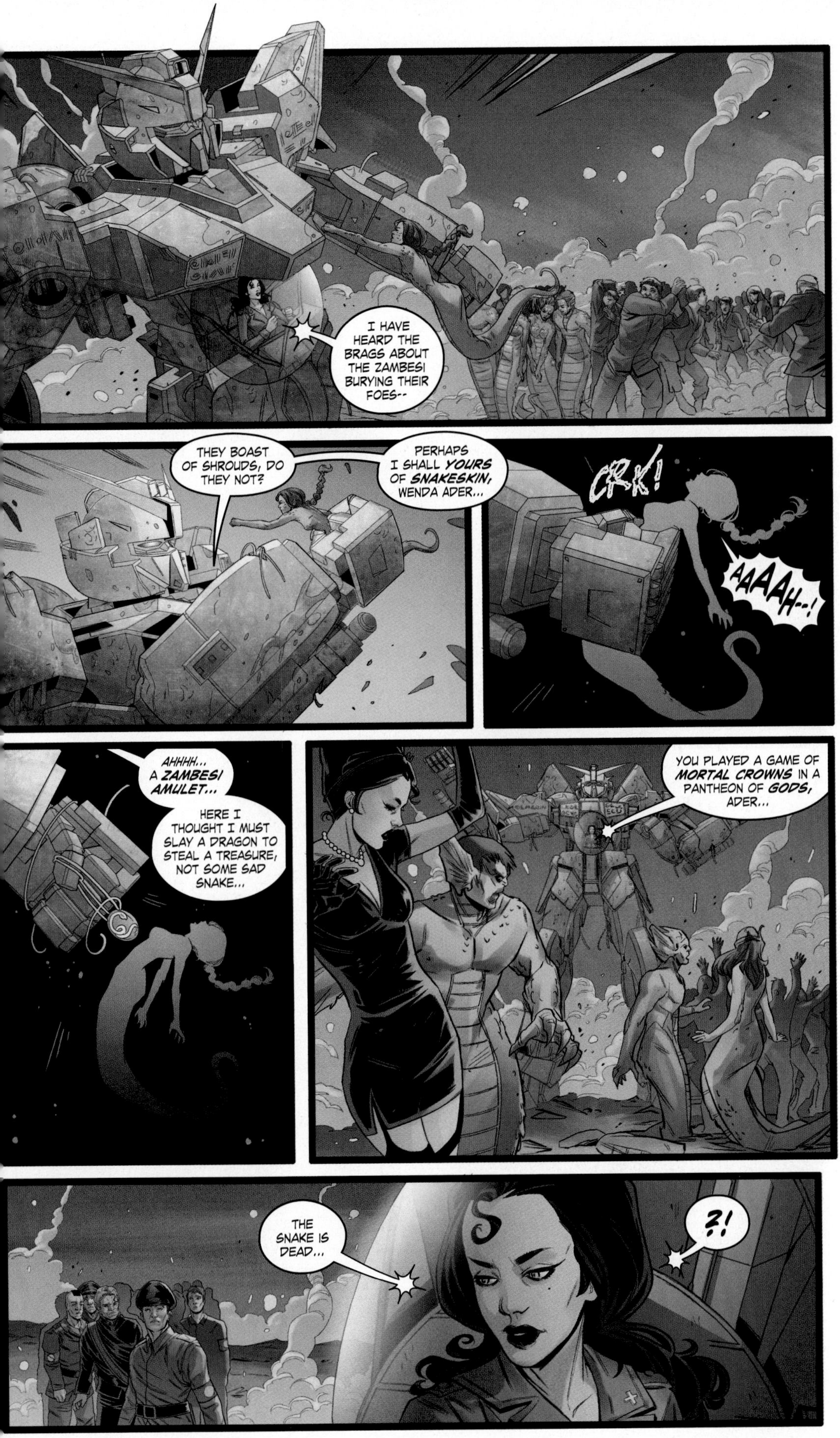
I HAVE HEARD THE BRAGS ABOUT THE ZAMBESI BURYING THEIR FOES--
THEY BOAST OF SHROUDS, DO THEY NOT?
PERHAPS I SHALL *YOURS* OF *SNAKESKIN,* WENDA ADER...
CRK!
AAAAH--!
AHHHH... A *ZAMBESI AMULET...*
HERE I THOUGHT I MUST SLAY A DRAGON TO STEAL A TREASURE, NOT SOME SAD SNAKE...
YOU PLAYED A GAME OF *MORTAL CROWNS* IN A PANTHEON OF *GODS,* ADER...
THE SNAKE IS DEAD...
?!

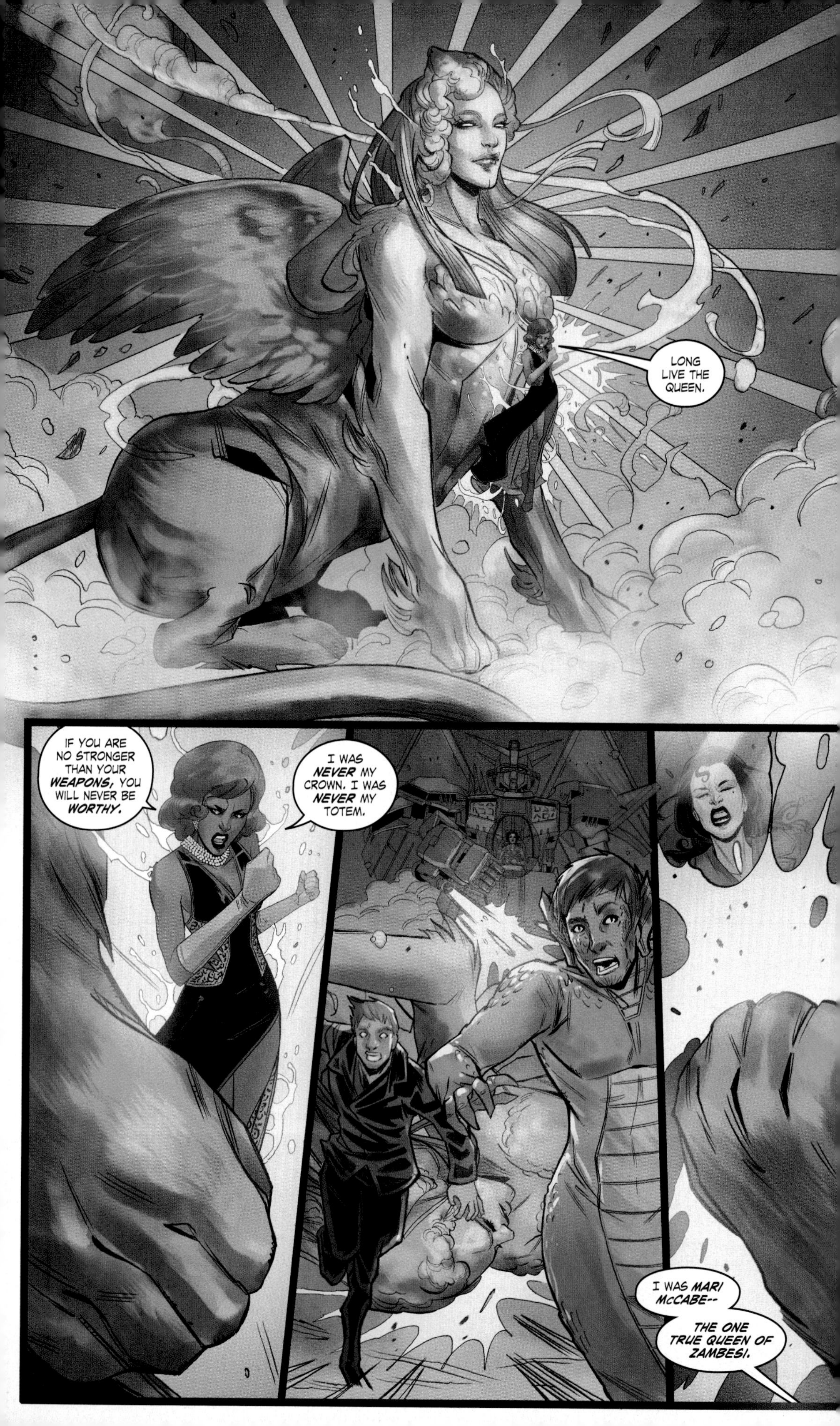
LONG LIVE THE QUEEN.
IF YOU ARE NO STRONGER THAN YOUR WEAPONS, YOU WILL NEVER BE WORTHY.
I WAS NEVER MY CROWN. I WAS NEVER MY TOTEM.
I WAS MARI McCABE--
THE ONE TRUE QUEEN OF ZAMBESI.

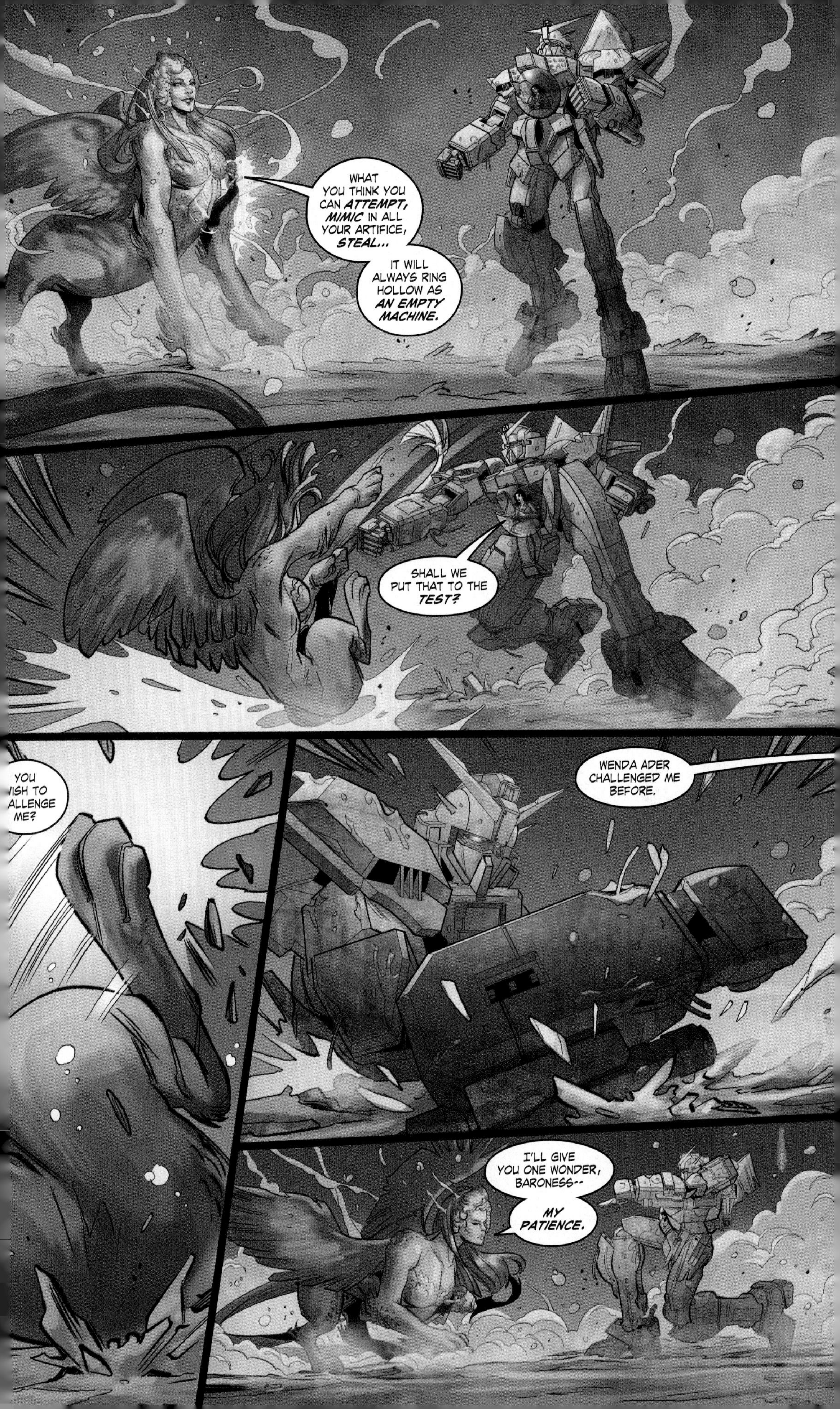
WHAT YOU THINK YOU CAN ATTEMPT, MIMIC IN ALL YOUR ARTIFICE, STEAL...
IT WILL ALWAYS RING HOLLOW AS AN EMPTY MACHINE.
SHALL WE PUT THAT TO THE TEST?
YOU WISH TO CHALLENGE ME?
WENDA ADER CHALLENGED ME BEFORE.
I'LL GIVE YOU ONE WONDER, BARONESS--
MY PATIENCE.

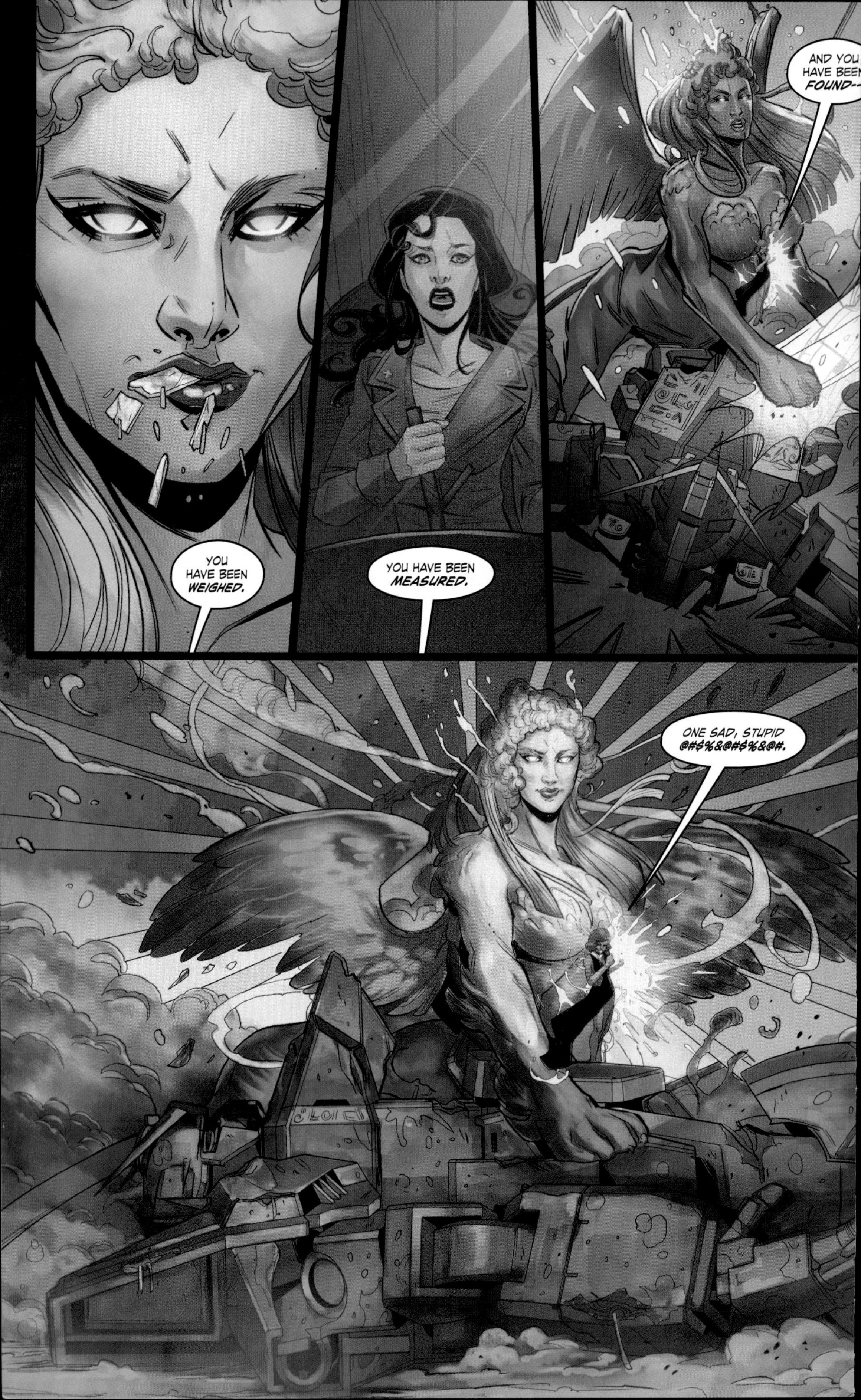
YOU HAVE BEEN WEIGHED.
YOU HAVE BEEN MEASURED.
AND YOU HAVE BEEN FOUND--
ONE SAD, STUPID @#$%&@#$%&@#.

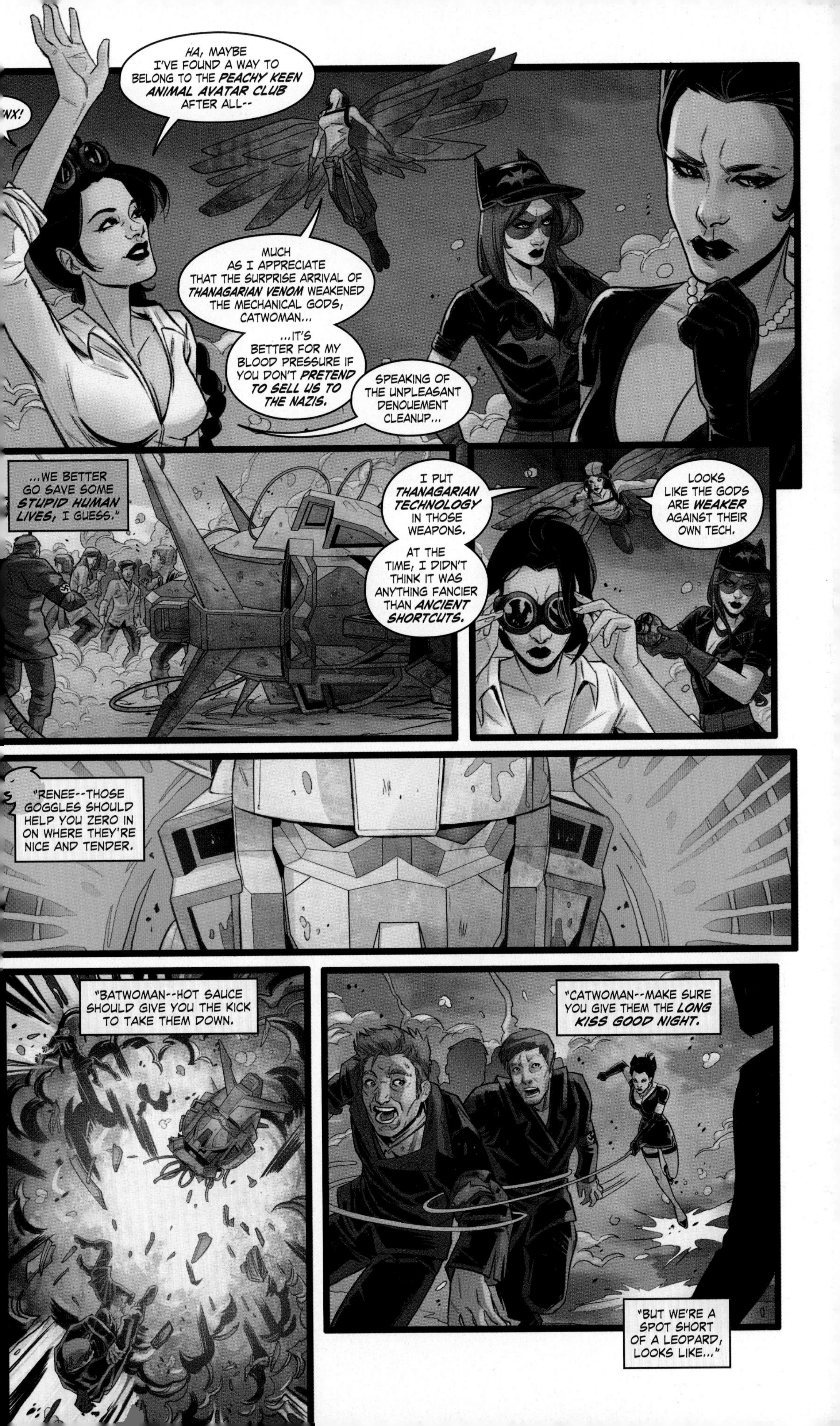
...NX!
HA, MAYBE I'VE FOUND A WAY TO BELONG TO THE PEACHY KEEN ANIMAL AVATAR CLUB AFTER ALL--
MUCH AS I APPRECIATE THAT THE SURPRISE ARRIVAL OF THANAGARIAN VENOM WEAKENED THE MECHANICAL GODS, CATWOMAN...
...IT'S BETTER FOR MY BLOOD PRESSURE IF YOU DON'T PRETEND TO SELL US TO THE NAZIS.
SPEAKING OF THE UNPLEASANT DENOUEMENT CLEANUP...
...WE BETTER GO SAVE SOME STUPID HUMAN LIVES, I GUESS."
I PUT THANAGARIAN TECHNOLOGY IN THOSE WEAPONS.
AT THE TIME, I DIDN'T THINK IT WAS ANYTHING FANCIER THAN ANCIENT SHORTCUTS.
LOOKS LIKE THE GODS ARE WEAKER AGAINST THEIR OWN TECH.
"RENEE--THOSE GOGGLES SHOULD HELP YOU ZERO IN ON WHERE THEY'RE NICE AND TENDER.
"BATWOMAN--HOT SAUCE SHOULD GIVE YOU THE KICK TO TAKE THEM DOWN.
"CATWOMAN--MAKE SURE YOU GIVE THEM THE LONG KISS GOOD NIGHT.
"BUT WE'RE A SPOT SHORT OF A LEOPARD, LOOKS LIKE..."

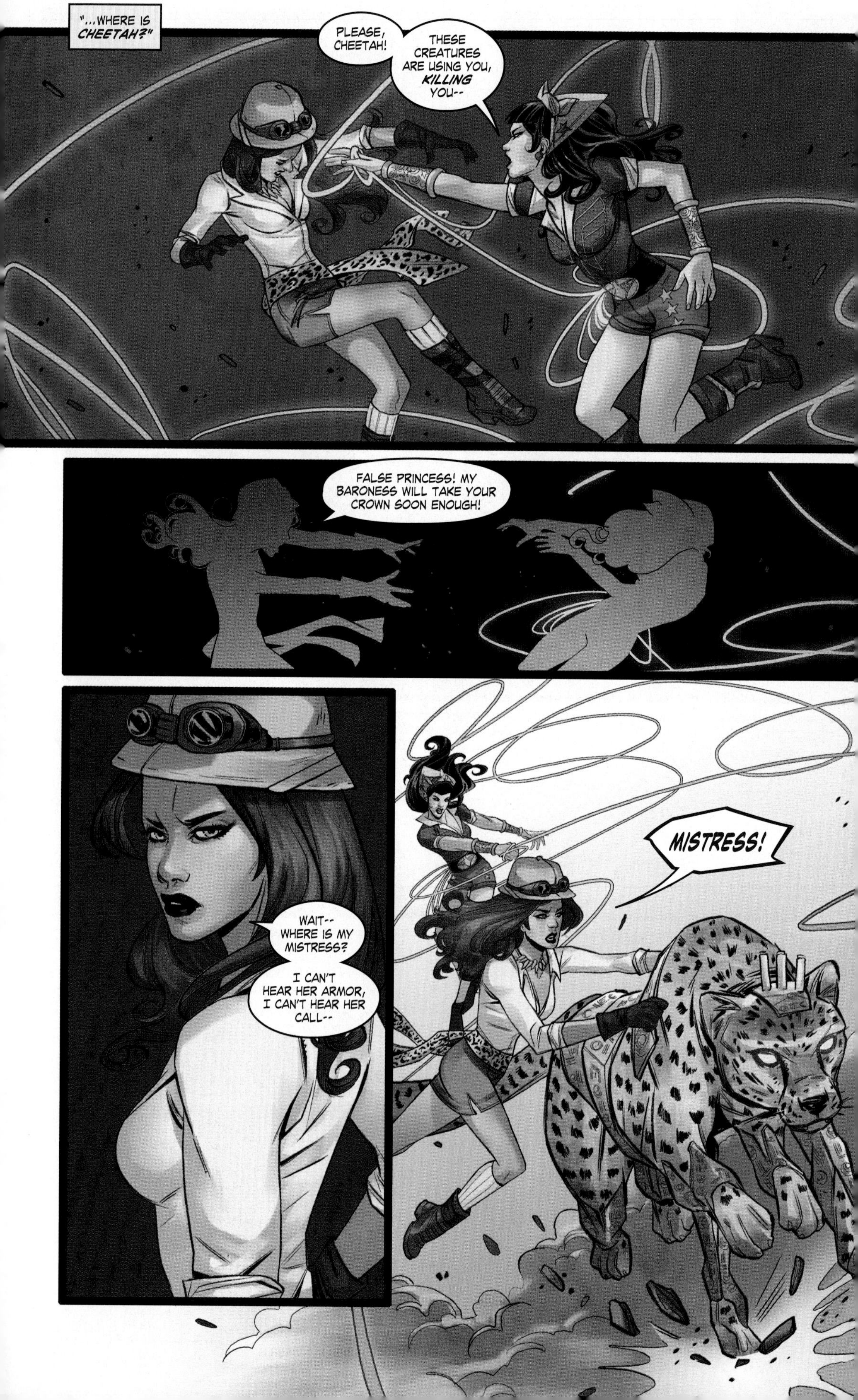
"...WHERE IS CHEETAH?"
PLEASE, CHEETAH!
THESE CREATURES ARE USING YOU, KILLING YOU--
FALSE PRINCESS! MY BARONESS WILL TAKE YOUR CROWN SOON ENOUGH!
WAIT-- WHERE IS MY MISTRESS?
I CAN'T HEAR HER ARMOR, I CAN'T HEAR HER CALL--
MISTRESS!

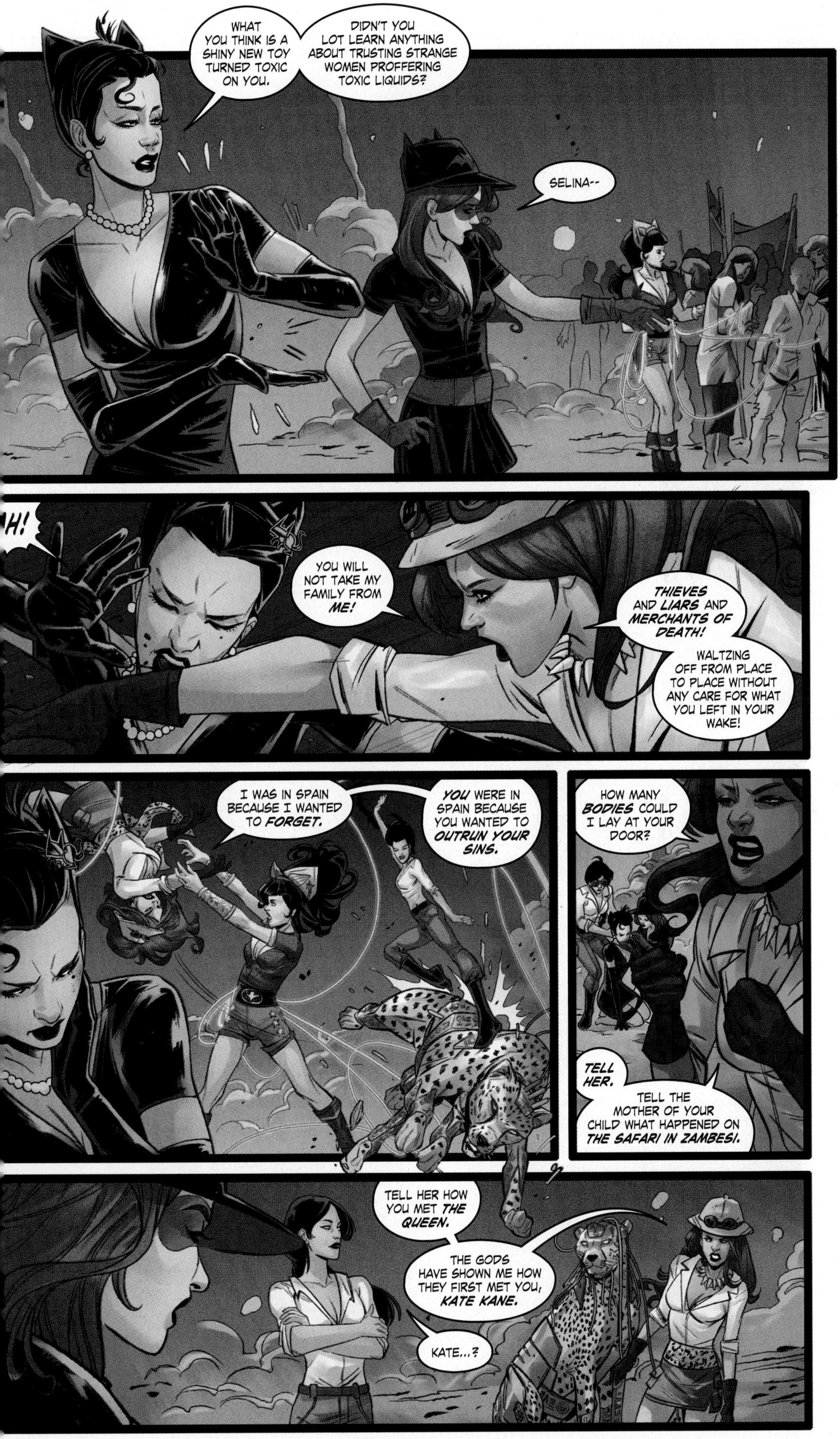
WHAT YOU THINK IS A SHINY NEW TOY TURNED TOXIC ON YOU.
DIDN'T YOU LOT LEARN ANYTHING ABOUT TRUSTING STRANGE WOMEN PROFFERING TOXIC LIQUIDS?
SELINA--
YOU WILL NOT TAKE MY FAMILY FROM ME!
THIEVES AND LIARS AND MERCHANTS OF DEATH!
WALTZING OFF FROM PLACE TO PLACE WITHOUT ANY CARE FOR WHAT YOU LEFT IN YOUR WAKE!
I WAS IN SPAIN BECAUSE I WANTED TO FORGET.
YOU WERE IN SPAIN BECAUSE YOU WANTED TO OUTRUN YOUR SINS.
HOW MANY BODIES COULD I LAY AT YOUR DOOR?
TELL HER.
TELL THE MOTHER OF YOUR CHILD WHAT HAPPENED ON THE SAFARI IN ZAMBESI.
TELL HER HOW YOU MET THE QUEEN.
THE GODS HAVE SHOWN ME HOW THEY FIRST MET YOU, KATE KANE.
KATE...?

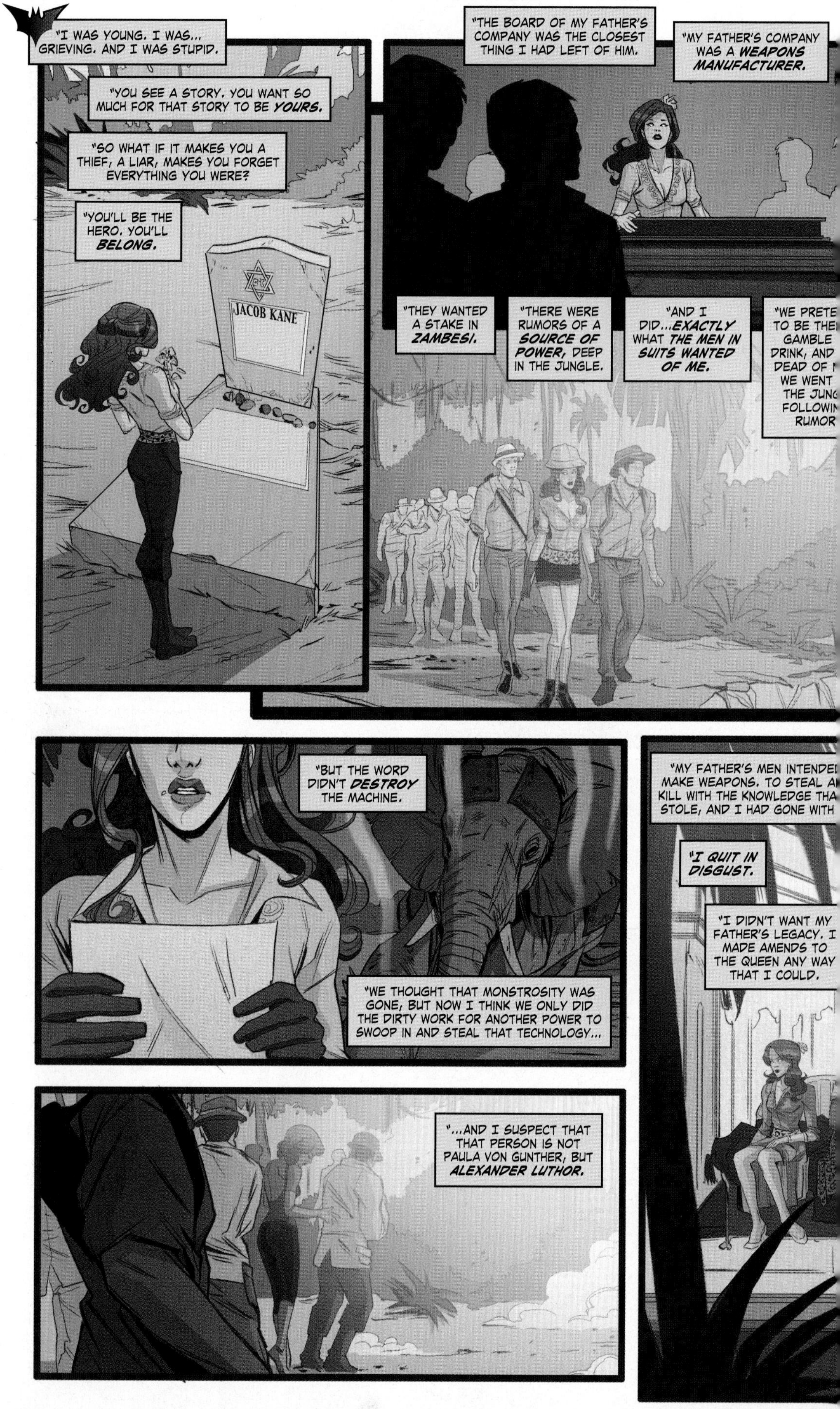
"I WAS YOUNG. I WAS... GRIEVING. AND I WAS STUPID.
"YOU SEE A STORY. YOU WANT SO MUCH FOR THAT STORY TO BE *YOURS.*
"SO WHAT IF IT MAKES YOU A THIEF, A LIAR, MAKES YOU FORGET EVERYTHING YOU WERE?
"YOU'LL BE THE HERO. YOU'LL *BELONG.*
JACOB KANE
"THE BOARD OF MY FATHER'S COMPANY WAS THE CLOSEST THING I HAD LEFT OF HIM.
"MY FATHER'S COMPANY WAS A *WEAPONS MANUFACTURER.*
"THEY WANTED A STAKE IN *ZAMBESI.*
"THERE WERE RUMORS OF A *SOURCE OF POWER,* DEEP IN THE JUNGLE.
"AND I DID...*EXACTLY* WHAT *THE MEN IN SUITS WANTED OF ME.*
"WE PRETE TO BE THE GAMBLE DRINK, AND DEAD OF WE WENT THE JUNG FOLLOWIN RUMOR
"BUT THE WORD DIDN'T *DESTROY* THE MACHINE.
"WE THOUGHT THAT MONSTROSITY WAS GONE, BUT NOW I THINK WE ONLY DID THE DIRTY WORK FOR ANOTHER POWER TO SWOOP IN AND STEAL THAT TECHNOLOGY...
"...AND I SUSPECT THAT THAT PERSON IS NOT PAULA VON GUNTHER, BUT *ALEXANDER LUTHOR.*
"MY FATHER'S MEN INTENDE MAKE WEAPONS. TO STEAL A KILL WITH THE KNOWLEDGE THA STOLE, AND I HAD GONE WITH
"*I QUIT IN DISGUST.*
"I DIDN'T WANT MY FATHER'S LEGACY. I MADE AMENDS TO THE QUEEN ANY WAY THAT I COULD.

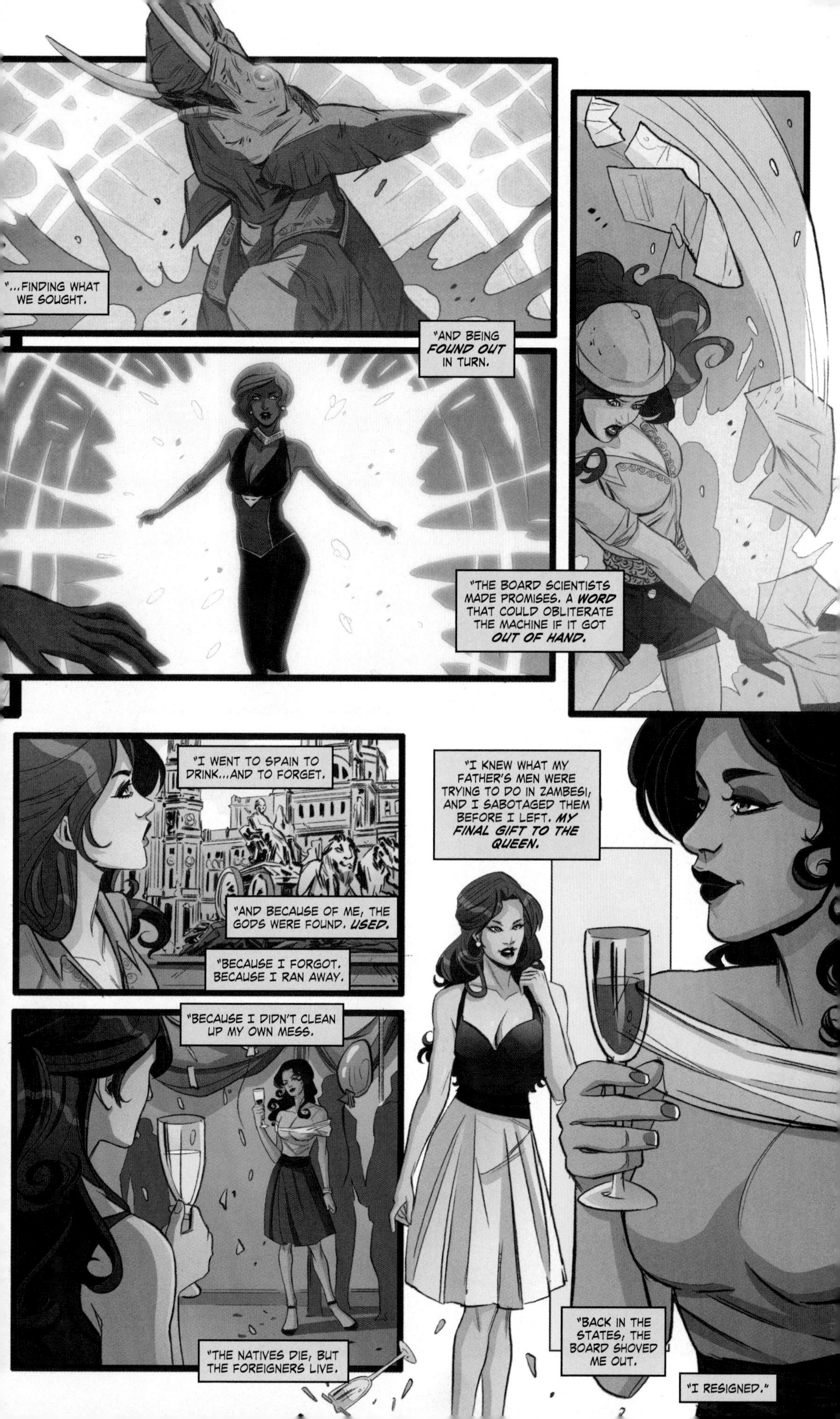
"...FINDING WHAT WE SOUGHT.
"AND BEING FOUND OUT IN TURN.
"THE BOARD SCIENTISTS MADE PROMISES. A WORD THAT COULD OBLITERATE THE MACHINE IF IT GOT OUT OF HAND.
"I WENT TO SPAIN TO DRINK...AND TO FORGET.
"AND BECAUSE OF ME, THE GODS WERE FOUND. USED.
"BECAUSE I FORGOT. BECAUSE I RAN AWAY.
"BECAUSE I DIDN'T CLEAN UP MY OWN MESS.
"THE NATIVES DIE, BUT THE FOREIGNERS LIVE.
"I KNEW WHAT MY FATHER'S MEN WERE TRYING TO DO IN ZAMBESI, AND I SABOTAGED THEM BEFORE I LEFT. MY FINAL GIFT TO THE QUEEN.
"BACK IN THE STATES, THE BOARD SHOVED ME OUT.
"I RESIGNED."

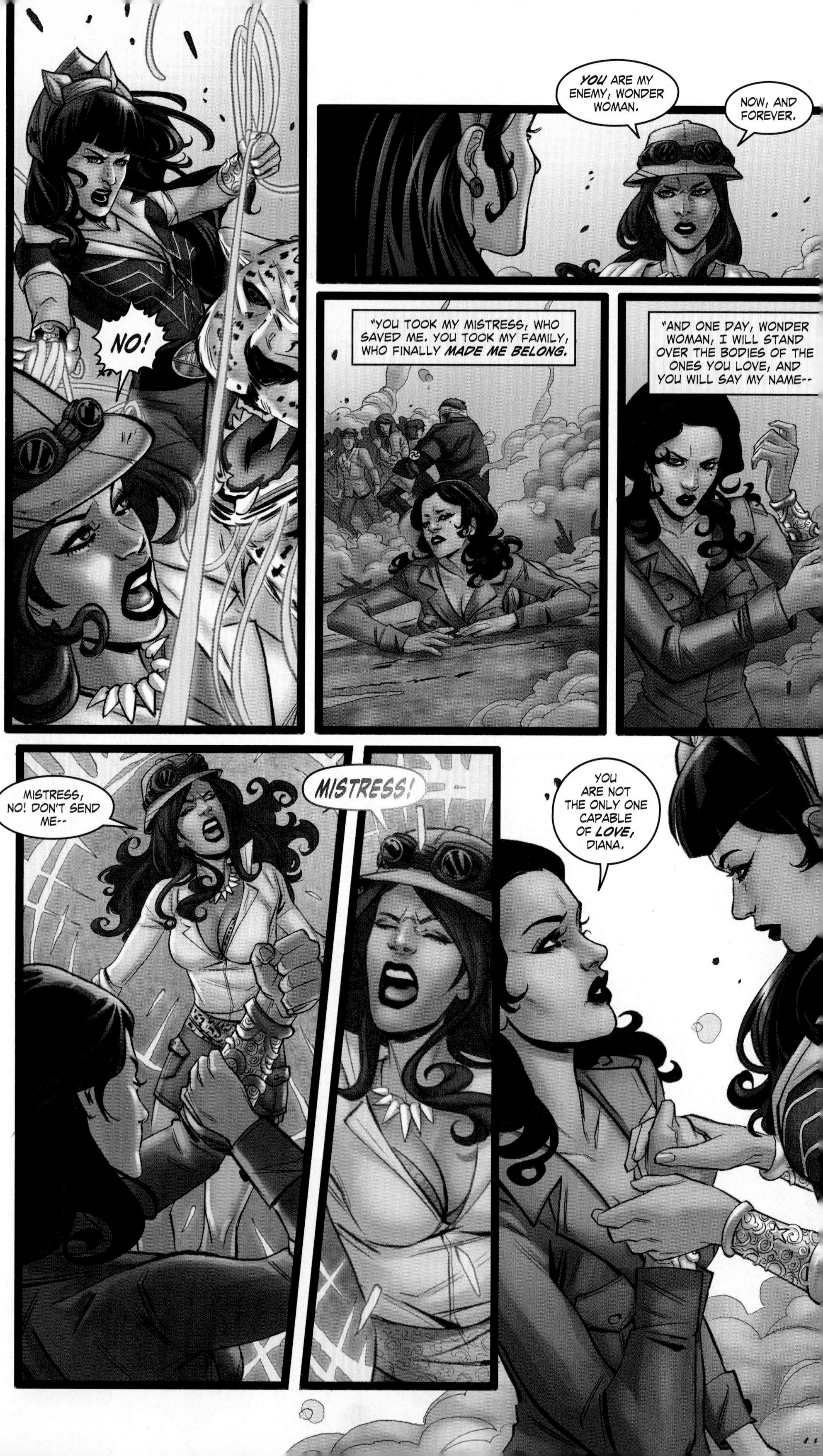
NO!
YOU ARE MY ENEMY, WONDER WOMAN.
NOW, AND FOREVER.
"YOU TOOK MY MISTRESS, WHO SAVED ME. YOU TOOK MY FAMILY, WHO FINALLY MADE ME BELONG.
"AND ONE DAY, WONDER WOMAN, I WILL STAND OVER THE BODIES OF THE ONES YOU LOVE, AND YOU WILL SAY MY NAME--
MISTRESS, NO! DON'T SEND ME--
MISTRESS!
YOU ARE NOT THE ONLY ONE CAPABLE OF LOVE, DIANA.

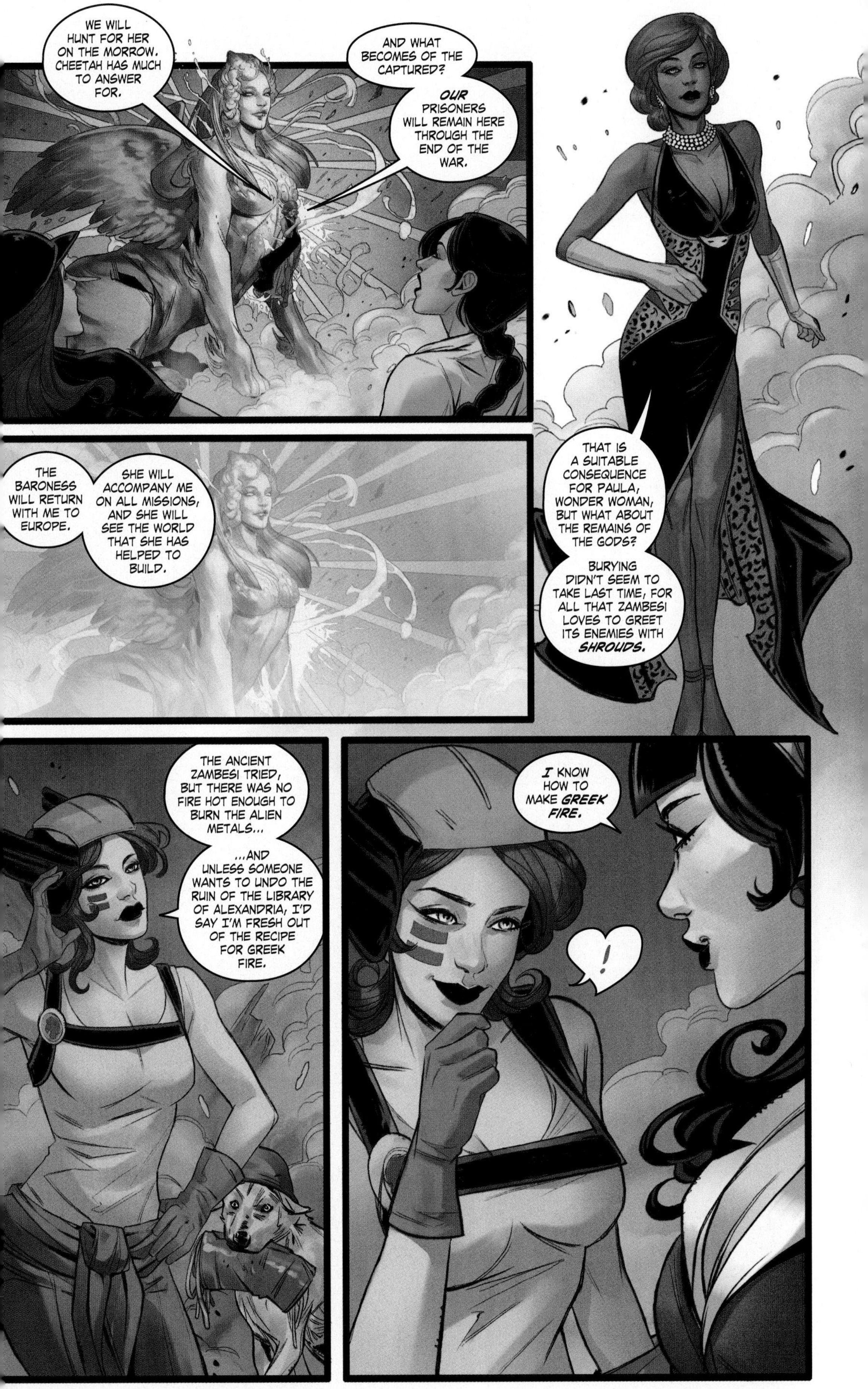

WE WILL HUNT FOR HER ON THE MORROW. CHEETAH HAS MUCH TO ANSWER FOR.
AND WHAT BECOMES OF THE CAPTURED?
OUR PRISONERS WILL REMAIN HERE THROUGH THE END OF THE WAR.
THE BARONESS WILL RETURN WITH ME TO EUROPE.
SHE WILL ACCOMPANY ME ON ALL MISSIONS, AND SHE WILL SEE THE WORLD THAT SHE HAS HELPED TO BUILD.
THAT IS A SUITABLE CONSEQUENCE FOR PAULA, WONDER WOMAN, BUT WHAT ABOUT THE REMAINS OF THE GODS?
BURYING DIDN'T SEEM TO TAKE LAST TIME, FOR ALL THAT ZAMBESI LOVES TO GREET ITS ENEMIES WITH SHROUDS.
THE ANCIENT ZAMBESI TRIED, BUT THERE WAS NO FIRE HOT ENOUGH TO BURN THE ALIEN METALS...
...AND UNLESS SOMEONE WANTS TO UNDO THE RUIN OF THE LIBRARY OF ALEXANDRIA, I'D SAY I'M FRESH OUT OF THE RECIPE FOR GREEK FIRE.
I KNOW HOW TO MAKE GREEK FIRE.
!

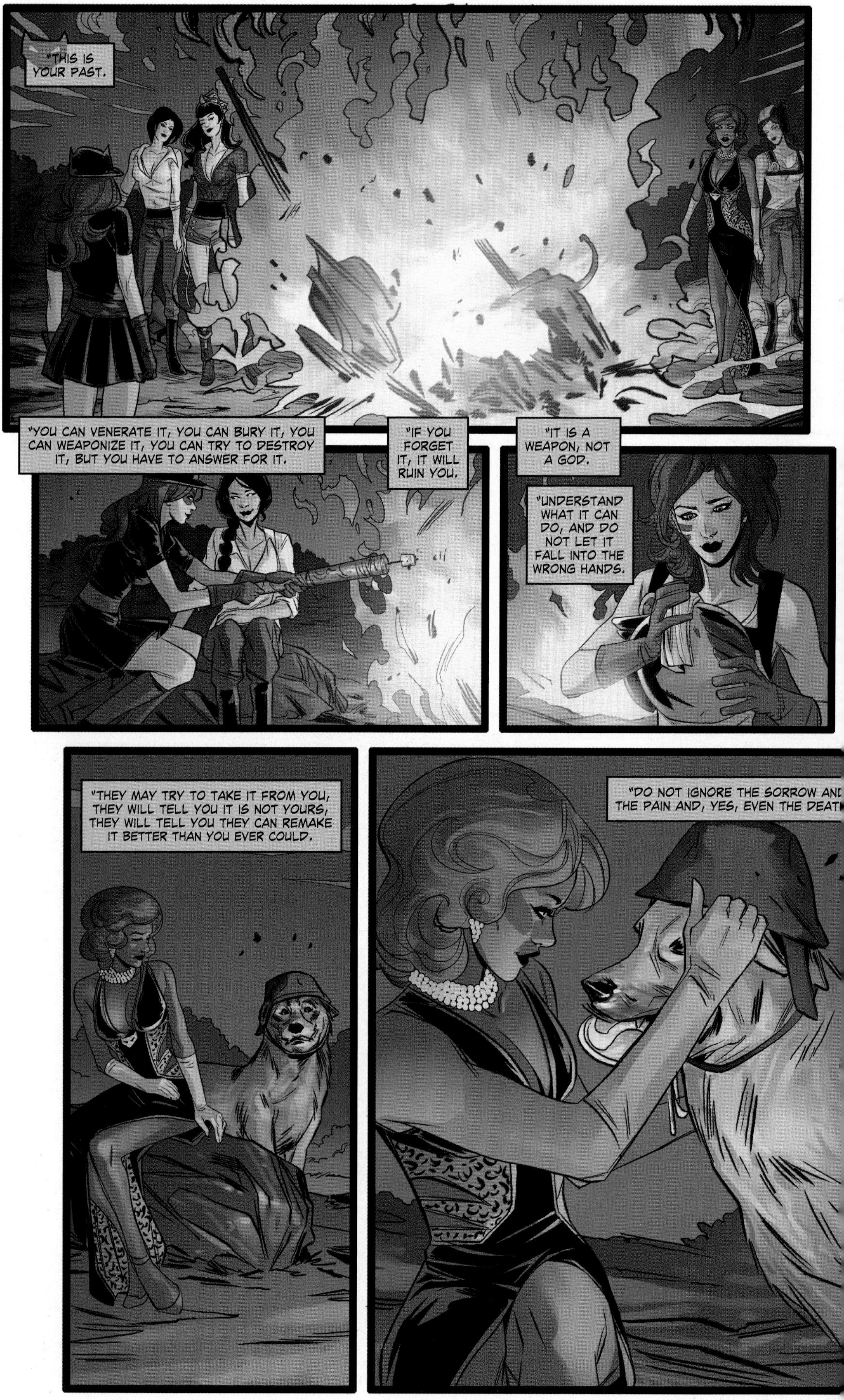

"THIS IS YOUR PAST.
"YOU CAN VENERATE IT, YOU CAN BURY IT, YOU CAN WEAPONIZE IT, YOU CAN TRY TO DESTROY IT, BUT YOU HAVE TO ANSWER FOR IT.
"IF YOU FORGET IT, IT WILL RUIN YOU.
"IT IS A WEAPON, NOT A GOD.
"UNDERSTAND WHAT IT CAN DO, AND DO NOT LET IT FALL INTO THE WRONG HANDS.
"THEY MAY TRY TO TAKE IT FROM YOU, THEY WILL TELL YOU IT IS NOT YOURS, THEY WILL TELL YOU THEY CAN REMAKE IT BETTER THAN YOU EVER COULD.
"DO NOT IGNORE THE SORROW AN THE PAIN AND, YES, EVEN THE DEAT

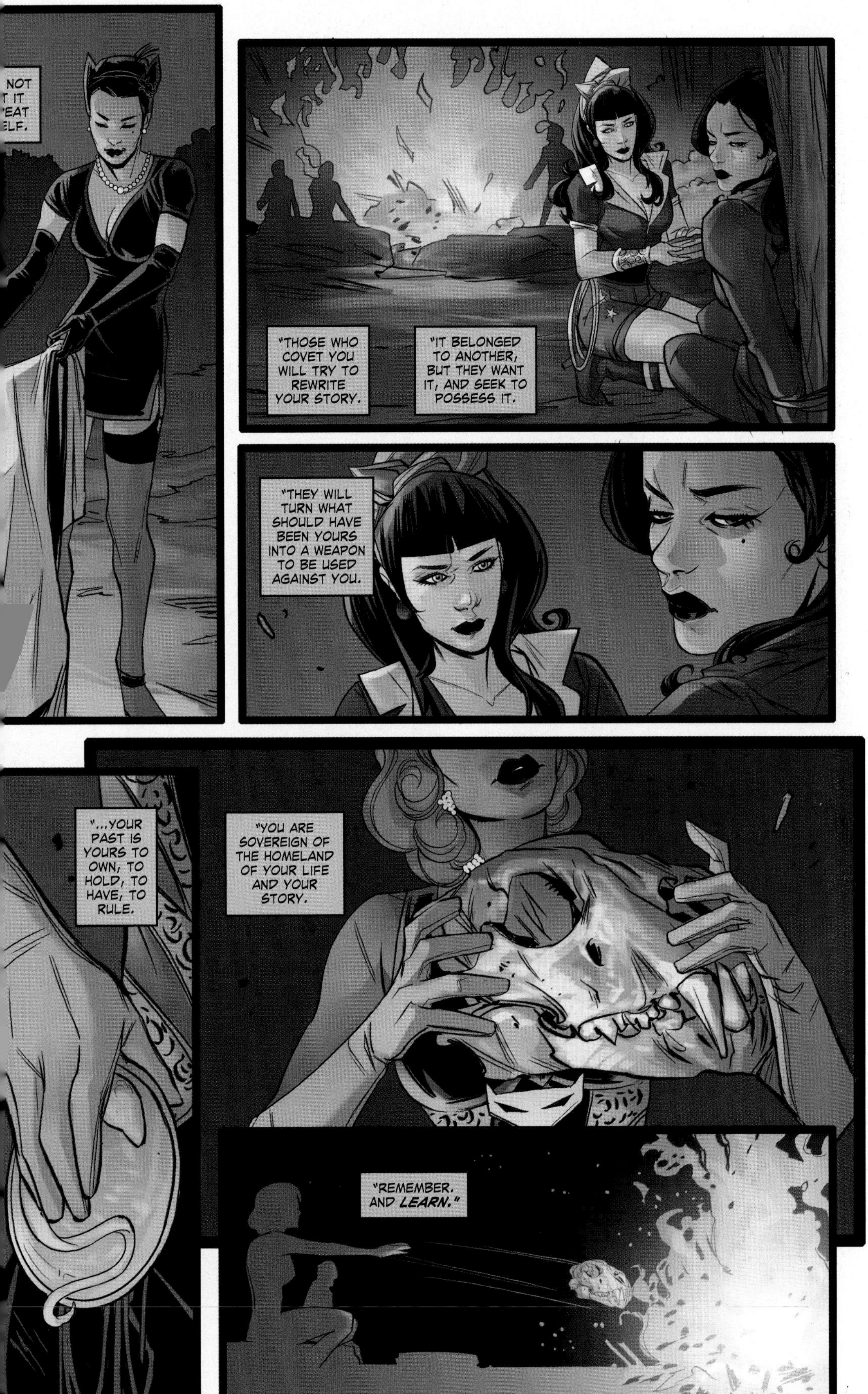
"THOSE WHO COVET YOU WILL TRY TO REWRITE YOUR STORY.
"IT BELONGED TO ANOTHER, BUT THEY WANT IT, AND SEEK TO POSSESS IT.
"THEY WILL TURN WHAT SHOULD HAVE BEEN YOURS INTO A WEAPON TO BE USED AGAINST YOU.
"...YOUR PAST IS YOURS TO OWN, TO HOLD, TO HAVE, TO RULE.
"YOU ARE SOVEREIGN OF THE HOMELAND OF YOUR LIFE AND YOUR STORY.
"REMEMBER. AND *LEARN.*"

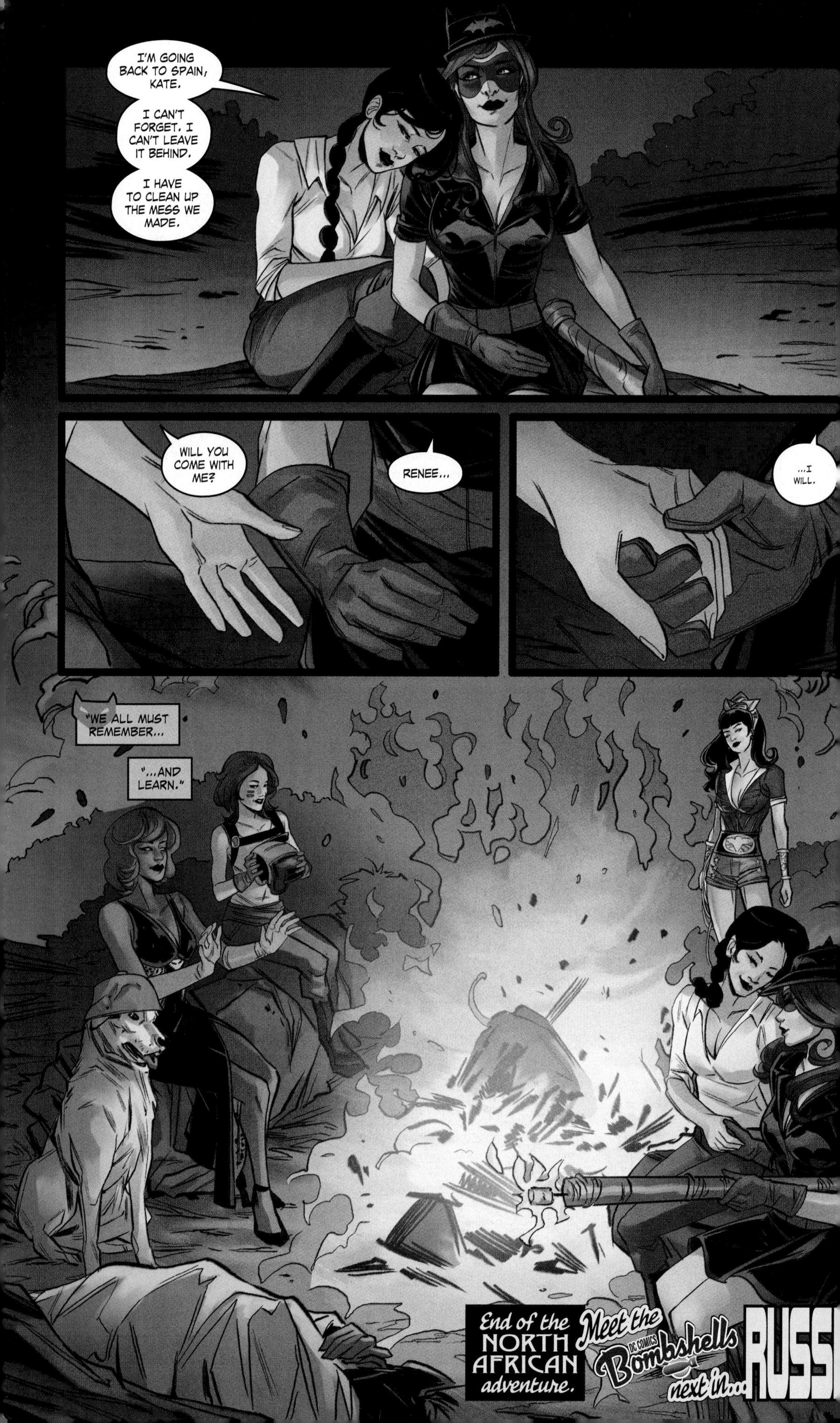
I'M GOING BACK TO SPAIN, KATE.
I CAN'T FORGET. I CAN'T LEAVE IT BEHIND.
I HAVE TO CLEAN UP THE MESS WE MADE.
WILL YOU COME WITH ME?
RENEE...
...I WILL.
"WE ALL MUST REMEMBER...
"...AND LEARN."
End of the NORTH AFRICAN adventure.
Meet the DC COMICS Bombshells next in... RUSS

COVER LAYOUTS
BY ANT LUCIA

C COMICS: BOMBSHELLS #19

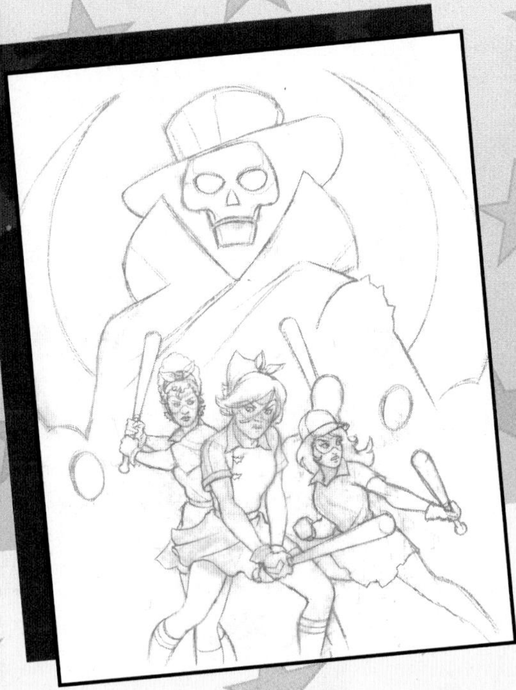

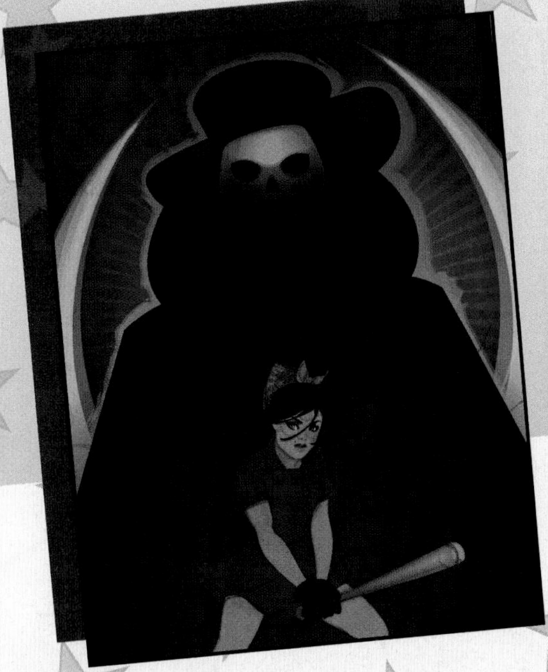

C COMICS: BOMBSHELLS #20

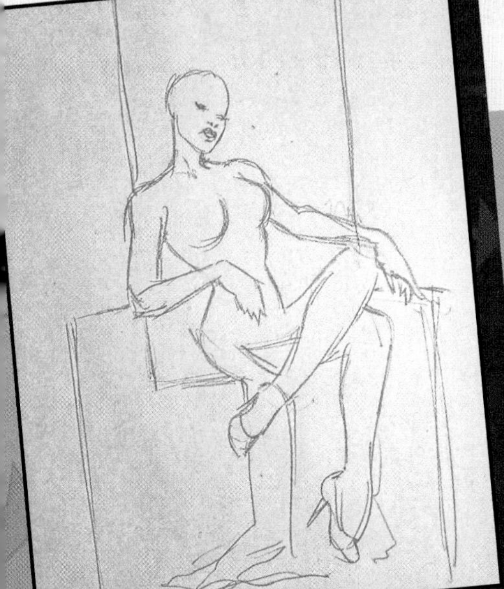

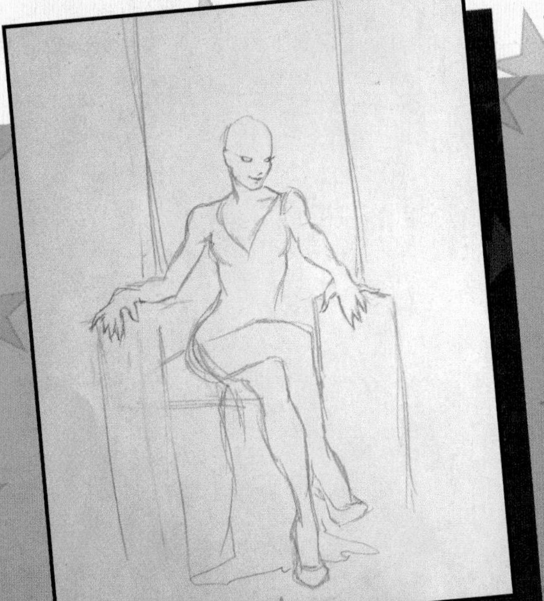

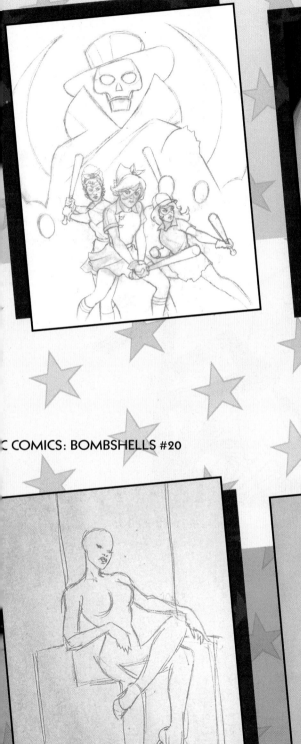

DC COMICS: BOMBSHELLS #22

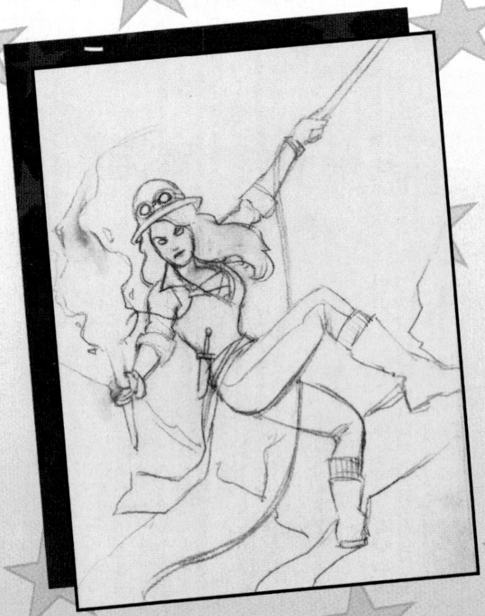

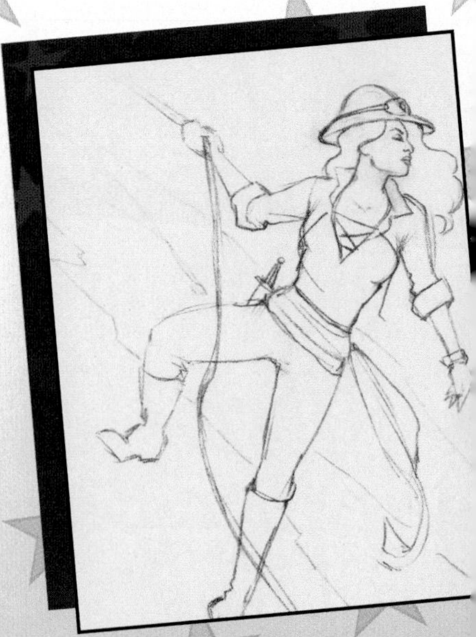

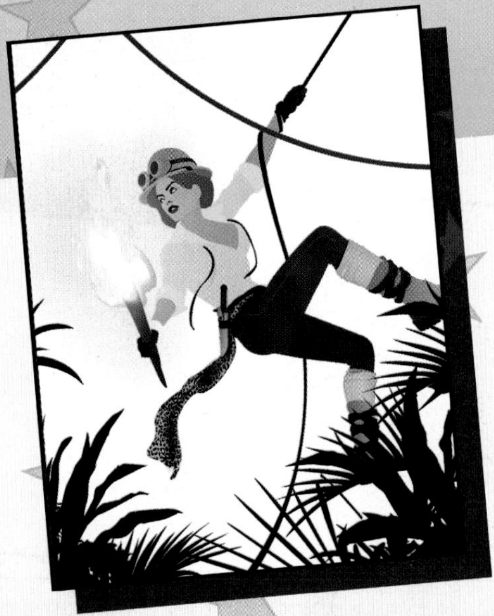

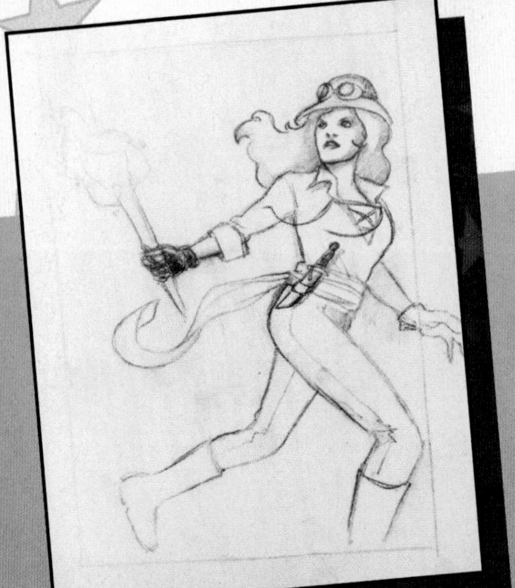

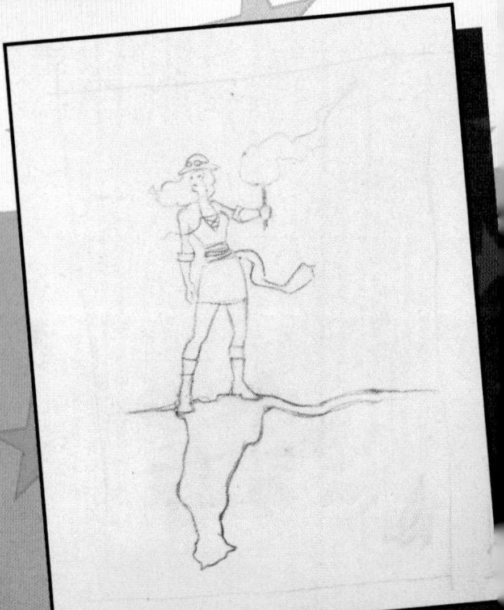

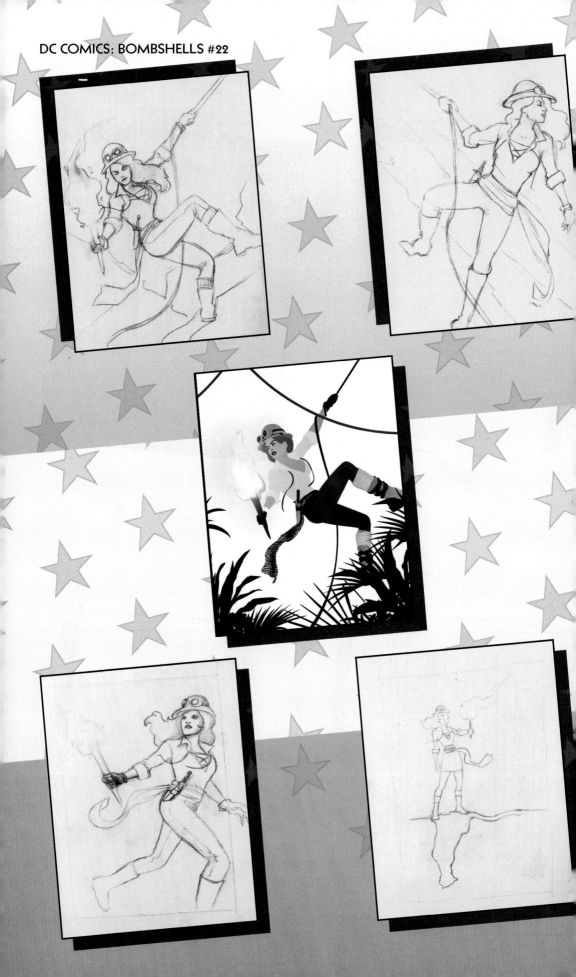

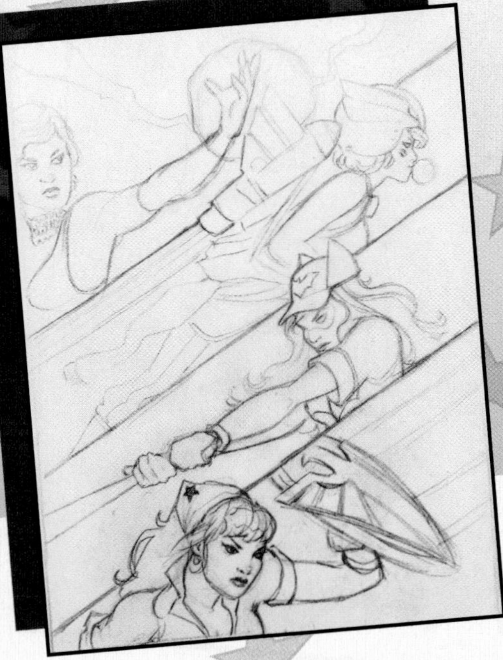

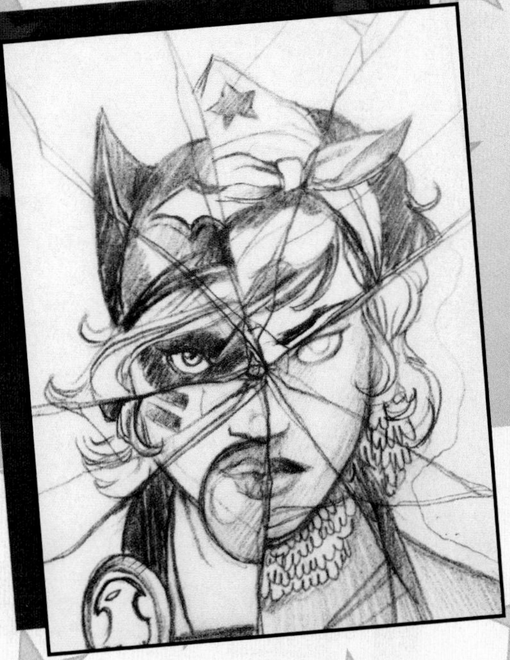

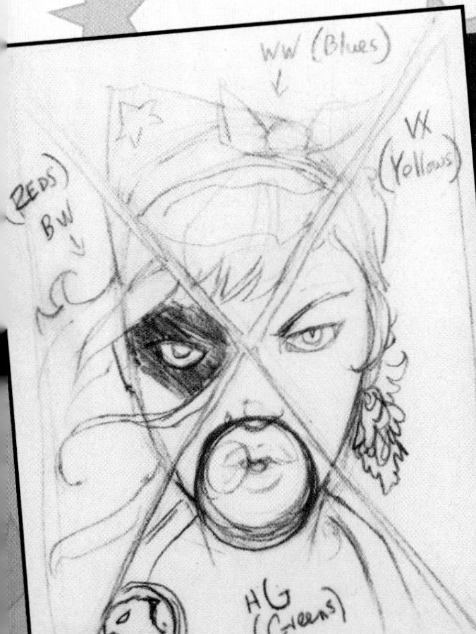
WW (Blues)
VX (Yellows)
(REDS) BW
HG (Greens)

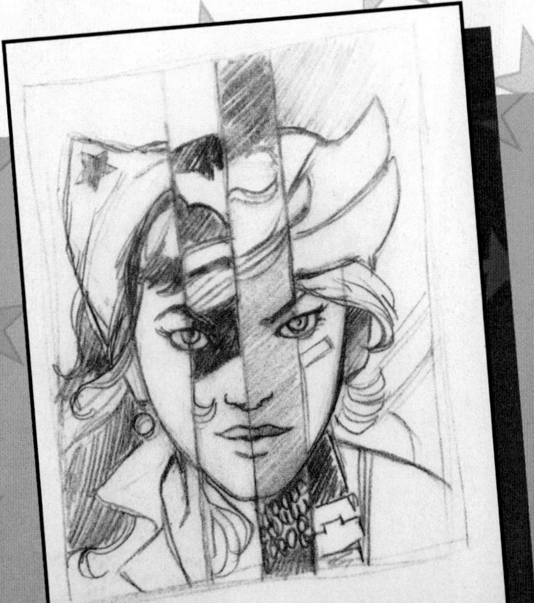

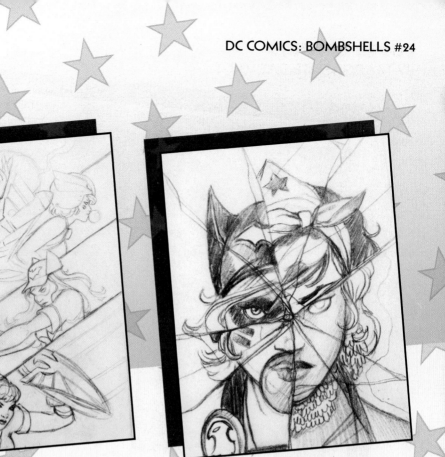

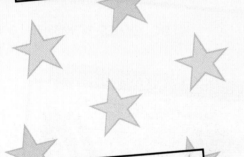

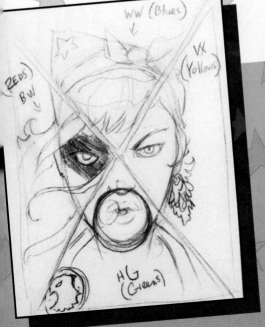

COVER LAYOUTS
BY MARGUERITE SAUVAGE

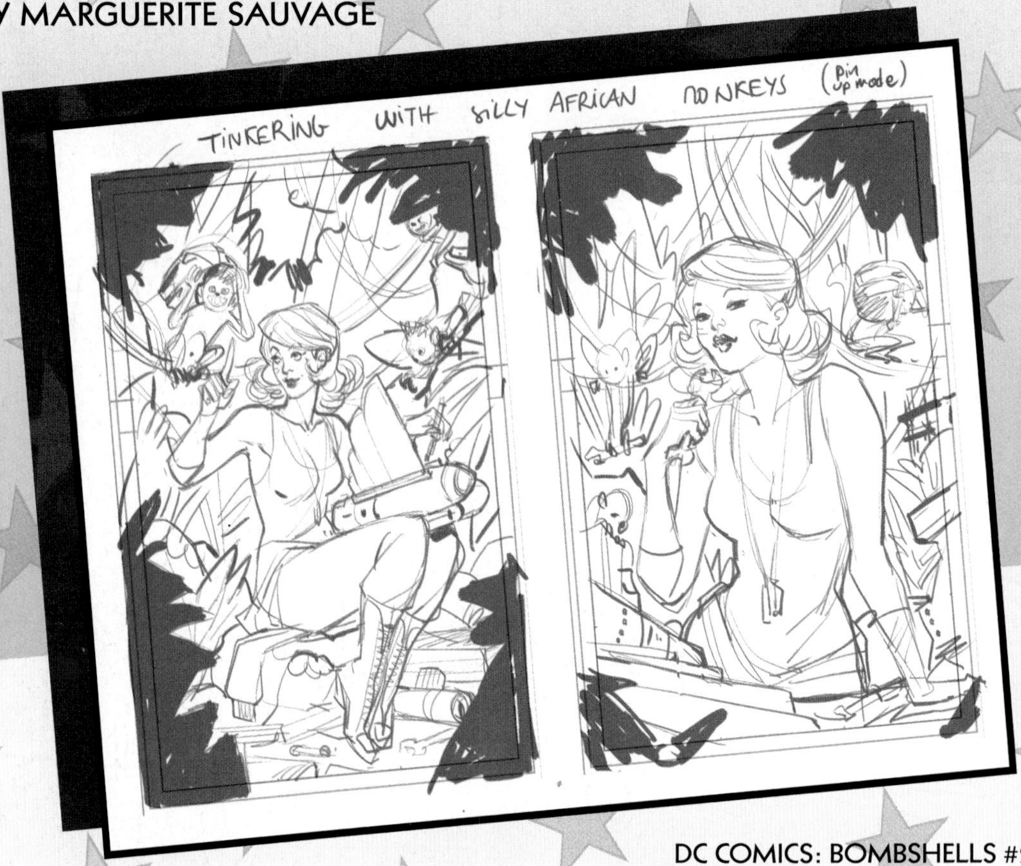
TINKERING WITH SILLY AFRICAN MONKEYS (pin up mode)

DC COMICS: BOMBSHELLS #21

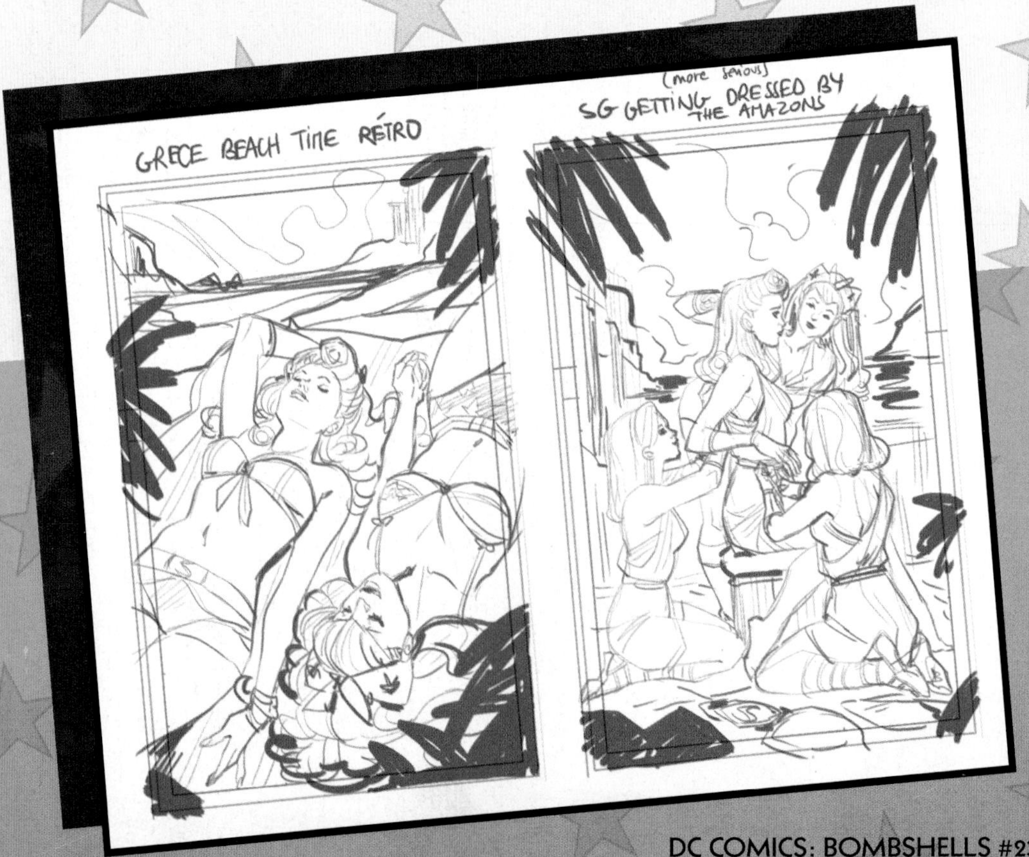
GRECE BEACH TIME RÉTRO
(more serious)
SG GETTING DRESSED BY THE AMAZONS

DC COMICS: BOMBSHELLS #23